Toward the Critique of Violence

Benjamin-Archiv
Ms 1858

TOWARD THE CRITIQUE OF VIOLENCE

A Critical Edition

WALTER BENJAMIN

EDITED BY
Peter Fenves and Julia Ng

STANFORD UNIVERSITY PRESS
Stanford, California

STANFORD UNIVERSITY PRESS
Stanford, California

English translation © 2021 by the Board of Trustees of the Leland Stanford Junior University. All rights reserved.

"Toward the Critique of Violence" was originally published in German under the title "Zur Kritik der Gewalt," © 1921, *Archiv für Sozialwissenschaft und Sozialpolitik*; all but two of Benjamin's other writings were first published in Walter Benjamin, *Gesammelte Schriften*, ed. Rolf Tiedemann and Hermann Schweppenhäuser, 7 vols., © 1972–91, Suhrkamp Verlag.

"Notes toward a Work on the Category of Justice" is a revision of the translation that first appeared in Peter Fenves, *The Messianic Reduction: Walter Benjamin and the Shape of Time*, © 2011, Stanford University Press.

"Literature for a More Fully Developed Critique of Violence and Philosophy of Law" is a translation of the previously unpublished "Literatur zu einer ausgeführteren Kritik der Gewalt und zur Rechtsphilosophie," WBA 508/16 [= I MS 1858], in the Walter Benjamin Archiv; both appear here with the permission of the Hamburger Stiftung zur Förderung von Wissenschaft und Kultur.

Selections from Hermann Cohen, *Ethics of Pure Will*, were originally published in German under the title *Ethik des reinen Willens*, © 1907, Cassirer.

Kurt Hiller, "Anti-Cain: A Postscript to Rudolf Leonhard's 'Our Final Battle against Weapons,'" was originally published in German under the title "Anti-Kain: Ein Nachwort zu dem Vorhergehenden," © 1919, *Das Ziel: Jahrbücher für geistige Politik*.

Selections from Georges Sorel, *Reflections on Violence*, were originally published in French under the title *Réflexions sur la violence*, © 1921, Marcel Rivière.

Selections from Erich Unger, *Politics and Metaphysics*, were originally published in German under the title *Politik und Metaphysik*, © 1921, Verlag David.

Emil Lederer, "Sociology of Violence: A Contribution to the Theory of Social-Formative Forces," was originally published in German under the title "Soziologie der Gewalt: Ein Beitrag zur Theorie der gesellschaftsbildenden Kräfte," © 1921, *Die weißen Blätter*, neue Folge.

Introduction and Afterword © 2021 by the Board of Trustees of the Leland Stanford Junior University. All rights reserved.

No part of this book may be reproduced or transmitted in any form or by any means, electronic or mechanical, including photocopying and recording, or in any information storage or retrieval system without the prior written permission of Stanford University Press.

Printed in the United States of America on acid-free, archival-quality paper

Library of Congress Cataloging-in-Publication Data available upon request.

Cover design: Rob Ehle

Frontispiece and cover image: Walter Benjamin, "Literature for a More Fully Developed Critique of Violence and Philosophy of Law." Akademie der Künste, Berlin, Walter Benjamin Archiv 508/16. Hamburger Stiftung zur Förderung von Wissenschaft und Kultur.

Text design: Kevin Barrett Kane

Typeset at Stanford University Press in 11/14 Arno Pro

Contents

Note on the Translation of Benjamin's Writings	vii
Acknowledgments	ix
Abbreviations and Conventions	xi

INTRODUCTION by Peter Fenves ... 1

"Toward the Critique of Violence" by Walter Benjamin ... 39

ASSOCIATED NOTES AND FRAGMENTS

1. Notes toward a Work on the Category of Justice ... 65
2. Vivification and Violence ... 67
3. From "Life and Violence" ... 68
4. On Morality ... 69
5. All Unconditionality of the Will Leads to Evil ... 70
6. On Kantian Ethics ... 71
7. The Spontaneity of the I ... 72
8. Ethics, Applied to History ... 73
9. Modes of History ... 75
10. Methodical Modes of History ... 76
11. Death ... 78
12. As Many Pagan Religions, So Many Natural Concepts of Guilt ... 79
13. On the Problem of Physiognomy and Prediction ... 80
14. The Meaning of Time in the Moral World ... 81
15. 1) World and Time ... 83
16. Morality, Ethics ... 85
17. The Right to Apply Force / Use Violence ... 86
18. Capitalism as Religion ... 90

19. Notes on "Objective Mendacity" I   93
20. Notes toward a Work on Lying II   96
21. Schemata for the Psychophysical Problem   98
22. Literature for a More Fully Developed Critique of Violence and Philosophy of Law /
Literatur zu einer ausgeführteren Kritik der Gewalt und zur Rechtsphilosophie   108

AFTERWORD: Toward Another Critique of Violence by Julia Ng   113

Hermann Cohen, *Ethics of Pure Will*
   Translator's Preface   161
   Excerpt, "Self-Responsibility"   167

Kurt Hiller, "Anti-Cain: A Postscript to Rudolf Leonhard's 'Our Final Battle against Weapons'"
   Translator's Preface   179
   Essay   185

Georges Sorel, *Reflections on Violence*
   Translator's Preface   194
   Excerpts   201

Erich Unger, from *Politics and Metaphysics*
   Translator's Preface   214
   Excerpts   220

Emil Lederer, "Sociology of Violence: A Contribution to the Theory of Social-Formative Forces"
   Translator's Preface   233
   Essay   237

Glossary   247
Notes   259
Note on the Translators   343
Index   345

Note on the Translation of Benjamin's Writings

During the period in which Benjamin wrote "Zur Kritik der Gewalt" (Toward the critique of violence), he was also translating the poetry of Charles Baudelaire and reflecting, in turn, on "Die Aufgabe des Übersetzers" (The task of the translator), to cite the title of the essay he wrote as a preface to his edition of Baudelaire's *Tableaux parisiens* (4:9–21; SW 1:253–63). Beginning with its first sentence, which identifies the "task" (39) at hand, "Toward the Critique of Violence" resonates with "The Task of the Translator"—so much so that the former became preparation for the latter, and the latter can be seen as a distillation of certain elements of the former. In translating Baudelaire, Benjamin had imposing predecessors, including Stefan George, perhaps the most prominent poet of the period; by contrast, in translating several long passages from Georges Sorel's *Réflexions sur la violence* (Reflections on violence) for inclusion in "Toward the Critique of Violence," he was on his own. Note 40 to the essay (see 288) is specifically concerned with the manner in which Benjamin addresses some elements of the "task of the translator" in relation to Sorel's work; more broadly, the striking choices Benjamin makes in his own translations of French political and legal terminology inform the translation of his writings throughout this volume. And in all of the commentary that accompanies "Toward the Critique of Violence," ranging from the Introduction through the endnotes to the Afterword, individual problems of translation come under discussion, while the Glossary at the end of the volume provides a brief summary of our lexical choices. With respect to the conflict between the two tendencies that circumscribe the "task of the translator"—fidelity to the original, on the one hand, and freedom in service to accessibility, on the other (4:17–19; *SW* 1:259–61)—the translations in this volume are more inclined toward the former than the latter, even as they seek to make Benjamin's work comprehensible to contemporary English-speaking readers in all of its alluring and disconcerting complexity.

Julia Ng is the translator of "Toward the Critique of Violence," while Peter Fenves translated the Associated Notes and Fragments, with the exception of the final one, Note 22, which Julia Ng prepared in conjunction with her editing of this hitherto unpublished text. Julia Ng consulted the manuscript originals whenever available and used them to establish the textual basis for the translations, which at times involved reconstituting and reformatting the texts; any deviations from existing published versions can be taken as corrections of the latter. Both editors reviewed and adjusted translations throughout the volume for accuracy and consistency. Benjamin's own notes appear as footnotes; the editors are jointly responsible for the endnotes to his writings.

Acknowledgments

The editors would like to thank Lisa-Marie Fleck and Nora Mercurio at Suhrkamp Verlag for working with us on the texts written by Walter Benjamin included in this volume. We are also grateful that the Hamburger Stiftung zur Förderung von Wissenschaft und Kultur and the editors of the new *Kritische Gesamtausgabe* of Benjamin's works granted us permission to include a previously unpublished manuscript located at the Walter Benjamin Archiv at the Akademie der Künste in Berlin. The editors thank Ursula Marx of the Walter Benjamin Archiv for making available facsimiles of the originals of the associated writings for our reference. In addition, Julia Ng would like to thank Dr. Gregor Wolff and Gudrun Schumacher at the Ibero-American Institute in Berlin for granting her access to the Walter Lehmann Archive.

The editors, furthermore, thank Dr. Harald Lützenkirchen, who, as the president of Kurt-Hiller Gesellschaft, e. V. Hamburg, granted us permission to publish an English translation of "Anti-Kain." We are grateful to Dr. Esther Ehrman for permission to publish a translation of passages from Erich Unger's *Politik und Metaphysik*. David Biale, Markus Hardtmann, Christine Helmer, Jörg Kreienbrock, Gary Saul Morson, Benjamin Sommer, Samuel Weber, and Jürgen Wehnert generously responded to queries concerning especially difficult terms, citations, and allusions. Ariel Weiner reviewed the final version of the manuscript, and Jonas Rosenbrück compiled the index. Finally, we are beneficiaries of detailed and helpful suggestions made by two anonymous readers of earlier versions of the translations in this volume.

Abbreviations and Conventions

In the body of the volume, citations of a multi-volume text in parentheses without any additional abbreviation, for example, "(2:179)," refer to the following edition, which is designated by *GS* whenever it is required: Walter Benjamin, *Gesammelte Schriften*, 7 vols., ed. Rolf Tiedemann and Hermann Schweppenhäuser (Frankfurt am Main: Suhrkamp, 1972–91). Citations to a single-volume text in parentheses, for example, "(217)," refer to this volume.

The following abbreviations are used throughout the volume:

GB	Walter Benjamin. *Gesammelte Briefe*. 6 vols. Edited by Christoph Gödde and Henri Lonitz. Frankfurt am Main: Suhrkamp, 1995–2000.
KGA	Walter Benjamin. *Werke und Nachlaß: Kritische Gesamtausgabe*. 21 vols. planned, 9 vols. to date. Edited by Christoph Gödde and Henri Lonitz in association with the Walter Benjamin Archive. Frankfurt am Main: Suhrkamp, 2008– . (References to a volume of this edition also include the names of its individual editors.)
TB	Gershom Scholem. *Tagebücher: Nebst Aufsätzen und Entwürfen bis 1923*. 2 vols. Edited by Karlfried Gründer, Herbert Kopp-Oberstebrink, and Friedrich Niewöhner in association with Karl Grözinger. Frankurt am Main: Jüdischer Verlag, 1995–2000.
Scholem Arc	Gershom Scholem Archive, National Library of Israel, Jerusalem.
Scholem Coll	Gershom Scholem Collection, National Library of Israel, Jerusalem.
WBA	Walter Benjamin Archive, Akademie der Künste, Berlin.

All translations throughout the volume are new; references to existing translations are given whenever available for the convenience of English-speaking readers. When references are made to existing translations of Benjamin's writings not included in this volume, the following abbreviations are used:

C   Walter Benjamin. *Correspondence*. Translated by Manfred Jacobsen and Evelyn Jacobsen. Chicago: University of Chicago Press, 1994.

O   Walter Benjamin. *Origin of the German Trauerspiel*. Translated by Howard Eiland. Cambridge, MA: Harvard University Press, 2019.

SW   Walter Benjamin. *Selected Writings*. 4 vols. Edited by Michael Jennings, Howard Eiland, et al. Cambridge, MA: Harvard University Press, 1996–2000.

Citations without abbreviations in the appendices to the volume refer to the original pagination of the relevant texts. References to Kant's writings throughout the volume use the following abbreviations:

AkA   Immanuel Kant. *Gesammelte Schriften*. 29 vols. to date. Edited by Königlich-Preußische (later, Deutsche) Akademie der Wissenschaften. Berlin: Reimer; later, Walter de Gruyter, 1900– .

A   *Critique of Pure Reason* (1781 edition)

B   *Critique of Pure Reason* (1787 edition)

For the Notes and Fragments, the following editorial conventions are used:

Single underline in the manuscript = italics
Double underline in the manuscript = underlined italics
Square brackets in the manuscript = { }
Editorial insertions = < >

In the Afterword, brackets in the original are indicated with { }.

Toward the Critique of Violence

INTRODUCTION

by Peter Fenves

Walter Benjamin wrote "Toward the Critique of Violence" in January 1921, while staying in his parents' house in an upper-middle-class district of Berlin.¹ Little more than two years had passed since a group of sailors in Kiel mutinied, the German Revolution began, and the First World War ended. When the German Revolution itself ended is a matter of dispute. In August 1919, Friedrich Ebert, the leader of the Social Democratic Party (SPD) who had recently been elected to the position of Reichspräsident, signed the constitution that had been drafted in Weimar as a reminder of Germany's cultural accomplishments; but the status of the new democratic-constitutional state was far from secure. "Toward the Critique of Violence" refers directly to the violence of the recent war only in relation to the law of universal conscription (45). With respect to the events of the German Revolution, it is similarly reticent. Nowhere does Benjamin mention, for instance, the revolutionary regimes in Munich or the assassinations of their leaders, including Kurt Eisner and Gustav Landauer; the battle around the *Vorwärts* building in Berlin or the subsequent assassinations of Karl Liebknecht and Rosa Luxemburg; the general strike in March 1920 that led to the defeat of the Kapp-Lüttwitz putsch, allowing constitutional governance to resume; or the continuation of the general strike in the Ruhr region, where it was brutally suppressed by governmental and right-wing paramilitary forces in tandem.² "Toward the Critique of Violence" draws attention only to a single and arguably minor incident in the "recently elapsed German revolution" (52): doctors going on strike, "as was seen in several German cities" (53).³ Kurt Hiller's "Anti-Cain," which Benjamin criticizes near the end of his essay, reproduces a newspaper report about doctors in Greifswald staging a walkout because the local Council of Workers and Soldiers had "forcibly [*gewaltig*]" (188) raised a red flag over the roof of the university hospital. Concerned more with a class of events than with any particular one, Benjamin does not identify the cities where doctors went on strike, nor does he mention the cause of the one Hiller denounces. As with Greifswald, so with the rest of Germany and beyond: "Toward the Critique of Violence" nowhere refers to the violent conflicts over council or soviet forms of governance.

These omissions are elements of its double focus. Near the beginning of the essay Benjamin notes that he will circumscribe the horizons of his investigation to the circumstances of "contemporary Europe" (42); in the concluding paragraph, by contrast, he criticizes any "gaze" (60) that would limit its purview of violence to what occurs only close at hand. The double focus of the essay makes it difficult for its readers to locate its author, determine where he stands, or what he stands for. Published in a prominent journal for the advancement of research in the social sciences, "Toward the Critique of Violence" maintains a tone of scholarly objectivity, which may lead readers to suppose for a moment that its author is coming from, or seeking entrance into, an established academic field. This impression is soon dispelled, however, for just as the essay does not associate itself with any political party or program, it remains aloof from standard scholarly affiliations. Yet the essay is not therefore relentlessly negative, "critical" of every position, left or right, within and beyond academic disputes—which would suggest that the author seeks to occupy the position of a "nihilist" who stands for nothing and affiliates with no one. Benjamin, to be sure, emphatically rejects the position advanced in "Anti-Cain," but this comes only after he has associated his line of argument with a heterogeneous group of thinkers and scholars, including Immanuel Kant, whose name signifies so much that it signals very little; Georges Sorel, none of whose major works had yet been translated into German; and Erich Unger, whose work was largely unknown in 1921, as it remains today.⁴ What do these associations add up to—some form of cosmopolitan-republicanism in conjunction with Kant's *Zum ewigen Frieden* (Toward eternal peace), a version of anarcho-syndicalism in relation to Sorel's *Refléxions sur la violence* (Reflections on violence), and an unknown "ism" connected with Unger's *Politik und Metaphysik* (Politics and metaphysics)? With respect to the only other scholar with whom Benjamin aligns his argument, Hermann Cohen, the body of work associated with this name certainly signifies a well-defined set of academic and political affiliations; but Benjamin indicates that the insight he draws from *Ethik des reinen Willens* (Ethics of pure will) came to its author inadvertently.

For all of these reasons, combined with the obscurity of its twenty-nine-year-old author, it is scarcely surprising that "Toward the Critique of Violence" generated almost no response during the Weimar period. Despite persistent rumors to the contrary, there is no evidence that any well-known intellectual of the period—Carl Schmitt is often mentioned in this context—responded to the essay, with the possible exception of the travel writer Alfons Paquet, who briefly sketches his own "critique of violence" in 1924.[5] In an unpublished academic exercise from 1926, Leo Löwenthal mentions Benjamin's essay in a footnote, but only to dismiss its argument as irrelevant to his concerns.[6] In 1929, a young political theorist and theologian, Karl Thieme, refers to the essay in a minireview of the first German translation of Sorel's *Reflections on Violence*.[7] Three years later, in a monograph on Sorel as "conservative revolutionary," Michael Freund indiscriminately associates Benjamin's essay with several disciples of Sorel who follow him in distinguishing life-affirming violence from stultifying power.[8] A similarly brief yet far more incisive remark appears in Thieme's essay "Una Sancta Catholica: Rückblick und Ausblick [Retrospect and prospect] 1933," which recommends Benjamin's "Theorien des deutschen Faschismus" (Theories of German fascism) as an antidote to Ernst Jünger's novels and refers without further elucidation to the "unfathomably deep analyses" undertaken in "Toward the Critique of Violence."[9] "Una Sancta Catholica" could not prompt further interest in Benjamin's essay, however, since it appeared in the very last issue of *Religiöse Besinnung* (Religious reflection), which the Nazis shuttered upon seizing power. A Hungarian jurist mentions the essay in a routine academic exercise that is worth recalling here only because it was published by a Berlin-based press in 1934. Appearing in alphabetical order among fifty-some articles and books concerned with the relation of violence to power, "Toward the Critique of Violence"—in title alone—slipped past Nazi-era censorship.[10]

In 1955, the Suhrkamp publishing house reprinted "Toward the Critique of Violence"—with a notable error—as the first item in a two-volume edition of Benjamin's writings edited by Theodor and Gretel Adorno.[11] Ten years later, responding to a surge of interest in Benjamin's thought, Suhrkamp published a slim follow-up volume titled *Zur Kritik der Gewalt und andere Aufsätze* (Toward the critique of violence and other essays), which concludes with an afterword by Herbert Marcuse that reflects on the "enormous distance" separating Benjamin's words and phrases from those currently in vogue.[12] The conditions under which Benjamin could still speak of "the culture of the heart" (50), for instance, have changed so drastically, Marcuse suggests, that, if a similar phrase were formed today, it would immediately prompt suspicions of false content and mendacious tone.[13]

Something of what Marcuse says about the words and phrases of "Toward the Critique of Violence" may already have been true when Benjamin submitted his essay to a publisher—and perhaps remains so today. Nevertheless, much has changed. Even if the terminology found in Benjamin's writings does not enter into what often passes for political discourse, it reverberates throughout a broad range of discussions conducted in numerous languages in and beyond scholarly contexts. With the publication of Jacques Derrida's *Force de loi*, Werner Hamacher's "Afformativ, Streik," Giorgio Agamben's *Homo Sacer*, and Judith Butler's *Parting Ways*—to name only a few prominent responses to "Toward the Critique of Violence" in European languages, each of which is vastly different from the others—the situation on the hundredth anniversary of its publication is utterly unlike the near silence with which it was originally greeted.[14]

The double focus of "Toward the Critique of Violence" is reflected in the structure of this volume. As a "critical edition," it does not compare various versions of the essay and seek to construct one that most accurately reflects the author's intention, for there are no extant manuscripts, only the published text, which was neither republished nor translated during the author's lifetime. The critical character of the edition lies, rather, in its annotation of the essay and in its two sets of associated writings—on the one hand, a large selection of Benjamin's closely related notes and fragments in which the relevant manuscripts are accurately reproduced, and on the other, selected passages from all of the contemporaneous books and articles Benjamin cites in his essay. The first set of associated writings allows readers to follow the variety of paths that he pursues in formulating the argument of the essay and in developing some of its premises, corollaries, and consequences; the second set allows readers to become familiar with the texts he approvingly cites in the essay—and in the case of "Anti-Cain," an argument he wholeheartedly rejects. Although placed at the end, the second set of associated writings is an integral part of the volume, for without the inclusion of other lines of argumentation, Benjamin would not have been able to complete his own. This is apparent from a letter he sent to Ernst Schoen in September 1919, where he exuberantly describes how his recent conversations with Ernst Bloch forced him to alter his previous attitude, which consisted in a stultifying rejection of "*every* contemporary political trend" (*GB* 2:46; *C* 148). Accepting *some* contemporaneous political trends—although, it should be emphasized, not Bloch's—is therefore a crucial element in the construction of Benjamin's essay, even if the trends with which he aligns its argument are incompatible with one another. As for the last item in this volume, Emil Lederer's "Soziologie der Gewalt" (Sociology of violence), Benjamin nowhere cites it in any of his extant writings; but Lederer was the first reader of the essay, and "Sociology of Violence" gives insight into the manner in which it was—and still is—received even by presumably sympathetic readers.

Prompted by "Toward the Critique of Violence," Lederer reiterates an argument that finds expression in the tension between the complementary nouns in the full title of his essay: "Sociology of Violence [*Gewalt*]: A Contribution to the Theory of Social-Formative Forces [*Kräfte*]." In the context of sociopolitical analysis, *Gewalt* is often translated by "force." One of Lederer's foremost predecessors, Friedrich Engels, wrote a treatise about Bismarck's politics of "blood and iron" under a title that reads in its English version *The Role of Force* [*Gewalt*] *in History*.[15] The translation of *Gewalt* as "force" is based on an argument that is similarly expressed in the relevant title: when violence assumes a dramatic role in the historical process, it reveals itself as a social-formative force. In his "Theory of Force [*Gewalt*]," Engels argues that no appeal to the "immoral" or "diabolical" character of violence carries any consequences at those crucial moments in history when violence helps form a society by destroying its antiquated political-juridical frameworks: "In the words of Marx," Engels concludes, "[*Gewalt*] is the midwife of every old society pregnant with a new one [and is thus] the instrument with the aid of which social movement breaks through, shattering dead, fossilized political forms."[16] Without reference to the images of dramatic or biological processes, Lederer immediately identifies *Gewalt* as a "tool" (238) and argues that, today—the winter of 1921—violence can no longer be cast in the coveted role of a social-formative force. *Gewalt* thus simply means "violence," which, as such, can never break through political impasses, much less assist with the birth of a new social order. As a "thing of yesterday" (237), despite its destructive capacity, it has neither histrionic nor maieutic power. "Sociology of Violence" doubtless addresses some of the major questions posed in Benjamin's essay; nevertheless, under Lederer's optic, whose historical vista extends no further than medieval Europe, its basic thesis is neither extended nor refuted but repressed. This thesis appears midway in the essay: "All violence as a means is either law-positing or law-preserving" (48). Every form of violence that conforms to a given end also aims either for the preservation of current law or for its replacement by still another one—except, Benjamin adds, in the case of contemporary police forces, which, as a "spectral mixture" (47), convert this either/or into an invasively violent both/and. In a formal sense, however, as the essay proceeds to show, this is not the end of violence, that is, not its only possible form; on the contrary, a preconception of violence as a "tool" or "instrument" is a function of a political unconscious that makes it impossible to conceive of, and thus actually evaluate, violence in general.[17] By surveying a vista that is at once much closer and much wider than Lederer's, Benjamin does not simply draw attention to certain stages in the history of law-related violence but envisages its "ending" (59) as well.

The following introduction, broken into three sections, does not further describe the reception of "Toward the Critique of Violence," nor does it attempt to grasp any of the ways in which its argument can be productively applied to contemporary circumstances. Rather, it is concerned solely with the circumstances surrounding the essay: first, the conditions of its publication, which include the nonpublication of a complementary essay Benjamin wrote under the alluring title "Der wahre Politiker" (The true politician) that unfortunately has been lost; second, the program of research in view of which he was able to complete two "political essays" (*GB* 2:101) in rapid succession during the winter of 1920/21; and finally, the epitome of this program as it appears in the "observations" (39) with which Benjamin begins "Toward the Critique of Violence." The goal of the introduction, in short, is to help readers grasp Benjamin's own introduction to his essay. A coda briefly describes what the volume lacks beyond the lamentable absence of "The True Politician."

"Archive" and "White Pages"

"Toward the Critique of Violence" was published in the forty-seventh issue of the *Archiv für Sozialwissenschaft und Sozialpolitik* (Archive for social science and social policy). Originally founded as the *Archiv für soziale Gesetzgebung und Statistik* (Archive for social legislation and statistics), the journal embarked on a "new series" with a revised title in 1904, when Edgar Jaffé became its managing editor and invited two innovative sociologists, Max Weber and Werner Sombart, to form its editorial board.[18] The introduction to the new series, cowritten by the three editors, describes the change in direction of the journal: whereas there was once only a desire for statistical information about the scope and scale of capitalist development, "the reawakening of philosophical interest in general" has generated a "hunger for social theory," the satisfaction of which will become the principal task of the rechristened *Archiv*.[19] The sociology of religion gained considerable prominence, as signaled by the second issue under the new title, which includes the initial installment of Weber's singularly influential study *Die protestantische Ethik und der "Geist" des Kapitalismus* (The Protestant ethic and the "spirit" of capitalism).[20] This was soon followed by Ernst Troeltsch's closely related treatise, *Soziallehren der christlichen Kirche* (Social doctrines of the Christian church).[21] By 1921, however, much had changed—above all, because of war and revolution. Jaffé supported the November 1918 Munich uprising and served under Kurt Eisner as the first and only finance minister in the short-lived People's State of Bavaria. With the collapse of the People's State and Eisner's assassination, Jaffé withdrew from professional life. He died in 1921 at the age of 55. Weber, a year older, died a year earlier. Sombart, who had been a supporter of the pan-German-nationalist "ideas of 1914," lived much longer; but the forty-seventh issue is the last one in which he is listed as coeditor. As his political views tended rightward, his relation to the journal frayed.[22]

Leadership of the *Archiv* fell to Lederer, who had played a role in managing the journal since 1910. He also published dozens of essays and articles in the fields of economic theory and social policy, especially as they concern class conflict, the status of white-collar workers, and the characteristics of the war economy.[23] Although a dedicated socialist, he studied with members of the Austrian school of economics, especially Joseph Schumpeter, who effectively replaced Sombart on the editorial board of the *Archiv* in the last years of the war. Another founder of the Austrian school of economics, Ludwig von Mises, contributed an essay to the forty-seventh issue, "Die Wirtschaftsrechnung im sozialistischen Gemeinwesen" (Economic calculation in the socialist commonwealth), which has long been recognized as a classic example of the school's style of reasoning, as it purports to demonstrate the economic irrationality of socialism in general.[24] If Benjamin's essay recalls the first issues of the newly renamed *Archiv* in which it sought to fulfill a desire for philosophically infused political theory, von Mises's contribution anticipates an era in which marginal theory and mathematical methods dominate social-scientific journals.

Beyond those already mentioned, the forty-seventh issue of the *Archiv* includes several other notable contributions, including Max Weber's posthumously published inquiry into the sociology of the city and Hans Kelsen's reflections on the "essence and value of democracy," which derive in large part from his experience in drafting the constitution for the new state of Austria.[25] Lederer made several contributions of his own, including an inquiry into the situation of labor unions during the German Revolution.[26] In his editorial capacity, he also opened the journal to younger scholars, who had no academic credentials beyond their PhDs. This characterizes Benjamin's situation at the time, and so too several other contributors—including, as it happens, Karl Marx. Gustav Mayer, a journalist who had recently published a biography of the young Engels, prepared an essay for the *Archiv* from a mass of papers that was later published in Moscow under the title *Die deutsche Ideologie* (The German ideology). Mayer's selection of pages could scarcely have been less topical, for the result of his editorial work was an essay, obscurely titled "Das Leipziger Konzil" (The Leipzig Council), which derived from the string of eviscerating attacks on Bruno Bauer that Marx launched in "Zur Judenfrage" (On the Jewish question) and continued in *Die heilige Familie, oder Kritik der kritischen Kritik* (The holy family, or a critique of critical critique).[27] At the beginning of the essay Mayer produced for the *Archiv*, Marx indicates why he finds it necessary to turn his attention yet again to Bauer: not only did "Saint Bruno" miss the point of the earlier attacks, but as a critic of every political trend, he attributes his own immunity from criticism to the "glory of 'pure critique.'"[28]

Marx did not, of course, intend to publish anything in the *Archiv*. Neither, surprisingly, did Benjamin. In a long letter he began to write to Scholem in early January 1921 but completed only at the end of the month, Benjamin notes in passing that Lederer had "commissioned [*bestellt*]" (*GB* 2: 127; *C* 172) an essay from him. He does not indicate how Lederer contacted him, nor does he describe the terms of the commission. Among Lederer's literary remains, there are unfortunately no records before 1922.[29] The most likely intermediary was Ernst Bloch, who befriended Lederer during his years in Heidelberg and became acquainted with Benjamin when they lived near each other in Switzerland. Lederer had commissioned Bloch to write a report on Swiss pacifism that eventually appeared in the forty-sixth issue of the *Archiv*.[30] Perhaps with a report of this kind in mind—written in a lively expressionist style—Lederer solicited a contribution from Benjamin. Only one aspect of Lederer's commission is certain, however: it came with a "fixed deadline" (*GB* 2:125) that Benjamin dutifully met. Resuming his letter to Scholem at the end of January 1921, he adds a second and final postscript in which he describes the status of the commission to which he had referred in the opening paragraphs of the letter: "I am finished with 'Toward the Critique of Violence' and hope that Lederer will bring it out in *Die weißen Blätter*" (*GB* 2:131; *C* 174; cf. *GB* 2:130; *C* 173).

Die weißen Blätter (The white pages) rather than the *Archiv* was thus the venue in view of which Benjamin wrote "Toward the Critique of Violence." This is an odd conjuncture of journals. In their original forms, they could hardly be more different. Even their titles indicate as much: whereas an "archive" preserves the past, "white pages" summon the future. Founded in 1913 as an "organ of the younger generation," *Die weißen Blätter* presents itself as the blank slate on which "the coming literature" was to have been written.[31] Thus proclaims its original editor, Ernst-Erik Schwabach, in its inaugural issue. And he was not deluded, for the journal did indeed play a significant role in the emergence of early twentieth-century German literature. The list of its authors includes—to name only a few whose works have appeared in English—Gottfried Benn, Else Lasker-Schüler, Heinrich Mann, Carl Einstein, and Robert Musil. Franz Kafka contributed a single item, "Die Verwandlung" (The metamorphosis), which appeared in the 1915 issue and earned its author the money associated with the Theodor-Fontane Prize, although the prize itself went to Carl Sternheim, another contributor to the journal.[32] Also in 1915, René Schickele assumed its editorship and sharpened its political focus. A pacifist with dual French-German nationality, Schickele fiercely opposed the war and accordingly made the journal into a forum for intra-European reconciliation, where citizens of belligerent nations could at least appear together in print.[33]

By 1920, Schickele had withdrawn as editor, and the publisher, Paul Cassirer, announced a change in format: *Die weißen Blätter* would henceforth appear only a few times a year, with each issue assigned a different editor who would choose a particular theme. In the last year of its monthly format, Lederer contributed an analysis of class conflicts during the German Revolution that concluded with the claim that the "situation is ripe" for the working classes finally to find an "objectively valid" conception of themselves.[34] Perhaps with the expectation that Lederer could contribute to this effort, Cassirer appointed him as the first—and as it turns out, the only—editor in the "new series" of the journal. Lederer thus enjoyed a proverbially clean slate for his issue of *Die weißen Blätter*. Its theme, though, is not entirely clear, despite the bland title printed on the frontispiece of the issue, "Sociological Problems of the Present."[35] Instead of describing these problems, Lederer opens his issue with a strangely dyspeptic preface, "Zur Einführung" (By way of introduction) that seeks to identify and dispel a new ghost haunting postwar Germany: "Until now," he writes in the opening paragraph of the introduction, "Germany has been the land of political romanticism. It is also starting to turn into the land of social romanticism. *Reality* does not act especially well upon the German intellectual; he is not in a position to see or handle it."[36] The theme of the issue can thus be understood in polemical terms: Lederer will launch a counteroffensive against the metamorphosis of the German ideology from political to social romanticism.

Writing to Scholem in February 1921, Benjamin describes the disposition of his essay as follows: "Lederer considered it too long and too difficult for *Die weißen Blätter*; but he has accepted it for the *Archiv für Sozialwissenschaft*, which he also edits" (*GB* 2:138). All of the essays in Lederer's edition of *Die weißen Blätter* are doubtless less difficult than Benjamin's, but this is arguably true of the essays in the *Archiv* as well, including Marx's and von Mises's. With respect to length, Benjamin's essay is an outlier; but at least in the case of Ernst Bloch's contribution to the issue, "Über den sittlichen und geistigen Führer" (On the moral and spiritual leader), Lederer seems to have received a longer version that he simply reduced.[37] Because of its breadth and complexity, "Toward the Critique of Violence" may have been less amenable to editorial intervention than Bloch's essay; but the main reason for the change of journals was in all likelihood its content. Insofar as Benjamin's essay maintains, for instance, that the "culture of the heart" (50) makes it possible for conflicts among individuals to be resolved without resorting to violence of any kind, Lederer may have seen it as a species of the very "social romanticism" against which the issue as a whole was directed. And syndicalism, strongly associated with Sorel's name, was, in Lederer's view, nothing more than a defunct petit-bourgeois ideology that should be abandoned, so that the working classes can gain an "objectively valid" conception of themselves.[38] Lederer in any case published his own reflections on violence in a slot that had doubtless been reserved for Benjamin's work.

Die weißen Blätter ceased publication after the first issue of its "new series," while the *Archiv* continued to thrive until the Nazis shuttered its operations. Benjamin was therefore uncharacteristically fortunate in the ultimate destination of his essay. Nevertheless, there are reasons to suppose that Lederer published "Toward the Critique of Violence" in such a way that it would immediately become, to use his own words, a "thing of yesterday" (237)—buried, as it were, in the archive of (in Marx's words) "critical criticism." Inasmuch as he commissioned an essay from Benjamin and received one within the assigned deadline, he could not in good conscience deny publication altogether. Nor could he parry the force of Benjamin's essay with a preface akin to the one with which he introduces his issue of *Die weißen Blätter*. Marx, however, could perform this service for him. The following passage from his contribution to the forty-seventh issue directly precedes Benjamin's: "Saint Bruno [Bauer] goes so far as to 'be able and be willing' to give us two items of the most profound information about the state-shattering power of critique [*staatsbrecherische Macht der Kritik*]—first, the information that 'critique and critics hold power in their hands [*haben die Gewalt in ihren Hände*], because' (a beautiful 'because'!) 'force [*Kraft*] [lies] in their consciousness,' and second, the information that these great fabricators of history 'hold power [*Gewalt*] in their hands' because they 'draw power [*Macht*] from themselves and from critique' (thus, again from themselves)—whereby, unfortunately, it remains unproven that anything at all can be 'drawn' from within 'themselves,' from within 'critique.'"[39] In revisiting the polemical pyrotechnics of the young Marx, readers of the *Archiv* not only can see that he was fully capable of playing with the semantic slippage around *Gewalt*, *Macht*, and *Kraft*; they are likewise induced to ask whether or not he ultimately mastered the slippage in his scientific work, beginning with *Zur Kritik der politischen Ökonomie* (Contribution to the critique of political economy) and continuing through the posthumously published volumes of *Capital*.⁴⁰ Within the pages of the journal itself, "The Leipzig Council" assumes another role as well: the thrust of Marx's attack on "Saint Bruno" extends to the next essay, especially its concluding paragraphs, where such seemingly sacral terms as "expiation" (56) and "pure divine violence" (60) are on prominent display. Did Lederer want readers to view Benjamin as "Saint Walter"? Perhaps not, but the *Archiv* resurrects Marx's literary corpus to exorcise another specter of "pure critique."⁴¹

And beyond the first essay Lederer received from Benjamin, he would publish nothing further. Benjamin offered him "The True Politician," which, from the evidence of the title alone, would have been an appropriate sequel to Bloch's "On the Moral and Spiritual Leader." According to Bloch, there can be no such thing as a "spiritual leader," and Benjamin may have argued in turn that the "true politician" cannot be a leader at all. Lederer, though, rejected "The True Politician" with the perfunctory words of an overworked editor: "maybe later." This is evident from a remark Benjamin makes in the postscript to the letter that records the progress of his work during the month of January: "[T]he 'True Politician' has definitely not been accepted [for publication], since Lederer, at least for now, does not want to bring it out" (*GB* 2:130; *C* 174).⁴² Benjamin immediately adds: "And of course I am not turning to Bloch now. We [Benjamin and his wife Dora] have still not had a line from him since the death notice [of Bloch's wife, Else von Stritzky, who died on January 2, 1921]" (*GB* 2:131–32; *C* 174). Benjamin, in other words, did not have the temerity to solicit a friend in mourning and ask him to intercede on his professional behalf.⁴³ As a result, "The True Politician" did not follow "On the Moral and Spiritual Leader" in the last issue of *Die weißen Blätter*.

"Politics" and "My Moral Philosophy"

In the spring of 1923, Benjamin encountered an editor who did want to publish "The True Politician": Martin Buber. This was a remarkable turn of events, for, several years earlier, Buber had asked Benjamin whether he would be interested in contributing an essay for one of his new publishing ventures, but after months of reflection, Benjamin declined the offer in a densely argued letter that Buber never directly answered.⁴⁴ Nonetheless, in 1923, the two of them entered into an agreement whereby Buber would publish "The True Politician" in a forthcoming series of volumes that would be guided by certain no longer extant "leading principles" (*GB* 2:333). The willingness on both sides to enter into this agreement can certainly be understood as the simple coincidence of an editor in search of contributors and an author in search of a publisher, but neither Buber nor Benjamin tended to conduct matters of publication in such a haphazard manner. And there is at least one compelling reason to suppose that these two occurrences, stretching across some eight years, are closely connected with each other: the title of the essay Buber accepted in 1923 resonates with the terms in which Benjamin rejected Buber's earlier request. It is as though—and both of them must have recognized this—the letter in which Benjamin described the reasons for his refusal to participate in Buber's earlier publishing project forms the blueprint of the essay Buber wanted to include in a later series of publications in lieu of a direct response to the letter itself.

Here, then, is a brief résumé of the earlier encounter between Benjamin and Buber. In the fall of 1915, Buber asked Benjamin whether he would contribute an essay to a journal he would soon be editing under the title *Der Jude* (The Jew). Benjamin was an unlikely candidate for inclusion in this journal, for, beyond his lack of expertise in Jewish matters, he had published nothing outside of youth- and student-movement periodicals, with the exception of the republication of "Das Leben der Studenten" (The life of students) in Hiller's journal *Das Ziel* (The goal), and even this, as he informs Buber, was a mistake, for he quickly recognized that he had nothing in common with Hiller's "activist" program (*GB* 1:327; *C* 81).[45] Buber, by contrast, was already a major figure in the German-speaking literary world. Among his many accomplishments, he had edited a prominent series of monographs under the rubric of *Gesellschaft* (Society); authored a Nietzsche-inspired novel titled *Daniel: Gespräche von der Verwirklichung* (Daniel: Dialogues on realization); translated into mellifluous German several collections of Hasidic tales; and most recently, called for "Jewish renewal" in a widely read manifesto, *Drei Reden über das Judentum* (Three discourses on Judaism), which establishes the tone and framework for the launch of *Der Jude*. Despite a degree of skepticism with respect to Buber's work in general, especially its constant invocation of "Jewish lived experience [*Erlebnis*]" (*GB* 1:75), Benjamin wrote a brief note to Buber in November 1915 indicating that he had persistently occupied himself with the theme of "Jewish spirit [*Geist*]" (*GB* 1:283) and would therefore consider submitting an essay to *Der Jude* after the two of them—perhaps with Scholem present as well—had a chance to discuss its content. The first item in the associated writings of this volume, "Notes toward a Work on the Category of Justice," may stem from Benjamin's reflections on a potential contribution to *Der Jude*. The only definitive result of these reflections, however, was a letter he sent to Buber in July 1916 in which he formally declines to participate in *Der Jude* "in its current stage" (GB 1:327; C 81).

As Benjamin indicates at the beginning of the 1916 letter, his decision was partly based on the intensity of his disagreement with several articles in the journal that expressed enthusiasm for the "European war" (GB 1:325; C 79). This doubtless included—although Benjamin was too polite to say so—the essay with which Buber introduced *Der Jude*, "Die Losung" (The watchword), where he claims that "assimilated Jews" for the first time in their scattered, largely meaningless lives feel responsible for their community "by virtue of the Jewish lived experience of this war."[46] Benjamin's antipathy to this kind of talk was not, however, the primary reason for his refusal to participate in *Der Jude*; the reason lay, rather, in his sense of what "politically effective writings" (GB 1:325; C 79) entail. After describing in an "apodictic" manner the relation between words and actions, such that the former are not conceived as cumulative motivations for the latter, Benjamin concludes that *Der Jude* does not accord with his "concept of an objective [*sachlichen*] and at the same time highly political [*hochpolitisch*] style and writing" (GB 1:326; C 80), which he summarizes in terms of a double movement: a highly political style leads to a point where words "fail" (*versagen*), while at the same time this failure eliminates all traces of "the unsayable." Insofar as the unsayable is evacuated, the failure of words cannot be mistaken for a—charismatic, authoritative, or authoritarian—intimation of a higher language that would confuse political writing with poetry or prophecy. Benjamin closes his letter to Buber in a cordial manner by indicating that he would consider submitting his work to an altered "stage" of *Der Jude*. He even proposes Heidelberg as a potential meeting place for a nonepistolary dialogue.

Neither of these occurred: Buber and Benjamin did not enter into a dialogue in Heidelberg, and Benjamin never submitted anything of his own to *Der Jude*. Still, Benjamin's letter to Buber may have been singularly effective on both sides of their missed encounter. For Benjamin, the letter clarified the elements of style that would guide his political writings, beginning perhaps with "The True Politician" and definitely encompassing "Toward the Critique of Violence." For Buber, the effect of the letter may have been even more profound: his mode of thought underwent a decisive change in July 1916. Not only did he reject his earlier view of the violence of the First

World War as a positive step toward the "renewal" of Judaism in particular and humanity in general; he also—and for this reason—began to replace the theme of "lived experience" with that of dialogical encounter. In *Ich und Du* (I and Thou), which first appeared in 1923, Buber presents the core of such a language-centered encounter in terms that closely resemble those he found in Benjamin's sketch of a nonprophetic and nonpoetic style that is nevertheless capable of achieving a "true effect" (*GB* 1:327; *C* 80).⁴⁷ And in the same year, the two of them resumed their interrupted correspondence by agreeing to include "The True Politician" in the first volume of Buber's new publishing project.

Despite the appearance of such works as Buber's *I and Thou* and Benjamin's translation of Baudelaire's *Tableaux parisiens*, 1923 was not an auspicious time for German publishers, nor for the Weimar Republic in general. It was the year of hyperinflation.⁴⁸ Buber was unable to secure support for a sequence of volumes that was probably modeled on the influential Gesellschaft series.⁴⁹ After Benjamin learned that Buber's publication plans were no longer viable, he asked him to mail the manuscript to an intermediary who was involved in the production of a collection of essays in honor of Gottfried Salomon, a sociologist at the University of Frankfurt whom Benjamin befriended in conjunction with his efforts to obtain his *venia legendi* (license to teach).⁵⁰ Salomon clearly appreciated both "The True Politician" and "Toward the Critique of Violence" (*GB* 2:385), and the latter may have convinced him to support a German translation of Sorel's *Reflections on Violence*; but the volume in honor of his thirty-second or thirty-third birthday never appeared. Benjamin's essay was thus left "homeless," prompting him to rename it "The Poor Politician" (*GB* 2:518).⁵¹ In a letter to Salomon from January 1925, he takes stock of the situation: "The arsenal of my political works encompasses only: 'The True Politician' and the 'Critique of Violence.' Yes, there are a series of interesting aphorisms for a planned third treatise; but I have the decency to give them out as such [that is, as aphorisms]. Still, I could not send them at this time in print-ready form" (*GB* 3:9–10).

This description of Benjamin's "arsenal" corresponds to remarks he makes in several letters in the early 1920s. In the first of these, dating from the fall of 1920, Benjamin addresses the journalist and "urban garden" activist Bernhard Kampffmeyer, asking his help in procuring some books that were difficult to find in Germany, especially Sorel's *Reflections on Violence*: "In a series of political essays on which I am currently working, I intend to write a treatise on

'The Dismantling of Violence' [*Abbau der Gewalt*], and for the development of my thoughts I would like to orient myself a little in the status of this question. It is, above all, the anarchist literature that comes under consideration. And within this literature, in turn, the kind that interests me the most is that which, concerning violence, not only rejects it with respect to the state but is more or less apologetic with respect to its revolutionary kind" (*GB* 2:101).[52] The title of the proposed essay is different from the essay that eventually appeared in the *Archiv*, but the direction of its argument is broadly the same. By reaching out to Kampffmeyer, whom he had never met, he demonstrates the degree to which he took seriously what he had written to Ernst Schoen in the aforementioned letter from September 1919: he no longer rejects "*every contemporary political trend*" (*GB* 2:46; *C* 148); on the contrary, in contacting Kampffmeyer, he goes out of his way to connect his line of thinking with at least *one* current trend.

In a letter to Scholem that dates from the beginning of December 1920, Benjamin outlines some elements of a book titled *Politics*.[53] Oddly enough—and Scholem seems to have misconstrued the letter because of this oddity—he proceeds backwards, starting with the topic of the project's third and final part: "the philosophical critique of [Paul Scheerbart's science-fiction novel] *Lesabéndio*" (*GB* 2:109; *C* 168).[54] Concerning the second part of the book, Benjamin says nothing of its content but gives its title: "Die wahre Politik" (The true politics). The second section is itself divided into two chapters. The first retains the title mentioned in the letter to Kampffmeyer, "The Dismantling of Violence," and Benjamin again indicates that he requires a "necessary book from France," presumably *Reflections on Violence*. The second chapter of the second part also appears in title only: "Teleology without Final Purpose" (*Teleologie ohne Endzweck*) (*GB* 2:109; *C* 168–69). About the title of the first part of the book Benjamin says nothing. This is perhaps because its content would have been obvious: consistent with scholarly protocols of the period—which he himself would use for his *Origin of the German Trauerspiel*—the proposed book would begin with a theoretical or methodological introduction to a bipartite treatise.

By New Year's Eve 1920/21, the plan Benjamin described at the beginning of the month had changed in a manner that is at once subtle and sweeping. In writing to Scholem at the very end of December, he no longer speaks of a two-part midsection titled "The True Politics." Rather, he announces the completion of "The True Politician": "Hopefully," he immediately adds, "this will soon come into print. After the New Year, I want to write the subsequent works that, with it, should constitute the 'Politics'" (*GB* 2:119; *C* 171). It seems, therefore, that "Politics" is now the title of a project rather than a book, for otherwise Benjamin would probably not plan to publish "The True Politician" as a separate essay. At any rate, during January 1921, he writes "Toward the Critique of Violence," which Lederer receives in the following month. Around the time of its publication in August, Benjamin tells Scholem that he will now turn his attention to "the next and last essay directed at politics [*Aufsatz zur Politik*], which will certainly become much larger than the previous ones" (*GB* 2:117; *C* 185). Benjamin thus returns to the formulation of his plans that appears in his letter to Kampffmeyer: "a series of political essays," the last of which, as he came to realize, would not conform with the style he adopts in the previous two parts. As he explains to Salomon several years later, the "third part" of his "arsenal of political works" is made up of aphorisms, and he has no intention of trying to turn them into a falsely unified treatise. This last part eventually became a book that Benjamin published in 1928 under the title *Einbahnstraße* (One-way street), which reprises, inter alia, a claim that may have been more fully developed in the first part: "The true politician reckons only in target dates [*Terminen*]" (4:122; *SW* 1:470).[55]

Beyond a single letter to Scholem at the beginning of December 1920, in short, there is no indication that Benjamin intended to write a book titled *Politics*. The letter indicates, however, the source of the broader program of research in view of which he was able to complete two "political essays" in the span of two months: it developed, in brief, out of an "altercation [*Auseinandersetzung*] with Kant and Cohen" (*GB* 1:441; *C* 119) that first took shape in his 1917 essay "Über das Programm der kommenden Philosophie" (On the program of the coming philosophy). Benjamin begins the sole description of his "Politics" project by referring Scholem to Salomon Friedländer's review of Bloch's *Spirit of Utopia*, which criticizes Bloch for finding "the Holy Spirit of apocalypse more intelligent than the holy-sober spirit of Kant."[56] Benjamin too had written a review of *The Spirit of Utopia*, which passed through the hands of the neo-Kantian jurist and SPD representative Gustav Radbruch, who in turn was supposed to have forwarded it to the editors of *Kant-Studien*.[57] For unknown reasons, *Kant-Studien* did not publish Benjamin's review, nor—for lack of funds—did the review appear, as Benjamin had expected, in a special issue of the journal *Logos*, which was the other principal literary organ of the period that dedicated itself to the advancement of Kant's philosophical legacy.[58] Like "The True Politician," Benjamin's review has since been lost; still, it is clear enough from the journals to which it was submitted that, like Friedländer's review, it placed Bloch's book under a Kantian optic. And the same optic guides the description of the "Politics" project Benjamin offered Scholem in early December 1920. With the ambiguous exception of "The Dismantling of Violence," all of the topics and titles in the putative *Politics* derive from Kant.[59] And in the case of "The True Politics," the citation of a phrase from one of Kant's works could scarcely have been more topical. The preamble to the Treaty of Versailles consists in the Covenant of the League of Nations, and the first session of its General Assembly convened in November 1920.[60] The name "Kant" does not appear in the covenant, of course; but *Toward Eternal Peace*, which is written in the form of an international treaty, is the most consequential program for the institution of a League of Nations within the history of European thought, as was emphasized at the time by the German signatory of the 1918 armistice and vice chancellor of the republic, Matthias Erzberger, whose manifesto in favor of the *Völkerbund* as the "way to world peace" was widely disseminated in several European languages.[61]

The following passage in *Toward Eternal Peace* is the source of the phrase Benjamin adopts for the title of the central part of his "Politics" project: "The true politics [*Die wahre Politik*] can therefore not take a step without having already paid homage to morality [*Moral*], and although politics by itself is a difficult art, its union with morality is no art all, for as soon as the two struggle against each other, morality into two cuts the knot that politics cannot dissolve [*auflösen*]. — The right of human beings must be held sacred [*heilig*], however great a sacrifice this may yet cost the dominant power [*herrschenden Gewalt*]" (Aka 8:380).[62] Like "Toward the Critique of Violence," *Toward Eternal Peace* combines a complex argument with a disarmingly simple thesis, which is discernible even in this brief passage: politicians must subordinate their policies to the universal and unconditional—hence "categorical"—imperatives that derive from moral self-consciousness. The complexity takes shape in the personification of morality, which can sever the knot with politics, but politics cannot do likewise, that is, "dissolve" or "annul" (*auflösen*) its connection to morality. This is a strange image of morality's great, Alexander-like power. Even stranger is Kant's choice of words, which suggests that the "true politics" is the opposite of its "empirical" counterpart: the latter cannot undo the knot, whereas the former would "redeem" (*erlösen*) the broken whole. Kant thus comes close to formulating a political version of the Lurianic image of "shattering the vessels," which Benjamin, for his part, will incorporate into the preface to his translation of Baudelaire's *Tableaux parisiens* (4:18; *SW* 1:260).[63] By repressing its connection with (personified) morality, (personified) politics breaks apart the whole, and only a redemption of some sort can repair the breach. In suggesting the term *erlösen* (redeem) through its association with the negation of its antonym, *auflösen*, Kant amplifies the theological resonance of the phrase "true politics," which then reverberates in the post-dash claim that a "great sacrifice" must be performed in honor of what "must be held sacred."

Whether or not Benjamin conceived of his "True Politics" as a response to the passage in *Toward Eternal Peace* where he found the phrase cannot be known—above all, because his work on this, the second part of the supposed *Politics*, may have stalled at its initial stages. Nevertheless, an element of what Benjamin planned to develop under the rubric of "true politics" can be discerned from the title of its second chapter, "Teleology without Final Purpose," which alludes to both sections of Kant's bipartite *Kritik der Urteilskraft* (Critique of the power of judgment). In the Critique of Aesthetic Judgment, he famously explicates the appearance of beauty under the categorial form of relation as "purposiveness without purpose" (*Zweckmäßigkeit ohne Zweck*) (*Aka* 5:251).[64] Benjamin retains the syntax of this formula and replaces its terms with those derived from the accompanying Critique of Teleological Judgment—as in the following passage, where the two terms are uneasily conjoined: "[W]e certainly find purposes in the world, and physical teleology [*physische Teleologie*] presents them in such measure that, if we judge in accordance with reason, we will ultimately have grounds to assume as a principle for research into nature that there is nothing at all in nature without a purpose; yet we seek in vain the final purpose [*Endzweck*] of nature in nature itself" (*Aka* 5:454). Even if little can be said for certain about the final purpose, this much is known: it somehow involves the existence of rational beings who transcend the conditioned character of nature by virtue of their receptivity to unconditional moral commands (see *Aka* 5:433–36). For now, the only such beings of which there is any knowledge are human beings as they currently occupy the surface of the earth.

It is to this argument that the title of the second chapter of Benjamin's "True Politics" responds: if "physical teleology" is granted, yet there is no final purpose, then nature must be so constituted that it is everywhere vivified by beings that relate to themselves and one another in a purposive manner; but at the same time, nature is thoroughly de-moralized and therefore, in a certain sense, de-humanized. The project named in the title "Teleology without Final Purpose" thus calls for a double-focused inquiry: the first of its two parts examines the biological sciences, while the second will be concerned with something like science fiction. For the latter, Benjamin chooses Scheerbart's "asteroid-novel" *Lesabéndio*, for which he had already sketched some "prolegomena" for its "critique" (*GB* 2:54). In regard to the biological sciences, Benjamin tells Scholem in February 1921 that he is currently occupying himself "with the epistemology [*Erkenntnistheorie*] of biology for the last or penultimate part of my political works" (*GB* 2:140). His principal guide in this regard is the *Habilitation* thesis that Richard Kroner published in 1913 under the direction of Heinrich Rickert, a neo-Kantian professor of philosophy whose classes Benjamin attended in Freiburg in 1912–13. Kroner's effort to modernize the Critique of Teleological Judgment in light of both Darwinian and Lamarckian theories of evolution largely consists in the construction of a concept of unidirectional "life-accomplishments," which cannot be reduced to reversible physicochemical processes.[65] In the same vein but from a different direction, Benjamin resumes his interest in the "psychophysical problem," perhaps as a result of his interaction with Unger, for whom the solution to this problem allows for an otherwise inaccessible connection of politics with metaphysics.[66]

The disparate areas of inquiry suggested by the phrase "Teleology without Final Purpose"—science fiction, the philosophy of science, the problematic science of psychophysics—are thus united around a missing element, which can be briefly described as "morality in the Kantian sense," generally designated by the term *Moral*. The absence of morality in the Kantian sense poses, however, a major question with respect to the "Politics" project: How can Benjamin retain the Kantian distinction between "the true politics" and its "empirical" counterpart, inasmuch as the former consists in the subordination of the latter to a morality whose source is supersensible? The titles of the two essays Benjamin completed in the winter of 1920/21 register the force of this question. Instead of producing a bipartite section titled "The True Politics," as he had proposed at the beginning of December, he completes a stand-alone essay under a revised title, "The True Politician," at the end of the month. And after the New Year, instead of "dismantling" violence, as he had earlier proposed, he returns to the initial word of the Kantian program and undertakes its "critique." The "toward" in the title of the second stand-alone essay consummates the titular transformation, as Benjamin adopts the first word in the title of the treatise where Kant seeks to distinguish true peace from perpetual preparation for war and thus produces a prototype for the recently convened League of Nations.[67]

With the completion of two "political essays" in the winter of 1920/21 Benjamin dropped from his correspondence any unambiguous reference to a book he wanted to publish under the title *Politics*. Nowhere in his extant notes, moreover, is there anything of the kind. On the contrary, as expressed in Fragment 17 in this volume—which most closely approximates the argument developed in "Toward the Critique of Violence"—the larger project involves not politics but rather moral philosophy: "The expounding of this standpoint [according to which 'only the individual has the right to apply force / use violence'] belongs to the tasks of my moral philosophy" (88). The "my" in this formulation is not a sign of some Nietzsche-inspired attempt to create a morality of one's own invention; indeed, Fragment 18 includes a skeletal analysis of an Übermensch-inflected "elevation" that, recognizing the religious character of capitalism, sets out to fulfill its every demand (91). The "my" of "my moral philosophy," by contrast, refers to the version of practical philosophy that would proceed from Benjamin's "altercation with Kant and Cohen," as briefly described in the following passage from "On the Program of the Coming Philosophy":

> It should by no means be overlooked that the concept of freedom stands in a peculiar correlation to the mechanical concept of experience and was developed accordingly in neo-Kantianism. Here, too, however, it is necessary to emphasize that the entire complex of ethics [*der gesamte Zusammenhang der Ethik*] can no more be absorbed into the concept of morals held by Kant, the Enlightenment, and Kantians than can the complex of metaphysics be absorbed into what they call "experience." With the new concept of knowledge, therefore, not only the concept of experience but also that of freedom will experience a decisive transformation [*Umbildung*]. (2:165; SW 1:105)

The range of notes and fragments in this volume attest to the fecundity and flexibility with which Benjamin elaborates a moral philosophy that is not indebted to a concept of experience in which the relation of cause-and-effect at once underlies the unity of nature and fosters the idea of a freedom that, in transcending all of nature, grounds a supranatural morality. In Fragment 4, Benjamin draws on the lexicon of phenomenology to expand the range of moral philosophy, so that, by including even the most seemingly mechanical—hence, "compulsive" (69)—actions, it can identify certain moments when motive-directed and goal-driven agency "falls away" (69). Fragments 5 to 7 directly derive from the same "altercation with Kant and Cohen" that produces his programmatic essay on "the coming philosophy." Note 8 belongs in this context as well, for in "applying" ethics to history, Benjamin interpolates a paragraph that identifies "guilt-debt" (*Schuld*) as "the highest category of world history": physical processes are in principle reversible, whereas historical occurrence is constitutively "unidirectional" (74). In the same context, Note 8 indicates why Benjamin would hesitate to describe any work of his own as a contribution to moral philosophy: "Moral philosophy is a stupid tautology" (74). This trenchant remark is a denigration of neither philosophy nor moral philosophy; rather, it asserts that philosophy as such is always moral, which means that it is impossible for moral philosophy to be pursued in isolation from the theory of possible knowledge, which morality does not so much reflect as "refract." Notes 9 and 10 accordingly outline certain "modes of history" that accord with a transformed concept of experience; phenomenology and philology are singled out in this context, because the phenomenological reduction suspends the "natural" presumption of causal connectivity, while philology grants the possibility of an altogether different kind of connection among its linguistic elements. Fragment 12 and Note 13 are associated, in turn, with Benjamin's inquiries into the relation of fate to guilt-debt, in which prediction of the so-called future is correspondingly dissociated from causal reasoning.[68]

Whereas Fragment 14 isolates the specificity of the concept of time in the "moral world," Fragment 15 replaces the theme of world and time with the more vexing problem of world and "coming world" (83). Note 16 summarizes Benjamin's attempt to survey and arrange the basic elements of "moral philosophy," understood as the "second part of the [coming philosophical] system" (74). And in Fragment 17, as Benjamin begins to sketch a line of argument that would occupy him in the composition of "Toward the Critique of Violence," the shape of "my moral philosophy" gains a higher degree of clarity. It proceeds in this way: unlike the schematizations of moral philosophy in

Notes 8 and 16, there will no longer be any place for "ethics"—neither as it "applies" to history nor as a form of practical reason through which "moral [*sittliche*] personality" (85) can be evaluated. As a result, the term "ethics" appears in "Toward the Critique of Violence" only when it cites the title of Cohen's treatise. Benjamin thus returns to the table of moral categories sketched in Note 1, which, as previously mentioned, may have been written in response to Buber's request that he publish a sample of his work in *Der Jude*. According to this schema—which seeks confirmation in ancient Rome, Athens, and Jerusalem—law and justice are the only categories of moral philosophy, and they are "essentially" separated from each other by virtue of an "enormous gulf" (66).

"More" and "Different"

Benjamin introduces "Toward the Critique of Violence" with a series of claims that epitomize a moral philosophy in which the critique of violence is an indispensable task. The term he uses to describe these claims, "observations" (*Feststellungen*) (39), suggests scholarly objectivity as well as steadfast reliability. Benjamin does not identify the source of his observations; but in view of the notes and fragments collected in this volume, they can be seen as elements of a moral philosophy that capture in brief a transformation of "the entire complex of ethics." They are not so much axioms as prolepses, which come into focus only in retrospect. Benjamin accordingly says of these "observations" that they contain something "more" as well as something "different" than may first appear. The aim of this, the final section of the introduction to the volume, is to amplify this easily overlooked remark by examining each of its parts in turn. The "observations" contain "more" than appears at first glance because they outline the skeleton of the coming moral philosophy; at the same time, however, their implications "differ" from what readers of a contemporary journal—whether it be the *Archiv* or *Die weißen Blätter*, although perhaps not *Der Jude* in a different "stage" (GB 1:327; C 81) of its existence—would expect to find in its pages:

> The task of a critique of violence [*Gewalt*] may be described as the presentation of its relation to law and justice. For however effective a cause may be, it becomes violence in the impressive sense of the word only when it intervenes in moral [*sittliche*] relations. The sphere of these relations is designated by the concepts of law and justice. With regard to the first of these, it is clear that the

most elementary basic relation in every legal order is the one between ends and means. Furthermore, it is clear that violence can first be sought only in the realm of means, not in the realm of ends. With these observations, something more and something different than may perhaps appear is given with respect to the critique of violence. (39)

The German word *Gewalt* can also be translated by a vast variety of terms, including "power," "force," "control" (as in "under my control" for *in meiner Gewalt*), and "authority" (as in an administrative authority that supervises certain mechanisms of power). The word is generally disambiguated from two broadly defined perspectives. As described earlier, *Gewalt* can be understood either as "violence" or as "force" from within the optic of sociopolitical reflection: it is "force" when it plays a significant role in a historical process, "violence" when it remains outside such processes. From the perspective of juridical reasoning, by contrast, *Gewalt* is generally disambiguated in accordance with a distinction between legitimate power, often associated with the Latin term *potestas*, and unsanctioned, nonconsensual, and imputable action that affects the physical or psychic state of (legally defined) persons and/or the disposition of their (accordingly defined) things. In this context, moreover, *Gewalt* functions as a "force" when it is dutifully "applied" to a situation that warrants such action. As is clear from the second of his "observations," Benjamin does not disambiguate *Gewalt* in either of these ways. Nor, despite drawing numerous citations from *Reflections on Violence*, does he seek to disambiguate *Gewalt* in accordance with Sorel's proposal for associated French terms, which inverts the sociopolitical optic by making violence the superior form: "[I]t would be very beneficial to adopt a terminology devoid of ambiguity by reserving the term *violence* for the latter sense ['act of revolt' rather than 'act of authority']; we will therefore say that the object of force is to impose the organization of a certain social order in which a minority governs, while violence tends toward the destruction of that order" (212).

Benjamin does not follow Sorel's suggestion. Nor does he distinguish "violence" from "force" in terms of their respective socially formative functions, or lack thereof. Still less does he adopt a classical juridical perspective that opposes *potestas*, rooted in authority, and *violentia*, which has none. Rather than proceeding in any of these various directions, Benjamin goes to the very source of the ambiguity of *Gewalt* by specifying the category from which all of its associated concepts derive. That category is causality, which is itself a certain determination of the categorial form of relation, specifically the relation of ground to consequence or cause-and-effect. Benjamin does not engage in detailed examination of the causal character of *Gewalt* but instead reapplies the category of causality to the word itself. The adjective with which Benjamin specifies *Gewalt* for its ensuing critique, namely *prägnant*, could be translated as "impressive," "compressive," or—following a convention in Gestalt psychology—"pithy"; since "compressive" is rarely used for linguistic units, however, and "pithy" suggests a causal character only in the phrase "pith helmet," "impressive" is probably the most effective English equivalent. However translated, *prägnant* has nothing to do with the "pregnancy" (*Schwangerschaft*) to which Marx and Engels refer in their analysis of situation in which violence becomes force; rather, it designates a species of causality, hence a subspecification of the category to which *Gewalt* in general belongs. Violence, in brief, for Benjamin, is always causal; but in its "impressive" sense, it does not designate a change in either corporeal disposition or psychic state but rather in "moral relations," which are themselves circumscribed by the relation between law and justice. This relation, for its part, cannot be represented in terms of the means-ends relation, since the latter solely belongs to the legal pole of the moral sphere. This implies at the very least that law cannot be seen as a "way" to justice. Furthermore, the sum of the "observations" implicitly denies that there is a third term in addition to law and justice that would serve as a mediating category. The "sphere of moral relations" is rigorously bipolar, without any meridians that would lead full circle from one pole to the other—with the result that the term *sittlich*, here translated as "moral," is ambiguous, oscillating between law and justice.

The absence of a third term in the "sphere of moral relations" is decisive, so much so that it establishes the task of submitting violence to a critique that transcends any attempt to evaluate the fitness of means or the rightness of ends. Why would a concept that mediates between law and justice obviate the need for a critique of violence? Because, as an additional moral category, it would generate a path along the sphere from one pole to the other, hence from law to justice or from justice, perhaps in the form of natural law, to positive legislation. From within the "entire complex of ethics" several such terms readily present themselves, including "ethics." Cohen's *Ethics of Pure Will* is particularly instructive in this regard, for it presents law in the form of "legal science" or "jurisprudence" (*Rechtswissenschaft*) as the "factum" from which moral reasoning derives and which thus generates the validity and reality of all moral categories.[69] To this—and countless other similar attempts to forge a path from law to justice or justice to law—Benjamin says "no." Recognition of the bipolarity of the sphere encompassing moral relations is the ultimate source of the theoretical data with which "Toward the Critique of Violence" begins.

In this way, Benjamin unambiguously aligns his argument with the last of Kant's attempts to formulate *his* moral philosophy, namely, his 1797–98 treatise *The Metaphysics of Morals*, which is itself divided into two parts, one identified as the *Doctrine of Law*, the other as the *Doctrine of Virtue*—without any transition from one to the other. The absence of any such transition is in a certain sense astonishing: virtue, for Kant, contributes nothing to law, and law has nothing to do with virtue.[70] In comparison with the fidelity with which Benjamin appropriates the structure of *The Metaphysics of Morals* at the beginning of "Toward the Critique of Violence," his modifications are relatively minor. One pole of moral philosophy remains unchanged, namely, the doctrine of law, whose basis, for Kant, is not the moral law per se but rather the autonomous logic of "right," which is discernible by reason and distinguished from justice per se. The other side of moral philosophy splits apart in accordance with the ancient distinction between justice as a particular virtue and justice as state or condition—a distinction Benjamin begins to recast in his 1916 notes on the "category of justice" (65). "Toward the Critique of Violence" proceeds to account for virtue under a variety of names, beginning with the "culture of the heart" (50), which suggests its rhythmic character. Just as Kant separates the doctrine of law from that of virtue, so Benjamin separates the exercise of virtue from the enactment of law: wherever the "culture of the heart" still beats, law is moribund; wherever there is law, the pulse of virtuous life is arrested. Instead of producing an extensive doctrine of virtue, Benjamin concentrates on probity, as a link perhaps between his reflections of violence and his portrait of "The True Politician." In the same vein, Benjamin draws up a series of notes on the opposite of individual probity, which he calls "objective mendacity" (93). And in the concluding paragraphs of the extant notes, he develops the consequences of what is implied in the relevant paragraphs of "Toward the Critique of Violence": insofar as probity is a virtue, insofar as virtue excludes law, and insofar as politics is related to law, there is no place for probity in politics—which does not imply that lying is a valid political technique but rather that truth must be connected to politics in another, as yet unspecified manner. This presumably forms the nucleus of any true-to-life portrait of "the true politician."

Just as the absence of a third term mediating between law and justice becomes evident when Benjamin's opening "observations" are compared with Cohen's *Ethics of Pure Will*, so another missing element becomes legible when they are brought into relation with the full spectrum of Kant's metaphysical doctrines. The missing term is "nature." A dozen years before Kant divided his moral philosophy into the *Doctrine of Right* and the *Doctrine of Virtue*, he produced a *Doctrine of Natural Science* that consists in the a priori construction of nature as a system of forces. In the second paragraph of "Toward the Critique of Violence," Benjamin briefly reflects on the concept of nature but only from the perspective of modern natural-law theory, which treats violence as a natural force and cannot therefore contribute to the critique of violence in its "impressive" sense (see 40). The fact that Benjamin does not include the word "nature" in his initial "observations" and subsequently excludes natural-right theory from further consideration does not mean that nature is absent from his essay; still less does it indicate that he naïvely adopts the then-standard academic distinction between the natural and "spiritual" or human sciences. When he determines violence in its "impressive" sense as the intervention into moral relations, it may seem at first glance as though he is excluding any use of the term "violence" in the context of natural events: a thunderstorm or earthquake, for example—precisely those events to which, incidentally, Kant refers in his elucidation of the word *Gewalt* in the *Critique of the Power of Judgment*, specifically in his opening discussion of the "dynamical" sublime.[71] This impression, though, is mistaken, for events of this kind enter into the sphere of moral relations under the rubric of fate—as interventions of a Zeus or a Poseidon, for example. The impossibility of excluding any occurrence in principle from the sphere of moral relations leads to the fulcrum of Benjamin's revision of Kantian critique.

By defining violence in the "impressive" sense in terms of its effect on moral relations, Benjamin transforms it into the inverse of freedom in its "transcendental" sense (A 533; B 561). Such freedom, Kant argues, consists in the ability of an agent to initiate a new causal sequence (A 451; B 479). Wherever the causality of freedom is actualized, there is an intervention into natural relations. Wherever, by contrast, the causality of violence occurs, there is an intervention into moral relations. In neither case can any relation be excluded from the possibility of the relevant intervention. Just as the concept of freedom in the "transcendental" sense is the "keystone" (*Aka* 5:3) of Kantian critique, so the concept of violence in its impressive sense is the starting point of Benjamin's revision. If Benjamin's critique is the inverse of Kant's, whereby Kant's "free intervention into natural relations" becomes Benjamin's "violent intervention into moral relations," then the following conclusion seems inevitable: there ought to be no violence in the "impressive" sense of the term. Whereas free beings ought to intervene in natural relations—this is, for Kant, what it means to be "free"—moral relations should remain as they are: free from interference. The critique of violence, so construed, would express itself as a manifesto in favor of total nonviolence. And if the sphere of moral relations were not divided into two poles or if these poles circumscribed a uniform field, then the conclusion would hold: there ought to be no violence; moral relations should remain unchanged.

The decisive question around which Benjamin's critical program forms thus concerns the character of the space within which the term "violence" in its "impressive" sense applies. For Kant, the two doctrines of moral philosophy, law and virtue, are indifferent to each other; Benjamin hyperbolizes this indifference by making them mutually repugnant: where there is justice, there is no law, and where law, no justice. The doctrine of law, though, cannot simply stand on its own; rather, it requires some assistance. And if assistance cannot be found in a doctrine of virtue—or alternatively, in a "systematics of ethical values" (85), in the prospect of "moral instruction" (2:48–54), or to use a more contemporary term, in the rigors and joys of "subjectivation"—then the only remaining source for its implementation lies in nature. Kant recognizes the entanglement of law with nature, for it is already discernible in the spatio-dynamic character of the word "right" (*Aka* 6:232–33). Instead of simply noting that legal force is intermittently dependent on physical force—for who would deny this?—Benjamin formulates the more exacting proposal that the relation between legal and physical forces should be understood as a matter of "fate," the sphere of which is "uncertain" and "ambiguous" (55): "uncertain" because legal and physical forces never in fact coincide; "ambiguous" because of the polarity that characterizes the "fateful order" (*schicksalhaften Ordnung*) (46). Whereas the sphere of moral relations is split by mutually repugnant poles, the "fateful order" attains a semblance of homogeneity by making all of its relations ambiguous—neither entirely moral (that is, legal) nor entirely extramoral (that is, natural). It is not, therefore, simply a matter of chance that Benjamin introduces the "fateful order" into his argument immediately after casting doubt on the adequacy of Kant's formulation of the categorical imperative, which, as he emphasizes, corresponds to what positive law, "wherever it is conscious of its roots," will claim for itself: "the interest of humanity in every individual" (46).

The primary theoretical datum with which Benjamin introduces "Toward the Critique of Violence" is that the relation between law and justice is disjunctive. The consequence of this datum is that law is originally identical with myth. This becomes apparent in relation to the establishment of borders, which are a fateful, hence "ambiguous" conflation of natural relations (where a body stands relative to other bodies in general) and moral relations (where each agent stands in relation to all others in particular). All "legal" borders derive from stipulative stories, which is to say, from "sayings," hence, *muthoi* in the original sense of the word. In *Toward Eternal Peace*, Kant derives the right to hospitality from the total traversability of the terrestrial surface, which is doubtless finite yet nevertheless unbounded (*Aka* 8:357–60). Benjamin, acknowledging Kant's insight, goes a step further and derives the mythic origin of law from the fateful character of all nonnatural boundaries. And it is in light of this derivation that "something different" (39) emerges from the "observations" with which "Toward the Critique of Violence" begins—different, again, from what readers of the *Archiv* or *Die weißen Blätter* would expect to encounter in a scholarly publication. Readers of a different *Der Jude* than the one currently in circulation would perhaps be better prepared. In any case, Benjamin does not describe the following passage as an "observation," but it marks the start of a new line of argumentation that, alluding to the opening sentence of the essay, finally specifies the "task" required of a critique of violence as the "annihilation" (57) of its law-related forms:

> Established and circumscribed boundaries remain, at least in primeval times, unwritten laws. A human being can transgress such laws unawares and thereby succumb to expiation [*Sühne*]. For the encroachment of law [*Eingriff des Rechts*], summoned by the violation of the unwritten and unknown law, is called expiation as distinct from punishment. (56)

This is one of the passages of "Toward the Critique of Violence" where its double focus becomes especially acute, for even as Benjamin refers to "primeval times," his inquiry into the "encroachment of law" recalls his previous analysis of an encroachment that takes place under the aegis of the police. The "spectral" (47) quality of the modern police is an expression of its entangled temporality: at once primordial and hypertopical. Wherever the police "intervene ... in countless cases where no clear legal situation exists" (48) for the supposed purpose of general "security"—or as Benjamin emphasizes, for the more pressing purpose of harassment and surveillance—there is an encroachment of law that results in a renewal of primordial "expiation" (*Sühne*). Benjamin's elucidation of the term *Sühne* likewise recalls his disambiguation of *Gewalt* at the beginning of the essay, for each term designates an invasive grasping that alters moral relations.[72] Benjamin further notes—but this can be found in any reliable dictionary—*Sühne* was originally a juridical term that refers to a process through which a conflict among competing groups is set aside and a certain conciliation attained.[73] In recovering the legal character of the term *Sühne* and contrasting it with *Strafe* (punishment), Benjamin is not suggesting that those who undergo a process of expiation do not suffer as a result of their imputed transgressions; on the contrary, their suffering consists in succumbing to law, which tautologically finds them guilty. In this way, they are "expiated" in the original sense of this Latinate term: completely "pietized," that is, subordinated to the legal-political order and in this way "moralized." The prefix *ex-* in *expiation* does not express "undoing," as it often does in Latin; rather, as in *excruciate* and *exacerbate*, for instance, the *ex-* of *expiation* denotes the completion of a process, which in this case is not the removal of sin or the rectification of evil but rather the "pietization" of *all* relations, including those that constitute the phenomenon of "mere natural life" (57).[74]

In a series of lectures Benjamin attended in the fall of 1913, Rickert laboriously constructed a distinction between "mere life" (*bloßes Leben*), which can be known through the methodologies of the natural sciences, and "completed life" (*vollendetes Leben*), which is the subject matter of a new philosophical discipline that would at once replace traditional "ethics" and transcend contemporary Bergsonian vitalism as well as Nietzschean *Lebensphilosophie*.[75] With stunning brevity, Benjamin adopts the term "mere life" and proceeds in the opposite direction—not with the construction of a counterconcept such as "completed life" but rather with a specification of the circumstance under which "mere natural life" succumbs to a process of complete pietization. Benjamin outlines this circumstance as follows: guilt-inducing blame, hence "inculpation" (57), delivers the living, "innocent and unfortunate," to the process of expiation that "expiates"—*sühnt* appears here in quotation marks—the very inculpation that finds the living guilty. Such finding is in the first place literal, for the "guilty" are found to have crossed a boundary of whose existence they were unaware, as there are no natural ones. The resulting process of expiation is a "release," a "trigger," or to use the corresponding chemical term, a "catalyst" (*Auslösung*). And what it catalyzes is the violence of law, which can count on an endless supply of material, for there is always more nature to be more pervasively and invasively moralized.[76] When, in 1955 and then again in 1965, Suhrkamp Verlag released an edition of "Toward the Critique of Violence" in which *Auslösung* is replaced by *Auflösung* (dissolve, annul), it effectively annulled any recognition of the self-perpetuating process Benjamin painstakingly abbreviates.

The process of expiation would indeed be perpetual, according to Benjamin's argument, if it were not for the reality of *Entsühnung*, which will henceforth be translated by the neologism "de-expiation" for reasons that will be explained in what follows. *Entsühnung* is a strange word to encounter outside of quotation marks in the pages of a journal dedicated to the advancement of the social sciences. The same is perhaps true of *Sühne*, but at least with this word, which Benjamin does indeed place in scare quotes when it is so warranted, there is a straightforward juridical origin. Its pairing with *Schuld* (guilt) was sufficiently well established that the phrase *Schuld und Sühne* could serve, for example, as a translation of the title of Dostoyevsky's *Crime and Punishment*.[77] It is under this familiar title that Kurt Eisner addressed the International Socialist Congress and identified the "true politician" with the prophet a few weeks before his assassination.[78] With respect to *Entsühnung*, by contrast, there is no equivalent juridical or literary catchphrase that would serve as a guide in the determination of its meaning. The following entry in the authoritative dictionary of modern High German begun by Jacob and Wilhelm Grimm gives an indication of why this would be so: "*SÜHNEN, vb. richten, (einen streit) beilegen, versöhnen, wiedergutmachen, genugtuung leisten, entsühnen*" (*sühnen*: verb, to judge, to settle [a conflict], to reconcile, to make amends, to obtain satisfaction, *entsühnen*).[79] In other words, as the successors to the Brothers Grimm note, *sühnen* and *entsühnen* are so closely related to each other that one can be used to define the other. Shortly before his death—which occurred while he was at work on the "F" volume of his dictionary—Jacob Grimm implicitly explains why *sühnen* and *entsühnen* are more or less interchangeable: simply put, the *ent-* in *entsühnen* mimics the function of *ex-* in *expiare*. Benjamin could certainly have been familiar with the following entry in the original volumes of the *Deutsches Wörterbuch*: "ENTSÜHNEN, *piare, expiare, versöhnen* [reconcile], *reinigen* [purify]," followed by three examples of its usage, all drawn from the final acts of Goethe's "classical" play, *Iphigenie auf Tauris*.[80] The implication of Jacob Grimm's elucidation of *entsühnen* is characteristically clear: just as *piare* and *expiare* are synonyms, so are *sühnen* and *entsühnen*, even if each term may acquire a slightly different inflection in any given context.

This, though, is not at all the case with Benjamin. On the contrary, in "Toward the Critique of Violence" *Sühne* and *Entsühnung* are strict antonyms, congruent with the disjunction between law and justice. Where there is *Sühne*, there is no *Entsühnung*, and vice versa. Later in the 1920s, Heidegger will hyphenate the word *Entfernung* (distance), so that it designates the opposite of its everyday meaning, where it is interchangeable with its root term, *Ferne* (distance, remoteness). For Heidegger, *Ent-fernung* means at bottom "de-distance," that is, existential "coming-nearer."[81] In advance of Heidegger—and without any attention-grabbing semantic gestures—Benjamin does something similar with *Entsühnung*. And this conjunction is perhaps no coincidence, for during the months in which Benjamin wrote "The True Politician" and "Toward the Critique of Violence," he was also occupied with Heidegger's *Habilitation* thesis on a late scholastic doctrine of categories and its corresponding theory of meaning.[82] Benjamin thereby undertook a systematic review of the structure and elements of Latin grammar in which the "transcendental" problem of securing the source of meaning in general becomes paramount. This problem gains concretion, as it were, in the case of *Entsühnung*, the meaning of which is unmistakably problematic. Instead of mimicking the completion function of *ex-* in Latin, the *ent-* in Benjamin's use of the word negates the root term, so that the word as a whole is best translated in Latinate form as either *ex-piation* or *de-expiation*, with a preference for the latter simply because it does not require any familiarity with Latin.[83] Since *Sühne* means "encroachment of law," *Entsühnung* designates a countermovement, hence "distancing from law." This is not a static juridical void, nor does it refer to a meandering "no-man's land" like those that materialized between the trenches during the recent war. Instead of turning to circumstances close at hand, Benjamin looks in the opposite direction and associates distancing from law, hence "de-expiation," with the biblical account of the destruction of Koraḥ and his "horde," as described in the book of Numbers, chapter 16: "The judgment strikes privileged ones, Levites; it strikes them unannounced, without threat, and does not stop short of annihilation. At the same time, however, precisely in annihilating, it is also de-expiating, and one cannot fail to recognize a profound connection between the bloodless and the de-expiating character of this violence" (57).

Abstracting from the immense commentary on Numbers 16, which is in itself confusing enough, Benjamin identifies "Koraḥ's horde" with a single trait: as Levites—like Aaron and Moses, who remain conspicuously unnamed—they are "privileged" (*Bevorrechtete*), which indicates that they are willy-nilly exponents of law in accordance with the recently articulated theorem "[A]ll law [*Recht*] was the privilege [*Vor-recht*] of kings or grandees" (56). Privilege equals law, even in the case of the grandee named Koraḥ, who expresses the identity of one with the other, *Recht* with *Vor-recht*, through an appeal to the supposed sanctity of "the whole community" (Num. 16:3). Benjamin makes nothing of the fact that "the children of Koraḥ" (Num. 26:11) survive the demise of their accursed ancestor, which would corroborate the argument advanced by Cohen in the very section of *Ethics of Pure Will* to which Benjamin draws attention (171–72). Nor does he follow Cohen and show how Abraham's prayer for the innocent inhabitants of Sodom reverberates in Moses' prayer for "the people over against Koraḥ's horde."[84] What draws Benjamin to the figure of Koraḥ is, rather, the stunningly inconsequential character of his demise. No boundaries of any kind are drawn; on the contrary, the site of devastation is erased and thus, in its own way, devastated too.[85] This stands in explicit contrast with the figure of Niobe, who, having turned into stone, forms "the border between human beings and gods" (55). And it stands in implicit contrast with other prominent occurrences of divine violence in the Hebrew Bible. After the earth opens up and swallows Koraḥ, not only is there no earthly or heavenly trace of this event, there is no ceremonial commemoration either: no rainbow in the heavens, as after the Flood; no desolation in the lowest region of the land, as in the destruction of Sodom; nor is there a yearly remembrance, as in the festival of Passover, above all. According to Numbers 26:10, Koraḥ and his company became a "sign," yet the Bible does not specify what they signify. Benjamin fills in the lacuna by making them into figures of "de-expiation"—which has nothing to do with atonement, propitiation, absolution, satisfaction, conciliation, forgiveness, or the like. The day of their destruction is no Yom Kippur.[86] It represents, rather, a paradigmatic countermovement to the encroachment of law over the surface of the earth.

By virtue of human habitation, Benjamin claims in Note 9 of this volume, the earth is a "*world*-historical individual" (75). Nowhere in the extant notes does he elaborate on this claim, and in Fragment 15, where he contrasts "world" with "coming world," he seems disinclined to do so, inasmuch as "earth" not only qualifies "world" but is identical with it: "[G]enuine divine violence can manifest itself *other than destructively* only in the coming world (of fulfillment). Where, by contrast, divine violence enters into the earthly world, it breathes destruction" (83). With the case of Korah in view, however, all of this is scrambled: "the earthly world" carries out his destruction by opening its mouth, swallowing, and closing its mouth without ever breathing a word or marking the site. Least of all is there a border one could pass unawares or vigilantly protect. Whereas in the case of Niobe a boundary marker is slowly erected and the earth thus eventually altered, in the case of Korah the agent is the earth, which immediately restores itself. This is the sole point of contrast between the two cases: there is no glorification of Korah's death, as though he deserved punishment or somehow underwent an expiatory process. It is only that the earth becomes a tablet on which law is inscribed in Niobe's case but returns to its unblemished condition in his. Once the earth is no longer a surface that is amenable to inscriptions jealously guarded by gods and law, other kinds of limits and delimitations may come to light. Benjamin begins to sketch them in Fragment 21, where, by schematizing the "psychophysical problem," he distinguishes not only the shapes of the "living body" (*Leib*) from the limits of the "somatic body" (*Körper*) but also the "boundaries of both over against nature" (100). These as yet unspecified boundaries between bodies and among different kinds of bodies are to be distinguished from the borders that define the "person," which, like Niobe, forms a "petrifact" (78). Emancipated from the petrifaction of legal personhood, boundaries "fluctuate," such that "the expansive proliferation of both [living body and somatic body] determines world occurrence" (100). All of this can become recognizable, however, only under a general condition that obtains in the strange case of Korah, where the earth is no longer a passive medium on which ambiguous borders are drawn, fate is solicited, and law thereby encroaches.

By emphasizing the bloodless character of the violence that destroys Koraḥ, Benjamin introduces an ultra-abbreviated intercalation of antiquity and contemporaneity that accords with the double focus of his essay—gazing afar, while examining circumstances near at hand.[87] In his introduction to *Der Jude*, "The Watchword," Buber does not explicitly claim that the word in question is "blood"; but he implies as much, for he urges those who are conscripted into the armies of boundary-destroying and boundary-setting states to seize the opportunity of life-and-death combat and open their ears to "the call of the deeper community of blood."[88] To this and similar appeals to the moral significance of blood, Benjamin responds in "Toward the Critique of Violence" with a transformation of the enigmatic principle that justifies the priestly monopoly on sacrifice against which Koraḥ and his cohorts rebel. The ancient doctrine, as expressed in Leviticus, runs as follows: "For the life of the flesh is in the blood" (Lev. 17:11). Its contemporary transformation reads: "For blood is the symbol of mere life" (57).[89] With this pithy theorem, almost as enigmatic as its biblical prototype, Benjamin transforms an ancient proscription on indiscriminate butchery into a modern counterpart—without appealing to any new laws that would generate new forms of inculpation, which, in turn, would offer more occasions for the release of legal violence. On the one hand, the symbolic character of blood means that it is not really a purgative agent that requires its handlers, the Aaronite priests, to separate themselves from everyone else; the life of creatures is not literally in their blood. On the other hand, blood *does* have a symbolic function, which means that it is not simply a chemical substance like any other. What it symbolizes, moreover—"mere life"—is dangerous, for blame accompanies bloodshed, and inculpation, born in blame, catalyzes the application of legal force. The absence of bloodshed does not guarantee blamelessness, of course; but Benjamin directs attention to the actions of the earth in the case of Koraḥ only to illustrate that law in its primordial form does not in at least one instance expand over its surface. The absence of expansion is, in effect, a contraction, even if it cannot be recognized with certainty as such. And as Benjamin argues in the final paragraph of his essay, where he adopts Kant's argument concerning the unrecognizability of genuinely moral action, the absence of indubitable recognition does not mean that "pure violence"—which intervenes in the sphere of moral relations by delegalizing them—is not still "pending" (60).

Coda—What's Missing

Beyond the previously mentioned essays—"The True Politician" and a review of Bloch's *Spirit of Utopia*—two other related items are missing: "Phantasie über eine Stelle aus dem Geist der Utopie" (Fantasy on a passage from the *Spirit of Utopia*) (*GB* 2:118; *C* 170) and a critique of Kurt Hiller titled "Es gibt keine geistigen Arbeiter" (There are no intellectual workers) (*GB* 2:76; *C* 160), although the latter may have been only a joke. Another lost essay, which is doubtless more serious, carries the title "Leben und Gewalt" (Life and violence), a few sentences of which are probably preserved in Fragment 3 of this volume. "Life and Violence" may also have functioned as a complement to another short essay, which appears here as Fragment 2. The editors of Benjamin's *Gesammelte Schriften* call this essay "The Centaur," but it is more broadly concerned with the theme of "Belebung und Gewalt" and is accordingly here titled "Vivification and Violence." Whereas "Life and Violence" is "highly topical" (*GB* 2:85; *C* 162), "Vivification and Violence," facilitated by Hölderlin, looks to the distant past, as it opens a vista onto the difference between Greek and Jewish conceptions of creation.[90] Finally, a pair of essays Benjamin mentions in conjunction with his plan to edit a journal under the title *Angelus Novus* may also be exponents of the same "complex of ethics" from which many of the Notes and Fragments in this volume derive. One is titled "Wucher und Recht [Profiteering and law]," the other "Recht und Gewalt [Law and violence]" (*GB* 2: 218); the first may be a revision of Fragment 18, "Kapitalismus als Religion" (Capitalism as religion), whereas the second may be a recapitulation or revision of "Toward the Critique of Violence." Benjamin does not identify himself as the author of these essays in his letters to the prospective publisher of the journal, perhaps because he does not want to suggest that it would be saturated by his own work, or perhaps because he was not in fact their author.

As for "Toward the Critique of Violence" itself, Benjamin was aware of its lacunae. This is evident in several passages of the essay and in certain parts of this volume, especially Note 22, "Literatur zu einer ausgeführteren Kritik der Gewalt und zur Rechtsphilosophie" (Literature for a more fully developed critique of violence and philosophy of law), which is published here for the first time in any language and for this reason appears in both German and English. As Benjamin prepared the fair copy of the essay for Lederer with the expectation that it would soon appear in *Die weißen Blätter*, he acknowledged that it does not address all aspects of violence, while summarizing his "hope" for its achievement: "There are still questions concerning violence that are not touched on in it; but I nevertheless hope that it says something essential" (*GB* 2:131; C 174).

"TOWARD THE CRITIQUE OF VIOLENCE"

Walter Benjamin

[§1] [2:179] The task of a critique of violence may be described as the presentation of its relation to law and justice. For however effective a cause may be, it becomes violence in the impressive sense of the word only when it intervenes in moral [*sittliche*] relations. The sphere of these relations is designated by the concepts of law and justice. With regard to the first of these, it is clear that the most elementary basic relation in every legal order is the one between ends and means. Furthermore, it is clear that violence can first be sought only in the realm of means, not in the realm of ends. With these observations, something more and something different than may perhaps appear is given with respect to the critique of violence. For, if violence is a means, one standard [*Maßstab*] for its critique might seem to be readily given. It imposes itself in the question of whether violence is, in certain cases, a means to just or unjust ends. A critique of it would then be implicitly given in a system of just ends. This, however, is not the case. For what such a system would contain, assuming that it is secure against all doubt, is not a criterion [*Kriterium*] of violence itself as a principle, but a criterion for cases of its use. What would remain open is whether violence in general, as a principle, is moral, even as a means to just ends. To decide this question, a narrower criterion is needed, a differentiation in the sphere of means itself, without regard for the ends they serve.

[§2] [2:180] The suspension [*Ausschaltung*] of this more precise critical interrogation characterizes a major trend in legal philosophy, perhaps as its most prominent feature: natural law.[1] This sees in the use of violent means for just ends nothing more problematic than human beings see in their "right" to move their bodies toward an intended goal. According to this view (which provided the ideological foundation for the terrorism during the French Revolution), violence is a natural product, a raw material, as it were, the use of which is entirely unproblematic unless one were to misuse it for unjust ends.[2] If, according to the natural-law theory of state, persons give up all their violence for the sake of the state, this is done on the assumption (which Spinoza, for instance, explicitly maintains in his *Tractatus Theologico-Politicus*) that the individual, in and for itself and before the conclusion of a contract in accordance with reason, would exercise de jure any violence whatsoever that it de facto has at its disposal.[3] Perhaps these views have been recently revived through Darwin's biology, which, in a thoroughly dogmatic manner, only regards violence as an original means alongside natural selection, and the only means appropriate to all vital ends of nature. Darwinian popular philosophy has often shown how small a step it is to move from this natural-historical dogma to the following, still cruder dogma of legal philosophy: the violence that is almost alone appropriate to natural ends is, for this very reason, also already in accordance with law.[4]

[§3] This thesis of natural law, which regards violence as a natural given [*Gegebenheit*], is diametrically opposed to the thesis of positive law, which holds that violence emerges in history [*Gewordenheit*].[5] If natural law can evaluate all existing law only through the critique of its ends, then positive law can evaluate every emergent law only through the critique of its means. If justice is the criterion of ends, then legality is the criterion of means. Regardless of this antithesis, however, both schools meet in the fundamental dogma they share: just ends can be attained by justified means, and justified means can be used for just ends. Natural law strives, through the justness of ends, to "justify" the means, and positive law strives to "guarantee" the justness of the ends through the justification of the means.[6] The [2:181] antinomy would prove insoluble if their shared dogmatic premise were false, if justified means, on the one hand, and just ends, on the other, were in irreconcilable conflict.[7] No insight could be gained here, however, until the circle is abandoned, and the criteria for just ends and justified means are established independently from one another.

[§4] The realm of ends and, therefore, also the question concerning a criterion for justness are, for now, suspended from this study. Instead, it focuses on the question concerning the justification of certain means that constitute violence. Principles of natural law are incapable of deciding on this question and only lead to a groundless casuistry. For, if positive law is blind to the unconditionality of ends, natural law is blind to the conditionality of means. By contrast, the positive theory of law is acceptable as a hypothetical foundation at the outset of this investigation because it draws a fundamental distinction with respect to kinds of violence independently from cases of their use. This distinction occurs between historically recognized, or so-called sanctioned violence, on the one hand, and nonsanctioned violence, on the other.[8] But even if the following considerations proceed from this distinction, this of course does not mean that given [forms of] violence [*gegebene Gewalten*] can be classified according to whether or not they are sanctioned. For, in a critique of violence, the standard by which positive law classifies forms of violence cannot undergo its application but rather only its evaluation. At issue is the question of what thus follows, for the essence of violence, from the fact that such a standard or differential can be applied to it at all, or in other words, what the meaning of this distinction is. For the fact that this distinction, supplied by positive law, is meaningful, that it is completely grounded in itself, and that it is irreplaceable by any other distinction, all this will be shown soon enough, while at the same time light will also be shed on the sphere in which alone this distinction can be found. In a word: if the standard established by positive law to assess the legality of violence can be analyzed only according to its meaning, then the sphere of its use must be criticized with regard to its value.[9] For this critique, it is a matter of finding a standpoint not only beyond the philosophy of legal positivism but also beyond natural [2:182] law. The extent to which only a historical-philosophical reflection on law provides this standpoint will emerge in what follows.

[§5] The meaning of the differentiation of violence into legitimate and illegitimate is not immediately obvious. To be decisively rejected is the misunderstanding arising from natural law in which this meaning would consist in the distinction between violence used for just ends and unjust ends. Rather, as was already indicated, positive law demands from every form of violence evidence of its historical origin, which under certain conditions conserves its legality, its sanction. Since the recognition of legal forms of violence [*Rechtsgewalten*] manifests itself most tangibly in the submission, without any resistance in principle, to its ends, the hypothetical ground for the classification of these forms should lie in the presence or absence of a general historical recognition of its ends.[10] Ends lacking such recognition can be called natural ends, while the others can be called legal ends.[11] The diverse function of violence, depending on whether it serves natural or legal ends, can be developed with the greatest lucidity on the basis of some specific set of legal circumstances [*Verhältnisse*]. For the sake of simplicity, the following discussions will refer to those of contemporary Europe.[12]

[§6] Characteristic of these legal circumstances, so far as they concern the individual person as legal subject, is the tendency to deny the natural ends of these individual persons in all cases where, in a given situation, such ends may be pursued purposively [*zweckmäßigerweise*] with violence.[13] This means: in all areas where the ends of individual persons could be purposively pursued with violence, this legal order insists on erecting legal ends that only legal authority can actualize. Indeed, this legal order insists on limiting by legal ends even those areas, such as education [*Erziehung*], in which natural ends are in principle widely admitted, as soon as those natural ends are pursued with an excessive measure of violent action, as is the case with laws limiting the powers within education to inflict punishment [*Strafbefugnis*].[14] It can be formulated as a universal maxim of contemporary European legislation that all natural ends of individual persons must [2:183] collide with legal ends if they are pursued with a greater or lesser degree of violence. (The contradiction between this and the right to self-defense will find a clarification in the course of the following reflections.)[15] It follows from this maxim that law sees violence in the hands of the individual as a danger undermining the legal order. As a danger thwarting [*vereiteln*] legal ends and the execution of law? No; for then, it would not be violence as such that would be condemned but only violence used for illegal ends. One will argue that a system of legal ends could not be maintained if natural ends can still somewhere be pursued with violence. This, however, is mere dogma. To counter it, one would perhaps have to consider the surprising possibility that law's interest in monopolizing violence vis-à-vis the individual is explained by the intention not of preserving legal ends, but rather of preserving law itself.[16] [This is the possibility] that violence, when it does not lie in the hands of law, poses a danger to law, not by virtue of the ends that it may pursue but by virtue of its mere existence outside of law. The same suspicion may be more drastically suggested by reflecting on how often the figure of the "great" criminal has aroused the secret admiration of the people, even when his ends were repulsive.[17] This can happen not on account of his deed but only on account of the violence to which it testifies. In this case, therefore, the violence that present-day law tries to take from the individual in all areas of action does, indeed, manifest itself as threatening and arouses the sympathy of the masses [*Menge*] against law even in defeat. The function through which violence can, with reason, appear so threatening to law, and be so feared by it, must show itself precisely where its deployment [*Entfaltung*] is still permissible, even in the present legal order.

[§7] This, first of all, is the case with class struggle in the form of the right to strike guaranteed to workers.[18] Today, organized labor [*Arbeiterschaft*] is, apart from states, perhaps the only legal subject that is entitled to a right to violence. Against this view, there is, of course, a ready-made objection: that the omission [*Unterlassung*] of actions, [2:184] a nonaction, which after all is what ultimately constitutes a strike, cannot be described as violence at all.[19] Such a consideration doubtless made it easier for state power [*Staatsgewalt*] to concede the right to strike once it was no longer avoidable.[20] The validity of this statement, however, is not unrestricted because it is not unconditional. It is true that omitting an action or even a service can be a pure means wholly lacking in violence if it amounts simply to a "severing of relations." And just as in the view of the state (or of law) the right to strike does not so much grant organized labor the right to use violence as a right to escape from the mediated [*mittelbar*] violence exercised by the employer, so it may undoubtedly occur from time to time that a strike of this kind happens, announced only as an "estrangement" or "alienation" from the employer. The moment of violence is, however, certainly introduced into such an omission in the form of extortion when it is undertaken with a readiness in principle to perform as before the omitted action under certain circumstances, which may have nothing to do with the action at all or only modify it superficially. And in this sense, the right to strike, in the view of organized labor, which is opposed to the view of the state, constitutes the right to use violence for the implementation of certain ends. The antithesis in the two conceptions emerges in stark detail in view of the revolutionary general strike. In the revolutionary general strike, labor will always appeal to its right to strike, but the state will always call this appeal a misuse, since the right to strike was not "so intended," and will issue special decrees [*Sonderverfügungen*]. For the state remains at liberty to declare that a simultaneous exercise of the strike in all industries is illegal, since the particular grounds for the strike specified by the legislator cannot be present in all of them. In this difference of interpretation, the objective [*sachlich*] contradiction of the legal situation is expressed, a situation in which the state recognizes a form of violence whose ends it treats at times with indifference as natural ends, but which in a situation in which everything is at stake [*Ernstfall*] (the case of the revolutionary general strike) it confronts with hostility. For, however paradoxical it may seem at first glance, even conduct undertaken in the exercise of a right can be described under certain conditions as violence. [2:185] And indeed such conduct [*Verhalten*], when it is active, can be called violence if it exercises a right that is vested in it by the power of the legal order so as to topple that very order. When passive, however, it is nonetheless to be described as violence if it constitutes extortion in the sense developed above. It therefore testifies to an objective [*sachlich*] contradiction in the legal situation, but not to a logical contradiction in law if under certain conditions law meets the strikers, as perpetrators of violence, with violence. For in the strike the state fears above all that function of violence which this study seeks to determine as the one and only secure foundation for its critique. For if violence were, as it appears at first glance, the mere means to secure immediately whatever incidental thing happens to be sought, it could fulfil its ends only as predatory violence. As such, violence would be wholly unsuited to grounding or to modifying circumstances in a relatively stable manner. The strike shows, however, that it can do this, that it is capable of grounding and modifying legal situations, however offended the feeling of justice may thereby find itself. One might object that such a function of violence is incidental and isolated. This objection can be refuted with a consideration of military violence.

[§8] The possibility of a law of war rests on precisely the same objective [*sachlich*] contradiction in the legal situation as can be found in strike law, namely, on the fact that legal subjects sanction forms of violence whose ends remain natural ends for those who sanction it and which can therefore come into conflict with the legal or natural ends of these same subjects in a situation where everything is at stake [*Ernstfall*].[21] Admittedly, military violence is at first directed altogether immediately toward its ends as predatory violence. Yet it is most striking that even—or perhaps particularly—in primitive circumstances that scarcely know the beginnings of constitutional [*staatsrechtliche*] relations, and even in those cases where the victor has established himself in a position of henceforth incontestable possession, a peace ceremony is definitely required. Indeed, the word "peace," understood as a correlate to the word "war" (for there is yet another, entirely different yet equally unmetaphorical and political meaning of the term, the one of which Kant [2:186] speaks in *Toward Eternal Peace*), really designates this a priori and necessary sanctioning of every victory, independently of all other legal circumstances.[22] This sanction consists precisely in recognizing the new circumstances as new "law," altogether independently from the question of whether or not they de facto require any guarantee of their continuing existence. If a conclusion may be drawn from considering military violence as an original and archetypal form of violence, it would be that there inheres a law-positing [*rechtsetzender*] character in all violence used for natural ends. The investigation will later return to the consequences of this insight. It explains the aforementioned tendency of modern law to divest at least the individual person as legal subject of all violence, even violence directed only to natural ends. In the great criminal, this violence confronts modern law with a threat: the threat of positing a new law, which, in spite of its impotence where it really matters, even today makes the people shudder as it did in primeval times. The state, however, fears this violence everywhere for its law-positing character, just as it must recognize violence as law-positing whenever foreign powers [*auswärtige Mächte*] compel it to concede the right to war, and [concede to] classes the right to strike.

[§9] If in the last war the critique of military violence became the point of departure for a passionate critique of violence in general—which taught at least one thing, that violence is no longer naïvely exercised or tolerated—it was nevertheless not only the object of critique for its law-positing character, but another function was evaluated in a perhaps even more annihilating manner.[23] For characteristic of militarism, which could only arise through universal conscription, is a doubleness in the function of violence. Militarism is the compulsion to the universal application of violence as a means to the ends of the state. This compulsion to use violence has recently been evaluated with as much, or even more, severity than the application of violence itself. In this compulsion, violence reveals itself in a function entirely different from its simple use for natural ends. It consists in the use of violence as a means to legal ends. For the subordination of citizens to laws—in the present case, to the law of universal conscription—is a legal end. If the first function of violence is [2:187] law-positing, then this second function of violence can be called law-preserving [*rechtserhaltende*].[24] Since compulsory military service is an application of law-preserving violence that is not in principle distinguished from other cases in which force is applied, a genuinely effective critique of it is far less easy than the declamations of pacifists and activists pretend. Rather, such a critique coincides with the critique of all legal violence—that is, with the critique of legal or executive power—and is not to be accomplished with a less ambitious program. Of course, unless one wants to proclaim a childish anarchism, critique is also not accomplished by saying that one acknowledges absolutely no constraints on the person and by declaring that "what pleases is permitted."[25] Such a maxim merely suspends reflection on the moral-historical sphere and thus on any sense that action might have; beyond this, however, it suspends reflection on any sense that reality as such might have—a sense that cannot be constituted if "action" is severed from the domain of reality.[26] More important is the fact that even the oft-attempted appeal to the categorical imperative and its indubitable minimal program—"act in such a way that at all times you use the humanity in your person as well as in the person of all others as an end, and never merely as a means"—is in itself inadequate for such a critique.*[27] For positive law, wherever it is conscious of its roots, will definitely claim [*beanspruchen*] to recognize and promote the interest of humanity in the person of every individual. Positive law sees this interest in the presentation and conservation of a fateful order.[28] While this order, which law claims with reason to safeguard, cannot escape criticism, every challenge made of it only in the name of an amorphous "freedom," which is itself unable to designate this higher order of freedom, remains impotent against it. It is most impotent, however, when it does not challenge the legal order itself root and branch but rather [only] individual acts of legislation [*Gesetze*] or legal customs that law, of course, takes under the protection of its power, a power that resides in the notion that there is only one fate and that [2:188] the status quo [*das Bestehende*], and especially what threatens the status quo, belongs inviolably to its order. For law-preserving violence is a threatening violence. And its threat does not carry the sense of a deterrent, as it is interpreted by liberal theorists.[29] A deterrent in the exact sense would involve a certainty that contradicts the essence of the threat and cannot be attained by any act of legislation, since there is always the hope of eluding its reach. In its threatening character an act of

---

* Doubts, on the contrary, may be raised about this famous demand—whether it does not contain too little, that is, whether or not it is permissible to use, or allow to be used, oneself or another also as a means in any respect whatsoever. Very good reasons for this doubt could be found.

legislation proves itself to be all the more like the fate that, after all, prescribes whether or not the criminal falls victim to it. The deepest meaning of the indeterminacy of the legal threat will emerge only later, from the subsequent consideration of the sphere of fate from which it originates. A valuable clue to the character of this threat can be found in the domain of punishments. Among those, ever since the validity of positive law has been called into question, the death penalty has provoked more criticism than all other forms of punishment. However little the arguments put forward by this critique were, in most cases, grounded in principles, their motives were and still are based on principle. Critics of the death penalty felt, perhaps without being able to justify their feelings, indeed probably without wanting to feel this way, that a challenge to the death penalty attacks not a punitive measure, not certain acts of legislation, but rather law itself in its origin.[30] For if violence, violence crowned by fate, is the origin of law, then one may readily suppose that in the highest form of violence, in the power over life and death, where violence appears on the stage of the legal order, its origins are represented as they burst into the status quo, manifesting themselves in a fearsome manner. In agreement with this is the fact that in primitive legal circumstances, the death penalty is imposed even for such offenses as property misdemeanors, to which it seems entirely out of "proportion [Verhältnis]." Its meaning is thus not to punish the infringement of law but to establish new law. For in the exercise of power [Gewalt] over life and death, law reinforces itself more than in any other form of law enforcement. In this event, however, something rotten in law also announces itself most perceptibly to finer feeling, which knows itself to be infinitely far removed from the circumstances in which fate in its own majesty would have shown itself through such law-enforcing acts. The faculty of understanding, however, must attempt to approach these circumstances all the more decisively if it wants to bring to a conclusion the critique of law-positing as well as law-preserving violence.

[§10] [2:189] In a far more unnatural combination than in the death penalty, in a spectral [gespenstische] mixture, so to speak, these two kinds of violence are present in another institution of the modern state: the police.[31] The police constitute a form of violence directed toward legal ends (under the law pertaining to orders [Verfügungsrecht]), but with the simultaneous authorization [Befugnis] to set these ends for itself within broad limits (under the law pertaining to regulations [Verordnungsrecht]).[32] The ignominy of such an authority [Behörde]—which is felt by few only because its authority rarely suffices even for the crudest interventions but is therefore allowed to range all the more blindly in the most vulnerable areas and against those with any degree of reflection [*Besonnene*], those from whom the state finds no protection through its laws—lies in the fact that with the police, the separation of law-positing and law-preserving violence is annulled [*aufgehoben*]. If it is demanded of the first kind of violence that it prove itself in victory, the second is subject to the constraint that it may not set for itself new ends. Police violence is emancipated from both conditions. It is law-positing—for its characteristic function is not the promulgation of laws but the adoption [*Erlaß*] of any given decree with the claim to legality [*Rechtsanspruch*]—and it is law-preserving because it places itself at the disposal of these ends. The assertion that the ends of police violence are always identical with, or even connected to, the ends of the remainder of law is thoroughly untrue. Rather, the "law" ["*Recht*"] of the police basically denotes the point at which the state, whether from impotence or because of the immanent connections of every legal order, can no longer guarantee through the legal order the empirical ends that it wishes to achieve at any price. Therefore, the police intervene "for security reasons" in countless cases where no clear legal situation exists, if they are not merely, without any reference whatsoever to legal ends, accompanying the citizen as a brutal harassment through a life regulated by ordinances, or quite simply surveilling him. In contrast to law, which recognizes in a "decision" that is fixed in place and time a metaphysical category through which it raises a claim to critique, reflection on the institution of the police encounters nothing essential.[33] The violence of this institution is shapeless [*gestaltlos*], like its nowhere-tangible, all-pervasive, ghostly appearance in the life of civilized states. And though policing may, in specific respects, look everywhere alike, [2:190] there can ultimately be no denying that its spirit is less devastating in absolute monarchies, where it represents the ruler's power [*Gewalt*], in which there is a unity of full legislative and executive power [*Machtvollkommenheit*], than in democracies, where its existence, elevated by no such relation, bears witness to the greatest conceivable degeneration [*Entartung*] of power [*Gewalt*].[34]

[§11] All violence as a means is either law-positing or law-preserving. If it lays claim to neither of these predicates, then it forfeits all validity. From this, however, it follows that every violence as a means, even in the most favorable case, itself participates in the problematic character of law as such. And if the significance of its problematic character cannot be ascertained at this stage of the investigation, law nevertheless appears in such an ambiguous moral light from the previous discussion that the following question becomes urgent: whether there are no means other than violence available for the regulation of conflicting human interests. The question makes it obligatory, above all, to establish that a fully nonviolent resolution of conflicts can never amount to a legal contract. A legal contract, however peacefully the parties enter into it, leads ultimately to possible violence. For the contract confers upon each party the right to resort to violence in some form or another should one party break the agreement.[35] Not only this: like the outcome, the origin of every contract also points toward violence. It need not be immediately present in the contract as a law-positing violence, but violence is represented in it insofar as the power that guarantees the legal contract is, in turn, of violent origin, if not itself legally established in this very contract by means of violence. If the consciousness of the latent presence of violence in a legal institution disappears, the institution falls into decay. In current times, parliaments constitute an example of this: they offer a well-known, woeful spectacle because they have not remained conscious of the revolutionary forces to which they owe their existence. Particularly in Germany, the most recent manifestation of such forms of violence [Gewalten] ran its course without any consequences for the parliaments. They lack the sense for the law-positing violence that is represented in them; no wonder they arrive at no resolutions that would be [2:191] worthy of this violence but instead cultivate through compromise a supposedly nonviolent manner of handling political affairs. Compromise remains, however, a "product situated within the mentality of violence, no matter how much it may disdain all open violence, because the effort toward compromise is motivated not internally but from outside, indeed by the opposing effort, for no compromise, however freely accepted, is conceivable without a compulsory character. 'It would be better otherwise' is the basic feeling belonging to every compromise."* — It is significant that the decay of parliaments has turned just as many minds away from the ideal of a nonviolent resolution of political conflicts as were earlier drawn to it by the war. Standing opposed to the pacifists are the Bolsheviks and the Syndicalists. They have submitted today's parliaments to an annihilating and altogether

---

* Erich Unger, *Politik und Metaphysik* (*Die Theorie: Versuche zu philosophischer Politik*, 1. Veröffentlichung [Berlin, 1921], 8).

fitting critique.³⁶ As desirable and gratifying as an advanced parliament may be in comparison [with today's versions], however, a discussion of the means of political accord that are in principle nonviolent cannot be concerned with parliamentarianism. For what parliamentarianism achieves in vital affairs can only be those legal orders [*Rechtsordnungen*] that are afflicted by violence in origin and outcome.

[§12] Is any nonviolent resolution of conflicts possible? Without a doubt. The relations between private persons are replete with examples of this. Nonviolent agreement [*Einigung*] can be found wherever the culture of the heart has placed pure means of accord [*Übereinkunft*] in human hands.³⁷ Indeed, nonviolent means may be set apart as pure means from legal and illegal means of all sorts, all of which are without exception [forms of] violence. Heartfelt courtesy, affection, peaceableness, trust, and whatever else might be named here are the subjective preconditions of nonviolent means. Their objective appearance, however, is determined by the law (whose tremendous [*gewaltige*] scope cannot be discussed here) that pure means are never means for immediate solutions but always only for mediated ones. They thus never relate immediately to the arbitration of conflicts between one human being and another but rather only by way of things [*Sachen*]. [2:192] In the most material [*sachlichsten*] relation of human conflicts to goods there opens up a realm of pure means. For this reason, technique [*Technik*] in the broadest sense of the word is its most proper domain. Its profoundest example is perhaps discussion [*Unterredung*] as a technique of civil accord. For, in a discussion, not only is nonviolent agreement possible, but the suspension of violence in principle can be altogether explicitly documented by something significant: impunity for lying. There is probably no legislation on earth that originally punished lying.³⁸ What is expressed in this situation is the existence of a sphere of human accord that is nonviolent to such a degree that it is wholly inaccessible to violence: the proper sphere of "coming-to-an-understanding" [*Verständigung*], language. Only at a late stage and by a peculiar process of decay has legal violence penetrated this sphere by penalizing fraud. For, whereas the legal order in its origin, trusting in its victorious power [*Gewalt*], is satisfied with striking down unlawful violence wherever it appears, and whereas fraud, since it has nothing of violence in itself, was penalty-free under the principle [*Grundsatz*] of *ius civile vigilantibus scriptum est* ("civil law is written for the vigilant"), viz., "eyes for money" [*Augen für Geld*] in Roman and Old Germanic law, the law of a later period, which lacked trust in its own power [*Gewalt*], no longer felt itself to be a match for all other forms of violence, as did earlier law.[39] Rather, fear of other forms of violence and mistrust toward itself give indication of its state of distress [*Erschütterung*]. It begins to set itself ends with the intention of sparing law-preserving violence still stronger [*stärkere*] manifestations. It therefore turns against fraud not out of moral [*moralischen*] considerations but for fear of the violent acts that it might trigger in the defrauded party. Since such fear stands in conflict with law's own violent nature from its origins, ends of this kind are incommensurate [*unangemessen*] with the justified means of law. In these ends, not only does the decay of law's own sphere manifest itself, so also does the diminishment of pure means. For, in prohibiting fraud, law sets constraints on the use of wholly nonviolent means, since they could reactively generate violence. The tendency of law, thus conceived, has also played a role in conceding the right to strike, which contradicts the interests of the state. Law grants this right because it restrains violent actions [2:193] it is afraid to confront. Previously, workers resorted straight away to sabotage and set fire to the factories. — To move human beings toward peacefully reconciling their interests independently of any legal order, there is, finally, apart from all virtues, one effective motive that often enough places pure rather than violent means into the hands of even the most obdurate wills: the fear of the mutual disadvantages that threaten to arise from violent confrontation, whatever the outcome may be. Such disadvantages are clearly evident in countless conflict-of-interest cases among private persons. It is otherwise when classes and nations come into conflict, since the higher orders that threaten to overwhelm both victor and vanquished alike are hidden from the feelings of most and the insight of almost all. The search for such higher orders and the common interests that correspond to them, which would yield the most enduring motive for a politics of pure means, would lead too far afield.* For this reason, only a pure means of politics as an analogue to the means governing the peaceful interchange between private persons may be indicated.

[§13] As concerns class struggles, under certain conditions the strike must be counted as a pure means. Two essentially different kinds of strike, whose possibility has already been considered, will now be characterized in greater detail. Sorel can be credited for having first differentiated between

---

* See, however, Unger, 18ff.

the two—more on the basis of political than purely theoretical calculations. He draws a distinction between the political and the proletarian general strike. There is also an antithesis between their respective relations to violence. About the partisans of the former he writes: "The strengthening of state power [*l'État / Staatsgewalt*] is the basis of their conceptions; in their present organizations the politicians (namely, the moderate socialists) are already preparing the ground for a strong centralized and disciplined power [*pouvoir / Gewalt*] that will be impervious to criticism from the opposition, and capable of imposing silence and issuing its mendacious decrees."*[40] "The political general strike demonstrates [2:194] how the state will lose none of its force [*force / Kraft*], how power is transferred [*la transmission / Macht*] from the privileged to the privileged, how the mass of producers will change their masters."† In contrast to this political general strike (whose formula, incidentally, seems to be that of the recently elapsed German Revolution), the proletarian general strike sets itself the sole task of annihilating [*Vernichtung*] state power [*Staatsgewalt*]. It "suspends [*supprime / schaltet aus*] all ideological consequences of every possible social policy; its partisans regard even the most popular reforms as bourgeois."‡ "This general strike clearly announces its indifference toward material gain through conquest by declaring its intention to abolish [*supprimer / aufheben*] the state; the state was really . . . the basis of the existence of the ruling groups, who profit from all enterprises whose burdens are borne by the public."§ Whereas the first form of work stoppage is a form of violence, since it only occasions an external modification of working conditions, the second, as a pure means, is nonviolent. For it takes place not in the readiness to resume work after external concessions and some modification of certain working conditions, but in the resolve to resume only an entirely transformed work that is not compelled by the state, an upheaval that this kind of strike does not so much occasion as consummate. The first of these undertakings is therefore law-positing, whereas the second is anarchistic. In connection with some occasional statements by Marx,[41] Sorel rejects from the revolutionary movement all kinds of programs, utopias of every kind—in a word, efforts at law-positing: "With the general strike, all

---

* Sorel, *Réflexions sur la violence*, 5th ed. (Paris, 1919 [sic]), 250.
† Sorel, 265.
‡ Sorel, 195.
§ Sorel, 249.

these fine things disappear; the revolution appears as a clear, simple revolt, and no place is reserved either for the sociologists or for the elegant amateurs of social reforms, nor for the intellectuals who have made it their profession to think for the proletariat."* This deep, moral, and genuinely revolutionary conception cannot be countered by any calculation that would like to brand the general [2:195] strike as violent because of its possibly catastrophic consequences. Even if one may rightly say that the modern economy, taken as a whole, is less comparable to a machine that idles when abandoned by its stoker than a beast that rages as soon as its tamer turns his back, nevertheless the violent character of an action can be judged no more by its effects than by its ends, but only by the law of its means. Of course, state power, which looks only toward effects, opposes precisely this kind of strike, which it presumes to be violent, in contrast to partial strikes, which are, for the most part, actually extortionary. With thought-provoking arguments Sorel has explained the extent to which such a rigorous conception of the general strike is liable to diminish the deployment of actual violence in revolutions. — By contrast, a conspicuous case of a violent act of omission [*Unterlassung*] that is cruder and more immoral than the political general strike, and which is akin to a blockade, is the doctors' strike, as was seen in several German cities.[42] The most unscrupulous use of violence [*Gewaltanwendung*] is revealed at its most repellent in a strike of this kind, an application of force that is positively depraved for a professional class that has for years "secured death its prey," without the slightest attempt at resistance, in order to then voluntarily abandon the cause of life at the very first opportunity.[43] — Means of nonviolent accord [*Übereinkunft*] have emerged in the millennia-old history of states more clearly than in recent class conflicts. Only occasionally does the task of diplomats who are mutually interacting with one another consist in the modification of legal orders. In essence, diplomats must, on analogy with the accord between private persons, resolve conflicts peacefully and without contracts, case by case, in the names of their states. A delicate task, which is more resolutely resolved by arbitration, but it is nevertheless a method of resolution that in principle stands higher than any method of arbitration because it is beyond every legal order and therefore beyond violence. In sum, like the interaction among private persons, dealing among diplomats has engendered

---

*   Sorel, 200.

its own forms and virtues, which may have become outward formalities but were not therefore always so.

[§14] Within the entire realm covering the forms of violence foreseen by both natural law and positive law, none is free from the [2:196] gravely problematic character of legal violence that has thus far been indicated. Since, however, every representation of any conceivable solution [*Lösung*] to human tasks [*Aufgaben*], to say nothing of a redemption [*Erlösung*] from the spell encircling [*Bannkreis*] all previous world-historical existential situations [*Daseinslagen*], cannot be accomplished if each and every form of violence is fully excluded in principle, the question necessarily arises concerning other kinds of violence than those envisaged by all legal theory. This is a question that at the same time concerns the truth of the basic dogma held in common by these theories: just ends can be attained by justified means; justified means can be used for just ends. How, then, would things stand if the kind of violence that is commensurate with fate, as it employs justified means, were to be in irreconcilable conflict with just ends, and if, at the same time, a different kind of violence should be foreseen, a kind of violence that definitely could not be either a justified or an unjustified means to those ends, and would, instead, relate to them not as means at all but somehow differently? This would throw a light on the strange and initially discouraging experience of the ultimate undecidability [*Unentscheidbarkeit*] of all legal problems (which in its hopelessness can perhaps be compared only with the impossibility of deciding conclusively on what is "correct" or "false" in evolving languages). Reason, after all, never decides on the justification of means and the justice of ends; rather, fateful violence decides on the former, while God decides on the latter.[44] [This is] an insight that is uncommon only because a stubborn habit prevails, a habit of conceiving of just ends as ends of a possible law, that is, not only as universally valid (which follows analytically from the distinguishing mark of justice), but also as capable of universalization, which, as can be shown, contradicts the distinguishing mark of justice. For ends that are just for one situation [*Situation*], universally recognized and in this sense valid universally, are so for no other, even if in other respects the situation [*Lage*] is ever so similar. — Everyday experience of life already shows a nonmediate [*nicht mittelbare*] function of violence like the one under investigation here. As regards a human being, rage [*Zorn*], for instance, leads to the most visible outbursts of a violence that is not related as a means to a predetermined end. This violence is not a means but a manifestation. And, in fact, this kind of violence [2:197] admits of thoroughly objective [*objektive*] manifestations in which it can be subjected to critique. It is of the highest significance that these can be found, above all, in myth.

[§15] In its archetypal [*urbildlichen*] form, mythic violence is a mere manifestation of the gods. Not a means to their ends, scarcely even a manifestation of their will, but in the first instance a manifestation of their existence. The legend of Niobe contains an outstanding example of this.[45] To be sure, it could appear as though the action of Apollo and Artemis were only a punishment. But their violence establishes a law far more than it punishes the transgression of an existing one. Niobe's arrogance conjures up the disaster that befalls her not because it injures law but because it challenges fate—challenges fate to a combat in which fate must triumph, bringing a law to light, if need be, only in its victory. How little such divine violence in the ancient sense was the law-preserving violence of punishment is shown by the legends of heroes in which the heroic protagonist, for example, Prometheus, challenges fate with dignified courage, combats fate with changing fortune [*Glück*], and is not left by the legend without the hope of one day bringing a new law to human beings.[46] It is actually this hero along with the legal violence [*Rechtsgewalt*] of the myth native to him that people still today seek to make present to themselves [*vergegenwärtigen*] when they admire the great malefactor. Violence thus closes in upon Niobe from the uncertain, ambiguous sphere of fate. This violence is not actually destructive. Although it brings bloody death to Niobe's children, it stops short of taking the mother's life, which it leaves behind as an eternal, mute bearer of guilt and as a stone marking the border [*Grenze*] between human beings and gods, a life now, through the children's death, more inculpated [*verschuldeter*] than before. If this immediate violence in mythical manifestations should prove closely related to, even identical with, law-positing violence, this would reflect back on a problematic trait of law-positing violence, insofar as the latter was characterized in the earlier exposition of military violence only as a certain kind of means [*mittelartig*]. At the same time, this connection promises to shed more light on the fate underlying legal violence in all cases and to bring its critique in broad strokes to a close. For the function of violence in law-positing is twofold in the following sense: the positing of law, which uses violence as its means, pursues as its end precisely *what* is to be [2:198] established [*eingesetzt*] as law; in the moment of instating as law [*Einsetzung*] the end at which it aims, however, law-positing does not simply relinquish violence; rather, now in a rigorous sense and, indeed, immediately, it turns this violence into the law-positing kind by establishing not an end that would be free of, and independent from, violence but, on the contrary, an end that, under the name of power, is necessarily and intimately bound up with it. The positing of law is the positing of power, and, in this respect, an act [*Akt*] of an immediate manifestation of violence. Justice is the principle of all divine end-positing, power the principle of all mythic law-positing.

[§16] The latter principle undergoes an immensely consequential application in constitutional law [*Staatsrecht*]. For in its domain, the establishment of boundaries [*Grenzsetzung*], which is carried out by the "peace" of all wars of the mythic age, is the original phenomenon [*Urphänomen*] of law-positing violence as such.[47] What appears most clearly in the establishment of boundaries is the fact that law-positing violence is supposed to guarantee power [*Macht*] more than even the most extravagant gain in possession. Where boundaries are laid down, the adversary is not utterly annihilated; indeed, he is granted rights even where the victor possesses the most superior force [*Gewalt*]. And these are "equal" rights in a demonic-ambiguous [*dämonisch-zweideutiger*] manner: it is the same line that may not be crossed for both parties to the treaty. Here appears in dreadful primordiality the same mythic ambiguity of laws that may not be "transgressed" about which Anatole France said, satirically: "Poor and rich are equally forbidden to spend the night under the bridge."[48] It also seems that Sorel touches upon a truth that is not simply cultural-historical but also metaphysical when he surmises that at its beginnings all law [*Recht*] was the privilege [*Vor-recht*] of kings or grandees—in short, of the powerful.[49] So it will remain, *mutatis mutandis*, as long as law continues to exist. For, from the viewpoint of violence, which alone can guarantee law, there is no equality, only at best equally sized magnitudes of violence [*gleich große Gewalten*]. The act of establishing boundaries is, however, also significant for understanding law in another sense. Established and circumscribed boundaries remain, at least in primeval times, unwritten laws. A human being can transgress them unawares and thereby succumb to expiation [*der Sühne verfallen*].[50] For this encroachment of law, summoned by the violation [2:199] of the unwritten and unknown law, is called expiation, as distinct from punishment. But with whatever misfortune expiation may befall its unsuspecting victim, its occurrence is, for the purpose of law, not an accident but rather fate, which here presents itself once again in its methodical ambiguity. In a passing reflection on the conception of fate in antiquity, Hermann Cohen already identified this "inevitable insight": "[O]rders [of fate] themselves seem to occasion and bring about this transgression, this defection."*[51] Even the modern principle that ignorance of the law offers no protection from punishment testifies to this spirit of law, just as combat over written law in the early period of ancient communities should be understood as rebellion against the spirit of mythic statutes [Satzungen].

[§17] Far from opening up a purer sphere, the mythic manifestation of immediate violence reveals itself to be at the deepest level identical with all legal violence and transforms a vague intimation of its problematic character into a certainty concerning the perniciousness of its historical function, the annihilation of which thus becomes a task. Precisely this task introduces once again and for the last time the question of a pure, immediate form of violence that might be capable of putting a halt to mythic violence. Just as God is opposed to myth in all spheres, so divine violence runs counter to mythic violence. Indeed, divine violence designates in all respects an antithesis to mythic violence. If mythic violence is law-positing, divine violence is law-annihilating; if the former establishes boundaries, the latter boundlessly annihilates them; if mythic violence inculpates [verschuldend] and expiates [sühnend] at the same time, divine violence de-expiates [entsühnend]; if the former threatens, the latter strikes; if the former is bloody, the latter is lethal in a bloodless manner. The legend of Niobe may be contrasted by way of example with God's judgment on Korah's horde.[52] The judgment strikes privileged ones, Levites; it strikes them unannounced, without threat, and does not stop short of annihilation. At the same time, however, precisely in annihilating, it is also de-expiating, and one cannot fail to recognize a profound connection between the bloodless and the de-expiating character of this violence. For blood is the symbol of mere life.[53] Now, the release [Auslösung] of legal violence stems (as cannot be shown here in greater detail) [2:200] from the inculpating [Verschuldung] of mere natural life, which delivers the living, innocent and unfortunate, into the hands of an expiation that "atones" ["sühnt"] for this inculpation [Verschuldung]—and doubtless also de-expiates [entsühnt] the guilty, not of guilt, to be sure, but of law.[54] For the domination of law over the living ceases with mere life. Mythic violence is blood-violence over mere life for the sake of violence itself; divine

---

* Hermann Cohen, Ethik des reinen Willens, 2nd ed. (Berlin, 1907), 362.

violence is pure violence over all of life for the sake of the living. The former demands sacrifice; the latter assumes it.

[§18] This divine violence acquires attestation not only through religious tradition; on the contrary, it also has at least one hallowed manifestation in present-day life. What, as educative violence, stands in its completed form outside of law is one of its forms of appearance. These forms are thus not defined by God immediately exercising divine violence in miracles but rather through moments of bloodless, striking, de-expiating implementation [*Vollzug*]. Through the absence, in the end, of all positing of law. To this extent, it is doubtless justified to also call this violence annihilating; but it is annihilating only in a relative sense, with regard to goods, law, life, and the like, never absolutely with regard to the soul of the living. — Such an extension of pure or divine violence will certainly, and especially today, provoke the fiercest attacks, and one will respond to this extension by saying that, directly in accordance with its justification [*Deduktion*], it unleashes lethal violence on human beings against one another under certain conditions. This is not to be conceded. For the question "May I kill?" begets an unshakeable answer in the form of the commandment, "Thou shalt not kill."[55] This commandment blocks the deed as though God were "preventing" it from happening.[56] But just as it ought not truly be fear of punishment that compels one to comply with the commandment, so the commandment remains inapplicable to, incommensurable with, the completed deed. No judgment of the deed follows from the commandment. And thus, neither the divine judgment of the deed nor the basis for this judgment can be foreseen. For this reason, those who base the condemnation of every violent killing of a human being by fellow human beings on the commandment are wrong. The commandment exists not as a standard of judgment but as a guideline of action for the agent [2:201] or community that has to confront it in solitude and, in terrible cases, take on the responsibility of disregarding it. Thus too did Judaism, which expressly rejected the condemnation of a killing done in self-defense, understand the commandment.[57] — But those thinkers [who raise the objection] refer to a more remote theorem on which they perhaps propose to base the commandment itself. This is the proposition concerning the sanctity of life, which they either apply to all animal or even vegetal life, or limit to human life. Exemplified in an extreme case by the revolutionary killing of oppressors, their argumentation looks like this: "If I do not kill, then I will never establish the empire of justice. . . . This is the reasoning of the intellectual terrorist.... We profess, however, that higher still than the happiness and justice of an existence—stands existence itself."* As certainly as this last sentence is false, even ignoble, it uncovers with equal certainty an obligation to seek the basis of the commandment no longer in what the deed does to the murder victim, but in what the deed does to God and to the perpetrator himself. False and lowly is the proposition that existence is higher than just existence, if existence [*Dasein*] is to mean nothing other than mere life—and this is the meaning of existence in the reflection above. But the proposition contains a powerful [*gewaltige*] truth if existence (or better, life)—words, whose double sense, just like that of the word "peace," is to be resolved by relating them to two spheres—means the unshakeable aggregate state of "the human being."[58] If the proposition wants to say that the nonbeing of a human being is more terrible than the (unconditioned: mere) not-yet-being of the just human being. The aforementioned proposition owes its plausibility to this ambiguity. Under no condition does the human being coincide with the mere life of a human being, just as little with the mere life in this being as with any of its states and qualities, indeed not even with the uniqueness of its bodily person. However sacred the human being is (or that life therein, which stays identical in earthly life, death, and living-on), its [physical] states are not sacred, nor its bodily life, which is vulnerable to injury by fellow human beings. [2:202] What distinguishes it, then, in essence, from the life of animals and plants? And even if these were sacred, they could nevertheless not be sacred in mere life, for the sake of their mere life. It would be worthwhile to track down the origin of the dogma of the sanctity of life. Perhaps, indeed probably, [the dogma] is too young, as the latest aberration of a weakened Western tradition, to seek the sacred one [*den Heiligen*], which it had lost, in cosmologically impenetrable things.[59] (The age of all religious commandments against murder provides no counterargument, since they are based on thoughts other than those underlying the modern theorem.) Finally, there is something in the thought that what is here called sacred is, according to ancient mythical thinking, the designated bearer of inculpation: mere life.

[§19] The critique of violence is the philosophy of its history. The "philosophy" of this history because only the idea of its ending [*Ausgang*] makes possible a critical, incisive, and decisive attitude toward its temporal

---

* Kurt Hiller in a yearbook of *Das Ziel*.

data. A gaze directed only at what is closest at hand can at most become aware of a dialectical back-and-forth in the formations of violence into its law-positing and law-preserving kinds. The law of its oscillation rests on this: all law-preserving violence, in its duration, indirectly, through its suppression of hostile counterforces [*Gegengewalten*], weakens law-positing violence, which is represented in it. (A few symptoms thereof have been documented in the course of this investigation.) This lasts until either new forms of violence or ones earlier suppressed gain victory over the hitherto law-positing violence, thereby founding a new law, with a new decay. A new historical era is founded on breaking through this cycle that spins under the spell of mythical forms of law, and on de-posing [*Entsetzung*] law together with all the forms of violence on which it depends, just as they depend on it, and finally, therefore, on de-posing state violence.[60] If, in the present, the domination of myth is already broken here and there, the new age does not lie in such an unimaginably lofty distance that a word against law would make no difference. But if, with respect to violence, its standing resource [*Bestand*] as pure immediate violence is also secured beyond law, this proves that, and how, there is a possibility of revolutionary violence, which is the name reserved for the highest manifestation of pure violence through human beings. Not equally [2:203] possible, and also less urgent for human beings is, however, the decision concerning when pure violence was realized in a particular case. For only mythic violence, not divine violence, can be recognized as such with certainty, unless it be through incomparable effects, for the de-expiating force [*Kraft*] of violence is not disclosed to human beings. Once again, all eternal forms that myth bastardized with law stand free and open to pure divine violence. Divine violence may appear in the true war [*wahrer Krieg*] exactly as it does in the divine judgment of the multitude [*Menge*] upon the criminal. To be rejected [*verwerflich*], however, is all mythic violence, the law-positing kind, which may be called attending [*schaltende*] violence. Also to be rejected is the law-preserving kind, the expended [*verwaltete*] violence that serves it. Divine violence, which is the sign and seal but never the means of sacred dispatch [*Vollstreckung*], may be called pending [*waltende*] violence.[61]

Walter Benjamin, "Zur Kritik der Gewalt," *Archiv für Sozialwissenschaft und Sozialpolitik* 47, no. 3 (1920/21): 809–32. No manuscript original has been preserved. An offprint along with a typescript containing several corrections in black ink and labeled "Hyne Caro's copy from 1921" are located at Scholem Arc 4° 1598 File 93. Translated by Julia Ng.

The following reproduces the table of contents for the "treatises" (*Abhandlungen*) published in the forty-seventh issue of the *Archiv*:

- Benjamin, Walter. "Zur Kritik der Gewalt" [Toward the critique of violence]
- Engels, Friedrich, and Karl Marx (ed. and intro. Gustav Mayer). "Das Leipziger Konzil" [The Leipzig Council]
- Engliš, Karl. "Die wirtschaftliche Theorie des Geldes" [The economic theory of money]
- Hirschstein, Hans. "Der englische Währungsbericht" [The English currency report]
- Kelsen, Hans. "Vom Wesen und Wert der Demokratie" [On the essence and value of democracy]
- Michels, Robert. "Dogmengeschichtliche Beiträge zur Verelendungstheorie I" [Dogma-historical contributions to the theory of impoverishment, pt. 1]
- Mises, Ludwig. "Die Wirtschaftsrechnung im sozialistischen Gemeinwesen" [Economic calculation in the socialist commonwealth]
- Moeller, Hero. "Zur Frage der 'Objektivität' des wirtschaftlichen Prinzips I" [On the question of the "objectivity" of the economic principle, pt. 1]
- Oppenheimer, Franz. "Das Bodenmonopol" [Monopoly of land]
- Salz, Arthur. "Über das Problem der 'Dekadenz' des Islam" [On the problem of the "decadence" of Islam]
- Strigl, Richard. "Der Kapitalzins als Residual-Rente" [Interest on capital as residual revenues]
- Szende, Paul. "Die Krise der mitteleuropäischen Revolution" [The crisis of the middle-European revolution]
- Weber, Alfred. "Prinzipielles zur Kultursoziologie" [Some principles for the sociology of culture]
- Weber, Max. "Die Stadt: Eine soziologische Untersuchung" [The city: A sociological investigation]

Associated Notes and Fragments

1.

\<Notes toward a Work on the Category of Justice\>

[*TB* 1:401] To every good, limited as it is by the spatiotemporal order, there accrues a possession-character as the expression of its transience. But possession, as something caught in the same finitude, is always unjust. No order of possession, however articulated, can therefore lead to justice.

Rather, this lies in the condition of a good that cannot be a possession. This alone is the good through which [whom] goods become possessionless.

In the concept of society one tries to give to the good a possessor that cancels its possession-character.

Every socialist or communist theory misses its goal precisely because the claim of the individual ranges over every good. If, for individual *A*, there is a need *z* that can be satisfied with good *x*, and if one therefore believes that good *y*, which is equal to *x*, may and should be given justifiably to individual *B* in order to calm the same need, one errs. For there is an entirely abstract claim of the subject in principle to every good, a claim that in no way leads back to needs but rather to justice, and whose ultimate direction does not point toward the possession-right of the person but possibly toward a good-right of the good.

Justice is the striving to make the world into the highest good.

The aforementioned thoughts lead to this conjecture: justice is not a virtue among other virtues (humility, love of the neighbor, loyalty, bravery); rather, it grounds a new ethical category that one must not perhaps even call a category of virtue but rather a category of the same order as virtue. Justice does not appear to refer to the good will of the subject but instead constitutes a state [*Zustand*] of the world. Justice designates the ethical category of the existent, virtue the ethical category of the demanded. Virtue can be demanded; justice in the final analysis can only be, as a state of the world or as a state of God. In God all virtues have the form of justice; the prefix *omni* in omnigracious, omniscient, and so forth points in this direction. Only a fulfillment of what is demanded [*TB* 1:402] can be virtuous; only a guarantee [*Gewährleistung*] of the existent (*no longer perhaps* to be determined through demands, nevertheless in any case not any arbitrary one) can be just.

Justice is the ethical side of the battle; justice is the power [*Macht*] of virtue and the virtue of power. The responsibility for the world we have protects from the instance of justice.[1]

The Lord's Prayer: Lead us not into temptation, but rather redeem us from evil [several words unreadable], is the prayer for justice, for the just state of the world.[2] The empirical individual act is related to the moral law somehow as a (nondeducible) fulfillment of the formal schema. Conversely, law [*Recht*] is related to justice [*Gerechtigkeit*] as the schema to its fulfillment. Other languages have designated the enormous gulf that essentially separates law from justice.

ius	θεμις [*themis*]	משפט [*mishpat*]
fas	δικη [*dikē*]	צדק [*tsedek*][3]

2.

\<Vivification and Violence\>

[7:26] The centaur belongs originally to those times of Greek nature in which creation became vivified [*belebt*] through the spirit of water and was developed through such spirit. "Roaming around," water is first an undirected force [*Gewalt*] still belonging to chaos; then it becomes a directed current—the beginning of vivification [*Belebung*] and cosmos. It is also at one moment stagnation and therefore death; it then turns the next moment into the roaring element, the living thing that vivifies. This existence [*Dasein*] of water in creation is doubtless what Thales meant when he found in water the first principle.[1] Moisture was life, but it was nevertheless at the same time shapeless [*gestaltlos*], almost that nonvivified element from which the living shaped itself; it was the medium of vivification. Because it was a medium, it was unity beyond oppositions. The concept of the centaur, Hölderlin says, was that of vivifying water.[2] The genuinely Greek sadness of these shapes, however, held true for their existence in the vivifying element, for any developing creation, and for the violence vivifying such creation. This is because whenever something is vivified, there is violence where spirit does not vivify. The latter, however, is the word. Where the word does not vivify, life takes a while to awaken, and where creation lingers for a while, it is sad. Such is Jewish cheerfulness in creation: that it emerges from the word, full of deep seriousness but full of elevated joy. Greek nature comes to itself blindly; it awakens sadly and finds no awakener. It awakens in the centaur.

3.

<From "Life and Violence">

[7:791] ... to be rejected as reprehensible. By contrast, orig[inal] violence, as it may exist, for example, in [self-]defense, is not at all reprehensible or to be rejected. The judgment of an action has absolutely nothing to do with whether it was accomplished with or without bodily force [*Gewalt*]. Therefore, the anarchistic demand that violence [*Gewalt*] be abolished makes sense only in relation to expended violence [*verwaltete Gewalt*]; therefore, its terroristic praxis does not stand in contradiction with its theory.[1] By contrast, the demand for complete nonviolence cannot be exactly defined (when does violence stop?); it is not only absurd in its consequence, which denies life and even suicide, but there is also, above all, no reason to instill it.

Therefore, violence cannot be fought with violence, and the question arises: How, then, should human beings in the free community of their life be secure? Only inclination [*Neigung*] disarms the evil act in such community; orig[inal] violence *as such*, however, is not *at all* affected.[2]

4.

On Morality

[6:54] Bavarian Prayer: ... And may you {God} also be beseeched for what you want to be beseeched. — Here can be found not only the usual intention of the one who prays (which expresses itself adequately in the first part of the prayer) but also a second intention, directed at the form of the first part of the prayer, which is related to the first intention in the following way: God should understand the prayer not so much in accordance with its prayerful intention as in accordance with the intention of making the first prayerful intention absolute, that is, intensifying its expression to the point where the intended correlate (that which is reverently beseeched) falls away, while nevertheless the prayer survives God [*vor Gott besteht*] on the basis of the first, absolute, correlationless intention.

Thus it is with compulsive neurotics: the action (for example, the ordering of objects on a table) should still retain its meaning if, regardless of every rationally intended correlate of such an order, the ordering act appears absolute. Thus it is with dogma: it is not a matter of the correlate of the first intention, not of what is meant in the credo, but rather of the second intention: even with the removal of the intentional correlate of what is meant in the first intention (which is removed, say, because of subjective incredulity), there still remains in place the full *virtus* of the dogma, which is therefore not viewed in terms of subjective conviction. Here, then, a second, actual intention is directed toward a certain intentional correlate of the first, a correlate that is conquered and held, regardless of the degree to which the first intention weakens and diminishes.

That second intention is always in the eminent sense directed at something that belongs absolutely to the order of action [*ein handlungsmäßiges*], that is, a moral moment in the zones of any given first intention, zones that are otherwise, in the rigorous sense, morally indifferent; the second intention is therefore of supreme value for insight into the essence of morality. Also of supreme value for the determination of the relation of action [*Handlung*] to deed and word [*Tat und Wort*], which occur only in the [above-described] first intentions.

5.

<All Unconditionality of the Will Leads to Evil>

[6:55] All unconditionality of the will leads to evil: ambition, lust are unconditioned tendencies of the will. The natural totality of the will, as theologians always recognized, must be shattered. The will must splinter into a thousand pieces. The components of the will [*Willensmomente*], having thus become diversified, reciprocally condition one another: the earthly, conditioned will emerges. Everything that, beyond them, requires the (supreme) unity of intention is not an object of the will: it does not require the intention *of the will*. Devotion [*Andacht*], however, may be unconditioned.[1]

6.

On Kantian Ethics

[6:55] In a certain sense, one can recuperate within Kantian ethics the inconclusiveness of the indivisible unity, the individual, who is the subject of ethics. The doctrine of "rational beings" as subjects of ethics has at least one thing in common with this inconclusiveness: it makes the number of ethical subjects independent of the number of human living bodies [*Leiber*], without, of course, recognizing that this number is a comparative, rival unity.[1] Its constituents are only human beings—and their *brothers* (for example, those on other planets).[2]

The concept of "inclination [*Neigung*]," which Kant considers an ethically indifferent or counterethical concept, is to be transformed through a change of meaning into one of the supreme concepts of morality in which it is perhaps called upon to take the position that "love" held.[3]

7.

<The Spontaneity of the I>

[6:55] The spontaneity of the I is definitely to be distinguished from the freedom of the individual.[1] The question concerning the freedom of the will is often and mistakenly also related to spontaneity, so that there is also, as a result, a question concerning the freedom of thinking-acts or mere living-bodily actions. There is no such freedom. The individual can be thought of as *free* only in relation to its actions. The question of the spontaneity of the I belongs in an entirely different (biological??) context.

8.

<Ethics, Applied to History>

[6:91] Ethics, applied to history, is the doctrine
>of revolution
>applied to the state, it is the doctrine
>of anarchy
>>Still other applications?

Cosmopolitanism [*Weltbürgertum*]	
World history	Divine history [*Gottesgeschichte*]
Judgment of the nations [*Weltgericht*][1]	

A   Pure ethics   Doctrine of freedom

    Applied ethics   I History: doctrine of revolution

                      II State: doctrine of anarchy

B   Pure philosophy of law

    Applied philosophy of law   I History: doctrine of world history as development

                      II Doctrine of dominion [*Herrschaft*]

                      (Monarchy — democracy)

[6:92] C Pure Morality   Doctrine of action   Doctrine of justice

    Applied morality   I History: doctrine of the judgment of the nations

                      II Morality: doctrine of theocracy

World history is distinguished from divine history in three moments:

1) What is unified in divine history is separated in world history
2) What in divine history has no temporal index has one in world history
   (e.g., revolution — beginning
   judgment of the nations — end)
3) In world history everything takes place in time
   (temporal revolutions, temporal judgments of the nations)

In order to guarantee the unidirectionality [*Einsinnigkeit*] of occurrence, the highest category of world history is guilt-debt [*Schuld*]. Every world-historical moment is inculpated and inculpating. Cause and effect can never be decisive categories for the structure of world history, for they cannot determine a totality. Logic is called upon to demonstrate the thesis that no totality as such can be a cause or an effect.[2] It is an error of rationalistic conceptions of history to view any given historical totality (that is, a state of the world [*Weltzustand*]) as a cause or an effect. A state of the world is, however, always only a debt [*Schuld*] (with respect to some other later one). Whether it is also inculpated in relation to an earlier one (analogous to how every mechanical phase is *cause* and *effect*) is to be investigated. (It's easily possible that this is not the case.) Once again: no totality is a cause or an effect, no cause or effect is a totality. That is, a totality can contain within itself a cause-effect system but can never be fully defined through such a system.

| The rebel [*Aufrührer*] | The historical individual |
| The ruler [*Herrscher*] | The historical person |

The relation between world history and divine history is to be methodically investigated and described through research into the series of historical numbers.

[6:93] "Morality" [is] the title of the second part of the system. "Moral philosophy" is a stupid tautology. Morality is nothing other than the refraction of action in knowability [*Handlung in der Erkennbarkeit*]; something from the region of knowledge. Morality is not: ethos [*Gesinnung*].

9.

Modes of History

[6:93] Natural history   Cosmogony

                              Ladder of phenomena

World history   Unidirectional causal nexus

Divine history   from whose standpoint

                              Natural history — history of creation

                              World history — revelation

There is natural history only as cosmogony or as the history of creation; Herder's conception of it is false, seen from the earthly standpoint; but because human beings live on it, the earth is already a *world*-historical individual.[1]

The nexus of phenomena is valid not only for the heavenly world but also for earthly nature (the world-historical nexus is also already valid for earthly nature); it is also valid for the *anthropos* as phenomenon, for example, as sexual being, to the very limit of history.[2]

Natural history does not reach the human being; just as little does world history, which knows only the individual. The human being is neither phenomenon nor effect but creature.

10.

Methodical Modes of History

[6:93] In general, history is a unidirectional process.

I. Pragmatic history proceeds temporally, in struggles.[1]

II. Phenomenon-history	Concerns the series of phenomenological (not temporal) presuppositions of phenomena; it too is unidirectional (areas of application, e.g., natural history and art history)
III. Philology	Concerns that process that is neither essentially temporal nor [6:94] exhibits essentially separate phenomena: the terminological process. Philology is transformation-history [*Verwandlungsgeschichte*]; its unidirectionality rests on this—that terminol[ogy] does not become presupposition but rather the material of a new [terminology], and so on. In philology the object has the highest continuity. Unidirectionality is modified in philology in a peculiar way, since it ultimately inclines toward the cyclical. This history has an end but no goal. (Example: the history of ideas [*Geistesgeschichte*], history of the Enlightenment)

It is very likely that phenomenon-history and pragmatic history can enter into no productive connection with each other; the contrary is the case with philology and pragmatic history (the study of sources and their transmission) as well as philology and phenomenon-history (interpretation); the older the pragmata and phenomena, the ever tighter the connection. Literary history and the history of philosophy are sciences of interpretation and cannot exist without rigorous philology and a fully developed doctrine of phenomena (which is called "morphology" in relation to nature; for philosophy and art, it lies in logic).[2] With the same justification or, more exactly, lack of justification, to which one would appeal in calling the history of literature and philosophy auxiliary sciences of the history of ideas [*Geistesgeschichte*], one would designate the study of documents [*Urkundenlehre*] an auxiliary science of history. Methodically subordinated, they nevertheless have entirely independent value.

11.

Death

[6:71] The *individual* dies; that is, there occurs a scattering. The individual is an indivisible yet inconclusive unity; death is in the realm of individuality only a movement (a wave movement). Historical life always elapses [*vergeht*] at some location; it is, however, immortal life in its entirety. The apparently *entire* (conclusive) individual is unimportant. This is the actual true meaning of metempsychosis

The *person* becomes petrifact   Old-agedness.

Only the person can remain faithful

The *human being* becomes free

The *living body* [*Leib*] elapses, shatters as a <u>manometer</u> that in the instant of supreme tension is blasted and, with the falling into pieces of the bond, becomes frail, superfluous.

12.

⟨As Many Pagan Religions, So Many Natural Concepts of Guilt⟩

[6:56] As many pagan religions, so many natural concepts of guilt. Life is always somehow guilty, the punishment for it is death.

>A form of natural guilt, that of sexuality, for enjoyment and for the procreation of life

>Another form, that of money, for the mere possibility of existing

>Other kinds of natural guilt?

Jewish[:] not life but, rather, only the acting human being can become guilty.[1] (Moral guilt. — Is this expression permitted?)[2]

13.

On the Problem of Physiognomy and Prediction

[6:91] The time of fate is the time that can always be made *simultaneous* [*gleichzeitig*] (not present [*gegenwärtig*]). Such time stands under the order of guilt-debt, which determines the connection in it. It is a nonindependent time, and there is in it neither present nor past nor future.

[6:683] — Character and comic
                Comic and innocence [*Unschuld*]
        Character-comedy (Molière)

[4:936] Expressionlessness [*Ausdruckslosigkeit*] — Caricature
        (Invisibility)   Maximum of the
                                                              expressive
                                                              [*Ausdrücklichen*]

[4:937] The death's head is maximum at both:
The maximum of the expressionless: the eye sockets
The maximum of the expressive: the grinning teeth.

E. Nevill Jackson. The history of silhouettes London 1911[1]

14.

The Meaning of Time in the Moral World

[6:97] In the legal institutions that allow for the establishment of fact and judgment with respect to far distant times, one is accustomed to seeing nothing but the intentions of morality itself, brought to their highest concision [*Prägnanz*]. What lends law such interest in and power over the distant past is, however—far from representing the presence of morality in law—a tendency that sets it apart from the moral world in the most precise manner: the tendency toward retribution [*Vergeltung*]. If in modern law, even in the extreme case of murder, retribution—as if shying away from exceeding the domain of one human life—is limited to a time frame of thirty years, hence a lifetime, still it is known from earlier forms of law that this retributive force [*Gewalt*] was able to extend itself into the series of more distant generations. Retribution is at bottom indifferent with respect to time insofar as it remains undiminished in force through the centuries, and still today a picture that is actually pagan arranges the Last Judgment [*jüngste Gericht*] in this sense: as the deadline [6:98] when all delay is canceled, with full retribution setting in. But this line of thought, which mocks delay as empty dawdling, does not comprehend the immense meaning [*Bedeutung*] of what is continually forced back from the hour of every misdeed [*Untat*], relentlessly fleeing into the future; the Day of Judgment [*Gerichtstag*] has this meaning. It does not disclose itself in the world of law, where retribution reigns, but only where, in the moral world, forgiveness confronts retribution. In order to struggle against retribution, however, this finds its powerful shaping [*Gestaltung*] in time. For time, in which Atē pursues the criminal, is not the lonely lull of fear [*Angst*] but rather the loud storm of forgiveness, roaring ahead of ever-approaching judgment, for which Atē is no match.[1] This [storm] is not only the voice wherein the criminal's cry of fear drowns; it is also the hand that erases the traces of his [misdeed], even if it must devastate the earth for this reason. Just as the purifying hurricane rolls past, ahead of the thunderstorms, so God's wrath roars through history in the storm of forgiveness so as to sweep away what would otherwise be forever consumed in the lightning bolts of divine weather.[2]

What is said in this image must let itself be grasped clearly and explicitly in concepts: the meaning of time in the economy of the moral world, in which time not only extinguishes the traces of the misdeed but also, by virtue of its duration—beyond all remembrance or forgetting—lends help in an entirely enigmatic way to forgiveness, though never to reconciliation.

15.

<1) World and Time>

[6:98] 1) World and time

In the becoming-revealed of the divine, the world—the setting [*Schauplatz*] for history—is subjected to a great process of decomposition, time—the life of the performer [*Darsteller*]—to a great process of fulfillment. The demise of the world [*Weltuntergang*]—the destruction and emancipation of a (dramatic) performance [*Darstellung*]. Redemption of history from [6:99] the act of performing [*Darstellenden*]. / But perhaps, in this sense, the deepest contrast to "world" is not "time" but rather "the coming world [*die kommende Welt*]."[1]

2) Catholicism—the process of the approach of anarchy

The problem of Catholicism is that of the (false, earthly) theocracy. The principle is here: genuine divine violence [*Gewalt*] can manifest itself *other than destructively* only in the coming world (of fulfillment). Where, by contrast, divine violence enters into the earthly world, it breathes destruction. This is why, in this world, nothing continuous and no shaping [*Gestaltung*] can be based on divine violence, to say nothing of dominion [*Herrschaft*] as its supreme principle. (Further, compare the notes toward the critique of theocracy.)[2]

3) a. My definition of politics: the fulfillment of unelevated humanness [*die Erfüllung der ungesteigerten Menschhaftigkeit*].[3]

b. It should not be said that the legislation of the profane is enacted through religion; rather, it should be said that the legislation of the profane is required by religion. Probably without exception, the Mosaic laws do not belong to such legislation. Rather, these belong (presumably) to the legislation concerning the domain of living-bodiliness [*Leiblichkeit*] in the broadest sense and have an entirely peculiar status; they determine the mode and zone of *immediate* divine influence [*Einwirkung*]. And immediately where this zone posits for itself its border, where it retreats, there abuts the domain of politics, of the profane, of the living-corporeality [*Leiblichkeit*] that is lawless in the religious sense.

c. The meaning of anarchy for the profane region is to be determined from the philosophical-historical place of freedom. (Difficult proof: the connection of living-corporeality to individuality appears to be the basic question here.)

4) In its current state, the social is a manifestation of ghostly and demonic powers, admittedly often in their greatest tension with God, striving out of themselves. The divine manifests itself in them only in revolutionary violence [*Gewalt*]. Only in community, never in "social organizations," does the divine manifest itself nonviolently or mightily [*gewaltlos oder gewaltig*]. (In this world, divine violence is higher than divine nonviolence; in the coming world, divine nonviolence is higher than divine violence.) Manifestation of this kind is not to be sought in the sphere of the social but rather in revelatory perception and ultimately and above all in language, first of all, in sacred language.

[6:100] 5) a. It is not a matter of the "realization" of divine violence.[4] This process is, on the one hand, itself the highest reality, and divine violence, on the other hand, has its reality in itself. (Bad terms!)

b. The question concerning manifestation is central.

c. "Religious" is nonsense. There is no essential difference between religion and confession, but the latter is a narrow concept and in most contexts not central.

16.

<Morality, Ethics>

[6: 684] Distinctions in degree   Morality [*Moral*]   Ethics [*Ethik*]

Distinctions in rank   Moral will [*sittl<icher> Wille*] // Moral personality [*sittl<iche> Persönlichkeit*]

Logical deduction

                                                               World-histor<ical> reflections

                   Good will [*guter Wille*]   Great will [*großer Wille*]
                                   are *entirely* different
                                   concepts <u>of the will</u>

Morals [*Sittlichkeit*]
⌒
Freedom / the supersensible

Ethics   Morality [*Moral*]   Systematics of ethical values

         Law [*Recht*]   not only (in general??)

                                 distinctions in degree but also in rank.

The *order* of values has nothing   ⌒ content of conflict
to do with systematics.
                                 Current and potential [*aktueller und potentieller*]

17.

The Right to Apply Force / Use Violence
Blätter für religiösen Sozialismus, I 4

Re I

[6:104] 1) It "is essentially the tendency of the legal order to react with coercion against the attempt to violate it and to maintain or restore the correct condition through coercion."¹

The justification of this correct proposition with reference to the intensive tendency of law toward its realization is skewed. It is a matter of law focusing on a subordinated reality. A matter of the violent [*gewalttätiges*] rhythm of impatience in which law exists and has its tempo, in contrast to the good² rhythm of expectation in which messianic occurrence takes its course.³

[6:105] 2) "Only the state has a right to apply force / use violence [*Gewaltanwendung*]" (and every application of force / use of violence, for its part, requires a particular law)

If the state is understood and posited as the supreme legal institution, the necessary validity of proposition 2) follows from proposition 1). And it is, indeed, irrelevant whether the state sets itself up as the supreme legal institution [*Machtvollkommenheit*] on the basis of its own or a foreign authority. In other words, 2) is also valid for earthly theocracy. A meaning of the state in relation to the legal order other than one of the two designated in the preceding proposition is unthinkable.

Re II

Critical Possibilities*†

A) Deny that the state and the individual have the right to apply force / use violence.

---

* Note. In the sense of these disjunctions, the individual does *not* stand in opposition to the living community; rather, to the state.

† For the state, the possibilities identified here are valid in relation to both other states and citizens.

B) Recognize unconditionally that the state and the individual have the right to apply force / use violence.

C) Recognize that the state has the right to apply force / use violence.

D) Recognize that only the individual has the right to apply force / use violence.

Re A): This view is designated by the author as ethical anarchism. His refutation of it is in no way to be considered correct. For 1) a "coercively" attained height of cultural standards, which should supposedly justify the application of force / use of violence, is a *contradictio in adjecto*. 2) It is a typically modern error, based on very mechanical habits of thought, to say that the order of any given cultural status can be built up from such minimal data as the securing of one's physical existence. Perhaps, in fact, indices of a cultural status can be recognized, and these indices can be posited as the goal of striving; but they are certainly not minimal data. 3) It is thoroughly false that the struggle for existence becomes in a constitutional state [*Rechtsstaat*] the struggle for law [*Kampf um Recht*].[4] On the contrary, experience shows in the clearest possible way the very opposite. And this is [6:106] necessarily so, because law asserts itself only apparently for the sake of justice, in truth for the sake of life. And indeed asserts its own life against its own guilt. In law, the genuinely normative *force* [*Kraft*] *always* belongs in the decisive case to the factical. 4) The deliberative thought that coercion, despite everything that the ethicist may have against it, "has influence on the inner attitude [*Haltung*]" rests on a crude *quaternio terminorum*,[5] insofar as an "inner attitude" is confused with a "moral attitude." For otherwise this argument is not demonstrative in an ethical deliberation. — By contrast, so-called ethical anarchism is faulty on the basis of entirely different considerations. See my essay "Life and Violence."[6]

Re B): This view, which the author puts forward in II under 2), is self-contradictory. For the state is not a person among others but rather the supreme legal institution, which, wherever it is recognized ethically as in the foregoing proposition, excludes an unconditioned recognition of the right to apply force / use violence for individuals. The author nevertheless seems to occupy this standpoint, since, without rejecting the state, he nevertheless potentially recognizes violence [*Gewalt*] of the individual against it.

Re C): This proposition can in principle be supported where the view prevails [*waltet*] that the moral order always assumes the form of a legal order that can then be conceived of only as mediated by the state. Law that is valid at any given moment demands the recognition of this proposition without accomplishing this recognition. (With regard to current conditions, its accomplishment is scarcely imaginable.)

Re D): This view, whose material impossibility seems so fully evident to the author in advance of any further reflection that he does not even clarify for himself its logical possibility as a particular standpoint but, instead, calls it an inconsistent, one-sided application of ethical anarchism—this view must be advocated where it is seen that, on the one hand (in contrast to A), there is no contradiction in principle between morals and violence [*Sittlichkeit und Gewalt*] and, on the other (in contrast to C), there is a contradiction in principle between morals [*Sittlichkeit*] and the state (viz. law). The expounding of this standpoint belongs to the tasks of my moral philosophy, in connection with which the term anarchism may certainly be used for a theory that denies moral right [*sittliche Recht*] not to violence as such, but rather only to every human institution, community, or individuality that awards itself a monopoly on violence or concedes for itself the right to violence in principle and universally from whatever perspective—instead of honoring it in the individual case as a gift of divine power, as plenipotentiary authority [*Machtvollkommenheit*].⁷

Two Remarks Concerning the Afterword of the Editor:

I) "Ethical anarchism" is, in fact, contradictory as a political program, that is, as a plan of conduct that is conceived with respect to the coming-into-being of a new cosmopolitan condition. Nevertheless, there is much to oppose in view of the other arguments against it. 1) If it is said that every "nonadult" has no other means to counter a violent attack, it can be said in response that the adult often has just as few means (and this, in general, has nothing to do with adulthood in the first place), and "ethical anarchism" does not want to propose anything like a means against violence. 2) Nothing at all is to be said against the "gesture" of nonviolence when it ends up in martyrdom, for example. In morality [*Moral*] and, indeed, with respect to all moral action, Mignon's dictum is valid without limits: "So let me seem until I become."⁸ No semblance [*Schein*] transfigures like this one. 3) As for the prognoses concerning the political success of this lack of resistance and the eternal dominion of violence on this earth, the greatest skepticism is not to be dismissed, especially regarding the last thesis, as long as physical action [*Aktion*] is understood under the term "force / violence."

Nevertheless (however spurious "ethical anarchism" is as politics), an action [*Handeln*] that is in accord with it (as already indicated in 2 above) may raise the morality [*Moralität*] of the individual or the community to the supreme level where they are suffering because violent resistance does not seem to be divinely commanded. When communities of Galician Jews let themselves be crushed in their synagogues without resistance, this has nothing to do with "ethical anarchism" as a political program; rather, here the mere "not-resisting-evil" enters into a hallowed light as moral action.[9]

II) It is necessary—and possible—to strike a universally binding decision about the right to apply force / use violence because the truth with respect to morality does not halt before the chimera of moral freedom. — However, if one ignores what is maintained above and engages in ad hominem arguments and discussions, a subjective decision for or against violent action [*gewalthaftes Handeln*] cannot actually be envisaged *in abstracto* because a truly *subjective* decision arguably seems to be imaginable only in view of determinate goals that one wishes to accomplish.

18.

Capitalism as Religion

[6:100] A religion is to be seen in capitalism; that is, capitalism essentially pacifies the same cares, agonies, unrest to which in earlier times so-called religions gave answers. The process of proving this religious structure of capitalism—not only, so Weber claims, as a religiously conditioned construction but also as an essentially religious phenomenon—would, today, still lead onto the stray path [*Abweg*] of a measureless universal polemic.[1] We cannot close [*zuziehen*] the net in which we stand.[2] Later, however, this will come into full view.

Three traits [*Züge*] are nevertheless already recognizable in the present with regard to this religious structure of capitalism. First of all, capitalism is a pure cult religion, perhaps the most extreme that has ever existed. In capitalism, everything has meaning only immediately in relation to the cult; it knows no special dogmatics, no theology. From this point of view, utilitarianism acquires its religious coloration. Connected with this concretion of the cult is a second trait of capitalism: the permanent duration of the cult. Capitalism is the celebration of a cult *sans trêve et sans merci*.[3] There is no "weekday," no day that would not be a festival day in the dreadful sense of an unfolding of sacral pomp, of the most extreme exertion of the worshipper. Third, the cult is inculpating. Capitalism is presumably the first case of a cult that does not de-expiate [*nicht entsühnenden*] but rather inculpates.[4] Thus does this religious system stand in the downward sweep of a tremendous movement. A tremendous consciousness of guilt that does not know how to de-expiate itself grasps for the cult, not for the purpose of thereby expiating [*sühnen*] this guilt but rather to make guilt universal, to hammer it into consciousness, and finally and above all to draw [6:101] God himself into this guilt for the purpose of finally securing his interest in de-expiation [*Entsühnen*]. De-expiation, therefore, is not to be expected in the cult itself, nor even in the reformation of this religion, which would have to be able to hold on to something secure in it, nor in its renunciation. This lies in the essence of the religious movement that is capitalism: holding out to the very end, until the final, complete inculpation of God, when the world condition of despair is attained, which is just about still *hoped* for. Therein lies what is historically unprecedented about capitalism: religion is no longer the reform of Being but, rather, its shattering. The expansion of despair into the religious world condition from which salvation is supposed to be expected. The transcendence of God has fallen. But he is not dead; he has been drawn *into* human fate. This passage of the planet "human" through the house of despair in the absolute loneliness of its path is the ethos defining Nietzsche.[5] This human being is the Übermensch, the first who, recognizing that capitalism is a religion, begins to fulfill it. Its fourth trait is that its God must be kept secret; he may be addressed only at the zenith of his inculpation. The cult is celebrated before an unmatured deity; every representation, every thought of this deity injures the secret concerning its maturity.

Freud's theory belongs also to the priestly dominion of this cult. It is conceived entirely capitalistically. The repressed, the sinful representation, is—by virtue of a profound analogy, yet to be thought through—capital, which pays interest on the hell of the unconscious.

The prototype of capitalist religious thought finds magnificent expression in Nietzsche's philosophy. The thought of the Übermensch locates the apocalyptic "leap" not in reversal, expiation [*Sühne*], purification, or penance, but rather in the apparently continuous, yet in the final analysis exploding, discontinuous elevation [*Steigerung*].[6] Therefore, elevation and development in the sense of *"non facit saltum"*[7] [are] incompatible. The Übermensch is the historical human, a being who has arrived without reversal and has perforated the heavens. Nietzsche judged in advance [*präjudiziert*] this exploding of the heavens by elevated humanness [*gesteigerte Menschhaftigkeit*], an exploding that, religiously (also for Nietzsche), is and remains inculpation. And similarly with Marx: nonreversing capitalism, [6:102] with simple and compound interest, which are functions of *guilt-debt* [*Schuld*] (see the demonic ambiguity of this concept), becomes socialism.

Capitalism is a religion [that develops] from a mere cult, without dogma.

Capitalism developed in the West parasitically on Christianity—as must be shown not only in Calvinism but also in the other kinds of orthodox Christianity—with the result that, in the end, Christianity's history is essentially that of its parasite: capitalism.

A comparison of the images of saints of various religions and the banknotes of various states. The spirit that speaks from the ornamentation of banknotes.

Capitalism and law. Pagan character of law. Sorel, *Réflexions sur la violence*, p. 262.[8]

Overcoming capitalism through wandering. Unger, *Politik und Metaphysik*, p. 44.[9]

Fuchs, *Struktur der kapitalistischen Gesellschaft*[10] or similar

Max Weber, *Gesammelte Aufsätze zur Religionssoziologie*, 2 vols., 1919–20.[11]

Ernst Troeltsch, *Die Soziallehren der christlichen Kirchen und Gruppen* (*Gesammelte Werke*, vol. 1, 1912)[12]

See, above all, the Schönberg bibliography under II[13]

Landauer, *Aufruf zum Sozialismus*, p. 144[14]

Cares [*Die Sorgen*]: a mental illness appropriate for the capitalistic epoch. Mental (not material) hopelessness [*Ausweglosigkeit*] in poverty, goliards-[*Vaganten*]-mendicant-monasticism. A condition so hopeless [*ausweglos*] is inculpating. "Cares" are the index of this guilt-consciousness, which knows that there is no way out. "Cares" originate in the fear [*Angst*] of community-related, not individual-material, hopelessness.[15]

During the time of the Reformation, Christianity did not promote the emergence of capitalism; rather, it transformed into capitalism.

Methodologically, it would first be a matter of investigating which connections of money entered into myth in the course of history, until money could draw from Christianity so many mythical elements as to constitute its own myth.

Wergeld[16] / Thesaurus of good works / Salary owed to the *priest*. Pluto as god of wealth.

Adam Müller, *Reden über die Beredsamkeit*, 1816, pp. 56ff.[17]

Connection of capitalism with the dogma of the dissolving [*auflösenden*] but also, for us, in this precise capacity, redeeming [*erlösenden*] and lethal nature of knowing [*Wissen*]: the balance sheet as a knowing that redeems and settles [*erledigend*].

This contributes to the recognition of capitalism as religion: recalling that the original paganism certainly did not conceive of religion in the very next instance as a "higher," "moral" interest [*Interesse*] but rather as the most immediate practical interest, and that, in other words, it was no more clear about its "ideal" or "transcendent" nature than contemporary capitalism is; on the contrary, it saw in the individual who was irreligious or of another faith an unmistakable member of its community, in exactly the same sense in which the contemporary bourgeoisie see its nonearning dependents.

19.

Notes on "Objective Mendacity" I

[6:60] Objective mendacity [*Verlogenheit*] is: not recognizing the situation of decision.[1]

That is the principle of practical (not theoretical-dogmatic) Catholic authority, of the court ruling or dispensation of justice in church discipline and confessional judgment. (In Islam, *kitman*.) Catholic, bad, postponement [*Verschiebung*] of Last Judgment (that is, of decision); Jewish, good, reprieve [*Aufschub*] from Last Judgment. (See Scholem's notes on justice.)[2]

Why "objective" mendacity? 1) It objectively dominates world-historically in this time. Anything that is not altogether great is *inauthentic* in our time. 2) It is not a subjective lie, for which an individual is clearly responsible. Rather, the latter is "bona fide."

Attempt at an outline:
I. The lie
    A. Conceptual investigations
        1. Correctness-incorrectness
        2. Truth-untruth ("an" untruth)
    B. Truth and Lie
        1. Truth and speech
        2. The lie ("the" untruth)
    C. Incorrectness {and Untruth}
        1. Untruths as forms of nonviolent [*gewaltloser*] convention
        2. Untruths as drawn weapons (children, women)
    D. Correctness as "betrayal"
II. Objective mendacity

A very pure type of objective mendacity of the era: The "false messenger" in Borchardt's *Verkündigung*.[3]

On the lie: Knut Hamsun, "A Real Rascal" (in *Slaves of Love*[4])
    Maxim Gorki, *Remembrances of Tolstoy* / Johan Bojer, *Macht der Lüge* (?)[5]
    Liliencron, *Leben und Lüge* / Nietzsche[6]
    [6:61] Anatole France, "In this Orient, land of lying," *Le génie Latin*, p. 2[7]
    Rudolph von Jhering, *Der Zweck im Recht*, vol. 2 (important!)[8]

"I don't socialize with people who display their sincerity [*Ehrlichkeit*] on their sleeves." — Fritz Heinle[9]

An investigation into the value, power, and necessity of flattery belongs here. Flattery, along with, or just under, money, [is] the greatest worldly power. — Also, praise of cleverness in this context.

Only human beings who are free from sincerity [*Ehrlichkeit*] can truly forgive—such that they therefore forget the harm done.[10]

The art of revocation. — "I take everything back and maintain the opposite." Fénelon's revocation after his condemnation by the Roman See in his controversy with Bossuet is exemplary.[11] — The denial of his ownmost conviction [*Überzeugung*] as an expression of his inner nobility and clarity. — What in the end is my own knowledge [*Wissen*] capable of? — And is even my uttermost and clearest knowledge worth the price of my life? These questions are decisive. The Jewish view rejects propaganda, and the staking of one's own life for some item of knowledge [*ein Wissen*] may never be dared; it allowed for a belief only under the gravest distress. Only repentance or toleration, never spirit or mind, may beat life into the ground.

Denial is adequate precisely for the deepest conviction. For only the determining [mode of] knowing [*Wissen*] is an object of conviction.[12] This [mode of] knowing, which determines the economy of moral life, distinguishes itself from other kinds of knowing, above all, in that it cannot enter into any complex of motives. If, therefore, I am a witness [*Zeuge*] of an unmoral action, the deeper my conviction [*Überzeugung*] of its immorality, the less I am able to become morally indignant, because the determinative element of that knowing, which is an object of my conviction, prevents such knowing from entering into my argumentation as an object. Be it through others or only through my own being, the determining [mode of] knowing cannot determine me, the knower, through my words, expressively [*ausdrücklich*], nor by way of motives; it can determine me only expressionlessly [*ausdruckslos*].[13] Now, in the innermost core of conviction, the more intense [*inniger*] it is, the deeper there prevails [*waltet*] the clarity concerning the romantic, dark dimension of its essence; for this reason, a deep conviction will least of all [6:62] posit the determining [mode of] knowing in the place of the commanding mode; least of all will it take the human for divine. This points to the fact that whoever is convinced grows dumb and does justice to his conviction only in the deepest silence, therefore when he verbally approves immorality, and accordingly condemns more deeply through the art of his approval than through dismissive words. Truth resides in the determining [mode of] knowing: it runs counter to the intention of cognition [*Erkenntnis*] and offers silence [*Schweigen*] in the face of expression. / Conviction is like hope, like conciliation [*Aussöhnen*], one of those thoroughly human, moral phenomena in whose life contemplative genius takes part. The philistine knows no convictions. He condemns denial. He cannot lie.

20.

Notes toward a Work on Lying II

[6:62] Comparison: facts [*Tatsachen*] (states of affair [*Sachverhalte*]) are comparable to serpents (something living) that one is not allowed to fondle [*tätscheln*]. One must avoid the path where serpents lie; they cannot be touched, unless one is prepared to look them in the eye, manned with the gaze of the sorcerer; in the same way, one is not allowed to touch states of affairs unless one does so with the ultimate and most rigorous intention toward truth. Otherwise, one has to circumvent them.

Lying is a dietetic necessity of life for every human being for whom the ultimate, rigorous intention toward truth is not continuously present, without any interruption. If states of affair are handled without this intention, there arises a pollution and congestion of life. It is no accident that the limitless "everything-must-be-said" is not seldom found among human beings who are also outwardly unclean (vegetarian types); in contrast to this, the outwardly well-groomed type of the diplomat.

Whereas, in any case, states of affairs may not be touched without the intention toward truth, it is possible, conversely, that this very intention to strike truth can resort to lies (not untruth). Thus, for instance, in the morally justified case of putting someone to the test: so that the truth is allowed to receive its due, someone falsely accuses himself in order to give someone else the necessary yet in no other way possible opportunity to forgive. Or: the case of sexual education is [6:63] typical for how the strike (smack) on the state of affairs can thwart the intention toward truth.

To distinguish: truth — untruth, from
correctness — falsehood. The word "lie" stands both for false information and untruth; only in the latter case does it cover something morally negative; by contrast, in the first case, it is something positive if it does not stand in coincidence [*Tateinheit*] with the latter.[1] And just as under certain circumstances false information can be compatible with truth, so correctness with untruth. (This is visible in the example of sexual education.) Likewise, untruth is thoroughly possible in combination with so-called bona fides, which for modern human beings is extraordinarily easy to procure (in

contrast to those living in the medieval period). Untruth in combination with correctness and (or) bona fides constitutes "objective mendacity" in contrast to (good and bad) lying.

The definition of untruth remains to be given.

Lying is not forbidden in the Ten Commandments.[2]

The innocence of lying described with respect to certain lies made by children.

Necessity of lying as a touchstone of the law of authoritarian powers [*Gewalten*]—state and parental power [*Gewalt*]. These forms of power [*Gewalten*] are genuine only if they show themselves to be superior to lying, which, for its part, is legitimate in its combative capacity as long as it has success. Not the demand for truth but, certainly, the demand for sincerity is in principle to be denied as a trustee of impotent and therefore unjustified authorities. The disorder of sincerity everywhere betrays the factually and morally untenable claim of the one who issues the demand.[3] — On the other hand, however, every revolutionary movement that does not methodically make lying obligatory for its supporters as a foundation of its struggle denounces itself as unfree and fascinated by the most dangerous suggestions of the ruling powers. These are the appearance of sincerity as well as of the so-called courage of conviction accorded the opponent. Both culminate only in delivering this opponent defenseless into their hands. Fearless readiness to declare one's belief is in its place only among the things of the credo. There is only a religious and not a political martyrdom. On the contrary, in the realm of politics, for those who are active, the protection of one's own life and those of one's [6:64] friends is an indispensable maxim. Every rebellion, in particular every anarchism that pays tribute to the moral idol established for the protection of society, is itself beholden to the ideologies of each of its forms of narrow-mindedness; it is simply an inverted yet equally juvenile patriotism.

The lie has a constitutive relation to speech [*Rede*] (so that a lie via silence is immoral). Truth does not have such a relation to speech but rather to silence.

21.

Schemata for the Psychophysical Problem

[6:78] I. Spirit and Living Body [*Geist und Leib*]

They are identical, different only as modes of viewing, not as objects. The term "shape" [*Gestalt*] designates the zone of their identity. The shape of the historical is in every stage of its existence spiritual-bodily; spiritual-embodiedness is, therefore, somehow the category of their "instant" [*Nu*], their momentary appearance as transient-nontransitory [*vergänglich-unvergänglicher*]. Living body and spirit in the sense that is identical with the living body are therefore the highest form-categories of world occurrence [*Formkategorien des Weltgeschehens*]—not, however, the category of its eternal content, which is how the George School views them.[1] Our living body is not, therefore, something drawn into the world process in itself; rather, it only stands in this process at any given moment; its modification from shape to shape is not the function of historical occurrence itself but rather a function of the abstracted connectedness [*abgezogene Bezogenheit*] with which a particular life attaches itself to such occurrence each time. Everything real may have a living body, but not as a substrate or a substance of its ownmost being, as is the case with the somatic body; rather, it may do so as an appearance in the exposure [*Belichtung*] of the historical "instant" [*Nu*]. Embodied spirit would perhaps most aptly be called "*ingenium*."[2]

This much can be said in general: everything real is shape [*Gestalt*] insofar as it is considered from the perspective of the historical process in such a way that it is meaningfully related to the entirety of this process in its "instant[,]" in the innermost core of its temporal presence. All shape of this kind can thus manifest itself in two identical modes, which perhaps stand in a polar relation to each other: as *ingenium* and as living body.

[6:79] II. Spirit and Somatic Body [*Geist und Körper*]

Whereas everything real can have living body and *ingenium* on the basis of the presence-relation of the real to the historical process (but not to God), somatic body, along with its accompanying spirit, is not grounded on a relation but rather on existence [*Dasein*] pure and simple. Somatic body is one among the realities that stand in the historical process itself. How it is distinguished from living body can be clarified at first through the example of the human being. Everything of which the human being in itself somehow has a shape-perception [*Gestaltwahrnehmung*], the entirety of someone's shape as well as its members and organs, insofar as they appear to this "someone" as shaped—all this belongs to the living body. All limitation that the human being sensuously perceives in itself likewise belongs as a shape to the living body. It follows from this that the sensuously perceived individual existence of the human being is a perception of a relation in which it finds itself—not, however, a perception of a substrate or its own substance, which is how the somatic body sensuously presents it. The latter manifests itself twofold in a peculiar polarity: as pleasure and pain. No shape whatsoever is perceived in either of these, nor indeed any limitation. When we know of our somatic body only or primarily through pleasure and pain, we know nothing of its limitation. It is now advisable to survey among the modifications of consciousness and look for those to which limitation is every bit as foreign as it is for states of pleasure and pain, which in their highest elevation [*Steigerung*] constitute ecstasy [*Rausch*]. Such states are, first of all, those of perception. Admittedly, with distinction according to degree. Least invested in limitation is perhaps visual perception, which, for instance, in contrast with the more centripetally directed perception of taste and especially tactile perception, can really be called centrifugal. Visual perception shows the somatic body, if not as unlimited, then nevertheless in a fluctuating, shapeless limitation.

This, therefore, can be said in general: insofar as we know about perception, we know about our somatic body, which, in contrast to our living body, extends without a determinate, shaped limitation. This somatic body is not, indeed, the final substrate of our being but is nevertheless a substance in contrast to the living body, which is only a function.[3] The somatic body is objective in a higher sense, and therefore the clarification of the spiritual "nature" of the living being that is bound to, or imprisoned by, the somatic body must be even more important than the illumination of the *ingenium*, identical as it is to the living body. Now, the difficult problem lies in the fact that "nature," whose belonging to the somatic body is asserted, nevertheless points in the strongest possible way to the restriction and particularity of the living being. The restricted reality that is constituted by the foundation of a spiritual nature in a somatic body is called the person. The person is, indeed, restricted but not shaped. It therefore has its uniqueness, which can be attributed to it, in a certain sense—not, however, from out of itself, so to speak, but rather from the area of its maximal extension. Thus, the same holds for its nature and its somatic body: they are not limited in a shaped manner but are still limited by a maximum of extension [*Ausdeutung* <sic>], the people.[4]

III. Living Body and Somatic Body

The human being belongs with living body and somatic body to universal interconnections. With each, however, to a different one: with living body, to humanity; with somatic body, to God. The boundaries of both over against nature fluctuate; the expansive proliferation of both determines world occurrence for the most profound reasons. The living body, the function of the historical present in the human being, grows into the living body of humanity. "Individuality," as the principle of the living body, stands higher than that of particular embodied [*leiblicher*] individualities. Humanity as an individuality is the completion [*Vollendung*] and at the same time the demise [*Untergang*] of embodied life—demise, because, with it, the historical life whose function is the living body reaches its end. Beyond the totality of the living, humanity is even partially able to draw nature into this life of the living body of humanity—and thus into this demise and this fulfillment—: the nonvivified [*Unbelebtes*], plants, and animals. And it can do all of this through the technology in which the unity of its life is formed [*bildet*]. Ultimately, everything that serves its happiness belongs to its life and its limbs.

Embodied [*leibliche*] nature proceeds toward its dissolution; somatic [*körperliche*] nature, by contrast, toward its resurrection. The decision about this lies too with the human being. The somatic body is, for the human being, the seal of its aloneness, and it will not break apart—even in death—because this aloneness is nothing other than the consciousness of its immediate dependence on God. What all human beings encompass within the range [6:81] of their perception, their pains and their supreme pleasure, is saved with them in resurrection. (This supreme pleasure has nothing to do with happiness, of course.) Pain is the governing principle of the somatic body[,] pleasure its valuing principle.

There are, therefore, two great processes in natural history: dissolution and resurrection.

IV. Spirit and Sexuality / Nature and Somatic Body

Spirit and sexuality are the basic polar forces of the "nature" of human beings. Nature is not something that belongs in particular to individual somatic bodies. Rather, nature in its relation to the singularity of the somatic body is comparable to the relation between currents flowing into the sea and individual drops of water. Countless such drops are seized by the same current. Nature is also certainly not the same in all human beings but is so in very many of them. And not only like, but indeed, in a proper sense, identical— one and the same. It is not constant; rather, its current changes with the centuries, and a greater or lesser number of currents are always to be found simultaneously. Sexuality and spirit are the two vital poles of this natural life, which disembogues into the somatic body and differentiates itself in it. Just like sexuality, spirit is, therefore, also in origin something natural and appears in the course of things as something somatic. The content of a life is dependent on the extent to which the living succeeds in somatically imprinting its nature. In the complete collapse of somatic corporeality, as the contemporary Occidental world experiences it, the torment of nature, which can no longer be contained in life and plunges in wild currents over the somatic body, remains as the final instrument of its renewal. Nature is itself totality, and the movement into the unfathomableness of total vitality is fate. The movement out of this unfathomableness is art. Because, however, total vitality has its reconciliatory effect only in art, every other form of expression must lead to annihilation. The presentation of total vitality in life has fate disemboguing in madness. For all lively reactivity is bound up with differentiation, whose most noble instrument is the somatic body. This is to be recognized as essential in its determination. Only the somatic body that is comprehended as an instrument that differentiates among vital reactions, and only this somatic body, is comprehensible according to its psychic [6:82] vivaciousness [*Belebtheit*]. All psychic activity [*Regsamkeit*] is to be differentially localized in it, which was undertaken by earlier anthroposophy in its analogy between the somatic body and the macrocosm. The somatic body has one of the most important determinations of differentiation in perception; the zone of perceptions, moreover, shows most clearly the variability to which the somatic body is subject as a function of nature. When nature changes, so do the perceptions of the somatic body.

The somatic body is a moral [*moralisches*] instrument. It is created for the fulfillment of commands. It was accordingly established at creation. Even its perceptions are characterized in terms of how far they withdraw it from, or lead it toward, its duty.

V. Pleasure and Pain

In the physical distinctions between pleasure and pain there lies the possibility of discerning their metaphysical difference. Among these physical distinctions two ultimately remain elementary and irreducible. From the perspective of pleasure, it is their lightning-like and uniform character that distinguishes it from pain; from the perspective of pain, its chronic and manifold character that distinguishes it from pleasure. Only pain, never pleasure, can become a chronic feeling accompanying constant, organic processes. It alone, never pleasure, is capable of extreme differentiation according to the nature of the organ from which it proceeds. An indication of this lies in language, which knows, in German, only the superlative of sweetness or bliss for the maximum of pleasure, and of these two, only the first is properly and unambiguously sensuous. The lowest of the senses, therefore, the sense of taste, lends the designation of its positive organ-sensation for the expression of every kind of sensuous enjoyment. Altogether different are designations of pain. In the words "pain," "woe," "agony," "suffering," something is pronounced in the clearest possible manner, which is indicated in the domain of pleasure's linguistic designation only by a word such as "bliss"—namely, that in pain, without any reliance on metaphor, the psychic [*das Seelische*] is immediately affected by the sensuous. It is possible that this is related to the fact that feelings of pain are incomparably more capable of genuine variability than feelings of pleasure, where variability is only a matter of degree. It is entirely certain, however, that there exists a connection between this more unbroken applicability of the feeling of pain to the [6:83] entire existence [*Wesen*] of the human being and the ability of pain to exist permanently [*Permanenz*]. And this permanence, in turn, leads immediately into the domain of those metaphysical differences between the two feelings that precisely correspond with, and explain, their physical differences. For in both the physical as well as metaphysical spheres, only the feeling of pain is capable of unbroken effectuation—of an, as it were, thematic treatment. The existence of the human being is the most perfect instrument of pain; only in human suffering does pain come to its purest adequate appearance; only in human life does it disembogue. Pain alone among all somatic feelings is, for human beings, like a navigable river, with waters that never dry up, leading them into the sea. Pleasure manifests as a dead end wherever human beings seek to follow it. It is, in truth, a portent of another world, not like pain, which is a connection between worlds. Organic pleasure is therefore intermittent, whereas pain can be permanent.

Connected with this relation between pain and pleasure is the fact that eidetic insight into human beings is indifferent to the occasion of their greatest pain, and yet, for such insight, the occasion of their greatest pleasure is very important. This is because every pain, even the most trivial, can lead all the way up to the uppermost religious pain; pleasure, however, is capable of no ennobling and has its entire nobility only by grace of its birth, in other words, that which occasioned it.

VI. Proximity and Distance

These are two relations that in the structure and life of the somatic body may be just as determinative as other spatial relations (up and down, left and right, and so forth). But they emerge, above all, in the life of Eros and sexuality. The life of Eros is ignited by distance. On the other hand, an affinity can be found between sexuality and proximity. — With respect to distance, Klages's investigations of dreaming are to be compared.[5] Even less well known than the effect of distance in somatic connections is the effect of proximity. Phenomena bound up with such connections were perhaps already rejected and suppressed thousands of years ago. — Further, there exists, for instance, a precise relation between stupidity and proximity: in the end, stupidity stems from a too close contemplation of ideas (the cow before the new gate). But [6:84] precisely this all too proximate (mindless) contemplation of ideas is an origin of enduring (not intermittent) beauty. Thus runs the relation between beauty and stupidity.

Literature

Ludwig Klages, "Vom Traumbewußtsein," *Zeitschrift für Pathopsychologie* III Bd. 4, Heft 1919 (see more there)

_____. "Geist und Seele," *Deutsche Psychologie* Bd. I, Heft 5 and Bd. II, Heft 6

_____. *Vom Wesen des Bewußtseins* (J. A. Barth)

_____. *Mensch und Erde* (Georg Müller)

_____. *Vom kosmogonischen Eros* (Georg Müller)[6]

VI. Proximity and Distance (Continuation)

The less a man is caught in the fetter of fate, the less he is determined by *that which is nearest*, whether it be circumstances or other human beings. On the contrary, a free human being, as a result of such freedom, has his proximity entirely to himself; he is the one who determines it. The proper determinateness of a life in accordance with its fate, by contrast, comes to the free human being from afar. He acts not with "retrospect" [*Rücksicht*] to what is coming, as though it might catch up with him; rather, he acts with "circumspection" [*Umsicht*] toward what lies in the distance, with which he complies. The interrogation of the stars—even understood allegorically—is, therefore, more deeply justified than brooding over whatever may ensue. For that in the distance which determines the human being should be nature itself, and nature does so all the more undividedly the purer the human being. It may thus frighten neurotics with its smallest portent, guide the demonic with the stars; yet it determines with its deepest harmonies—and with these alone—only the pious. Nature, however, affects all of them not in their action but in their life, which alone can be fateful. And here, not in the domain of action, does freedom have its place. Precisely its power releases the living from the determination by particular natural occurrences and allows the living to let its existence be led by the existence of nature. Led the living is indeed, but as one who is sleeping. And the perfect human being alone in such dreams from which he does not awake in life. For the more perfect the human being, the deeper the sleep—the sounder and the more limited to the primordial basis of his being. Hence, a sleep in which dreams are not occasioned by nearby noises and the voices of surrounding world [6:85], a sleep in which the surf and the spheres and the wind can be heard. This sea of sleep in the deep ground of all human nature has its flood time at night: every slumber says only that it splashes upon a shore from which, during waking hours, it withdraws. What stays behind: dreams that—however wonderfully formed [*geformt*]—are still only the dead from the womb of these depths. The living remains secure in the dead and on the dead: the ship of waking life and the fish as mute booty in the nets of artists.

The sea is thus the symbol of human nature. As sleep—in the deeper, figurative sense—it bears the ship of life along with its current, which is led by wind and stars from the distance; as slumber in the authentic sense, it arises at night like the tide on the shore of life, on which it leaves dreams behind.

Proximity {and distance?} are, incidentally, as determinative for dreaming as for eroticism. Nevertheless, though, in an attenuated, deteriorated way. The essence of this difference would still be something to locate. Extreme proximity in itself certainly takes place in dreams;—and—perhaps!—nevertheless also extreme distance?

As concerns the problem of the reality of dreams, this much is to be established: the determination of the relation between the dreamworld and the waking world, that is, the *real world*, is to be rigorously distinguished from an investigation into its relation to the *true world*. In truth, or in the "true world," there is no longer dreaming and waking as such; they may at most be symbols of their presentation. For in the world of truth the world of perception has lost its reality. Indeed, perhaps the world of truth is not a world of any sort of consciousness at all. What this means to say is: the problem of the relation of dream to waking is not "cognitive-theoretical" but rather "perception-theoretical." Perceptions, however, cannot be true or false; rather, they are problematic only in consideration of the jurisdiction of their meaning-content [*Zuständigkeit ihres Bedeutungsgehalts*]. The system of such possible jurisdictions in general is the nature of the human being. The problem here, therefore, is what in the nature of the human being concerns the meaning-content of dream perception and what the meaning-content of waking perception. For "cognition," both are important in precisely the same way, namely, simply as objects. [6:86] — Particularly in regard to perception, the customary way of posing a question concerning the superiority of one or another of these modes of perception according to the fulfillment of a greater abundance of criteria that prove their validity is senseless, because it must first be shown 1) that there is such a thing as *consciousness of truth* in general, and 2) that it is characterized by such proving-valid in regard to a relative majority of criteria. In reality, 1) comparison in truth-theoretical investigations is senseless, and 2) for consciousness in general, the relation to life alone is relevant [*zuständig*], not the relation to truth. As concerns life, neither of the two modes of consciousness is "truer" than the other; rather, for life, there exists only a difference of their meaning.

Complete balance between proximity and distance, in perfected love, "comes winged and spellbound."[7] — Dante places Beatrice among the stars.

Yet the stars could be close to him in Beatrice.[8] For in the beloved, the forces of distance appear near to the man. In this way, proximity and distance are the poles in the life of Eros; therefore, presence and separation are decisive in love. — The spell [*Bann*] is the magic of proximity.

Eros is what binds in nature, the forces of which are everywhere unbound wherever Eros does not hold sway [*waltet*]: "A great daimon, Socrates, {is Eros}, for everything demonic is in the middle, between god and mortal. — What force does it have? I asked. — To announce, and to convey to the gods what comes from the human being, to the human being what comes from the gods. From one, prayers and sacrifices, from the other, tasks and replies to sacrifices. The demonic fills the space between the two, so that the whole is bound up in itself. Through this demonic force, even prophecy and the art of the priest proceed into the sacrifices and consecrations and songs and all the divination and enchantment. God does not consort with human beings; rather, [proceeding] through this [demonic force] is the entire interaction and dialogue of gods with human beings in waking and in sleeping." *Symposium* 202d–203a.[9] The prototype and primordial phenomenon of binding, which is to be found in every particular bond, is, however, that of proximity and distance. It is, therefore, beyond all others, the original work of Eros.

Particular relation of proximity and distance to the sexes. For the man, the forces of distance should be the determining ones, whereas the forces of proximity are those from which he determines others. [6:87] Longing [*Sehnsucht*] is a [state of] being-determined. Which is the force from which the man determines his proximity? It has gone missing. Flight is the movement from longing. Which is the spellbinding [*bannende*] movement that determines proximity? Spell and flight are unified in the type of dream in which one flies low over the earth. (Nietzsche's life is typical of mere distance-determinateness, which is the disaster [*Verhängnis*] for the highest among finished human beings [*fertigen Menschen*].)[10] As a consequence of the failure of spellbinding force, they can do nothing to "keep their distance." And everything that penetrates into their proximity is unbound. Proximity, therefore, has become the region of unboundedness, as it becomes terribly apparent in the closest proximity of the married couple's sexuality, which Strindberg experienced.[11] But unscathed Eros has binding, spellbinding force [*Gewalt*] also in whatever lies nearest.

"Die Verlassenen" by Karl Kraus is a counterpart of Goethe's "Selige Sehnsucht."[12] In the latter, movement of wing and flight; in the former, spellbound standstill of feeling. Goethe's poem, a powerful uninterrupted movement; Kraus's poem, an enormously intermittent one, halting the middle strophe, which separates the first and final ones like an abyss of secrecy. The abyss is thus the primordial fact that is experienced in every intense erotic proximity.

22.

Literatur zu einer ausgeführteren Kritik der Gewalt und zur Rechtsphilosophie[1]

Fries: Philosophische Rechtslehre und Kritik aller positiven
    Gesetzgebung
Grotius: Drei Bücher über das Recht des Friedens
    und des Krieges
Beccaria: Über Verbrechen und Strafen
Dante: Über die Monarchie
Rosenstock: Der ewige Prozeß des Rechts gegen den Staat
    (E. Rosenstock)
Lessing, Th.: Studien zur Wertaxiomatik (Reine Ethik und
    reines Recht)
Machiavelli: Vom Staat
Platon: Die Gesetze
Zeitschrift für Rechtsphilosophie in Lehre und Praxis
Somló: Juristische Grundlehre

} Verlag Felix Meiner

Stammler, Rudolf: Theorie der Rechtswissenschaft
Adolf Menzel: Naturrecht und Soziologie Sonderabdruck aus der Festschrift für den 31<.> deutschen Juristentag Wien 1912
Année sociologique hg von E Durkheim (Nachschlagewerk)
Rapaport, M. Das religiöse Recht und dessen Charakterisierung als Rechtstheologie Beiheft 12 für die Vereinigung von Rechts- und Wirtschaftsphilosophie Berlin und Lpz Dr. W. Rothschild 1913
H. von Eiken: Geschichte und System der mittelalterlichen Weltanschauung
    (betr. die Theokratie) 2te Aufl. Stuttgart u Berlin 1913 Cotta
Kelsen: Staatslehre (?) – Allgemeine Staatslehre | Soziologischer und juristischer Staatsbegriff |
Wielikowski: Die Neukantianer in der Rechtsphilosophie München 1914 Beck
{Büttner, Georg: Im Banne des logischen Zwanges Lpz 1914 (E. Wunderlich) (Ethisch-erkenntnistheoretisch.)}

Görland: Ethik als Kritik der Weltgeschichte Lpz Teubner (Wissenschaft u Hypothese Bd 19)
: Die Idee des Schicksals in der Geschichte der Tragödie Tübingen Mohr
Natorp: Recht und Sittlichkeit Kantstudien XVIII (bei mir)
Savigny: Über den Beruf unseres Zeitalters zur Gesetzgebung
Reinach: Über die apriorischen Grundlagen des bürgerlichen Rechts (Jahrb. f. Philos. u. phänomenologischen Forschung 1913)
~~Gustav Radbruch~~ Gustav Radbruch: Grundzüge der Rechtsphilosophie Lpz 1914 Quelle u Meyer
Stammler: Recht und Macht Berlin 1918
E. Jung: Das Problem des natürlichen Rechts Ztschr. f. Rechtsphilosophie I 111 (1916)
Kurt Latte*: Heiliges Recht (Sakrales Recht in Griechenland) Tübingen 1920
Georg Fränkel: Die kritische Rechtsphilosophie bei Fries und Stammler 1912
Binder: Rechtsbegriff und Rechtsidee Lpz 1915
Stammler: Sämtliche Schriften
Radbruch und Tillich: Religionsphilosophie der Kultur (darin *Radbruch*: Religionsph. des Rechts) Berlin 1921²
Joseph Kohler: Das Recht der Azteken (evt von Lehmann zu erborgen)
Felix Kaufmann: Logik und Rechtswissenschaft Tübingen 1922 || Kritik der neukantischen Rechtsphilosophie
~~Wilamowitz-Möllendorf: Griechische Verskunst Berlin 1921 p31~~
Max Ernst Mayer: Rechtsphilosophie Berlin 1922 (Springer) {Enzyklopädie der Rechts- und Staatswissenschaft}
H. de Bonald: Die Urgesetzgebung Mainz 1825 (oder Französisch) = Législation primitive considérée dans les derniers temps par les seules lumières de la raison 1817
Lucas: Aus der Geschichte der Todesstrafe Der Greif 1914 August-Heft
Karl Schmitt-Dorotić: Die Diktatur München u Lpz 1921 (Dorotić)
: Politische Romantik München u Lpz 1919
: Politische Theologie 1923
Nelson: Die Rechtswissenschaft ohne Recht

22.

Literature for a More Fully Developed Critique of Violence and Philosophy of Law

Fries: Philosophical Doctrine of Right and Critique of All Positive Legislation
Grotius: Three Books on the Law of Peace and War[2]
Beccaria: On Crime and Punishment[3]
Dante: On Monarchy[4]
Rosenstock: The Eternal Process of Law against the State (E. Rosenstock)
Lessing, Th.: Studies on the Axiomatics of Value (Pure Ethics and Pure Law)
Machiavelli: On the State[5]
Plato: Laws[6]
Journal for the Philosophy of Law in Theory and Practice
Somló: Fundamental Doctrine of Law

Publisher: Felix Meiner

Stammler, Rudolf: Theory of Jurisprudence
Adolf Menzel: Natural Law and Sociology offprint from the commemorative publication of the 31st Meeting of German Jurists Vienna 1912
The Year in Sociology ed. by E Durkheim (Reference work)
Rapaport, M. Religious Law and Its Characterization as Theology of Law Supplement 12 of the Society for Legal and Economic Philosophy Berlin and Leipzig Dr. W. Rothschild 1913
H. von Eiken: History and System of the Medieval Worldview
    (ref. theocracy) 2nd edition Stuttgart and Berlin 1913 Cotta
Kelsen: Theory of State (?) — General Theory of State | Sociological and Juridical Concept of State |
Wielikowski: The Neo-Kantians in the Philosophy of Law Munich 1914 Beck
{Büttner, Georg: In the Thrall of Logical Compulsion Leipzig 1914 (E. Wunderlich) (ethical-epistemological.)}

Görland: Ethics as Critique of World History Leipzig Teubner (Science and Hypothesis Volume 19)
 : The Idea of Fate in the History of Tragedy Tübingen Mohr
Natorp: Law and Morals Kant Studies XVIII (at home)
Savigny: On the Vocation of Our Age for Legislation[7]
Reinach: On the Apriori Foundations of Civil Law (Yearbook for Philosophy and Phenomenological Research 1913)[8]
~~Gustav Radbruch~~ Gustav Radbruch: Fundamentals of the Philosophy of Law Leipzig 1914 Quelle and Meyer[9]
Stammler: Law and Power Berlin 1918
E. Jung: The Problem of Natural Law Journal for the Philosophy of Law I 111 (1916)
Kurt Latte*: Divine Law (Religious Law in Greece) Tübingen 1920
Georg Fränkel: The Critical Philosophy of Law of Fries and Stammler 1912
Binder: The Concept of Law and Idea of Law Leipzig 1915
Stammler: Complete Writings
Radbruch and Tillich: Religious Philosophy of Culture (including *Radbruch*: Religious Philosophy of Law) Berlin 1921[10]
Joseph Kohler: Law of the Aztecs (possibly to be borrowed from Lehmann)
Felix Kaufmann: Logic and Jurisprudence Tübingen 1922 || Critique of Neo-Kantian Philosophy of Law
~~Wilamowitz-Möllendorf: Greek Art of Poetry Berlin 1921 p.31~~
Max Ernst Mayer: Philosophy of Law Berlin 1922 (Springer) {Encyclopedia of Jurisprudence and Political Science}
H. de Bonald: Primitive Legislation Mainz 1825 (or French) = Primitive Legislation Considered in Recent Years Solely in the Light of Reason 1817
Lucas: From the History of the Death Penalty The Griffin 1914 August Issue
Karl Schmitt-Dorotić: Dictatorship Munich and Leipzig 1921 (Dorotić)[11]
 : Political Romanticism Munich and Leipzig 1919[12]
 : Political Theology 1923[13]
Nelson: Jurisprudence without Right

AFTERWORD

Toward Another Critique of Violence

by Julia Ng

Walter Benjamin left open a number of questions when he finished writing "Toward the Critique of Violence" in January 1921. Chief among them is the one with which the essay implicitly closes: What happens after the "ending" (*Ausgang*) of the "philosophy of the history" (59) of violence, the very "idea" of which Benjamin suggests will make possible a departure from the apparent dialectic of law-positing and law-preserving violence? In the concluding paragraph of the essay, he had summarized the findings of his investigation as a "document" of some "symptoms" of the following law of motion: as long as law-preserving violence persists, law-positing violence weakens. The "symptoms" he had diagnosed included several instances when the state uses its legal capacities to suppress law-positing "counterforces" such as the right to strike, the right to self-defense, and war, for the sake of preserving itself, tacitly understood in the context to be coextensive with the rule of law. The cycle of symptom and solution, however, self-perpetuates: in the instance when previously suppressed forms of law-positing violence intensify to a degree that they overcome the violence or authority that had hitherto posited law, the relation is upended and a "new law, with a new decay" (60) is founded. One proposal for a breakthrough out of the cycle suggests that "state violence," and the positive-legal apparatus identifiable with it, be "de-posed," meant in the sense of relieving the state of its law-positing capacities altogether. What, then, would remain—law-preservation with no end? The possibility of an unending preservation of law certainly resonates with the heading of a chapter he had proposed to compose for a project on "Politics," "Teleology without Final Purpose" (*Teleologie ohne Endzweck*) (GB 2:109; C 168–69), but would entail a wholesale reconsideration of "nature" and "natural law," inasmuch as these terms have generally been understood to denote participation in a realm of unchanging final ends, or moral order. A second possibility would see the separation of the *Staat* (state) from its *Gewalt* (authority, power). This, however, would imply the perhaps not unwelcome prospect of reconceiving of the state in its foundations, but also the infinitely more troubling idea of separating *Staat* from *Rechtsstaat*, that is to say, conceiving of the state without or at odds with the rule of law, its constitution. A third possibility lies in the idea of another species of violence altogether, one that preserves itself as a "standing reserve" (*Bestand*) beyond law, that is, without being spent in positing or capacitating law. This suggests an expansion of the repertoire of actions to include species of nondoing, withdrawal, and perhaps silence; but it is therefore also "not disclosed to human beings" (60).

In the end, Benjamin signals that he has to be satisfied with a neologism for the moment, derived from a quasi-negation: a "pending violence" (*waltende Gewalt*) that, in withholding expenditure, is nonmythic, has nothing to do with the illusion of having "free disposal" over things, and saves some constitutively nondeterminate signified encrypted behind "sign and seal" (60). But "Toward the Critique of Violence" also gives indications of a number of other outstanding concerns to which, it suggests, its author might one day return. To prepare the way "toward" the critique, the "question concerning a criterion for justness" (40) was suspended, so that Benjamin could pose the question of whether there are any violent means that are moral. The discussion in the essay was restricted to matters pertaining to "contemporary Europe" (42) for the sake of giving contour to preconstitutional relations (such as peace ceremonies), images of individual violence (the great criminal, Prometheus), the death penalty, and unwritten laws. The law "that pure means are never means for immediate solutions but always only for mediated ones," which governs the objective appearance of the subjective conditions for nonviolent means such as "heartfelt courtesy, affection, peaceableness, [and] trust," has a "tremendous scope" that is yet to be elaborated (50). And the "higher orders" (51) that threaten to overwhelm victor and vanquished alike and that would yield an enduring motive for a politics of pure means were yet to be sought. Together with the essay's closing proposal, these are signals that Benjamin gives of the questions he had to leave aside, but they also lay out the ground on which the prolegomena for any future critique of violence stands and which a more fully developed critique must endeavor to cover. Benjamin admits as much to Gershom Scholem in a letter from January 1921 in which he announces the completion of his essay: "[T]here remain questions concerning violence that it does not touch" (GB 2:131; C 174).

Six years later, in 1927, three events take place in respect to Benjamin's intellectual biography that give an indication of his progress with these remaining "questions concerning violence." One of these is an interview Benjamin conducted for the journal *Die literarische Welt*, which appeared on September 16 as part of a pair devoted to the theme of "Dictatorship" (4:1035).[1] Benjamin's subject was Georges Valois, a French journalist and fascist politician he describes as a "pupil of Sorel" (4:489). Sorel himself is lauded in the interview as "the great, truly significant theorist of syndicalism" (4:489), echoing Benjamin's earlier evaluations of the author of *Reflections on Violence* whose theory of the revolutionary general strike was so central to his conception of an extraparliamentary and thus nonviolent political means in "Toward the Critique of Violence." As the interview suggests, however, Benjamin's encounter with Valois compels him to reconsider Sorel's legacy in light of the fact that it had effectively provided "the best plant nursery for fascist leaders" (4:489).[2] Under Sorel's tutelage, Valois had started out as a student of socioeconomics but had in that very capacity joined the editorial staff of the *Action française*, the journalistic arm of the far-right monarchist movement known by the same name; he subsequently founded Le Faisceau, the first fascist party outside of Italy (see 4:489). In spite of any differences he discerns between Sorel's and Valois's precise definitions of the general strike, Benjamin wonders whether the "bloodless revolutions" of which Sorel spoke were a rhetorical "trick" (4:490) amenable to being appropriated for the fascist cause—a far cry from Benjamin's earlier contention in "Toward the Critique of Violence" that Sorel's "rigorous" conception of the general strike dissociated it from any "actually extortionary" actions (53) and would therefore "diminish the deployment of actual violence in revolutions" (53). The most telling moment of the interview comes when Benjamin stages the high stakes of precisely this train of thought: "As I lose myself quietly in these reflections," he writes, "my gaze falls upon a revolver that my discussant [*Unterredner*] has left lying in front of him on his desk. This prompts me to proceed without further digression to a summary of the conversation" (4:491). In "Toward the Critique of Violence," Benjamin had described "discussion" (*Unterredung*) as a "pure means" (50) of agreement that is free from violence inasmuch as it is reached without compulsion or threat by law. In 1927, Benjamin finds himself confronted with a "diplomat" (4:490) advocating for a reconception of government as the immediate representation of popular and bioproductive "forces" (4:492) in the name of overcoming parliamentarism and the movement with which it imagines itself transfixed in mortal combat, "Bolshevism" (4:491). Realizing that he had not reckoned with the prospect that a certain kind of "ruling" (*Regieren*) might become "second nature, if not [the] first" (4:490), Benjamin registers in the interview the new need to critique a kind of violence that disguises itself *as* pure means: the violence that attends the very positing of an immediate equivalence between being beyond law and being beyond violence.

A few months earlier—and this is the second event of 1927—Benjamin had in fact announced that he had moved beyond a certain earlier conception of the parameters of the critique of violence. The essay that would come to be published in the *Archiv für Sozialwissenschaft und Sozialpolitik* in 1921 belonged, at different points in Benjamin's thinking, to a shifting complex of politically oriented writings in various stages of conception. The project on a "futuristic politics" that Benjamin first mentioned in June 1919 in conversation with Scholem (*TB* 2:452) had, over the years, taken on a number of guises, sometimes envisioned as a book with several articulated chapters, sometimes as a series of essays, sometimes simply designated within quotation marks as "Politics."[3] His final mention of the project as such occurred in 1927, when in July he wrote in a letter to Scholem that during his recent trip to Corsica, a "convolute of irreplaceable manuscripts" containing "years' worth of preliminary studies [*Vorstudien*] pertaining to 'Politics'" (*GB* 3:281) had gone missing. What is curious about this moment is how little it seems to register for Benjamin as a real loss, for Benjamin never speaks of "Politics" again, let alone the misplacement of its "irreplaceable" *Vorstudien*. Instead, what we have is a laconic, almost matter-of-fact addendum: what he lost was not just the *Vorstudien* to "Politics" but "the original manuscript [*Urschrift*] of 'Einbahnstrasse' [One-way street], which nevertheless contains only very little that does not exist in duplicate and diverse allotria" (*GB* 3:281). Indeed, some months later, on November 18, Benjamin announces to Scholem that the proofs of *One-Way Street* were ready (*GB* 3:301); the book manuscript itself was finished by September 18 of the previous year (*GB* 3:197; *C* 306).

In short, all signs point to the probability that the "peculiar organization or construction," to which he eventually gave the name "One-Way Street" in July 1926 (GB 3:181), was created, initially, for a set of "aphorisms" he had begun around 1923 and which in January 1925 he still considered "a series of interesting aphorisms for the planned third treatise" of the "Politics" project (GB 3:9). Though in 1925 he had not yet decided on an appropriate print format for them (GB 3:9), he had already settled on the following formula: the pendant to the essay on the critique of violence is a book of aphorisms, jokes, and dreams (GB 2:510). Writing to Hofmannsthal in a letter on February 8, 1928, Benjamin elaborates: aphorisms do not document a "compromise" with the tendencies of the day but rather "an internal struggle" with them, the "object" of which is to "take actuality as the other side [*Revers*] of the eternal in history and to take an impression of this concealed side of the coin" (GB 3:331; C 325). For critique, the internal struggle and its object remain opaque. The aphorism, joke, and dream, by contrast, are able to retain marks of a perennial problem that intervenes from the other side of manifest history—and, specifically, of the eternal, concealed, other side of the history of violence. By 1927, Benjamin had written *One-Way Street* as a treatment of the manners in which forces, undercurrents, and anxieties irrupt into the phenomena that a critique of violence may behold. Besides "Toward the Critique of Violence," *One-Way Street* was the only part of the "Politics" project to make its way into print.

Yet alongside the production of these aphorisms and their eventual collation into *One-Way Street*, and even as he confronted the legacy of one of his major sources and the limitations of the 1921 essay, Benjamin continued to work on a critique of violence. The evidence for this documents 1927's third and final event in respect to his thinking on the critique of violence: there was one item that he did not misplace in Corsica, and it did not belong to the "convolute" of *Vorstudien* for "Politics" but was rather an outline of an independent endeavor. The evidence in question is a bibliography to which he gave the title "Literature for a More Fully Developed Critique of Violence and Philosophy of Law," and it is published for the first time in this volume as Note 22. This bibliography was among the papers Benjamin took with him when he fled Paris in June 1940; after his death, it came into Adorno's hands and became a part of the first set of materials to constitute Benjamin's posthumous archive. Its existence has been known to the editors of the *Gesammelten Schriften* since at least 1989, when volume 7 was published. There, however, the manuscript's name is mis-transcribed by the editors in the prefatory remarks to the "Verzeichnis der gelesenen Schriften" (Roster of books read): instead of *ausgeführteren* ("more fully developed"), they write *ausgeführten*, that is, "developed," which carries with it the determinate sense of having been "executed" (7:724). Apparently the editors thought Benjamin saw the critique of violence as a program to be implemented, at the end of which violence and the need for its critique will have been totally eradicated; their slip registers a sentiment shared by interpretations that take the essay to be a self-enclosed manifesto with no resonance with its textual conditions or the broader intellectual context of the problems that it treats. Mysteriously, the list itself was never published in the *Gesammelten Schriften*. Evidently the editors also assumed, as they assumed with regard to the many other working bibliographies Benjamin was in the habit of maintaining while outlining his various projects, that he mostly never read the works he named (7:724).

Yet he did read them (313), and the list on which they appear documents the scope of Benjamin's expansion of the groundwork that he had laid down in "Toward the Critique of Violence." Depending on which edition Benjamin used of some of the works he lists—those by Felix Somló, Hans Kelsen, or Carl Schmitt—the bibliography suggests that he might have continued working on a development of the critique of violence until 1927 or 1928, perhaps even producing the list after he had abandoned the academic career path. Moreover, in spite of never producing the "fuller development" of the critique of violence that the bibliography's title announces, and despite having no interest, so far as we know, in pursuing a *Habilitation* in legal philosophy, Benjamin's book list is precisely the kind of bibliography one might produce for a postdoctoral degree in that field. What this suggests is the following. When he was composing "Toward the Critique of Violence," he decided to align himself with one political trend: anarchism, because, as he writes in a letter to Bernhard Kampffmeyer, he wished to associate himself with the literature that "treats violence in a particular way, not only rejecting violence in respect to the state but also more or less defending the revolutionary kind" (*GB* 2:101). From October 1920 to as late as January 1921, Benjamin hastily gathered together some of the literature he had solicited or been recommended on the topic. He settled eventually on Sorel and Erich Unger as corroborators for his argument against the compulsion he saw in every respect of our relation to the state, which he tacitly understood to be synonymous with its constitution, the rule of law. By 1927, in contrast, Benjamin had had the time to immerse himself in the literature, for which he no longer had the need to ask for personal recommendations, because the books would have been widely accessible in any German law library. Moreover, having written the essay in 1921 with the help of a rapidly compiled anarchist book list, from which he included only two titles in the essay itself, Benjamin took a cue from the rest and decided to advance his argument by turning to the philosophy-of-law shelves: major and canonical works representing the most recent developments in positive law and natural law, constitutional law, comparative law, and legal ethnology.[4]

The aim of this Afterword is to pursue the question of why Benjamin turned to these juridical trends for the advancement of the critique of violence. It does so, in the first instance, by adopting the standpoint of the reader to whom the bibliography addresses itself, namely, a juridically trained scholar with access to a wide variety of historical and contemporaneous standpoints on questions of the state and law. In doing so, the Afterword is guided by the following assumption: after concluding "Toward the Critique of Violence," Benjamin does not stop thinking about the critique of violence but instead continues to pursue, via self-study, the answers to the remaining "questions concerning violence" (*GB* 2:131; *C* 174) the essay did not touch. The sum of these questions can be restated in the following form. If we do not assume that the state is necessarily equivalent to the rule of law, we must also discard the associated premise that natural law exclusively denotes the doctrine according to which we are in possession of natural forces that we agree to give up in order to enter the social contract. Since this associated premise also regards the social contract as a state of compulsion, we also need to revisit the concepts of nature and natural law if we are not to simply advocate, as Valois and the "new fascism" (4:491) did, for a new kind of compulsion under the guise of a political mystification of our innate capacities.

Section 1 of the Afterword shows how these considerations prompt Benjamin to revisit the antinomy of positive and natural law with which "Toward the Critique of Violence" began, pointing out ways in which he subsequently found his opening paragraphs to be insufficient. As the bibliography shows, Benjamin was particularly invested in filling in the lacunae in his 1921 essay with the help of a debate that, in the history of law and violence, defined some of the most trenchant concerns in constitutional legal theory: the debate between Hans Kelsen and Carl Schmitt on constitutional guardianship in the Weimar era, which famously culminated in a series of heated exchanges on the respective roles of judicial review and executive authority, published in the early 1930s. Section 2 demonstrates that Benjamin was already deeply familiar with both sides of the Kelsen-Schmitt debate through the publications in which it took place throughout the 1920s. Reconstructing this debate in the form Benjamin would have encountered it, section 2 also shows that Benjamin saw the critique of violence expanding into his own response to the debate, a response that took the shape of the analysis of seventeenth-century sovereignty he included in his *Habilitation* thesis, *Origin of the German Trauerspiel*. Section 3 demonstrates how Benjamin uses a fundamental insight from "Toward the Critique of Violence," which he cites in a later section of the *Trauerspiel* book, to identify a lacuna he perceives in the debate on constitutional theory itself: a lack of consideration of the myths of transition and origination that are involved in any thesis on the source of law. Section 4 speculates on how Benjamin intended to fill this lacuna by extending the critique of violence in one crucial direction: beyond the "modern European" confines of the 1921 essay and toward a decolonial philosophy of the history of violence. This section is based on new archival findings in the personal papers of Walter Lehmann, Benjamin's lecturer in Mesoamerican cultures, to whom Benjamin dedicated an offprint of "Toward the Critique of Violence"; the Afterword contends that Lehmann is also the intended addressee of an aphorism in *One-Way Street*, in which Benjamin expands the scope of the critique of violence beyond the Weimar-induced dream that Europe is the world. Finally, section 5 concludes with a reflection on the prospects Benjamin holds out for a philosophy of the history of violence in respect to German imperialism.

1. Revisiting the Antinomy of Natural and Positive Law

The bibliography to which Benjamin gave the title "Literature for a More Fully Developed Critique of Violence and Philosophy of Law" is a remarkable snapshot of the state of the field of legal philosophy in 1920s Germany. For one, it documents the extent to which German jurisprudence operated with a framework that, on the one hand, was still bookended by the new acquisition of an allodium (with German unification in 1871), and on the other hand, remained unperturbed by the transition from the imperial to a republican constitution in November 1918. That Benjamin takes this framework as his own starting point can be gleaned from a first glance at the selection of works Benjamin includes in his list. Among them are several classics of political philosophy published in German translation in a series then recently acquired by the Felix Meiner Verlag, advertisements for which Benjamin might have come across in the back matter of one of his other books.[5] The titles Benjamin includes address the foundational questions raised in his essay: the origin of law-giving (Plato), the death penalty (Beccaria), the foundation of modern natural law (Grotius), the legitimacy of the rule of law (Dante), and the constitutive role of dissent in the republic (Machiavelli). For such an ostensible "shopping" list, however, it is notably specific. It does not include names one might expect to be relevant for a critique more fully developed in terms of accounting for all the different ways in which violence might be sanctioned and placed in service of law's self-preservation: Hobbes, for instance, for whom natural law is the practical imperative to submit to political authority as an escape from the state of generalized private violence, or Rousseau, for whom one must accede to general will as a protection against private violence, or Hegel or Marx for that matter. Evidently, he felt that the scaffolding of violence as he envisioned it in 1921 had not yet been dismantled; furthermore, Benjamin revisited that scaffolding in its reconstitution as an inheritance of the German Empire, which he now set out to consider through classics that had felicitously been republished in German translation in tandem with the founding of the new nation-state, by a publisher who was also a jurist-philosopher personally involved in the inaugural years of the Reichstag.[6]

In 1920, Benjamin once briefly considered but then promptly turned away from conceiving of his project on violence as an *Abbau der Gewalt* ("de-cultivation of violence"; *GB* 2:101), an ambiguously worded, quasi-anarchist phrase with an anti-Semitic affiliation.[7] The bibliography demonstrates his awareness of a deeper, more insidious, and associated problem: the body of knowledge that undergirds the legal discourse of his time evinces a remarkable continuity with the legal philosophy of the nineteenth century. In "Toward the Critique of Violence," a version of this continuity was registered in the use of practically every piece of contemporaneous legal code Benjamin retrieved from police law, strike law, criminal law, and so forth: much of what constituted "modern" law in 1921 had been codified in the legal code of the Prussian federation.[8] The composition of the bibliography makes evident Benjamin's awareness of a correlating continuity on the level of legal philosophical terminology: the publication dates of the volumes he includes range into the 1920s, but they begin, with few exceptions, with the later years of the German Empire. What this realization must have suggested to Benjamin, for one, is that the legal code he knew existed in a space and time that was independent of anything like what he had described as a dialectic of law-preserving and law-positing violence. While new law can certainly be posited or superseded in relation to extrajuridical forces, legal code projects its own space and time in which it relates, primarily, to other legal code.[9] Relatedly, Benjamin must have sensed that the essay's working definitions of legal-philosophical categories, too, are imbricated in their own intrajuridical histories not unrelated to the history of the establishment of the field and the rise and fall of its various schools of thought. As the bibliography attests, Benjamin set out to inform himself of these scholarly debates.

Foremost among them is one that suggests that Benjamin detected a certain insufficiency in his conception of natural law. In "Toward the Critique of Violence," Benjamin had described natural law as a "major trend in legal philosophy" (39) based in a conception of the individual use of force, or "violent means," as a "natural product" (40), but only within the framework of its wholesale expenditure prior to the individual's entry into the social contract. While expedient for the purpose of suspending from consideration the question of ends, "for now" (40), in order to be able to pose the question of whether any violent means are ever legitimate, this essentially ahistorical conception overlooks a complexity that resides in the very way in which natural law had been taken up as a "trend" in the philosophy of law.[10] One of the titles listed by Benjamin in his bibliography, a book by Adolf Menzel titled *Naturrecht und Soziologie* (Natural law and sociology), discusses this complexity. In Menzel's account, modern natural law as a disciplinary designation is a secular variant of the medieval doctrine of state that formed a part of Christian theology, which jurisprudence adapted for the purpose of explaining and evaluating social phenomena; a trace of this theological origin is detectable in the way modern natural law purports to both describe phenomena and abstract from them general laws with which conclusions may be drawn about future development.[11] In the process, natural-law theory forgets that the social contract, the main instrument with which it explains the relinquishment of individualism in respect to the collective, is merely formal and not a prophetic index of the reality of progress. A case in point is the arc through which he sees Fichte's theory of state developing, over the course of his several writings on the topic, beyond anarchism and back to it again, which demonstrates, for Menzel, that the social contract as an explanatory means is of a purely formal character as opposed to sociological fact. Or, to paraphrase a review of Menzel's book by Hans Kelsen from 1915: the opposition between individual and collective exists only from the perspective of the state, and so is a posteriori to legal normativity.[12] As Max Ernst Mayer, another of Benjamin's bibliographic references, writes in his 1922 *Rechtsphilosophie* (Legal philosophy): since the beginning of the nineteenth century natural law had been invoked in its guise of eternal, inalienable right as a source of legitimation in liberatory political projects ranging from the abolition of slavery and the development of the constitutional movement to the formulation of a "humane" international law.[13] In light of Menzel and Mayer, Benjamin's sense of "natural law" in "Toward the Critique of Violence" (40) must appear restricted, based as it is on a connection between "natural ends" and their use as an "ideological foundation" for the "terrorism during the French Revolution" without making manifest that it is from the perspective of the state that this "provision" of natural law holds.

By the same token, the natural-law "trend" was also amenable to other purposes. After 1918, cruder variants of the same call flooded the literature in the form of brochures and newsletters—as Mayer notes, "Revolution and natural law have . . . always been good friends"—but they were invocations of natural law in an altogether different vein.[14] Mayer describes one exemplary work in this vein as a "shriek for natural law": Alfred Friters's *Revolutionsgewalt und Notstandsrecht* (Revolutionary violence and emergency law; 1919), which asks whether "carriers of revolutionary power / violence [*Gewalt*] exercise law-giving power [*gesetzgebende Gewalt*]." "Law-giving power" is a technical term that Friters treats as synonymous with "law-positing power" (*rechtsetzende Gewalt*), an expression that he borrows from the constitutional theory of the separation of powers.[15] The example he gives of "law-positing power" is the command, which, he argues, is the form that law takes in war and times of revolution and as such cannot amount to a legal norm. Given this fact, according to Friters, the natural-law conception of the source of law must be sufficient for the creation of a legal order. In support of his argument, Friters refers to Leonard Nelson's *Rechtswissenschaft ohne Recht* (Jurisprudence without right; 1917), a work that appears on Benjamin's bibliography.[16] Similar sentiment abounded after the German Revolution in 1919, which saw an array of antiliberal theorists call upon natural law to serve as a bulwark against the revolutionary forces that seemed to threaten the order of things. In the decade after 1919, the turn to natural law increasingly became coupled with nationalist, antiparliamentary, antidemocratic sentiment, with essays on natural law and fascism appearing in a leading journal of public law.[17] Indeed, there had been similar anxieties about the nature of natural law as a trend already prior to the war. Adolf Menzel, for instance, points out in *Natural Law and Sociology* that the social contract had also been used by conservative politicians to legitimate the privilege enjoyed by the nobility and property owners. As an example he cites Justus Möser, author of the multivolume work *Patriotische Phantasien* (Patriotic fantasies; 1775–86), who proposed that society be seen in terms of a social contract that is not one but double: one exists between the "original landowners," by which he meant those who had acquired their possessions through conquest or colonization; and a second exists between owners and latter-day immigrants whose economic activity on the land is strictly regulated for the sake of protecting the owners' privileges.[18] All of the above are aspects of the "trend" of natural law that Benjamin "suspends," "for now" (40), in his summary account of the question of natural law at the outset of "Toward the Critique of Violence," where he associates natural law solely with the idea of rational self-rule, albeit later perverted by social Darwinism.

The bibliography documents Benjamin's recognition of a further nuance with respect to the "trend" of natural law: that these various turns toward natural law all occurred within the context of a backlash against legal positivism, which had, in the years before the war, established itself as a synonym for "legal philosophy" (*Rechtsphilosophie*). In this regard, Benjamin's bibliography also expands on his abbreviated proposal, in "Toward the Critique of Violence," that natural law is "diametrically opposed" (40) to positive law. Benjamin's intent to supplement his formula takes the form, first and foremost, of his inclusion of Rudolf Stammler three separate times in his list.[19] Widely regarded as responsible for the "renaissance of legal philosophy" in the twentieth century, Stammler was chiefly known for his concept of "correct right" (*richtiges Recht*), which he develops among other places in his *Theorie der Rechtswissenschaft* (Theory of jurisprudence; 1911), one of the titles in Benjamin's bibliography.[20] Like natural law, Stammler argues, correct right or law purports to "judge" (*richten*) law, that is, to separate it into good and bad varieties; in contrast to natural law, however, correct right is not found above or beyond existing law but within it.[21] The criterion for determining "correct" from incorrect is, therefore, found in the idea of law: whatever law corresponds with this ideal is correct. This ideal has to be universally valid, however, if relativism is not to ensue. The idea of law is therefore also purely formal, not determined by its content as in the case of natural law. Stammler's *Recht und Macht* (Law and power; 1918), another of the titles listed by Benjamin, then submits the concept of correct law to the question, as the book's title suggests, of "law and power."²² This, Stammler elaborates, is "the question of the justification of one by the other," and in the course of applying the question to correct law Stammler reaffirms that law may need power for its implementation and protection.²³ Nevertheless, he argues, the "objective correctness" of a law is judged by the idea of law, manifest for instance in the idea of a "pure community," which supplies the meanings of an inalienable and autocratic will, the overcoming of special interests, and nonpartisanship, all of which would lead to the unconditional surrender of the right to self-defense.²⁴ Stammler does not deny that there are certain conditions that need to be met in order to arrive at the actual cessation of war—specifically, he writes, the German Empire would need an "allodium" as a basis for its law and justice—and he suggests that what looked like feud in the legal sense yesterday (that is, an instance of the right to self-defense) looks like nonpartisan state power today (*Staatsgewalt*): in other words, war, too, is an institution of law.²⁵ But like Felix Somló (*Juristische Grundlehre* [Fundamental doctrine of law]) and Julius Binder (*Rechtsbegriff und Rechtsidee* [The concept of law and idea of law]), Stammler insisted on circumscribing legal philosophy within the theory of the concept and idea of law, free from predetermined content or considerations of ethical striving, with its scope limited to systematically investigating the value of law in order to facilitate the evaluation of positive laws.

In "Toward the Critique of Violence" Benjamin had, perhaps unintentionally, nodded to Stammler's program of seeking within law itself the criterion for judging the correctness of law (*Richtigkeit des Rechts*), which is to say the justness of law (*Gerechtigkeit des Rechts*), when he wrote that "[n]atural law strives, through the justness [*Gerechtigkeit*] of ends, to 'justify' the means, and positive law strives to 'guarantee' the justness of the ends through the justification [*Berechtigung*] of the means" (40). Latent in Benjamin's formulation, though, is also a criticism that was sometimes levied against Stammler and legal philosophy at large. This criticism circled around the following observation: the idea that positive law should seek to guarantee justness through justification confuses the juridical sense of *Recht* ("law") with the ethical sense of the word ("right"), leading to charges of empty tautology.²⁶ A sign that Benjamin later sought out a juridical basis for articulating his own sense of this objection can be gleaned from the fact that the most prominent legal theorist to expand on this criticism, Gustav Radbruch, was someone Benjamin hoped would promote his "Politics" project and appears in his bibliography.[27] Radbruch's *Grundzüge der Rechtsphilosophie* (Fundamentals of the philosophy of law; 1914) met Stammler's purported abstraction with the counterproposal of "relativism," that is, the introduction of a value-related concept of culture as law that is oriented toward but also only ever approximating the idea of law. In "Über Religionsphilosophie des Rechts" (Religious philosophy of law; 1919), Radbruch addresses the relation between value and nonvalue, which, he argues, is another way to pose the question of how law relates to justice. As a means for overcoming their opposition while also keeping them separate, he proposes the philosophy of religion. For Radbruch, legal norms take the character of an imperative, and ethical norms say what one ought to do under compulsion. In contrast to both, religious norms presuppose a person's guilt, only to redeem and liberate him or her from law, as an act of "übermoralisch" (supermoral) grace.[28] In Radbruch's account, religion was therefore a means of affirming whatever exists, regardless of its value or lack thereof; it presented a third way beyond the opposition of natural and positive law and therefore away from the charge of empty tautology, because it opened the possibility of a source of law different from legal or ethical normativity altogether.

Several other titles on Benjamin's bibliography move in the direction of "religion" as one of many other possible, culturally saturated ways in which human beings negotiate, without collapsing, the gap between legal norms and moral norms, proceeding, if not axiomatically as Radbruch does, then historically in a broad sense of the word: Mordché Rapaport's *Das religiöse Recht und dessen Charakterisierung als Rechtstheologie* (Religious law and its characterization as theology of law), Hermann Lucas's "Aus der Geschichte der Todesstrafe" (From the history of the death penalty), and Kurt Latte's *Heiliges Recht* (Sacred law).[29] Benjamin also includes Erich Jung's *Das Problem des natürlichen Rechts* (The problem of natural law), a work that, in spite of its name, belonged to the Free Law Movement associated with Rudolf von Jhering and Hermann Kantorowicz. In his book, Jung sought to base legal judgments in sources that were other than logical and derived from preceding legal concepts; such alternative sources included the idea of the judge's own freedom and historical community.[30] As varied as these works are when taken individually, their collation in Benjamin's bibliography suggests one thing above all. In the opening paragraphs of "Toward the Critique of Violence," Benjamin had identified an "antinomy" of natural and positive law. He constructed the antinomy from what he saw as their "shared dogmatic premise," namely, that "just ends can be attained by justified means, and justified means can be used for just ends" (40), as well as an assumption that natural law was synonymous with rational self-rule. Constructing this antinomy allowed him to proceed on to two things: the articulation of a need for "insight" (40) into the dependence of the antinomy's solution on a circular premise, and the announcement that the circle would be "abandoned" by "suspending," "for now" (40), consideration of one part of the premise, a criterion for determining the justness of ends. The result was an investigation of whether violent means can ever be justified, with the exclusion of natural-law principles that he regarded as unsuited to the task because they do not appear to differentiate between means. It also resulted in his speculation on the possibility of a wholly "different kind of violence" than can be "envisaged by all legal theory" and that therefore relates to law and legal ends not as means at all but "somehow differently" (54).

By 1927, the bibliography suggests, Benjamin has left behind the antinomy for an altogether different manner of envisaging the relation between the reality and the value of law. Instead of regarding the criterion of the justness of ends as extrajuridical because it can be discovered only within an antinomy, Benjamin begins to abandon the antinomic structure altogether. A critical mass of titles in the bibliography suggests that he entertained the possibility of another relation to law that, while being neither "justified" law nor the (moral) idea of law, was also not merely outside law. Whether such a relation to the evaluation of law is cultural, religious, historical, or personal, it is also situated within law. It is a possible source of law that, being neither logically nor morally derived, however, reserves the possibility of affirming all existing law regardless of its value—or, as the case may be, suspending law altogether.

2. Benjamin and the Kelsen-Schmitt Debate

As a snapshot of the debates surrounding legal positivism from which the resurgence of interest in natural law emerged as a backlash, the bibliography suggests a new way in which Benjamin regarded contemporary natural-law doctrine around 1927. In 1921, Benjamin had conceived of natural law along rationalistic lines, that is, as a synthesis of what is and what ought to be; this implied, first, that norms can be recognized from observing reality and that law and nature are therefore essentially the same; and second, that ideals of justice and morality are universally accessible to any rational and educated citizen prior to membership in a community. By 1927, natural law designated for Benjamin a realm that its proponents conceived as simultaneously eternal and radically subjectivistic. In this respect, Benjamin's bibliography demonstrates a remarkable awareness of the debates that were taking place contemporaneously around the problem in the construction of the source of law. These debates would culminate in a series of papers published in 1932 by Hans Kelsen and Carl Schmitt, two of the period's most influential constitutional theorists, in the aftermath of the so-called *Preußenschlag* (strike against Prussia), the enactment of emergency decrees by Franz von Papen, chancellor of the Weimar Republic, on July 20, 1932. Authorized by Article 48 of the Weimar Constitution, the emergency decrees gave von Papen the authority to depose the government of Prussia with the aim of bringing an end to the street violence resulting from clashes between the communists and the Nazis, but essentially delivered Prussia's executive power into the hands of the federal government. Kelsen's and Schmitt's opposing responses to this event circled around the question of whether the judiciary should have the power to challenge the legality of the decrees (Kelsen's position) or whether the authority to restore the situation of normality belonged to the executive (Schmitt's view).[31] Their assessments of the judgment, however, were just the latest episode in a long development that unfolded over the course of the preceding decades. The publications in which Kelsen and Schmitt lay out their respective positions in the 1920s and earlier also found their way into Benjamin's bibliography. Allowing us to reconstruct how Benjamin encountered the debate between Kelsen and Schmitt, the bibliography also establishes a basis on which Benjamin can be seen to fashion his own response from an extension of an argument he made in "Toward the Critique of Violence."

The charge that natural law was eternal and radically subjectivistic was, notably, the thrust of Hans Kelsen's criticism of Erich Kaufmann's position paper on the idea of equality before the law, a principle that was codified in Article 109 of the new Weimar constitution. Article 109 was one of the topics for debate at the conference of the Vereinigung der Deutschen Staatsrechtler (Association of German Constitutional Lawyers) on March 29 and 30, 1926, which marked the height of the *Methodenstreit* (quarrel over methods) within jurisprudence between the classical legal positivism represented by Kelsen and the Vienna school, on the one hand, and various antagonists including Kaufmann and Carl Schmitt, on the other.[32] In his statement to the association, Kaufmann had sought to revive a version of natural law in the Aristotelian-Christian sense. He argued that neither rationalistic natural law nor abstract positive norms suffice to account for personal creativity in legal judgment (such as the exercise of conscience) and the belief in a "higher perspective" corresponding to the "telos" of life and material circumstances that are necessarily involved in ensuring that, for instance, equality before the law is upheld even where the written law draws unjust distinctions or else fails to name those who might be treated differently.[33] In response, Kelsen calls Kaufmann's embrace of natural law "juridical metaphysics"—specifically, a "shriek for metaphysics" that, in his view, failed to recognize that an objective natural law, which alone would cut through the chaos of the many different and opposing natural laws that ensue from the attempt to base legal judgments on personality and conscience, is achievable only as a species of revealed religion, that is, another kind of legal positivism.[34]

Kelsen's position in 1926 is a restatement of a point he had made some years earlier in respect to another nascent constitution—the 1920 Austrian Constitution, which he had helped draft. He had elaborated this point in an article entitled "Vom Wesen und Wert der Demokratie" (On the essence and value of democracy; 1921), which was published in the same issue of the *Archiv für Sozialwissenschaft und Sozialpolitik* in which "Toward the Critique of Violence" appeared. Like many of his contemporaries who immediately recognized its significance, Benjamin likely read this article, as suggested by the number of Kelsen's other writings Benjamin subsequently included in his bibliography.[35] In the article, Kelsen argued that turning to divine inspiration as a source of the equality of all under the law is merely an assertion of authority against democracy.[36] As Kelsen writes, the idea of the social contract relies on the agreement of signatories who are free at any moment to leave the community and withdraw their recognition of its validity; the legality of the objective legal order requires a gap between "the content of the order and the content of the will subordinate to it."[37] Equality before the law must therefore be a fiction of representation, an image that cannot in itself lead to the idea of freedom, which can only be approximated by the idea of an absolute majority, since we experience the legal order only as something into which we are born and which we might at the most alter or perpetuate.[38] The majority principle in parliamentary democracy derives from this hypothetical unanimity; actual unanimity, or equality before the law, by contrast, is merely "mechanical" and leads directly to autocracy. A case in point is the notion that the freedom of minorities is protected by direct democracy, which leads, as Lenin illustrates for Kelsen, to a "dictatorship . . . of individual persons" produced from the simplification of social functions and the dissolution of the bureaucratic, namely, representational apparatus, and who, lacking superiors, now embody the authoritarian task of reorganizing all of economic and social life.[39] Kelsen takes his description of the dictatorship of the proletariat as a dictatorship of individual persons from Karl Kautsky's pamphlet *Terrorismus und Kommunismus* (Terrorism and communism; 1919), in which Kautsky singles out Trotsky for transforming the revolutionary proletariat into a new class of administrators, resulting in the return of an absolutist bureaucracy and new forms of corruption and profiteering.[40] For Kelsen, therefore, the freedoms of minorities are necessarily protected by proportional representation, which guarantees that the minority, too, could become the majority; neither majority nor minority is absolutely wrong or without rights, and an insistence to the contrary amounts to asserting that law should be based simply on the might of the many.[41] The turn to natural-law metaphysics thus acquires for Kelsen a political meaning: the tendency to diminish the authority of positive law, and to discover behind it neither absolute truth nor absolute justice, but only "the Gorgon's head of power."[42]

It is uncertain when exactly Benjamin would have started reading Kelsen intensively; he likely did so upon reading "On the Essence and Value of Democracy" when it appeared alongside "Toward the Critique of Violence," though its radically different evaluation of parliamentary democracy as well as Kelsen's use of the term *Gewalt* exclusively in its legal-institutional sense would have marked out unfamiliar terrain.[43] Nevertheless, the bibliography attests to Benjamin's eventual immersion in the major works published in the earlier decades by Kelsen as well as by the other major figure in the *Methodenstreit*, Carl Schmitt. Their debate, insofar as it unfolds in the works listed in Benjamin's bibliography, would have looked as follows. Kelsen, arguably since his doctoral thesis on Dante's *On Monarchy* in 1905, had been concerned with discovering the historical and doctrinal roots of the rule of law or constitutional state (*Rechtsstaat*); in the thesis he argues that the modern state is the continuation of the medieval constitutional order in virtue of its bureaucracy and its impersonality.[44] Schmitt, in contrast, finds in Dante's Christian Middle Ages a foil for the German Romantics' subjectification and negation of all normative consistency.[45] In his next writings, beginning with the *Hauptprobleme der Staatsrechtslehre* (Main problems in constitutional legal theory), Kelsen took pains to express his confidence in the juridification of the state's functions and his understanding that the state derived its authority from state-building rather than sheer power; he does this by constructing a science of law based on a concept of the norm as the basic and common denominator of all the fields of law and strictly differentiating law's formal existence from its content (that is, distinguishing between "is" and "ought").[46] Schmitt, again in contrast, sees "all law [as] 'situational law'" and "every general norm [as] demand[ing] a normal, everyday frame of life to which it can be factually applied and which is subjected to its regulations," which a jurist cannot simply "ignore" as "external presupposition" since it "belongs precisely to its immanent validity."[47] In his *Allgemeine Staatslehre* (General theory of state) from 1925, Kelsen outlines a first version of the normative-positivistic constitutional theory that would in 1934 become the title of his most recognizable work, *Reine Rechtslehre* (Pure theory of law), which sought to "purify" jurisprudence and accounts of the generation and validity of a legal order of any moral, political, and ideological influences.[48] Schmitt discovers, already in his 1921 study of *Die Diktatur* (Dictatorship), that "even the seventeenth-century authors of natural law understood the question of sovereignty to mean the question of the decision on the decision," and that across a variety of different legal orders, "dictatorship means a form of government that is genuinely designed to resolve a very particular problem ... [:] the successful defense of a case to which the opponent's will is diametrically opposed."[49] For Schmitt, equality before the law leads to a distinction between friend and enemy, pitting an "us" against another group in collectively defined difference; this distinction is the basis of what makes politics possible for Schmitt and is the catchphrase for "democracy" that is formulated in his *Concept of the Political*, to which Benjamin later refers in manuscript notes to his essay on Karl Kraus.[50]

Benjamin's immersion in this quarrel over the source of law probably continued till 1928, if not longer: Benjamin might have used a 1928 edition of Kelsen's *Der soziologische und der juristische Staatsbegriff* (The sociological and the juridical concept of state), and in one of a set of loose leaf pages he kept under the heading *Zum "Kunstwerk im Zeitalter"* (On the "artwork in the age") he cites an excerpt from Schmitt's 1929 lecture "On the Age of Neutralizations and De-politicizations," which was in turn cited by Karl Löwith in his article "Max Weber und seine Nachfolger" that, as Benjamin notes, appeared in Thomas Mann's journal *Maß und Wert* in "January/February 1940" (7:673).[51] Benjamin's continuing interest suggests a familiarity with both sides of the Kelsen-Schmitt debate that was deep enough for him to consider his own response already in the *Origin of the German Trauerspiel*. Benjamin's engagement with Schmitt in his *Habilitation* thesis is, of course, well documented: in a letter to the publisher Richard Weissbach from 1923, Benjamin refers to *Political Theology*'s importance for his work on the *Trauerspiel*.[52] Some nine months later, writing to Gottfried Salomon, Benjamin specifies that he has been spending some time investigating the constitutional theories of the Baroque.[53] The book list, however, suggests that Benjamin regarded Schmitt as Kelsen's antagonist, that is, as someone who reconstructs the constitutional state of the seventeenth century as a legal order based, for its beginning and its end, in personality. "Sovereignty," Schmitt writes in *Political Theology*, replaces "divinity" as source and protection for the state in the stage of "secularization" in which the seventeenth century found itself.[54] Personality, that is, sovereignty, relates to the state as its creator and at the same time as its guardian; in place of God, who occupies the place of the absolute beginning, the prince of this world contends with the prospect of his terminating one order (law) for the sake of the other (the state) with each action he takes. This is contrary to Kelsen's view, according to which we are born into law; the pretense that we are not is a foil for power. Thus, according to Kelsen, we must presuppose the validity of the first, historical norm, as the origin is from the technical-normative point of view an extrajuridical consideration.[55] For Schmitt, "law" is therefore politics: the democratic principle that we are absolutely equal before the law expresses itself as the "general good," as war of all against all, and a "decision" regarding what constitutes public order and when it is threatened must therefore be made.[56] As Schmitt asserts, "Sovereign is he who decides over the state of exception"; he "produces and guarantees the situation in its totality" and "decides whether [the] normal situation," which must exist for any legal order to make sense, "actually exists" at all.[57] Insisting, contra Kelsen, that "[t]he juristic form is . . . not the form of technical precision, because the latter has a goal-oriented interest that is essentially material and impersonal," Schmitt then embellishes on how he sees "juristic form" manifesting: not, as "the idea of the modern constitutional state" would have it, "together with theism . . . [, as] banish[ing] miracle from the world [and along with it] the sovereign's direct intervention in a valid legal order," but rather as pervasive and "inexplicable" state intervention "everywhere," as evidenced in the work of counterrevolutionary thinkers and the literature of positive jurisprudence alike.[58] In fact, he protests, "the state intervenes everywhere. . . . [T]here always exists the same inexplicable identity: lawgiver, executive power, police, pardoner, welfare institution. . . . [T]here appears a huge cloak-and-dagger drama, in which the state acts in many guises but always as the same invisible person."[59]

It is in view of Schmitt's significance as Kelsen's antagonist that Benjamin's modification of Schmitt's thesis on seventeenth-century sovereignty as a pervasiveness of the political, viz. personal, decision must be read. As he writes, "The sovereign represents history. He holds historical occurrence in his hand like a scepter. This conception . . . is based on ideas about constitutional law. . . . If the modern concept of sovereignty boils down to a supreme executive power on the part of the prince, the Baroque concept develops out of a discussion of the state of exception and makes it the most important function of the prince to foreclose this state" (1:245; O 48–49). With this reformulation, Benjamin evidently sought to discover the grounds for the state of exception as a "conception"—though not of jurisprudence, as Kelsen would have argued, but of "ideas about constitutional law," that is, legal theory, which, in this context, is the debate between Kelsen and Schmitt and the latter's defense of power against the threat of its neutralization by law. In what Benjamin identifies as the quintessential scene of constitutional theory, the tyrannicide, the theory of the usurper becomes crucial, and "especially controversial," he writes, as it inspired a "continuing debate" in regard to whether the people, a rival prince, or only the curia could authorize the move to depose a tyrant (1:245; O 49–50). The seventeenth-century concept of sovereignty, as described by Schmitt, shores up the doctrine that the power to depose a rival lies absolutely with the prince, rather than the church; but the result, in Benjamin's account, was a "demand for a principality whose constitutional status guarantees the continuity of the commonweal" (1:246; O 50) that played out in the arts and in theology—that is, in theory. The sense of being driven toward catastrophe, and the need to demand that its political and juridical institutions multiply and blossom in an effort to put a halt to time: these were, for Benjamin, descriptors of a legal theory driven to hyperbolic distraction in its anxiety about its own foreclosure in the "inexplicability" of the source of law. In Kelsen's terms, this opacity translates into our need to simply presuppose the validity of the first, historical norm.

Thus, Benjamin writes, directly contradicting Schmitt, "it will not suffice to refer only to the greater stability of political relations in the eighteenth century" (1:246; O 50) to explain natural law in the seventeenth. In reshaping "natural law" into personal decisionism, Schmitt had declared that "the vivid awareness of the meaning of the exception that was reflected in the doctrine of natural law of the seventeenth century was soon lost in the eighteenth century, when a relatively lasting order was established."[60] Benjamin points toward the reliance of the doctrine of state on what Schmitt called "the interesting spectacle of the two tendencies facing one another, the rationalist tendency ... and the natural law tendency," and therefore also to the incompleteness of his picture of decisionism.[61] Neither a stabilized eighteenth century that, for Schmitt, is epitomized by Kelsen's neo-Kantianism, nor the "situational" picture of the seventeenth-century understanding of exception derived in Schmitt's view from an opposition to the perceived stability of the eighteenth century, suffice for Benjamin to explain the Baroque state of affairs. What does suffice, in contrast, are the countless literary phenomena that attest to the feeling of worldly despotism that accumulates as a bulwark against the threat of a state of exception, "the exalted forms of Baroque Byzantinism," "extracted" from a beyond that has been "emptied of everything" (1:246–47; O 51). Benjamin, in short, reads Schmitt polemically as an aesthetic theory—which he does by taking Schmitt's metaphor of the cloak-and-dagger drama literally, for instance, and grappling with an altogether different picture of the source of law as a result. In the *Origin of the German Trauerspiel*, this other source is indicated by the artistic and literary portrayals of the indecisiveness of the tyrant "with whom rests the decision on the state of exception, [and who] shows that, at the first given situation, resolve is nearly impossible for him" (1:250; O 56) because of the sheer arbitrariness that decisionism implies: with actions no longer unquestionably determined by thought, the ruler at the zenith of his power is simultaneously the point where history and power meet and a victim of his own unelevated humanness.

The "indecisiveness" he diagnoses in Schmitt's construction of the tyrant is based on a paradigm that Benjamin retrieves from "Toward the Critique of Violence." In the terms of that essay, the claim that a person suffers absolutely no constraints "merely suspends reflection on the moral-historical sphere and thus on any sense that action might have" (46); without any moral or historical "sense" to give it direction, reality, too, is deprived of its "sense" and reduced to sheer causality. Several years later, Benjamin suggests that when there is no sense to action, there can also be no decision. In "Toward the Critique of Violence," Benjamin had attributed the suspension of moral-historical considerations to "childish anarchism" (46); in regard to early modern constitutional theory, it is the tyrant who suspends reflection on the moral-historical sphere—and eliminates the grounds on which Schmitt determined his action to be a decision. Schmitt, in short, is secretly a legal positivist. Benjamin articulates this thought in an inversion of Schmitt's formula for sovereignty: "[T]he tyrant's business is the restoration of order in the state of exception: a dictatorship whose utopia will always be to put the iron constitution of natural laws in the place of fluctuating historical occurrence" (1:253; O 59). On this account, Schmitt's theory of sovereignty eliminates itself by virtue of its own insistence that all legal and executive power is a matter for moral and historical consideration: the argument that power guards the rule of law suspends the framework within which power can be considered the source of law. Sovereignty merely describes the situation in which action has no sense and decision is not possible, leaving just execution, implementation—and "dictatorship."

Benjamin's intent to address Schmitt's concept of dictatorship is suggested by a letter he sent to Schmitt on December 9, 1930, announcing the shipment of a copy of his *Trauerspiel* book to him, in which he refers to Schmitt's *Dictatorship* as "a confirmation of my art-philosophical research methods in your constitutional-philosophical methods" (*GB* 3:559). Like Kelsen's "On the Essence and Value of Democracy," Schmitt's *Dictatorship* responds to Kautsky's pamphlet on *Terrorism and Communism* (1919).[62] Unlike Kelsen, however, to whose argument he surreptitiously refers in the "Preliminary Remarks to the First Edition" of 1921, Schmitt argues that it does not follow from the idea that the dissolution of an elected parliament will result in the abolition of democracy that a dictatorship (of the proletariat) will necessarily result in "the rule of a minority over the majority," for "objections of principle cannot be raised against the recourse to democratic reforms."[63] Rather, Schmitt writes, law is merely the means to the maintenance of society, and if law fails to save society, "then force intervenes. . . . This, then, is the 'rescuing act of government' [*die rettende Tat der Staatsgewalt*] and the point in which the law coincides with politics and history."[64] Dictatorship thus refers to "any direct exercise of stately power," which may include as its aim "saving" democracy, though by definition it will not conform to the legal norms of that toward which it is directed—for "dictatorship is like the act of self-defense" and does not regard "the specific technical means of his action" as having a binding legal basis that the attacker shares.[65] The dictator has no particular task, and also no particular means that would or need to be considered "legitimate" for his action; his is a "constituent power" that, "without being itself constitutionally established, nevertheless is associated with any existing constitution in such a way that it appears to be foundational to it" and from which "new forms emerge incessantly" that it also has the capacity to destroy at any moment.[66]

For this ephemeral, contentless will Schmitt nevertheless sought a rather more "organic" figure, namely, the "organ," with which he hoped to illustrate the role that sovereign dictatorship plays in facilitating historical progress without falling into the rote mechanism of task fulfillment. This "organ," however, is nevertheless a figure that, given that dictatorship is a decision on the exception, would seem to always entail the possibility of deciding an exception to organic life itself.[67] Indeed, the apparently paradoxical character of Schmitt's "organic" dictator might have served as a reference point for Benjamin's extrapolations on "dictatorial power" (*diktatorische Gewalt*) (1:245–46; O 49), which he describes as the power that the ruler is destined to possess if faced with a state of exception: at the height of his power, the dictator is simultaneously the guarantor of historical progress and the denier of human perfectibility and life, while acting in the name of preserving life. As a result, Benjamin writes, the dictator reverts to a state of petrification that the organic metaphors belie, a state in which, on the one hand, he has no particular means and therefore any means whatsoever at his disposal, and on the other hand, being liberated from any prescribed ends, he has also abdicated any particular functionality and is therefore somewhat less like the decider than the senior administrator who does not realize his actions are, like those of defective equipment, not fit for the purpose. In insisting that sovereignty does not take the form of "technical precision" with a "goal-oriented interest," Schmitt fails to recognize the decay immanent to the concept of dictatorship.[68] For Schmitt, dictatorship is a name for the "inexplicable" state intervention that appears everywhere and in multiple guises as the preconstitutional act of personality that is ineluctable for the existence of legal norms. For Benjamin, dictatorship thereby reduces itself to a sort of obsession with technicity without a goal. Shortly after completing the *Trauerspiel* book, Benjamin revisits this thought in the interview he conducts with Georges Valois on the topic of "dictatorship" in 1927, in which he describes Valois sitting at his desk with a servant handing him his papers from behind. For Benjamin, Valois is an illustration of the "future dictator" whose virtue it is to "calculate every movement by its effect"; he who signs documents in such a manner is the one for whom "ruling" has become "second nature" (4:489–90). If, for Schmitt, "sovereign is he who decides over the state of exception," for Benjamin it is the bureaucrat who has become the sovereign.[69]

3. Natural Law and Natural History

"Second nature" entails a specific kind of decay: a decay of the dictatorial power driving history, which distinguishes this power from natural law. The emergence of this distinction, in turn, engenders a world of such sheer arbitrariness that dictatorship seems like nature again. Benjamin likely adapted the term from Georg Lukács, whose *Geschichte und Klassenbewußtsein* (History and self-consciousness; 1923) he read when he moved to Capri in 1924 to write the *Trauerspiel* book; in a letter Benjamin describes to Scholem his expectation that "the foundations of my nihilism will manifest themselves in [Lukács's] oppositional altercation with Hegelian concepts and the allegations of dialectics against communism" (*GB* 2:483; *C* 248). For Lukács, second nature describes the reification produced by commodity relations that appear uncreated by us, out of our control and thus as forms to which our consciousness is subjugated.[70] The term does not appear as such in *Origin of the German Trauerspiel*, however; instead, Benjamin describes in similar terms the moral world into which tragedy was ahistorically thrust in the nineteenth century by the philosophy of tragedy, which wanted to see in ancient tragedy the *Trauerspiel* world of generalized "guilt" and "expiation." According to this view of tragedy, the moral world of generalized guilt operates according to a principle of natural causation that turned "tragic fate" into the "state of affairs" dictating the individual's relation to the "lawfully ordered environment."[71] In this light, Benjamin's later identification of a certain kind of "ruling" with "second nature" in his interview with Valois probably refers back to a passage in the *Trauerspiel* book where Benjamin describes the depiction of the tyrant's fall as occurring not just in his own name but "in the name of historical humanity" (1:251–52; *O* 57). In its enactment in the *Trauerspiel*, Benjamin writes, the tyrant comes close to being a martyr, and the dictatorial power that drives history comes close to becoming naturalized relations of dominion and subjection. A term like "second nature" dehistoricizes the power that drives history by eliminating from view the historical dimension of the process of naturalization that power undergoes. "Second nature" would, in this view, correspond to a flattening of the "concave mirror" through whose "distortions" alone the moral world was "displayed before the eyes of the Baroque" (1:270; O 80) and acted out in the *Trauerspiel*. Instead of "second nature," Benjamin thus refers to the "complete secularization of the historical in the present state of creation," as "history wander[ing] into the setting" (1:271; O 81), and as "natural history": a generalization of creaturely guilt as fate across the created world, which presents causality as fate's instrument in the form of drama (1:308; O 128–29). The principle of this artwork, and of the theory of the moral world that it contains, must therefore not be causality but fate. Unlike causality, fate "is the elementary natural violence [*Naturgewalt*] in historical occurrence, [though] it itself is not thoroughly nature, since the present state of creation still reflects back the rays of the sun of grace, albeit mirrored in the murky waters of Adamic inculpation" (1:308; O 128). For Benjamin, this "not thoroughly natural" character of "natural violence," the minimal gap between natural law and the moral sphere, is the ground of action that the work of art manages to capture, inasmuch as it reflects ideas in a "field of guilt" (1:308; O 128–29).[72]

In using "natural history" in place of "second nature," Benjamin also pinpoints a corresponding inadequacy in the principle he associates with the latter, via Schmitt and later Valois and the "new fascists": the principle of equality before the law regardless of representation. Benjamin's shift of focus from determinism to inculpation as the ground of action harks back to an argument from "Toward the Critique of Violence," which he rearticulates in an art-historical and contracted form in the *Trauerspiel* book. In the essay, Benjamin discussed "power [as] the principle of all mythic law-positing," which he said has "an immensely consequential application in constitutional law" (56). In the *Trauerspiel* book, Benjamin refers back to this passage as an illustration of one consequence of the picture that the *Trauerspiel* gives of the equalization of all before law. In "Toward the Critique of Violence," he argued that one can "succumb to expiation" without "knowingly" transgressing a boundary, as though, as Hermann Cohen wrote, "the orders of fate themselves ... bring about this transgression" (57). According to the *Trauerspiel* book, one can be "torn," "guiltless, into the chasm of general guilt" by "nothing but the act" (1:310; O 131), as though the entirety of life were "inculpated" and subjected to the "law of natural life" (1:310; O 130), and thus subject to "expiation" through no participation of the will. In both contexts Benjamin speaks specifically to the conception of fate in antiquity, but, as he notes in "Toward the Critique of Violence," this conception of fate also finds an expression in modern jurisprudence, inasmuch as ignorance of the law also does not spare one from punishment (57). In its "application" to constitutional law, "power" as the "principle of all mythic law-positing" (56) thus corresponds with the sheer arbitrariness that Benjamin later diagnoses in Schmitt's "democratic" principle of equality of all before the law: Schmitt's theory of constituent power purports to be directionless and ends up suspending the moral-historical framework within which power could be indicated as the source of law. Benjamin suggests that Schmitt's "democratic" principle also inadvertently rejuridifies history, even as it eliminates the frame within which it would recognize it as anything other than determinism. Schmitt's generalization of prelegal power, in other words, delivers creation up to one of the most basic preconstitutional principles of law: the *Schuldverhältnis*, which can be translated as *obligatio*, quasi-contract, or literally, the "relation of debt or guilt." *Schuldverhältnis* underlies all contractual obligations and includes what might be considered its first cousins: the sale of goods, owner-occupier relations, vindication, and restitution. Furthermore, *Schuldverhältnis* includes the "act of self-defense" too, which is how Schmitt described dictatorship; dictatorship would deliver creation to an obligation that it alone, as the expression of the basic impulse to defend one's interests, is in a position to enforce and, in so doing, transmute into law.

Generalized as *Schuldverhältnis*, the act of self-defense underwrites the transition from one state of law to the next; correspondingly, Benjamin's discussion thereof in the *Trauerspiel* book reads as a theory of the origin of law-giving and the guarantee for the constitution. This Benjamin develops from his account of mythic law-positing in "Toward the Critique of Violence." Benjamin considers the transition of might to right as a transformation of the tyrant into the martyr, and expands on the provenance of the martyr drama, and thus the generalization of guilt, in his discussion of the portrayal of the death of Socrates as contrasted with that of the tragic hero. The difference between the tyrant and the martyr is based in their respective relations to death as the horizon for their liability and indexes for Benjamin the difference between the ancient and modern conceptions of the foundation of the legal condition. To illustrate the former, Benjamin draws on a "felicitous formulation" (1:294; O 110) attributed to Erich Unger, whose *Politik und Metaphysik* (Politics and metaphysics) had provided him with support for his argument against compromise as an example of law-positing violence in "Toward the Critique of Violence" (49). The tragic hero, Benjamin writes in the *Trauerspiel* book with reference to a "lost essay plan" (*GB* 2:206) drawn up by Unger, is fully determined by the "power of the frame" (*Gewalt des Rahmens*): the idea that his "spirit-living-bodily" [*geist-leibliche*] (1:294; O 110) existence fully determines the whole of his existence as well, such that the hero has no content other than the form that his death, in bordering his life as a whole, lends to his life. The phrase traces back to a letter from 1915 in which Unger proposes, as an antidote to the unfruitful and petrifying "endlessness of our ideas," the "bordering frame" (*begrenzender Rahmen*) that ancient drama provides to "occurrence," which gives occurrence an end and thus its sense and historical character; in finding its "end" in the frame, occurrence is able to "disclose itself in its own essence and its own power."[73] In tragedy, according to Unger, tragic life receives its sense and its historicity from its immanent end. In Benjamin's words, the tragic hero "shudders and shrinks back from the power of death as from a power that is familiar, his own, and ensnared with him" (1:293; O 109). By the same token, Benjamin argues, the hero who does not seek to justify himself before the gods, and thereby stands in a relation of obligation to the gods, thereby "enters into a contractual, as it were, process of expiation [*Sühneverfahren*]" (1:294; O 111).

For his elaboration of the legal situation arising from the conception of life as contractual expiation, Benjamin then turns to the work of Kurt Latte, the Jewish classical philologian whose *Heiliges Recht* (Sacred law; 1920) he marks with an asterisk in his bibliography for the expansion of the critique of violence (109). Latte argues that this scene of expiation is indicative of the way ancient law saw its relation to its own primal scene, which took place as the contractual struggle between the individual exercise of violence (in the form of the right to "self-defense" [*Fehderecht*] and "self-redress" [*Selbsthilfe*]) and the law's need to regulate it.[74] As Latte emphasizes, however, the need to regulate arises not from the attempt to arrive at a "judicial decision" but rather at "an expiatory negotiation [*Sühneverhandlung*]."[75] In fact, Latte argues, even where the "state" (*Staat*, which he uses in reference to "Hellas," in the sense of "Greece" as a whole legal-territorial entity, rather than the Athenian *polis*) succeeded in containing self-given authority (*Eigenmacht*), legal proceedings had as their goal not "to discover absolute right but to convince the offended party to renounce vengeance, [so that] the sacral forms of proof and verdict, given the impression that they could not fail to make even on those defeated, necessarily assumed an especially high significance."[76] In other words, ancient criminal law proceeded as a dialogue between accuser and accused, "without official intervention," and sought out conciliation as a form of expiation. Indeed, *Eigenmacht* was sometimes legitimate, for instance in the case of *exoulēs dikē* (act of ejectment), whereby a claimant could raise a suit against a debtor who refused to hand over property whose ownership a court had already decided in favor of the creditor.[77] In place of written law, the court relied on religious forms for security.[78] Synthesizing for his part Florens Christian Rang's theory of the agon with his reading of Latte, Benjamin elaborates by referring to the "Dionysian interruption," the "drunken, ecstatic word" in the form of which "a higher justice could arise from the force of conviction in living speech than from the trial of clans combatting one another with weapons or predetermined verbal forms" (1:295; O 112).[79] For Latte, such a form would have been the juridical oath (*Eid*), which, again, "aimed not at the clarification of guilt but at the avoidance of feud and the reconciliation [*Aussöhnung*] of the parties involved. The oath following the judgment gave the winning party the opportunity to strengthen his claim of innocence, not so much for the court as for the opponent so that he may lay his doubts to rest."[80] The oath, in other words, served merely to guarantee the justness of the judge's utterance in the moment rather than decide between right and wrong, but in so doing invoked a "higher order that tells the disputing parties to relinquish their self-given authority."[81] Latte recalls that the oath represented a call upon the gods as well as an "outflow of divine will" (*Ausfluß göttlichen Willens*).[82]

In contrast to the tragic hero's death, the death of Socrates represents the transition to the "modern" constitutional state, inasmuch as Benjamin detects traces of the early modern martyr drama portended in the Socratic episode. Its major difference from tragic death, Benjamin writes, is found in its prospects for an ensuing community. Unlike the tragic hero, Socrates accepts his sentence and goes without defiance to his death. Thus, first, unlike the tragic hero, whose death remains within the remit of the personal and "frames" his life, Socrates dies, at least in appearance, in "a sacrifice that expiates in accordance with the letter of an ancient law, a sacrificial death that establishes a community in the spirit of a coming justice" (1:292; O 108–9). Socrates therefore also dies, "like the Christian hero of faith[,] . . . of his own free will, and of his own free will, in unspeakable superiority and without defiance, he goes mute where he stays silent" (1:293; O 109). Whereas in ancient law the defendant (the tragic hero) is "defensive" even in silence and the court upholds his "right" to self-defense even in judgment—since the judgment is technically a reconciliation based on the mutual relinquishment of self-given authority and a verbally invoked divine guarantee of the resolution's justness—Socrates' silence is nondefiant. It is accepting of his sentence by the court—and therefore also ironic and pedagogically oriented toward a community to come, his disciples. Through silence, then, he knows he has secured a discursive community, and in death too he knows that he will be redeemed in language: "Like a mortal, Socrates looks death in the eye . . . but he acknowledges it as something alien, beyond which, in immortality, he expects to find himself again" (1:293; O 109). Socrates breaks out of the tragic "power of the frame" because he meets his demise willingly, parodying tragic death.

Furthermore, inasmuch as it is enacted in the "sober light of Plato's dialogs," Socrates' linguistic redemption is staged at the end of the *Symposium* as a discussion of the "genuine poet" who "contains" both tragedy and comedy in the same measure, and thus their "dialectic" (1:297; O 114). Broadly following Nietzsche, who declares "Socratism" to be the death of tragedy at the hands of a new "art form," the logical syllogism, which "annihilates" itself in the "bourgeois drama," Benjamin describes Socratic "rationalism" as "the language of the new drama and so all the more the language of the *Trauerspiel*" (1:297; O 115).[83] For this very reason, it is implied, Socrates' death also narrates the transition into a post-ancient basis for modern law: whereas in ancient law the legal proceedings ended in situations where no known law applied, only the oath as the correlate to self-redress, Socrates' ironization of his own death affords a basis on which law applies, which is to say, beyond the individual's claims and grievances and to a community before the law. The death of Socrates represents the myth of this transition out of ancient law. For this point Benjamin supplements an insight from Latte, who had envisioned the transition out of the oath and the religion it is based on as the transition out of legal Hellenism altogether.[84] He also adapts from his thesis in "Toward the Critique of Violence" that "power," as "principle of all mythic law-positing" (56), indexes the continuity between ancient and modern law, leading to spectral results. In Benjamin's account of the *Trauerspiel*, Socrates' truths cannot appear except as ventriloquized in dialog form; because his death is no longer his own but that of the disciples, of Plato, and of the community, the dying Socrates represents the myth of transition at the source of law.

Similarly, Benjamin suggests, the unity of time, place, and action, which he understands as an invention by latter-day Aristotelianism, corresponds with the emergence of jurisprudence, the practice of delimiting court sessions by the measure of the passage of time as centered on the rotation of the sun, for instance, and the harmonization and standardization of legal proceedings (1:296; O 113).[85] In the case of Socrates, therefore, it is no longer the individual who is on trial but, as in the case of the martyr dramas, a being who in his very limited consciousness is able to gather focus on something absolute (1:291; O 107–8). The implication of this is at least twofold. First, Socrates' conscious and willing meeting with death divides death itself—this is what occurs in mourning, in the attitude of which, Benjamin notes, "death thereby becomes salvation: crisis of death" (1:286; O 100). Second, mourning is therefore a state in which we accept death as a penalty meted out justly by law, the state's successful pacification of self-authorized uses of violence for the sake of the rule of law, which in this sense would seem to be coextensive with the state. In short, even as it refers to the transition out of myth, Socrates' death mythologizes the transition to the constitutional state, in the light of which the modern state appears as a state of mourning: as a state of conscious ironization of the "tragic death" that stood for the right to self-defense, the legitimate use of self-authorized violence. And thus the modern state, the transition into which is mythically represented by Socrates' death, is also revealed to be a mythologization of our having freely relinquished this self-authorization in the name of the rule of law. It follows that the court of law, too, is a setting for our nondefiant submission to the state's monopoly over life and death.

By choosing the term "natural history" over "second nature" to describe the world of historical occurrence in the *Trauerspiel* book, Benjamin shifts focus from determinism to inculpation as the ground of action. With reference to "Toward the Critique of Violence" and his bibliography for its subsequent expansion, he also demonstrates that the principle of equality of all before the law, which leads into the debate on the "dictatorship" of individual persons and the question of power at the source of law within constitutional theory, neutralizes from view that which its proponents, such as Schmitt, inadvertently presume to be the actual motive force of history: the generalization of guilt across creation. Hand in hand with this presumption is a rejuridification of history, in view of which all relations, including those of self-defense, constituent power, and "dictatorship," are recast in the shape of the transition from might to right. Benjamin draws attention to the mythic character of this theory of the transition into law, an account of which he finds absent from the theories on the source of law in constitutional theory. In so doing, he removes both personal will and the constitutional court from consideration as sources of law—or, to be precise, he removes from consideration the question of law as the focal point of a transition, be it from power or another law, and so removes the guardianship of law from the end goal of his inquiry.

What Benjamin leaves himself with, within the narrow scope of his question, however, is immense: the entire field of *Schuldverhältnisse*, that is, obligations, quasi-contracts, and "debt / guilt relations" underlying contractual obligations from goods exchange, possession and occupation, vindication, and restitution. These debts and promissory notes fill, as his brief remark on Valois and the Sorelian legacy suggests, the terrain that appears as "second nature" to the unchecked and directionless personal will. It is a terrain that otherwise appears as a history of commodity exchange and reification of relations that modern capitalism produces in the guise of the "natural laws" of society.[86] It is also a terrain that is filled with a "wealth of things" that the Baroque "extracts" from a "beyond" that it "empties of everything in which even the faintest breath of world wafts," in order to reimagine it as available for extraction work: the catalog of Byzantine orientalism, which provided the Baroque with an ostentation of pure materiality for its plays (1:246–48; O 50–53). From this trove of materials, extracted from extra-European ground and its world-character annihilated and therefore appearing as dead nature, the Baroque availed itself of materials for its own repurposing into an exaltation of its princes as deities, each one the center of his own solar system (1:247–48; O 52). Each prince whose glory is fashioned from the labor of extraction is a sun that cannot countenance the coexistence of another except in the form of a solar eclipse. Each act of extraction that contributes to this cosmology therefore participates in a myth of origination, specifically one whose scope is incompatible with the "constitutional-political reason" that "juridically affixes the sovereign's position" on the interior of the state but is fully in synchrony with the Baroque's "effusive ideal of world domination," which sees each prince ensnared in a perpetual and paranoid struggle with the other, his own shadow (1:247; O 52). Benjamin makes it clear that the two aspects of the prince, the sovereign of the constitution and the aspirant to extraterritorial dominion, are sides of the same allegorical engraving, and that the critique of power as the principle of mythic law-positing must also therefore critique the violence of origination of that power. As he writes, "the Baroque extracts a wealth of things that tend to withdraw from all shaping and, at its zenith, brings them to the light of day in drastic shape in order to clear out a last heaven and put it in the position of a vacuum that will one day annihilate the earth with catastrophic violence" (1:246; O 50–51).

4. Aztec Baroque

In *Origin of the German Trauerspiel*, Benjamin draws on an image to illustrate the cosmic struggle in which he finds seventeenth-century princes to be commonly depicted: emblem LXXVII of Diego de Saavedra Fajardo's *Idea de un príncipe político-cristiano representada en cien empresas* (Idea of a Christian political prince, presented in one hundred emblems; 1640), of which Benjamin refers to a German edition published in Cologne in 1674.[87] Saavedra's work is born out of his extensive travels around Switzerland, northern Italy, and various German states while based in Bavaria as Philip IV's diplomatic representative during some of the most devastating battles waged during the Thirty Years' War. The book of emblems was aimed at counseling the Christian prince against Machiavellian opportunism and advocated for a return to "true" church doctrine; it was written during the years when its author regarded Catholic Spain's influence on the continent as under threat by the sovereignty of other states. Emblem LXXVII, *Praesentia Nocet* (Presence injures), depicts a sun whose light is eclipsed by a crescent moon, which causes it to cast a broad shadow onto the surface of the globe below. The accompanying text, part of which Benjamin cites, specifies that this is an emblem of the art of diplomacy; but the diplomacy it depicts is an art that emerges from the fracturing of the vision of a unified European Christendom, which Saavedra amalgamates with natural astrology (in the form of a warning that "great shadows and other inopportune events" might arise from an eclipse) as a way to make discernible a divine order (and Catholic doctrine) as a resource for unity and security.[88] Undergirding the emblem is also a strange cosmology, according to which suns can behave as moons and block out the rays of the other. The image is so strange that Benjamin feels compelled to add "(sc. *lunae*)," "that is, of the moon," to clarify whose "presence injures" (1:248; O 52). And in this very act of clarification, Benjamin illuminates an additional aspect of the image raised by the diplomat: "inopportune events" threaten to lay waste to the world-political order in the shadow of the unanimity that state sovereignty, in its most anxious phase, seeks to impose over the surface of the earth.

Benjamin had a long-standing and well-documented interest in the cosmology of violence exacted by the imposition of moral unanimity, particularly in respect to the global aspirations of Catholic Spain. This interest moves in the orbit of the critique of violence; in 1922, Benjamin sent an offprint of his then recently published "Toward the Critique of Violence" to the director of ethnology at the National Museum in Berlin and docent in Mesoamerican languages and cultures, Walter Lehmann, together with a dedication inscribed on its inside cover: "To my revered teacher, Herr Professor Lehmann, presented most devotedly by its author."[89] In return, something in the essay prompted Lehmann to recommend a book to Benjamin, who includes the title in his bibliography for a "more fully developed" critique of violence: Josef Kohler's *Das Recht der Azteken* (Law of the Aztecs), which, as Benjamin notes in the bibliography, he would "possibly borrow from Lehmann" (111).[90] Finally, Benjamin responds to Lehmann in the form of an aphorism in *One-Way Street*, in which Benjamin expands the scope of his critique of violence beyond the Weimar-induced dream that Europe is the world. The following discussion elaborates on the exchanges above to propose how Benjamin extended the critique of violence beyond the "modern European" parameters he set for his 1921 essay and moved toward a decolonial philosophy of the history of violence, in respect to the Spanish conquest—and German imperialism's own, belated relationship to it.

While a student at the University of Munich, Benjamin wrote a letter to his friend Fritz Radt enthusing about a number of "precious vessels" that stood around the office and library of a docent whose course he was attending with unique relish that term (*GB* 1:291). Benjamin was so enthusiastic about the course that when he once had to miss class, he penned an extravagant letter of apology to its instructor—who, in turn, kept it stashed among his personal papers, unpublished and undiscovered till now. "Dear Professor," he wrote on February 4, 1916—the same year in which, according to the book's dedication, he "conceived" of the *Origin of the German Trauerspiel*—"I had to miss yesterday's lecture due to something that came up at the last minute. I hope you will forgive me. With the expression of the highest esteem, your most devoted Walter Benjamin."[91] The docent in question was Lehmann, then an assistant professor who had recently completed a *Habilitation* in ancient American languages and ethnology and was working as a curator for the Ethnographic Museum in Munich while also teaching a seminar on ancient Mesoamerican language and culture at his home.⁹² Lehmann's *Habilitation* thesis drew on linguistic and archaeological materials he had gathered during a trip to Central America from 1907 to 1909 on behalf of the Ethnological Museum in Berlin that was funded by a foundation endowed by the French and American antiquarian and philanthropist Joseph Florimond Duc de Loubat. His documentation of indigenous languages, including several just prior to extinction, formed the basis of his *Habilitation*, which he completed in 1915. The published version, *Zentral-Amerika*, is still regarded as a standard reference work, though it was not published until 1920, owing, ostensibly, to personal health issues and the intervening war.⁹³ Lehmann's research was also enabled by the economic and social networks that underpinned German capitalist activities in Central America. His contacts with consular officials and expatriate elites gained him access to excavation sites and contacts with plantation owners whose indigenous workforce provided him with vocabularies of their languages, body measurements for his anthropological research, and labor for his archaeological work. The German Club in Costa Rica was the meeting place where Lehmann conducted business with local antiquities dealers.⁹⁴ As a result of his trip, Lehmann acquired several valuable collections for the Ethnological Museum, including a vast collection of gold objects from Costa Rica. After his return to Germany, Lehmann was named to the Ethnographic Museum in Munich, completed his doctoral and *Habilitation* theses, and began teaching, often in the format of seminars held at his home using materials he had amassed on his trip for his personal collection.⁹⁵ One of these seminars was the one Benjamin attended.

Lehmann's later career trajectory is noteworthy for another reason. Soon after the publication of *Zentral-Amerika*, Lehmann was named to an associate professorship in Munich, and a year after that awarded his *Habilitation* anew at the (then) Friedrich Wilhelm University of Berlin and appointed to the directorship of the Ethnological Research Institute of the State Museums of Berlin. After a second research trip from 1925 to 1926 to Mexico and Guatemala, Lehmann was named the director of the African, Oceanic, and American division of the Ethnological Museum in Berlin in 1927. On September 8, 1933, however, Lehmann was put on early retirement effective from January 1, 1934; the official reason given was "rationalization and cost reduction" as a result of the enforcement of a new law concerning civil servants. It has been suggested that the proximate cause for Lehmann's removal was the seizure of power by the National Socialists; personal documents show, however, that Lehmann was a registered member of the National Socialist German Workers' Party (NSDAP) and Sturmabteilung (SA) Reserve from April 30, 1933, until September 1935, after which he left the SA for health reasons.[96]

Lehmann was the protégé of Eduard Seler, at the time the only professor of pre-Columbian American archaeology in Germany. Seler had, notably, earned his *Habilitation* with the first "systematization" of the field, which he based on an analysis of a set of codices Alexander von Humboldt had brought to Berlin ninety years earlier.[97] In 1903, Seler applied his adapted natural-scientific methods to an extensive commentary on the Codex Borgia, a divinatory and ritual manuscript among the few believed to have been written before the Spanish conquest. His aim, as he had written in an earlier major essay on the topic, was to arrive at a "system of chronology" in use across all of ancient Mesoamerica. His discovery, on which this system hinged, was that the Mesoamericans harmonized their vigesimal divinatory calendar known in Nahuatl as the *tonalamatl* with the 365-day solar year governing profane life not by intercalating the missing days or by simple division of one into the other after a requisite period of cycles, but by assigning successive years of both chronologies to the four cardinal directions, which allowed the Mayans and later the Aztecs to "obtain a fixed chronology by reckoning the days," the exact passage of which they computed based on observations of planetary motions.[98] In another set of essays, Seler argued that the Mayans tracked with notable accuracy the period of revolution of the planet Venus, whose appearances first as the morning star and then as the evening star enabled them to connect the solar year with the book of days with "perfection on the numeric-theoretical side."[99]

Benjamin would not only have learned of these arguments in the winter semester of 1915/16; he would have heard them presented in a way that, by his own account, inspired hours of conversation with a fellow seminar attendee, Felix Noeggerath, on "mythological" and "ethnographic" problems. These conversations extended to "the concept of historical existence [*Dasein*] and of history" as well as "all the other essential problems [that] seemed for us to develop" from the "centrality" (*GB* 1:300) of the problem of history. Something of the content of these seminars is indicated by an article Lehmann published in 1916 on "Ein kostbares Räuchergefäß aus Guatemala" (A precious smoker vessel from Guatemala), which was likely not dissimilar to the "precious vessels" Benjamin admired around Lehmann's apartment.[100]

Standing around 58 centimeters high, the clay vessel was shaped as a "grotesque human figure" with a large face and its nose and cheeks adorned with spikes. Lehmann identified the figure with Itzamná, an older Mayan god of the west associated with rain and fruitfulness, and, recalling another ancient god associated with fruitfulness and the west, as well as the first day sign of the *tonalamatl*, realized that they pointed to the probability that hidden behind the (younger) Mexican rain god Tlaloc, who was linked to the east, was an older moon god whose proper domain lay in the west—and that, therefore, the reckoning system could not have derived simply from a crude phenomenology of the periodic movement of Venus as it rose in the east and set in the west. As Lehmann wrote in a concluding footnote, sometimes the element *cauac* (rain) can denote "day," sometimes "night"; "even more significant is when the hieroglyphic element *ahau* (meaning 'lord' or 'sun') is sometimes used as a synonym for *cauac*—but there is no space here to get into this in more detail."[101]

Lehmann did in fact get into this in more detail—it was to be his preoccupation for the next decade and a half—though his work never made it into published form.[102] Nevertheless, Benjamin would have learned of these "wholly fundamental discoveries in the domain of mythology, of which the first publications are in progress" (*GB* 1:300), during his extensive conversations with Noeggerath, who was Lehmann's research assistant at the time. The fourteen original manuscripts comprising this project depart, as one might expect, from a revision that Lehmann undertakes of Seler's speculations concerning the harmonization of the divinatory and the profane reckoning systems.[103] To promote the theory that the appearance of Venus was paramount for this harmonization, Seler had recalled that the morning star was associated with Quetzalcoatl, a feathered-serpent Aztec deity who was not only "considered the first priest and inventor of every art" but was also the "king of the mythical forebears of the Mesoamerican peoples, the Toltec race." "Toltec" describes a culture that is referenced in Aztec sources as the origin of the arts and sciences and based in a place called Tollan, but the historical existence of a Toltec "race" is disputed; the concept of the "Toltecs" as an actual ethnic group whose territory spanned across Central America was an ideological construction by the Aztecs, who sought to use it to shore up the legitimacy of their own conquest over the Basin of Mexico, into which their ancestors had migrated just under three hundred years earlier, by claiming descendance from a pan-Mesoamerican race. Ethnologists around the late nineteenth to twentieth century, such as Seler, partook of the ideology by suggesting that Toltec nature myths, such as one associating the morning star with the deity Quetzalcoatl, also had their basis in actual historical figures and events. On the basis of this conflation of myth and history, Seler concluded that the arrangement of the *tonalamatl* was fundamental for both the Mayans who originated it and the Aztecs who adopted it, thereby also asserting the historical supremacy of the Aztecs.[104]

Lehmann, by contrast, opens his treatises with the appellation "Kucumatz-Quetzalcoatl," thereby referring also to the earlier, Mayan name of the deity; furthermore, he writes, "Kucumatz-Quetzalcoatl was originally a moon god."[105] If it is as the lunar god and not as Venus that Quetzalcoatl originally appears as the "inventor" of the calendar, time, and the time periods with which they are measured, then not only the calendar but time and its periods must be "lunar" in character as well. Significantly, the lunar calendar anchored its calculation of days on the cardinal directions that followed not the path of Venus as it moved from east to west, morning to evening, but the path of the moon as it visibly traveled through its four phases in the night sky, starting with the moonrise in the west. This, Lehmann writes, "is the ancient sacred cycle of the monthly lunar orbit, whose direction is the reverse of the apparent daily orbit of the sun but is nevertheless the same again as the direction of the course of the solar year."[106] According to Lehmann, the significance of his discovery extends beyond what he describes as an astronomically more consistent method of telling time. Seler had had to resort to what he called "naming" in order to harmonize the days and years.[107] Lehmann, by contrast, claims that the lunar day and solar year were already harmonized in Mayan manuscripts, and that any time-reckoning and naming of years on the basis of the solar day, such as in the use of the divinatory *tonalamatl*, was therefore an intervention made in virtue of a "younger solar system" introduced as a result of a "transition" from one view of the universe to another. As a product of this "transition," the years were named and the commencements of cyclical periods were marked in accordance with the (solar) days of the divinatory calendar. In short, prophecy and reality were harmonized by virtue of "transition"—Lehmann's word for "colonization." Traces of these ideas made their way into Benjamin's remarks from this time; in a note written not long after resuming his studies with Lehmann in the summer of 1916, Benjamin remarks that "the historical numbers are names" (6:90), and at the end of a set of notes in which he outlines a project on the "Category of Justice" in the late summer or early fall of 1916, which is included as Note 1 in this volume, one finds the addendum that "[t]he problem of historical time is already posed through the peculiar form of historical time-reckoning. The years are countable but, in contrast to most countables, not numerable"—that is, nameable, if the historical numbers are in fact names (294).[108] And around two years later in another set of notes, included in this volume as Note 8, Benjamin similarly notes that "[t]he relation between world history and divine history is to be methodically investigated and described through research into the series of historical numbers" (74).[109]

Lehmann had also conducted research precisely into the series of historical numbers *qua* names: the *tonalamatl* and the "peculiar form of historical time-reckoning" it presented, namely, a harmonization of prophecy and reality on the basis of a temporal unit measured on an apparent unidirectional movement from east to west. This had been taken by Seler as a means for standardization in favor of the solar day. What Lehmann claims to have discovered, in contrast, was that harmonization's symbolic originator, "Quetzalcoatl, was, as proto-historical personality, not actually the inventor of the calendar . . . but only a reformer."[110] Lehmann's statement is a peculiar conflation of ideological positions. First, he, like Seler, assumes Quetzalcoatl to be the quasi-historical king of the Toltecs and mythic forebear of the Aztecs; indeed, he sets out this view in an entry he wrote on "Toltecs" for the 1911 edition of the *Encyclopaedia Brittanica*, in which he writes that "it is possible that the legendary wanderings of Quetzalcoatl . . . are mainly a mythological description of the moon's periodic course[,] but even in that case there can be no doubt that the nature-myth has been embellished with details derived from an actual race movement which took place in prehistoric times."[111] Quetzalcoatl thus resets the calendar to a new zero; but in Lehmann's account, the *origo*, which institutes the end of myth and the beginning of historical time, is transformed into the scene of a historical-philosophical problem. To calibrate the 360-day lunar year to the 365-day solar year, the Aztec reformation inserted a set of intercalary or "leap" days—*Schalttage* in German—during which time, as the myth recounts, Kucumatz-Quetzalcoatl descended to earth to end the year on a new day marked by the glyph *ahau*, meaning lord or sun, which in turn was indissociable from the glyphs for the rain, moon, and the region where the sun is black and out of sight.[112] The myth of Aztec imperial unity emerges from this origin, which it posits as historical and unique, but this origin is also a setting in which night is day and day is night, a prehistorical scene of indeterminacy where phenomena bear within themselves the propensity to overturn themselves—and reveal themselves as hybrid, discontinuous, and indicative of some unspecified violence. Lehmann gave the name "luni-solar" to this region of time and noted that it has left traces of its existence even in calendars based on the solar day: namely, wherever lunar presence is interpreted as a solar eclipse. One of Benjamin's formulations in the *Origin of the German Trauerspiel* succinctly rearticulates the problem as follows: "the category of origin is not therefore . . . a purely logical one, but a historical one" (1:226; O 25). To this one might add, with Lehmann: origin is conquest. Yet Lehmann is unable to fully grasp the significance of his finding, inasmuch as his instinct is to fully conflate the natural-mythic and the historical; just as he declared the Toltecs to be an actual race whose origin myth is legitimated by historical fact, so he declares the "luni-solar" to be a "system" that he discovers across the world's religions up to the present day.[113]

According to Scholem, Benjamin also indicates this much to him, twice: communicating a mixture of fascination and repugnance with regard to Lehmann, Benjamin reportedly remarks to Scholem in August 1916 that "it is this man's fortune that he does not know what he knows, for otherwise he would have long gone insane. His lack of knowledge makes him into a scientist."[114] In a letter to Scholem from November 1919, Benjamin, who has in the interim recommended Lehmann's seminars to Scholem, writes: "I am surprised that he is still of sound spirit. His moral person cannot be regarded all that highly" (*GB* 2:57; *C* 152)—a remark that raises the possibility that Benjamin had already then intuited a fascist tendency that blinded Lehmann to the importance of his own insights and that Lehmann would later formalize through his NSDAP affiliation in the following decade. Still, two years later, Benjamin reacquaints himself with Lehmann and begins attending his lectures again, this time in Berlin, where, in the winter semester of 1921/22, Lehmann taught a course on "Astronomie und Kalender in Zentralamerika" (Astronomy and the calendar in Central America).[115] Something in these lectures, which presumably would have contained part if not all of the "fundamental discoveries" Lehmann had been advancing since 1916, then prompted Benjamin the following June to send Lehmann an offprint of "Toward the Critique of Violence," which in turn prompts Lehmann to recommend Josef Kohler's *Das Recht der Azteken* (Law of the Aztecs). Like the "precious vessel" Benjamin once encountered in Lehmann's study, Kohler's book is an artifact acquired through networks of prestige, capital, and fantasies of national and territorial belonging. For this reason, it too provides a focal point for questions concerning the fabrication of historical continuity, this time within legal theory.

Law of the Aztecs is an exemplum of comparative jurisprudence, the field of which Kohler was a founding figure; a compendium of laws public and private, it belongs alongside an array of other works in which Kohler sought similarly to give as complete and systematic a picture as possible of non-European and noncontemporary legal cultures: Assyrian, Babylonian, Talmudic, Arabic, Mohammedan, Indian, and Chinese, to name a few he had compiled by 1920.[116] Such work, especially in regard to contemporaneous non-European cultures, was of practical relevance for colonial authorities; Kohler himself had designed a "Fragebogen zur Erforschung der Rechtsverhältnisse der sogenannten Naturvölker, namentlich in den deutschen Kolonialländern" (Questionnaire for the investigation into the legal relations of so-called primitive peoples, specifically in the German colonies), in which he set out to "give guidance to travelers and colonial administrators in regard to how to observe and describe the legal relations and the associated mores (legal mores [*Rechtssitten*]) that belong to the so-called '*Naturvölker*'" and to "point the researcher to the tendencies of the soul that prevail [*waltend*] under the threshold of the juridical."[117] Kohler was also convinced of the contribution that comparative jurisprudence could make to "universal legal history" and a "genuinely living philosophy of law," as opposed to the "bloodless" variety he identified in "a priori philosophy."[118] In the case of *Law of the Aztecs*, which Kohler compiled with the help of Eduard Seler, the result was a portrait of the Aztecs who were, like their modern European counterparts, conquerors and lawful beings capable of constitutional relations, in spite of lacking the Europeans' a priori concepts of law.

Aspiring to construct "Aztec law" as it was "authentically" yet in his self-image as a naturally lawful European, Kohler paints a picture of natural law that was not reducible to the demands of reason—a prospect that Kant, for instance, in *Toward Eternal Peace*, had rejected out of hand as illusional in the absence of "the higher point of view of anthropological observation" that would be required.[119] Kohler describes an elaborate array of norms comprising the legal lives of the Aztecs, subdivided into constitutional and international law, social law, personal and family law, property law, and so forth. Its "moderate monarchy," he writes, had its power checked and balanced by an adjacent priesthood, and the king, who was elected, was supported by an administrative hierarchy of ministries and councils. From the federation of states to the colonized states, nobility, free common people, and prisoners of war, together with all conceivable aspects of social life from water consecrations to trade, every relation was regulated by a norm. Kohler's reconstruction of the legal life of the Aztecs is nevertheless consistently couched in the language of European jurisprudence, which is especially evident in his description of penal law. "Mexican penal law," he writes, "is a testament to moral rigor, a harsh view of life, and significant state-building capacity."[120] This, according to Kohler, hinged on the fact that although the Aztecs sought to apply the death penalty as often and as broadly as they could—Kohler's text at this point is a litany of ways in which one could be sentenced to die under Aztec law—nevertheless there was no right to self-redress because "one was not permitted to interfere with the state's penal authority."[121] Indeed, self-redress—and, with it, the right to self-defense—was itself punishable by death. In other words, the Aztec state had a monopoly on the use of violence over life and death, and upholding this monopoly was the single most important quasi-principle for Kohler, and presumably for the colonial authorities among his readers, that facilitated its transition from a state of nature to a civil state.

In "Toward the Critique of Violence," Benjamin had written that the right to self-defense is in contradiction with the "European legislation that all natural ends of individual persons must collide with legal ends if they are pursued with a greater or lesser degree of violence" (42) because violence in the hands of the individual is regarded as existing outside of law and therefore as endangering law itself. The "objective contradiction" (44) therein, Benjamin noted, was that law-threatening violence has in fact been permissible in the European constitution, for instance as seen in the right to strike, the law of war, and at least in what Benjamin designates as the "law of a later period" (51), fraud. In "Toward the Critique of Violence," however, Benjamin had still supposed that "primitive circumstances," which he implied to be anything outside of "contemporary Europe," "scarcely [knew] the beginnings of constitutional relations" (44). Benjamin's inclusion of Kohler's work in his bibliography for the further development of the critique of violence suggests that he later saw modern European legal principles in the way Kohler saw Aztec law: as species of statecraft constructed as a fantasy of the state's monopoly on the power over life and death. Both, therefore, are also constructed as continuations of the same colonial project, as though sharing a horizon in regard to the natural ends of individuals smoothed out the historical and systemic imbalances in power between the colonizing European state and the colonized non-European. As an extension of the monopoly on power over life and death within the sovereign European state, colonialism aspires to erase its own traces and reestablish equilibrium by codifying the pacification of individual, that is, indigenous exercises of self-defense in the idealized image Europe has of its natural legality and constitutional propensity. The success of the colonial project is measured by how successfully the colonized mimics the colonizer in this regard.

Baroque *Trauerspiel*, after all, was nearly coeval with "Aztec law," that is, the colonial reconstruction of it as an archaeological object. As Kohler painstakingly notes, the earliest "authentic" sources available to him were a small archive preserved by an Aztec historian during the first century after the Conquest that circulated widely into the seventeenth century and a translation authenticated in the sixteenth century.[122] Benjamin also suggested that the transition from tragedy to *Trauerspiel* was anchored in a process by which the early modern state acquired its legal force from our forfeiture of the right to exercise self-authorized violence in seeking to right a wrong (1:296–97; O 114). "Aztec law" is, in a sense, therefore a species of Baroque *Trauerspiel*, though not in any symmetrical sense, as Kohler's work made evident; for what might be designated as "Aztec law," however "authentic" it is purported to be, is evidently reconstructed through later documents that include missionary accounts, histories of art, lexica, and other types of archaeological artifacts dating to after the Conquest—in short, voiced in the idiom of having been conquered, even as its content speaks of conquest. As an archaeological object, "Aztec law" is supremely ambiguous: it is a European fabrication circulating as an excavated artifact onto which the European colonial process is projected—the invention of the death penalty. It is, therefore, also supremely mimetic, though what it mirrors back—the evidence of subjuridical "legal mores" that make a people amenable to a more advanced state of self-administration—also enables the remembrance of its foundation in the relinquishment of the right to self-defense, albeit couched in the protohistorical (and therefore quasi-mythic) language of self-authorization.[123] Benjamin had sketched out some related thoughts in 1918 in a set of notes he titled "Methodical Modes of History," included as Note 10 in this volume. The "study of documents [*Urkundenlehre*]", he writes there, should not be regarded merely as an "auxiliary science of history" but rather as possessing an "entirely independent value," since they are the components of what he calls "pragmatic history," the mode of history that "proceeds temporally, in struggles" (76). As "pragmata," which Benjamin might have understood in Kant's sense of the word as that which "a free-acting being makes of himself, or can and should make of himself," documents are both means and end to the self-fashioning of what Kant calls the "citizen of the world."[124] From a "pragmatic" point of view, one might say that "Aztec law" documents the origin of the constitutional state as a "struggle" that registers as *Trauerspiel*: as a "mournful" absence of recognition of the tragedy that ensues from the annulment of the right to defend oneself against the encroachment of the administration of life and death, and from the "free-acting being's" consent to its apotheosis, the death penalty.

In 1927, Benjamin writes a third missive to Lehmann. This time, it takes the form of an artifact he himself has excavated from a dream that he would later publish as part of the third section of his planned project on "Politics," the only section thereof other than "Toward the Critique of Violence" to make it into print, namely, *One-Way Street*.

> **Structural Engineering Works** [*Tiefbau-Arbeiten*]
> I saw in a dream a bleak terrain. That was the marketplace of Weimar. Excavations were taking place there. I too scraped a bit in the sand. There the spire of a church tower emerged. Highly pleased, I thought to myself: a Mexican shrine from the time of pre-animism, from the Anaquivitzli. I awoke with laughter. (Ana = ἀνά [upward]; vi = vie [life]; witz [joke] = Mexican church{!}) (4:101; KGA 8:28)

In the dream, the narrator finds himself in a setting reminiscent of Benjamin's own first encounters in Lehmann's study in 1916 with the "precious vessels" and the codices and lexica from which "Aztec law" would emerge. It is a marketplace of modern European intellectual exchange and the site where a new constitution would soon be conceived (Weimar), a central node in the networks of capital, prestige, and fantasies of national and territorial belonging that define a Germany on the cusp of becoming a new republic. One might expect to encounter seamless trade and the continuous functioning of law in such a marketplace, but the site presents itself instead as "bleak terrain," a barren surface into which one must first cut and perform an act of violent extraction from its subsoil before artifacts emerge. From this struggle with the world just beyond, an object presents itself, but the ensuing attempts at identifying it provoke laughter that awakens the narrator. He initially identifies the artifact, a church spire, as a Mexican shrine, but the object he finally arrives at outside of the dream, a "Mexican church(!)," exists in the same mode as the invented Nahuatl word *Anaquivitzli* to which it refers within the dream: as a mosaic of word and image fragments drawn from several nonadjacent systems, which decomposes in the same moment that a key to its construction is applied. The likeliest provenance of this "joke" is the bilingual Spanish-Nahuatl dictionary composed by the missionary linguist Fray Alonso de Molina, *Vocabvlario en lengva castellana y mexicana*, which was first published in 1555; Scholem recalls that he saw Molina's dictionary on Benjamin's desk in Berlin sometime after 1916, when Benjamin apparently undertook the project to learn Nahuatl.[125] Going down the list of transliterated Nahuatl words beginning with *ana*, then *ane*, as a learner of the language might, however, one finds a possible but ultimately false equivalence to the word recomposed in the dream from the mispronunciations, displacements, and insistence of an explorer-settler of a new linguistic continent: the word Molina transcribes as *Anequiliztli* and defines as "lo mesmo es que aneconi" (the same as *aneconi*), which he in turn defines as "cosa no necessaria, ylicita y sin provecho" (thing of no necessity, of illicit nature, and without benefit).[126] An artifact itself—like Lehmann's compendia of Mesoamerican languages and practices, Molina's missionary-linguistic enterprise participates in the colonization and pacification of indigenous forms of intellection and expression—the *Vocabvlario*, if that is indeed the provenance of Benjamin's "joke," enacts the explorer's fantasy of having free disposal over all things by virtue of naming them, only to find these very things he deems to be readily transferable and convertible mirroring back the violence of his desire in not one but two names for that which has been removed from use, from any sort of means-end schema it might have been embedded in, and which is in this sense "illicit" and indeed sacred, like a shrine.[127] But were one to proceed in accordance with the dream's logic through the lexicon from its manifest content, and thus from *campana* (church bell; a metonym for church) and *campanario* (church tower) to *campanero* (bell ringer) and the Nahuatl equivalents Molina gives for each of them, none of which remotely resemble *Anaquivitzli*, one arrives at a surprising discovery: for *yglesia* (church) Molina has given the Nahuatl word *teocalli*, the actual term for an Aztec flat-top pyramid.[128]

The Spanish flat-top pyramid is an artifact unlike the others. Lehmann's "precious vessel" was a fabrication of historical continuity, hybrid, discontinuous, and attesting to some unspecified violence inasmuch as it arose from the imposition of a moral unanimity with cosmological underpinnings. "Aztec law" was a product of historical continuity fashioned in the image of European "natural legality" at the expense of the indigenous right to self-defense. A Spanish *teocalli*, in contrast, is an object excavated from a dream whose emergence is the result not of a promise, contract, or gift but of a struggle and a violent act of extraction. For the one who mistakes it for the "Mexican church (!)," that colonial-cosmological emblem par excellence, the joke is on him as much as it is on any excavator who expects to disinter an origin, only to discover a mimetic object constructed in the image of his own idea of freedom. But the Spanish *teocalli* is freely given and free to give back, in the same sense that a looted object or territory is free to be repatriated or reparations are freely undertaken. Given back to Lehmann, the Spanish *teocalli* is Benjamin's experiment with what it might mean to give back the excavated object: a reparation that lets the struggle surface instead of forcing it to settle.

5. Not Recognizing the Situation of Decision

Around 1922–23, Benjamin drew up two sets of notes pertaining to a project on what he called "objective mendacity," included as Notes 19 and 20 in this volume. In them, Benjamin proposes a "solution" to the problem of having to decide between personal will and basic norm as the source of law: "Objective mendacity [*Verlogenheit*] is: not recognizing the situation of decision" (93). This statement recalls the observation Benjamin makes in "Toward the Critique of Violence" that, originally, fraud was not punishable by law: lying can go on for as long as people want until it induces violence, whereupon law intervenes in respect to persons lying about goods for fear of the unleashing of more violence on the part of the defrauded party. In its original form, however, lying is unpunishable, indicating that there is a sphere in which agreement may be arrived at under no compulsion whatsoever, and so without violence. In the notes to "Objective Mendacity," Benjamin elaborates as follows: untruths may constitute a form of nonviolent convention. Conversely, "sincerity" (*Ehrlichkeit*) is associated with correctness, cognition, unforgiveness, and holding on to harms done. If the latter set of terms is associated with the kinds of determinative judgments that can unleash legal decisions and therefore legal violence, and if lying can go unpunished, then, Benjamin seems to suggest, "sincerity" is what law requires as a guarantee of its ongoing operation.

Some years later, Benjamin again recalls this notion in the *Trauerspiel* book when he refers to Kurt Latte's account of the sacred oath (*Eid*). The oath is what Latte says the judge must swear in order to invoke a higher order so as to guarantee the sincerity of his word as a means of convincing opponents to lay down arms—as though his word alone were objectively untenable, even if sincere. What this might imply, according to a related remark in "Objective Mendacity," is that "decision" itself has a "situation" in which it is embedded and over which it does not simply "decide." In turn, this "situation" of decision is one that has been "decided" over, namely, by the powers and authorities (*Gewalten*) that need to demonstrate they have overcome lying for their own legitimacy. For not only every judgment but also every action taken has to respond to a state of affairs that, for the judge or the one taking action, is "true"; but the "truth" of this state of affairs consists in the "intention toward truth," as Benjamin writes in the related set of "Notes toward a Work on Lying II." This "intention toward truth" holds things as property or obligations as real, for instance, but if it intends without interruption, it would constitute an unbearable restriction on activity, as there would then be no opportunity to switch ownership, exchange beyond barter, fulfill obligations to third parties—or forgive, restore, repel force with force (as in overthrowing a tyrant), or overturn an unviable situation (that is, revolution). In these sets of notes, Benjamin therefore also calls "objective mendacity" an "art of revocation": not in the subjective sense, but in the "objective" sense of the necessity for legal definition to be "continuously present, without any interruption" (96).

Prior to the "situation of decision," therefore, there is no sense in talking about legal propositions and concepts as being the creations of law-making functions—or law-positing violence. In the words of Adolf Reinach's "Über die apriorischen Grundlagen des bürgerlichen Rechts" (On a priori foundations of the civil law), one of the titles in Benjamin's bibliography for a more fully developed critique of violence:

> [T]he structures (*Gebilde*) which one has generally called specifically legal have a being of their own just as much as numbers, trees, or houses, [and] this being is independent of its being grasped by men.... It is not only false but ultimately meaningless to call legal entities and structures creations of the positive law, just as meaningless as it would be to call the founding of the German empire or some other historical event a creation of historical science."[129]

Reinach, whose work in a species of proto–speech act theory was also of great interest to Benjamin in other contexts, suggests the following. Before the law, there is no equality in the sense of equal might before right. Nor is there equality in the sense of proportionality. Rather, before the law is the limitless scope to not-be the one for whom law intends. A de-posing of law.

HERMANN COHEN, FROM *ETHICS OF PURE WILL*
Translator's Preface

With the publication of the first edition of *Kants Theorie der Erfahrung* (Kant's theory of experience) in 1871, Hermann Cohen initiated one of the major trends in the broad philosophical program associated with the phrase "Back to Kant!" The imperative implies that philosophy should steer away from both metaphysical speculation and natural-scientific reductionism.[1] The argument Cohen pursues in and beyond *Kant's Theory of Experience* is directed against both of these trends, namely, interpretations of Kant's "critical idealism" that seek to preserve a belief in the real (rather than methodological) existence of things-in-themselves lying beyond experience, on the one hand, and, on the other, interpretations of the first *Critique* that, responding to the growth of interest in psychology as a natural science, fail to recognize the insuperable difference between knowledge and sensation. Transformed into the "critique of knowledge" (*Erkenntniskritik*), philosophy thus distinguishes itself from both metaphysics and natural science, as it demonstrates the inherent rationality (or "logic") of knowledge-generative methodologies. This version of neo-Kantianism came to be identified with the University of Marburg, where Cohen successfully submitted his *Habilitation* thesis and thereby became a Privatdozent in 1873. With his appointment to full professor in 1876, he became the first Jewish chair-holding professor (*Ordinariat*) in philosophy in any German-speaking land at a time when it was very rare for (unbaptized) Jews to hold university positions at all. Alongside his readings and revisions of the Kantian corpus, he sought to elucidate the rationality of Jewish monotheism and to demonstrate, in turn, that socialism was an essential element of the messianic idea. In *Deutschtum und Judentum* (Germanism and Judaism; 1915–16) he argued that the monotheism of the Hebrew prophets and the humanism of Herder, Goethe, and Kant are intimately related to each other: Germanism and Judaism are at bottom informed by the same future-oriented idealism.[2] Beginning in 1902 with *Logik der reinen Erkenntnis* (Logic of pure knowledge; 2nd ed. 1914), proceeding through *Ethik des reinen Willens* (Ethics of pure will; 1904, 2nd ed. 1907), and culminating in *Ästhetik des reinen Gefühls* (Aesthetics of pure feeling; 1912),[3] Cohen produced a "system of philosophy" in accordance with the tripartite structure of Kant's *Critiques*. Cohen expected to complement his system with a fourth volume that would treat universal human culture as the genuine form of the transcendental unity of consciousness. But instead of producing a volume of "psychology" in the last years of his life, he wrote *Religion der Vernunft aus den Quellen des Judentums* (Religion of reason out of the sources of Judaism), which appeared in 1919, after Cohen's death on April 1, 1918.[4]

Ethics of Pure Will is the main work in which Cohen elaborates his moral philosophy.[5] A core idea animating this work is that ethics may be conceived as in some sense arising from "law" (*Recht*).[6] Thus, Cohen's *Ethics* combines moral philosophy with a philosophy of law, and this combination is a decisive feature of the analysis undertaken in the section titled "Self-Responsibility" (*Selbstverantwortung*) that we present here for the first time in English translation.

Cohen's conception of ethics as arising from law is founded in his approach to retrieving and making Kant's *Critiques* newly productive in a philosophical and scientific milieu different from the one in which they were originally produced. The "critical idealism" Cohen develops in all three volumes of his "system of philosophy" takes its starting point from the so-called *factum* of science. In the first volume, *Logic of Pure Knowledge*, the *factum* in question is that of mathematical-natural science, which provides the basis for the discovery of the a priori lawfulness that accounts for the unity, continuity, and objectivity of experience. Cohen postulates that a certain kind of experience, namely, a cognition that takes place according to specifiable principles, is present in any science deserving of the name. Taking this cognition as a *factum*, Cohen proceeds to inquire into the conditions of its validity, hence its lawfulness.

In the arena of philosophical ethics, Cohen takes legal science or jurisprudence (*Rechtswissenschaft*) as the "*factum* of science" for ethics. Law thus occupies a role analogous to that of mathematical physics in theoretical philosophy.⁷ *Ethics of Pure Will* undertakes numerous analyses of juridical *facta* for the purpose of elucidating certain ethical principles and their corresponding realization. These analyses are informed by a view of the history of political-juridical institutions that proceed along a trajectory of moral-political progress. Cohen's inquiry is thus geared toward identifying strands in contemporary legal-political life that will promote such progress, and accordingly, he identifies moral beliefs that he sees as detrimental to progress.

The following section from the *Ethics* is part of a long chapter laying out aspects of the "autonomy of self-consciousness." For Cohen, ethics, law, and politics are not grounded in an individual subject or moral agent but form, instead, a generative process of *Allheit*. He thus examines ethical-political experiences for how they generate such a totality, or "all-ness," which encompasses both self-consciousness and action. His model for the subject of ethics and politics is thus not a preconstituted individual psychophysical person or citizen but rather an essentially collective subject that is continually generated or produced. This subject is also open-ended in the sense of being oriented to, or generated along with, future ethico-political tasks. This model of subjectivity is distinguished from ideas of societies as aggregates or pluralities made up of preconstituted and already individuated psychophysical subjects.

There are important points of contact between Cohen's *Ethics* and the philosophy of religion he derives from Jewish sources, the most famous and complete version of which can be found in *Religion of Reason*, particularly in its chapter titled "Atonement" ("Die Versöhnung").⁸ In the following section from the *Ethics* on "Self-Responsibility," Cohen broaches a topic that he elaborates more fully in *Religion*: the classification of sin as שגגה (*shegagah*), that is, unwitting or inadvertent sin. The idea that wrongdoing goes along with ignorance is, for Cohen, a discovery common to (Jewish) religion and Socratic ethics.⁹ The notion that there is to be atonement before God generates, on the one hand, the ethical notion of responsibility and, on the other, the modern understanding of criminal law, whose purview is the crime for which one is to be convicted or acquitted—and not, as in what Cohen calls "myth," personal guilt and expiation.

— *Dana Hollander*

Hermann Cohen is the only contemporary author cited in "Toward the Critique of Violence" in whom Benjamin had more than a passing interest—and the only one whom he quotes elsewhere in his published writings.[10] At the same time, his interest is characterized by varying degrees of ambivalence, generated at least in part by the sheer magnitude of Cohen's legacy. In June 1917, Benjamin told Scholem that he must postpone a reckoning with Kant and Cohen despite the urgency of the task, for an adequate study of their work will require "great expanses of time" (GB 1:362; C 88). Later in the year, however, he probably wrote "On the Program of the Coming Philosophy," which adopts certain elements of Cohen's *Logic of Pure Knowledge* while also criticizing the Marburg School for an insufficiently radical revision of Kant's concept of experience. In schematic terms, Benjamin sees in the "coming philosophy" a completion of Cohen's "annihilation" (*Vernichtung*) of the metaphysical schema, according to which a cognizing subject acquires knowledge by experiencing a recognizable object; at the same time, however, Benjamin takes issue with the governing rationale for Cohen's innovation, namely, its attempt to eliminate metaphysics from philosophy altogether. Metaphysics, for Benjamin, manifests itself after the critique of knowledge annihilates subject-object schemata with such radicality that a "pure systematic continuum of experience" can emerge. This continuum becomes the locus of metaphysics, which takes the form of "doctrine" (*Lehre*) (rather than "science"), from which the "authentic meaning of experience" (2:164; SW 1:105) is to be discovered.

In the spring of 1918, Benjamin tells Scholem that a "further altercation [*Auseinandersetzung*] with Kant and Cohen must be postponed" (GB 1:441; C 119). Soon after Scholem arrives in Bern in the summer of 1918, the two of them convene a reading group around *Kant's Theory of Experience*; but after several meetings, they disband in disappointment, with Benjamin complaining about Cohen's "transcendental confusion."[11] Nevertheless, Benjamin continued to adopt and critique Cohen's thought. Of particular importance in this regard is Benjamin's use of such terms as "intensive" and "intensity," which derive from Kant's analysis of the "Anticipations of Perception" in the first *Critique*, on the one hand, and Cohen's exposition of the infinitesimal method, on the other.[12] The culmination of the "altercation with Kant and Cohen" occurs in a paragraph of the "Erkenntniskritische Vorrede" (Epistemo-critical preface), where Benjamin argues that "the category of origin is not ... as Cohen contends [in his *Logic of Pure Knowledge*], a purely logical [category] but is, rather, historical" (1:226; O 25). Just as the title of Benjamin's preface adopts a cardinal term in Cohen's revision of Kantian thought, so the title of the work as a whole contains an abbreviated criticism of this revision, which, so he argues, fails to see that origin is a "thoroughly historical category" (1:226; O 24).

In preparing for the preface to his translations of Baudelaire's *Tableaux parisiens*, Benjamin "pored over" Cohen's *Aesthetics of Pure Feeling*, but this effort was "futile" (GB 2:146; C 177).[13] In other contexts, though, Benjamin found Cohen's *Aesthetics* of considerable value. This is especially so in conjunction with his essay on Goethe's *Elective Affinities*, where he favorably contrasts Cohen's treatment of the figures in the novel with several other commentators (1:134; SW 1:304). And in the final pages of his essay Benjamin says of Cohen that his view of Goethe may surpass that of all other interpreters, for he sees that tears alone grant the novel its "unities" (1:191; SW 1:348).[14] In 1937, however, as Benjamin reflects back on Cohen's attempt to complete his revision of Kantian thought with an aesthetics that is itself generated through the "pure feeling" of *humanitas*, he summarily identifies its decisive fault, namely, a "complicity with positivism" that expresses itself in its lack of "exact historical fantasy" and in the corresponding "rigidity" with which it "adhered to the strategic positions of the eighteenth century" (3:565).

This blunt public assessment from the late 1930s contrasts with the subtlety with which Benjamin privately mocks *Religion of Reason* in a letter he wrote to Scholem on the occasion of the latter's twenty-third birthday in 1920. Two books, Benjamin writes, are tempting him away from the pressure exerted by his own studies: Samuel Krauss's *Das Leben Jesu nach jüdischen Quellen* (The life of Jesus according to Jewish sources) and Cohen's *Religion of Reason Out of the Sources of Judaism*. The reason for this pairing lies in the similarity of their subtitles: with the help of Jewish sources, Krauss discovers Jesus, Cohen religion. Benjamin adds that Cohen's book is "clearly highly remarkable" (GB 2:107); he makes no remark, though, about what he finds remarkable—nor does he say whether he succumbed to the temptation to pause in the pursuit of his own work and actually read it. Much of Krauss's critical edition of the *Toledot Yeshu* was in any case, for him, a closed book, as Scholem would have known, for it is largely composed of passages in Hebrew and Aramaic.[15]

The supreme moment of Benjamin's ambivalence with respect to Cohen's work comes, however, as he prepares the final version of "Toward the Critique of Violence." After indicating to Scholem that he has produced a fair copy of the essay, he adds the following: "In writing the essay I had to deal with the *Ethics of Pure Will* a little bit. What I read there quite [*recht*] saddened me. Clearly with Cohen, the intimation of truth was so strong that he had to make the most unbelievable leaps in order for him to turn his back on it" (*GB* 2:130; *C* 173). In light of this memorable image of turning away from the truth, which may allude to a fabled event in Moses' life, the basic schema of Benjamin's essay can be seen as its precise reversal: justice does not emerge from law, as Cohen argues in his *Ethics*; rather, justice and law are mutually repugnant. It is even possible that the intensity of Benjamin's exposition of this repugnance in 1921 derives in part from the certainty with which he rejects Cohen's attempt to view the "science" of law as a *factum* that generates moral philosophy as a whole.

— *Peter Fenves*

HERMANN COHEN, FROM *ETHICS OF PURE WILL*

Self-Responsibility

[357] Just now we stated that in order to ensure that the ethical concept of self-determination can be applicable in reality, one need only acknowledge the psychological *factum* of intention [*Vorsatz*].[1] But here we might nevertheless still suspect a gap. While we did locate the starting point [*Ansatz*] of action in intention, this starting point can be impeded, so that the action is not carried out. But this impediment must lie outside the dispositions of the agent himself. If the [358] impediment comes about through the agent himself, then the intention is finished; it ceases to represent the concept of intention. In which of the moments that, in their combined effect, make up the pure will has the relapse or renunciation taken place?

What is decisive here is not some externally measurable time span. Rather, these decisions, that is, intentions, can arise or change in a flash. It is not a question of whether the deliberation that flowed into the intention took a long time, or of how long it took—given that such a duration cannot be measured. We also cannot, for example, say that the longer the deliberation would be, the more fully developed it will be. Such a deliberation might, instead, have lodged and entrenched itself in such a way as to hamper the agility of thought and judgment, while an intention that arose rapidly might have emerged from a free and bright elucidation of the circumstances to be weighed. Thus, when a change in intention has occurred, it could certainly be attributed to the changed causal judgment. Our question would thus be answered—and in such a way that the concept of intention would not be affected by this individual case.

What becomes of the concept of self-determination, however, if the change had been produced by the *share of affect* in the intention? An aftereffect of the view that will and intellect are identical is that the moment of affect is found to be less important than that of causal cognition. In other words, where there is a correct causal cognition, one does not seriously doubt that affect also played a role. The clear cognition of a causal link is for good reason understood to be the sure symptom of mental concentration and mastery of one's whole consciousness, so that the possibility of a quasi-motor paralysis becomes completely discounted.

Significant experiences, however, serve to qualify such a view, which once again shatters the applicability of self-determination. Perhaps one ought to deemphasize the problem of [359] so-called *weakness of will*; for the question is whether in such a case causal cognition can in fact achieve the acuity and determinacy that was provided by the first prerequisite. In that case, what would be lacking here is not only affect but rather causal thinking, that is, the energy of causal thinking. In this view, we may perhaps perceive the aftereffect of the other thesis, which sublates the intellect into the primordial foundation [*Urgrund*] of the will, making it into an appendix of the will. Furthermore, this case can be staved off by means of the opposite case, that of an explosion of affect—in the manner of *reflexive movement*—except that, in the first case, the role of intelligence was not suspended [*ausgeschaltet*]. Instead, causal thinking was carried out with such energy that, having become all-powerful, it produces the movement. Was it really affect that was so forceful here, or was it not causal thinking instead? Here one need only recall the tale of the rider in the wood, who, by vividly imagining the danger, falls prey to it.

From all these considerations, we wish to conclude that *the question about the share of affect* in intention poses no significant difficulty for the application of self-determination. The weakness of affect stands opposed to its impulsivity, and they perhaps even stand side by side. Normally, causal thinking and affect combine in such proportions as to bring about the intention.

But what about the *normality of causal thinking*, as the first and fundamental prerequisite of moral action and of self-determination? Is this prerequisite, in fact, to be assumed as a psychological *factum*? What if the precision or correctness of this causal cognition were in doubt, if causal cognition were, instead, the product of a mechanical compulsion, exerted from outside and from inside, so that what is prompted and maintained is only the appearance or illusion that action is self-determined? This is the grave and great question that appears to give *the possibility of ethics* over to skepticism.

Is it only ethics, however, that [360] is imperiled by way of this question? Is *logic* not at the same time also affected by it? If the precision, thoroughness, and clarity of causal thinking is merely an illusion of the self's own activity [*selbsteigene Tätigkeit*]; if it is, in fact, only the work of a music box within ourselves, then the founding principles that are conceived by logic in order to secure its doctrinal-theoretical edifice would, indeed, be no more than subjective after-experiments, attempts to trace and copy the unknowable objective foundation based on its superstructure. What would be produced in the process would be no picture [*Abbild*] but only, and at best, a purposive sketch [*Zeichnung*]. Given that such sketches of founding principles—which would stem only from the theoretical edifice, and for which there was otherwise no instruction or guidance—it would be remarkable, and beyond this, the most authentic example of a miracle, if practical experimental experience were to adapt in each individual case to conform to those sketches, so that a complete agreement would be produced between this theory erected on such shifting sands and experience, or reality.

This is not the place to defend the legitimacy [*Recht*] and sense of logic; we simply note, in consequence of the above, the circumstance that, in accordance with the basic law of truth, wherever real ethics is called into question, logic is also drawn into skepticism. And from here we are led to the consequence *that theoretical skepticism will essentially be destroyed along with ethical skepticism*. If, however, we return to the question that led us to this discussion, we see that while the logical certainty of causal cognition cannot be subjected to doubt in principle, the question may, indeed, be asked regarding the *individual* case of intention—not only from the point of view of affect but with respect to causal thinking. With what certainty is it possible to know that causal thinking was accomplished [*vollzogen*] in the normal way, so as to enable self-determination? *What ethical principle authorizes* this assumption and prerequisite, considering that it is, after all, indisputable that [361] the demonstrable necessity of this assumption entails, in each individual case, irresolvable difficulties? What necessity can there be for ethics, in spite of these difficulties, to maintain the assumption and to make an exception only for the individual case? With this question we face, in our pursuit of the question of freedom and autonomy, a step toward which we must develop that question further.

The question that we asked about what we can briefly term the freedom of causal thinking interests us at this point in our development of the ethical problem principally in the positive sense: What does this freedom of causal thinking mean for self-determination, that is, for the determination and continual new generation of moral self-consciousness? This question must, of course, also be directed negatively at the nongeneration of the moral self, and thus at the generation of evil. But the question must take as its point of departure the emergence of the good; only by starting in this way is it possible to treat the other question, which takes its guidance from the first question. Instead, however, it is common to be primarily interested in the *origin of evil*. This is why the question concerning the freedom of causal thinking is understood, above all and primarily, as the question of voluntary transgression of the moral law. In this way, the problem of freedom in self-determination becomes the question concerning, and even the interest in, the generation of evil. Self-determination is supposed to satisfy the interest in the self-generation of evil [*Selbsterzeugung des Bösen*].

That is the wrong starting point for ethics. Ethics must, instead, at every new stage in the development of its fundamental concepts, always begin from the positive problem. That is its logic: it must search for the law and must not begin from the exceptions. Science [*Wissenschaft*] is always and in all problems directed toward the law, and the exceptions only incite it all the more urgently to implement the law. Wherever interest attaches itself primarily to the origin of evil, we must suppose that it is not ethics that is the guiding principle and not science in general. What then, however?

[362] One will suppose that it is *religion*, then, that remains. This, however, is an error that can be cleared away, much to the advantage of religion. For religion, too, insofar as it is concerned with digging out its moral primordial force [*sittliche Urkraft*] and purifying it of false admixtures, turns its gaze away from the origin of evil and directs it, instead, to the origin of the good. It is not actually religion that here opposes ethics. Rather, it is naked mythology [*nackte Mythologie*] that we must recognize in this interest [*Interesse*].

It would be merely an aftereffect of this mistaken idea whose trail we are tracing here if one were to assume that *myth* is uninterested in, and pays no attention to, the appearance and idea of the good—or even that the good is not present to its consciousness. This is not at all the case. But the arousals of mythic consciousness are too elemental to be able to fade out in contemplative deliberations; they are always convulsions [Erschütterungen]. This is why it is the more stirring power of evil that arouses the original interest. The good is considered natural; it yields itself from the coincidences and conjunctures that are already established and ordered. Evil is an incursion [Einbruch] into those orders, in which, after all, the indestructible, the law, or nature otherwise is presented as without any exceptions [ausnahmslos]. And the miracle is all the greater in that evil is presented not only as a transgression of these orders; rather, it is these orders themselves that seem to occasion and bring about this transgression, this defection [dieses Heraustreten, diesen Abfall]. This insight, which becomes inevitable, enhances the astonishment at these exceptions with respect to what has come before [dem Herkommen], and they thereby become a living miracle.

Myth, however, cannot stop at seeing the cause that effects the defection as inherent in what has come before and in the universal order itself. Myth does not stop at thinking about circumstances and things; rather, myth personifies things and circumstances. The cause everywhere becomes for myth the arche-person [Urperson]; and for it, it is only out of the arche-person that there emerges the person. [363] Even where it might appear that it is only circumstances and situations that are being identified as the ground of evil—these things and circumstances are nonetheless thought as persons. Thus, myth proceeds from out of the concept of fate [Schicksal]. Disaster [Das Verhängnis] (εἱμαρμένη) is the supreme concept, the supreme god. It stands above the father of gods, Zeus.

What, however, is the basic thought in the concept of fate? One might say that it is the thought of domination [Herrschaft], of supreme domination that can be resisted by no one and nothing. But with that one would only be naming a hierarchy when, in fact, the supreme concept is the central one. Therein lies the center of gravity of the entire mythological system. It is, rather, always in the defection from fate that fate accomplishes itself and shows itself.

The fundamental concept that forms the authentic core of fate is the concept of *guilt*. Atē spans a generation, a privileged lineage [Geschlecht],[2] in which human fate illustrates itself. The domination exercised by fate consists in subordinating to itself the individuals in this lineage. Are the individuals thereby deprived of self [entselbstet]? Myth does not raise this question. Myth does not yet see any difference between the individual and its lineage, just as Zeus does not cease to be an individual god by virtue of being subordinated to fate [*Fatum*]. *Evil is guilt. And guilt is disaster.* Myth takes no offense at this conjunction of concepts. Woe to you if you are a descendant. "Woe" here signifies not something like pity, but verdict.

The connection of blood is felt to be nature and to be compelled by nature [*Naturzwang*]. The *soul* of the departed is, at first, a haunting ghost that will bring harm. It is for this reason that in the soul there lives on the connection between the dead and the living. Despite this, however, it is no less the son's own deed that awakens in him the soul of the father. *This natural connection is what* [364] *is presented by the guilt of fate.* There is no contradiction and no difference between the guilt of the descendant and that of the ancestor. The guilt of the descendant is at the same time the guilt of the ancestor. And the guilt of the ancestor is nonetheless also the guilt of the descendant. There is unity among them in guilt, because guilt is also assumed [*angenommen*] in their natural essence. *This unity accomplishes* [*vollzieht*] *precisely fate*,[3] which cannot be thought except in conjunction with lineage.

It is thus that the concepts of fate, guilt, and lineage are connected. Here the *individual* is not a particular concept; it is contained and caught up in its lineage, and thus in its fate, and thus in its guilt. Hence guilt constitutes the basic motif in the concept of fate, and thus also in the concept of lineage. *The lineage, however, represents* [*darstellt*] *the human being. Thus, the concept of guilt in myth becomes the basic motif of the human being.*

For this reason, the history of moral culture can be traced by looking at the development of the concept of guilt. Progress branches off from myth always in two directions: that of *religion* and that of *poetry* [*Poesie*]. It is difficult to determine which branch is the earlier, decisive one. We noticed repeatedly that religion and art become combined very early on, and that each enters this combination not only for its own purposes but for the sake of the problem of community that freedom itself poses. Freedom must become a problem in both poetry and religion, because it is in both poetry and religion that the individual emerges and detaches itself from its lineage. Freedom is an idea that shows up in poetry and religion but that does not come to fruition in either.

It is with freedom that theoretical culture begins, and it is to theoretical culture that the concept of freedom belongs. It is only science—ethics—that rends the veil covering the *individual*. In myth, it is the power of the secret, of the mystery, that joins together fate and guilt in the lineage. Freedom elucidates this secret by [365] bringing to light the individual. Now guilt and fate become separated from lineage. *The individual's own guilt becomes his own fate*, for the individual is the author of his deeds. Myth knows of no such author.

The separation of the individual from the lineage takes place in *tragedy* only in the direction of the problem; after all, it is still fused with myth. Nevertheless, Atē will not remain the sole sovereign. When suffering is humanized as the suffering of a hero, guilt too becomes subject to psychological motivation and thereby becomes unmistakably individualized. Now fate can no longer be the sole focal point that it originally was in drama. The fate of the lineage must become linked to the guilt of the individual. And guilt no longer retains the appearance of the *Erinys*, which represents the morality of lineage. Darkness is illuminated; the solution emerges in the direction of self-consciousness, in *catharsis*.[4]

This purification and liberation could not arise in the spectator if it did not originally present itself in the hero. His death, his earthly life to the end, accomplishes his redemption, his liberation from the guilt that he took upon himself: it was in taking on this guilt that he, too, arose. *Thus, the force of virtue is added to the guilt*. Guilt remains, but it falls back onto fate; and only insofar as guilt is necessary as a foil for human virtue, as a component of virtue, and for the force of the hero does it also remain as a shadow in the lustre of virtue. This time, however, it is a shadow over against the light of the individual—no longer in the darkness of lineage and of fate.

We saw in *Ezekiel* how the individual emerged in *religion*.[5] Now a basic concept is wrenched from *Mosaism*, detaching it also from its connection with myth. This concept not only accords with Socratic ethics, it also founds the *connection between ethics and law: sin without knowledge (shegagah)*. [366] All sin, insofar as it can be expiated [*gesühnt*] by means of sacrifice, is declared to be sin without foreknowledge. By contrast, whatever cannot be expiated by sacrifice cannot be considered a sin. Instead, it falls to the criminal judge; it is a crime.

Thus, sin is recognized and declared to be a human weakness.

We see that *religion treads the reverse path from that of poetry*. Tragedy generates the individual in the hero, in the demigod; and it generates and transfigures [*verklärt*] his guilt through his *heroic suffering*. Religion, by contrast, generates the individual in the human soul and in its sin. But it brings about redemption in the knowledge of human weakness. *Weakness becomes the attribute of human morality.*

Thus, the religious solution to the question is also only an ideal solution: it hands the actual treatment of the question over to *law*. What ought to happen with the criminal? How is the crime to be judged, from the point of view of self-consciousness and self-determination? Self-determination unmistakably mediates, after all, the connection between ethics and law. Does the ultimate conclusion of wisdom lie, for law, in recognizing only monomania and psychosis in *crime*, and thereby giving up altogether on a real verdict?

The only correct way to begin with this question is: fundamentally and in every sense to ward off and exclude the question of guilt. It is a mistaken—ethically mistaken—idea that the question of guilt is to be postponed to the *future of law*. Rather, law must be for all future time disconnected from the question of guilt, and this because it is disconnected from the question of guilt in principle. Guilt is a matter only for the divine judge. It is a problem of myth, tragedy, and religion. Law knows guilt only as *dolus* or *culpa*.[6] Both rest on *imputation* [*Zurechnung*], which, in turn, rests on self-determination and is rooted in it.

[367] Imputation is responsibility. It is self-imputation, and thus self-responsibility. Above all, one must now keep in view that self-responsibility, which imputes an action to the self, rests on self-determination, on the determination that generates the self. A different view of guilt returns to the old *metaphysics*, which in its turn returns to mythology. With respect to this decisive point, it was necessary for us to point out that the thing-in-itself of the intelligible character has not yet detached itself precisely and clearly enough from that metaphysics of rational psychology.

And when even *Schopenhauer* excludes the intellect from the intelligible character, he ceases to offer any real insight, let alone satisfaction; for the question regarding freedom points, as we have seen, to self-determination.[7] Self-determination, however, consists mainly in the determination of action on the basis of the determinateness of causal thinking, and thus of the intellect.

Thus, imputation, or self-responsibility, is connected precisely with self-determination. However fluid might be the distinction between *dolus* and *culpa*, it is nevertheless *dolus* that constitutes the fundamental question. The *dolus* is the intention, the determination of the self. Thus, the question steps out of the obscurity of the will and thereby also out of the mystery of guilt. Self-determination accomplishes not only its first step but the entire extent of its path in the activity of causal thinking. If imputation, as self-responsibility, rests on self-determination, then causal thinking is its most important prerequisite and therefore its surest criterion. The most serious interest in the question of guilt can now be related to a theoretical question—but to a preliminary question, namely, the question concerning the accomplishment of causal thinking.

This thought is attenuated in a way that is not unproblematic when *von Liszt* simply equates *intention* with the notion of *causality*.[8] As we have seen, intention also contains the starting point that consists in the cooperation of an affective element. For this reason, *intention* and *decision may not be distinguished*, not even psychologically in reference to deliberation. When it comes to self-responsibility, what is decisive is self-determination, and the latter rests—and is active primarily in—causal thinking, but by no means only in causal thinking. The affective element may not be suspended [*ausgeschaltet*]. Otherwise, the will will be sublated into the intellect. In that case, however, the question of law would become flattened out, and the question of guilt would be merely circumvented, in that it would appear leveled into the Socratic question of knowledge.

It would now turn out as if the criminal judge had only to establish whether the action had been performed on the basis of a normal causal thinking. And the normalcy of this thinking would at the same time decide the guilt borne by the author of the action. If the judge could himself be satisfied with such a solution to the big question, however; if a way out were thereby to be found for law, the question would still remain as to whether the criminal would have thereby been well served. And since we do not think law apart from its connection to ethics, this question would go back to law.

If the difference between ethics and logic is sublated, this can serve law no less than it can ethics. In essence, however, this is what it amounts to whenever intention is restricted to causal thinking. For with that, action is equated with thought. That the affective element makes the difference—this is overlooked. The ethical meaning of affect for the concept of pure will is not grasped, because one sees causal thinking as being the sole criterion that can guide the judge. No other way out is thought to exist for evading the question of guilt. With this, however, one abandons self-responsibility on the part of the criminal. *With this, the crime becomes a mistake of thinking.*

We assert the thesis that imputation must in principle be separated from the question of guilt for the judge; but by no means for the [369] criminal himself or, in him, for the moral human being. He would give up this character.[9] He would become a thinking machine, or in any case a thought-organism, or at best a thinking unity, but he would forfeit self-consciousness and would have no command of it, for self-consciousness is a moral concept of value. If, therefore, the moral individual is in need of the concept of guilt, then the share of affect, for which we allow latitude in intention, is a reference to this requirement of the legal subject [*Rechtssubjekt*] insofar as it is a moral individual. It is again, however, a question whether the concept of guilt when it is transferred from the judge to the criminal proves itself to be a more just judge in the latter than it does in the former.

The question arises already with *culpa*, [that is] negligence [*Fahrlässigkeit*]. It is carelessness, whereas circumspection is a prerequisite. Is this prerequisite correct and just? May one presume this theoretical capacity and sureness of circumspection as an unfailing prerequisite? And what distinguishes negligence from distraction [*Zerstreutheit*] or lack of concentration if, indeed, it is not to be leveled into a mistake of thinking? Thus, *culpa* comes to merge with *dolus*—with the difference that in *dolus* direct, positive intention becomes effective.

If, however, intention becomes effective only in the energy of causal thinking, the difference between *dolus* and *culpa* would dissolve into being a difference of degree; whereas in fact the concept of *dolus*, after all, rests on the circumstance that the *actual starting point of the action*, which surely cannot reside only in thinking, is attributed to the human being. Is that mythology? Is that a vestige of the old metaphysics? Or is it, rather, ethics? *This is and remains the great question of criminal jurisprudence.* And the inner connection that exists between ethics and law here becomes evident and penetrating. For this fundamental question of law is the universal question of the human being, the question of human culture. Culture ceases to be a human culture when it is relieved of asking the question whether human beings are the authors of their actions.

[370] We have seen that this question is not, however, in the purview of law; it may not even be postponed to the future of law. How, then, are we to understand that the question of guilt nevertheless should be retained as the fundamental question of human culture? Should this question perhaps be delegated to poetry, since, after all, myth has died off, and religion can apparently only rejuvenate itself in myth if it insists on original sin? To what direction of culture does the task belong of bringing this fundamental question of human culture to clarity and to a solution?

Here we recognize, along with its connection with law, the distinctiveness [Eigenart] of ethics, its own formulation and treatment of the question of moral self-consciousness. And here we also must recognize the *progress* that *self-responsibility represents beyond self-determination*. Even more emphatically than in self-determination and self-legislation, in self-responsibility the self emerges as the actual problem that all questions revolve around. Without self-responsibility, self-determination can also not arrive at certainty or clarity. Without self-responsibility, self-legislation in fact still remains bounded. When thinking self-legislation, I must already think self-responsibility along with it. By positing, through self-legislation, the self as the actual goal, I authorize the self to answer all questions that life poses to the human being, in which life calls the self into question. *This answering of all questions of fate from the perspective of the self signifies self-responsibility.* Self-responsibility makes the question of fate into the question of guilt, and it takes the question of guilt upon itself.

The self burdens itself with the consciousness of guilt because it recognizes that it would otherwise have to give itself up. It can no longer reach for the remedy of interpreting its transgression as an *accident* and on the basis of this interpretation free itself from this guilty conscience by means of a sacrifice. It also cannot be considered a moral [371] purification if I attain my *redemption* from guilt by means of faith in a *God who has sacrificed himself for my sin*. I can only seek and wish to find my salvation in the judgment of moral cognition. And I cannot be relieved of this judgment of moral cognition by any remedy of heaven or of hell. Otherwise, I would lose my center and my moral weight. *The judge may have to suspend judgment—namely, moral judgment—about me, but I may not do so.* For what is at issue is I myself, my self. Not even a judge's acquittal settles the matter of responsibility to oneself.

Nor, however, can the psychological view of the pathological changes to which the consciousness of thinking, as of the will, is in principle exposed influence the state of affairs that obtains for *the self-consciousness of the possibly ill criminal*. Insofar as he acknowledges himself before himself to be ill and renounces to himself the authorship of his actions, he thereby departs from the problem of self-responsibility and of moral self-consciousness. If, however, the criminal were to take personal advantage of the judgment of the medical expert about him, while for his part having no doubts about his health, he would thereby face the alternative of either giving up his self or instead permitting a difference [*Differenz*] between the juridical judgment and the moral judgment about himself. The forum for the question of guilt must always remain the self.

The question becomes all the clearer when confronting the general doubt about freedom, which recent times have popularized in the problem of *heredity*. In what way the judge must attend to these experiences and insights and exactly how he is in a position to be able to attend to them is something we will consider soon. Here, however, we are dealing with the criminal himself: Should he, based on such statistical conclusions drawn from medical histories, in case symptoms of the same or similar sort have perhaps been found in his own case, [372] with philosophical calm quit his moral self-consciousness? Does theoretical truthfulness really demand this moral suicide from him? It is indisputable that this must in fact be forbidden. For the statistical average entails no theoretical insight about the individual. The individual cannot be worked out into a fraction of a probability. Consequently, it could only be an interest of probability, and not of ethical necessity, that would entail such a self-destruction. But if guilt were to become an illusion with respect to the one individual, it would strictly speaking also have to become so with respect to every other individual. For who is immune to doubt about whether he is not ill, even if the doctor is not at all, or not yet, able to recognize this?

And if guilt becomes an illusion, then it will be no less so for *virtue*, for one who is ill can certainly afford to get up the force required for the frippery of virtue, just as he can also, in games of skill and wit, keep up with a given normal person. Virtue would also be subjected to these doubts, just as guilt would be if it, too, were subject to the verdict of the judge. Positive morality, however, is certainly founded in self-legislation; *thus one must also leave unassailed negative moral judgment, guilt as self-knowledge. It is merely self-knowledge,* self-responsibility. The judge, by contrast, must cognize neither guilt nor virtue; he must not make judgments about either. Both guilt and virtue escape his knowledge in the same manner. He not only oversteps his authority, and not only confuses his problem by way of this outlying interest, but by doing so he moves the border that has been marked out for the innermost property [*Eigentum*] of the self.

—*Trans. Dana Hollander*

KURT HILLER, "ANTI-CAIN: A POSTSCRIPT TO RUDOLF LEONHARD'S 'OUR FINAL BATTLE AGAINST WEAPONS'"

Translator's Preface

Having dispatched the Hohenzollern monarchy and Kaiser Wilhelm II practically overnight in November 1918, the German revolutionaries splintered into camps supporting either social democracy or a government of soviet-style councils. Many of them met with the brutality of counterrevolutionary forces including the paramilitary *Freikorps*, with much of the bloodshed attributable to the successive governments in Berlin and elsewhere that were proving short-lived and largely ineffective. Hiller's essay "Anti-Cain" analyzes many such events in these turbulent months, including the infamous Spartacus uprising of January 1919, a series of strikes and mass demonstrations in Berlin that resulted in armed conflict among the centrists in Friedrich Ebert's Sozialdemokratische Partei Deutschlands (Social Democratic Party of Germany; SPD), the left-wing Unabhängige Sozialdemokratische Partei Deutschlands (Independent Social Democratic Party of Germany; USPD), and Germany's new Kommunistische Partei Deutschlands (Communist Party of Germany; KPD), previously known as the Spartacus League.

Hiller spent the revolutionary period arguing for neither soviet councils nor social democracy but instead for a *Logokratie* (logocracy), a hegemony of intellectual elites in the tradition of Plato's philosopher-kings. Born in Berlin in 1885 to an assimilated German-Jewish family, Hiller had studied law with Franz von Liszt and philosophy with Georg Simmel, arguing in his dissertation for the right to self-determination and thus for the decriminalization of abortion and homosexuality.[1] He fought for gay rights with Magnus

Hirschfeld and others in the Scientific-Humanitarian Committee and the Institute for Sexual Science. He was also among the founders of literary expressionism, active in its Berlin cabarets and a frequent contributor to its journals and anthologies.

In 1914, the advent of World War One pushed Hiller away from expressionism and instead to what he called Activism, which considered art a political tool and called upon intellectuals to engage directly in political affairs. The Activist organ was Hiller's yearbook *Das Ziel* (The goal), which first appeared in 1916 and was quickly banned by the government because of its "revolutionary, antireligious, antimilitarist, feminist-pacifist and homosexual articles."[2] "Anti-Cain" appeared in the first half of the third volume of *Das Ziel* in 1919. Hiller seems to have finished the essay in April of that year. He called it a "postscript" to the two-page article that directly preceded it in the volume, "Endkampf der Waffengegner" (Our final battle against weapons) by Rudolf Leonhard, a writer and revolutionary who had just left the USPD for the KPD. Like "Anti-Cain," Leonhard's contribution argued that no one involved in the current political struggle should resort to armed force, and that complete disarmament was the best means of defense and path to peace. Along with many left-wing intellectuals of their generation, Leonhard and Hiller had been converted by the horrors of the war to pacifism, which became one of the key themes of *Das Ziel*. Hiller would go on to become an important voice in the Deutsche Friedensgesellschaft (German Peace Society).[3]

Hiller's pacifism was inseparable from his conception of logocracy. In the second volume of *Das Ziel* he wrote: "We must work so that the mindset that upholds the miracle of life becomes action; we must bring this mindset to power; we must bring intellect [*Geist*] to power."[4] The closest he ever came to realizing this goal was during the short-lived revolutionary council movement, when he led the *Rat geistiger Arbeiter* (Council of Intellectual Workers) that took its place alongside the workers' and soldiers' councils in the Berlin Reichstag. Their program included many of the agenda items Hiller argues for in "Anti-Cain," including the end of conscription and a prohibition on new military facilities. Plagued by political naïveté and the disillusionment of many members and supporters, the council ultimately disbanded shortly after its national congress in June of 1919.[5] Hiller continued to argue for pacifism, Activism, and logocracy, attempting to build a movement in which the proletariat and the intelligentsia would join forces in anticapitalist struggle.

Benjamin and Hiller first became aware of each other in Berlin's expressionist cabarets in the early 1910s. In June of 1911, Benjamin wrote to Herbert Blumenthal that he had read with interest Hiller's biting critique of the Swiss novelist Jakob Schaffner (*GB* 1:31–32), which defended Robert Musil and especially Heinrich Mann against Schaffner's anti-intellectualism.[6] In November of 1915, Benjamin wrote three letters to Hiller (probably the only ones he ever wrote to him), in response to Hiller's request for a list of Benjamin's most important writings to date (*GB* 1:284–88). The list was required for the appendix to the inaugural issue of *Das Ziel*, which included "Das Leben der Studenten" (The life of students), an essay based on two lectures Benjamin had given in Berlin and Weimar.[7] Of this Benjamin rather immediately expressed his regret, writing to Gershom Scholem that all the other contributions to the volume—with the exception of Franz Werfel's critique of Hiller's Activism—seemed to him less than meritorious (*GB* 1:314).[8] The relationship between Hiller and Benjamin collapsed, and they would always remain quite critical of each other's work. The year before "Toward the Critique of Violence" was finished, Benjamin conceived but likely never completed an essay rejecting Hiller's Activism and the council form it had taken; the title of the essay was to have been "Es gibt keine geistigen Arbeiter" (There are no intellectual workers); *GB* 2:76, 79.

"Toward the Critique of Violence" has little in common with "Anti-Cain," except perhaps their shared conviction that the Weimar governments have betrayed "the revolutionary forces to which they owe their existence" (49). Indeed, one of the problems Benjamin diagnoses in the Weimar parliaments (and in parliamentarism in general) is their failure to exercise the lawmaking violence they represent. Hiller's "Anti-Cain" had expressed some understanding for revolutionary "counterviolence" but could not ultimately justify it. Its criticism of the Weimar government under President Ebert and Defense Minister Gustav Noske focused primarily on their hypocrisy in punishing Spartacists and others on their left for the same kind of "terrorism" they themselves engaged in.

Hiller is a pervasive presence in Benjamin's essay, in ways not indicated by the brief quotation and footnote that come late in the text. The thoroughgoing critique of violence Benjamin wanted to carry out was necessitated at least in part, he thought, by the talk of "pacifists and activists" like Hiller about militarism and compulsory military service—talk that utterly failed to account for the "law-preserving" (45) function of legal violence. The faith Hiller expressed in "Anti-Cain" that "the League of Nations or the world community" would ensure international peace must have conveyed this naïveté to Benjamin, for whom every contract is based on the possibility of violence and every legal institution thrives on "consciousness of the latent presence of violence" (49) it contains.

And while Benjamin does not quote them, the final sentences of "Anti-Cain" are clearly in his sights as well: "Thou shalt not kill. Thou shalt not kill even for the sake of an idea. For no idea is more sublime than the living" (193). Hiller's essay advocated for deployment of the biblical commandment throughout German society as a means to peace; Benjamin responds by noting the permissibility of self-defense in Judaism and writes: "No judgment of the deed follows from the commandment. . . . [T]hose who base the condemnation of every violent killing of a human being by fellow human beings on the commandment are wrong" (58). Where Benjamin *does* quote Hiller directly, his concern is to reject the "dogma of the sanctity of life" (59) that motivates much of "Anti-Cain" and leads Hiller to read the biblical commandment as he does. The passage from Hiller reads: "If I do not brutalize, if I do not kill, then I will never establish the empire of justice, of eternal peace, of joy. This is the reasoning of the intellectual terrorist, of the noblest Bolshevik; this was the reasoning of the Spartacist leaders who were deliberately and treacherously slain. . . . We profess, however, that higher still than the happiness and justice of an existence—stands existence itself. We demand that no one be permitted to take the life of one brother in order to bring freedom to another" (186). Hiller condemned the violence of the Spartacists as well as the violence used by the government against them, denouncing even revolutionary force on the basis of the inviolable sanctity of "existence itself." Benjamin finds Hiller's thinking on this point "false and lowly" (59). Its naïve simplicity regarding the nature of existence leads Benjamin to introduce his now famous notion of "bare" or "mere life" (*das bloße Leben*), which is, contra Hiller, subordinate to justice. Moreover, in the "sanctity of life," Hiller had attributed to biblical antiquity what was in fact a modern Western dogma, and a nostalgic one at that (59).

In the years after "Anti-Cain" was written, Hiller would repeat one of its central arguments: that disarmament was a necessary condition for peace as well as for national and international security. In other ways, his thinking about peace and violence evolved significantly. During and immediately after the war, he said later, many had found only absolute pacifism to be an appropriately radical response. But by the time he founded the Gruppe revolutionärer Pazifisten (Revolutionary Pacifists Group) in 1926, Hiller was keen to distinguish between "violence" (*Gewalt*) and "violation" (*Vergewaltigung*), to stipulate that pacifism was not about protecting life per se but rather about protecting one's right and desire to live from the state as currently constituted. In the tradition of Ferdinand Lasalle, revolutionary pacifism held that because capitalism led inevitably to war, and because the dictatorship of the ruling class was unlikely to end without a fight, the path to peace could include revolutionary violence. Pacifism thus became, for Hiller, a doctrine of ends, without specification of a program through which means would be thereby justified: the end is a world whose economic interrelations are characterized as socialist. This may accord with Benjamin's essay, even if he does not himself identify the character of the postrevolutionary era. It is impossible to say whether the changes in Hiller's thinking over time were in any way influenced by Benjamin's writings (if so, he certainly would not have admitted it). But it is possible that Benjamin does echo in Hiller's insistence, in 1927 and very much in line with "Anti-Cain," that no one should be forced to join in class struggle (for example, via conscription into a Red army) who finds that cause less important than "naked life" (*das nackte Leben*).[9]

Those positions were advanced in *Der Sprung ins Helle* (The leap into light), a collection of Hiller's writings that appeared in 1932, which prompted Benjamin to publish a negative review. While expressing sympathy with some of Hiller's intentions (avoiding future wars, abolishing the death penalty, building a united front among leftists), he rejects Hiller's logocratic model as ahistorical and devoid of any real political meaning. Hiller's aim to politically empower private citizens of an intellectual "characterological type" seems to Benjamin not only quixotic but also potentially dangerous (see 3:350–52). Repeating some of these arguments two years later in a speech called "Der Autor als Produzent" (The author as producer), Benjamin counts Hiller among those left-wing intellectuals whose intentions were good but whose deeds were ultimately reactionary and counterrevolutionary (see 2:689–90; *SW* 2:772–73).

Hiller was arrested and sent to concentration camps soon after the Nazis came to power. He fled to Prague and London and founded a number of exile groups. He returned to Germany in 1955 and attempted, unsuccessfully, to reestablish the Scientific-Humanitarian Committee. In 1956 he founded

Hamburg's New Socialist League, which engaged in antiwar activism. In exile and afterwards he remained extremely critical of Benjamin, calling *his* work "counterrevolutionary" (and too jargon-laden). As he wrote to Theodor Adorno in 1965: "Walter Benjamin—yes, I included him in the first volume of *Das Ziel* in 1916, not because I 'recognized his genius' (I do not recognize it even today), but rather because I wanted to encourage a student whose orientation was at that time close to my own, he in his early twenties and I thirty years old, and so I made the effort to tolerate and overlook that which was banal and immaterial in an essay not devoid of talent. I recall that I found Benjamin's contribution to be the weakest in the volume. As soon as it appeared Benjamin defected from me and from us all. Suddenly he declared our (humanitarian) Activism to be flat and false; he preferred analytic contemplation, the attempt to understand rather than change the world; he was pivoting, I noticed, toward the Hegel-Husserl-Kassner line. The aphorisms and essays of his 'heyday,' which I read many years later, seemed to me of a certain standard but also deadly boring, completely superfluous, truly spokes put in the wheel of the spirit [*Geist*] rolling toward humanistic attainment" (quoted in 2:916–17).

There were many spokes in the wheel of Hiller's logocratic Activism. Its pacifism was impeded significantly by a series of internecine struggles: between Germany's organizational and revolutionary pacifists over allegiance to French versus Russian political models; between splinter groups of revolutionary pacifists over the permissibility of violence for the purpose of raising class consciousness. Already anachronistic when Benjamin quoted it two years later, "Anti-Cain" captures a moment before these emerging struggles devolved into irrecoverability—a moment of radical pacifism and rousing optimism in the immediate aftermath of the most destructive war humans had yet experienced.

— *Lisa Marie Anderson*

KURT HILLER, "ANTI-CAIN: A POSTSCRIPT TO RUDOLF LEONHARD'S 'OUR FINAL BATTLE AGAINST WEAPONS'"

Here especially, the skeptical smirk of "common sense" comes cheap. Of course, man is not good, but rather must become good;[1] and against violence only violence can prevail [*gegen Gewalt kommt nur Gewalt auf*].[2] But now that a few millennia have proven not that Cain is ineradicable but rather that Cain's instrument has not eradicated him, perhaps the idea finally suggests itself to attempt to be Abel. An experiment? And these times are too serious, too challenging for experiments? Surely, however, an Abel experiment cannot fail any more unhappily than our age-old attempts with Cain's methods. Abel would have to believe in it, you say, like the Abel of biblical myth? Myth creates an earthly state of being, the eternal validity of which we dispute, we who believe in becoming, we who devote our energy to the realization of a world we have seen in the mind [*im Geiste*], a not-yet-world.[3] A phantom world? No, we *can* realize it, we can, difficult and complex though it may be—and if not us, then those who come after us. Without such assurance, anything that calls itself intellectual action would in fact be senseless and mere self-gratification, and I would rather till the fields. We *can* realize the good here, despite the bad people around us, and only in this way will they, who are always in the majority, be overcome—only then will their majority cease to be also a supremacy. But someone has to start. We must make a start.

We revolutionaries must make a start. Abhor Cain's instrument unconditionally. Stand to the left of Spartacus, perhaps, in terms of policy—but stand there without the instruments of death. Opposition to the instruments of death is itself a policy, one to the left of any policy that continues to work by killing, and thus to the left of the Spartacists. The radical pacifist—whom I can only conceive as an opponent of injustice and power politics in the economic sense, as well, that is, of capitalism—sits to the left of the Bolshevik in the parliament of humanity. The Bolshevik wants war: not a war of nation against nation but an international war of class against class—another bloody war with the same terrible weapons. In his methods, the Bolshevik is just the inverse of the old Russian-Prussian militarist. The friends of Lenin are not concerned with the abolition of violence, only with "the class content of violence," as it says in the tenth of their "Theses on Social Revolution." And Radek, their Ultra, portrayed their ideal at the Communist Party Congress in Berlin: the allied armies of the German and Russian proletariat in a victorious battle on the Rhine against Franco–Anglo-Saxon imperialism.[4] The only difference from Ludendorff: the ethos of the final goal.[5] In fact, all our experience seems to indicate that intellect [*Geist*] cannot prevail by its own means; that it cannot renounce means that are contrary to it without forfeiting the realization of its goals; that renouncing violence means betrayal to anti-intellect [*Widergeist*], which in the case of socialism means capitulation before capital. If I do not brutalize, if I do not kill, then I will never establish the empire of justice, of eternal peace, of joy. This is the reasoning of the intellectual terrorist, of the noblest Bolshevik; this was the reasoning of the Spartacist leaders who were deliberately and treacherously slain by military officers loyal to Ebert.[6] We profess, however, that higher still than the happiness and justice of an existence—stands existence itself [*Dasein an sich*]. We demand that no one be permitted to take the life of one brother in order to bring freedom to another. We endorse what René Schickele wrote in the December issue of his journal *Die weißen Blätter*: "I am a socialist, but if I were convinced that socialism could only be realized via Bolshevist methods, then I—and not only I—would forgo its realization."[7] Indeed: eternal injustice for all is preferable to the killing of a single individual! Let fanatics call this disposition weak, sentimental, unheroic, cowardly, bourgeois, reactionary, criminal, base, common... or, perhaps worst of all, "eudaemonic"—I will never relinquish it. The notion that hundreds of thousands should be deprived of the fleeting miracle of existence so that millions can fare better is monstrous and hardly enforceable. The morality of this notion is insane. We desire not to replace international war with class war but to replace war with struggle [*Kampf*]. What kind of struggle? Struggle by all available means that leave life inviolate. Whose struggle? The justified struggle of the poor against the rich, certainly—but primarily the struggle of the intellectual against half-intellect and un-intellect and anti-intellect.

We anti-terrorists must make a start. Abhor Cain's instrument unconditionally. We cannot simply hurl terror against terror. On December 6 in Berlin, the government watched as machine gun fire was peppered into a crowd of unarmed Spartacist demonstrators. On December 24 the government ordered that grenades be fired on the sailors in the palace (without just cause, as I attempted to show in an article that appeared in the *Freiheit* and in the *Republik* on January 1, 1919).[8] This is the same government that is sorely lacking in positive developments toward revolutionary economic or cultural policies. Lie after lie about it in the newspapers. And so the Spartacus uprising of January 5 was more than provoked. We cannot justify it: it made use of armed force, which is reprehensible. Once it had been put down, however, the survivors met with more brutality than the Hohenzollerns would have used against the November 9 revolt, had their power been sufficient to suppress it. Some were put up against the wall, defenseless; the rest were imprisoned and condemned—according to the letter of a fifty-year-old law based in fear, meant to protect the monarchy from revolution. On February 12, the Munich Workers' Council rightly adopted, almost unanimously, *Landauer*'s motion to demand a government decree "that all political paragraphs of the criminal code that the revolution itself has violated, are hereby revoked."[9] Who could fail to be disgusted? The beneficiaries of a successful uprising prepared by their opponents, one they tried to prevent up until the very last moment, now celebrate themselves as heroes of freedom and determine that the organizers of an *un*successful revolt, which was in its motives at least equally respectable, are insurrectionists and breakers of the peace. They offer them up to prosecutors and judges who come from the now dispatched system, from the old school of anti-intellectualism—judges who promptly and bestially treat the idealism of the idealist as an aggravating circumstance against him, and pronounce far milder "punishments" upon others who participated for mercenary or foolhardy reasons, or out of such other questionable motives as there certainly were, than upon students like *Heinrich Appel* and *Adolf Steinschneider*, who acted intellectually and responsibly and have had to pay dearly for that decision.[10] Kaiser-ism knew class justice against one social stratum; the reign of terror of these bandwagon socialists exacts a much more disgraceful class justice against a moral type: the intellectual who acts on his experience of logos to the point of self-sacrifice. No one is in a worse position in this grotesque revolution than the revolutionary. He is its bête noire; any miscreant in a uniform can arrest him at the drop of a hat. There is hardly an opposition leader (not only Spartacists but also staunch anti-Bolshevists like *Kautsky, Vorst, von Beerfelde* . . .[11]), hardly an unpopular soul whom some bastard officer or petty officer of the White Guard hasn't pulled from his home, arbitrarily and without a warrant, and dragged through their sleazy prisons—to say nothing of the organized, brutal, and still deliberately unpunished killing of *Liebknecht* and *Rosa Luxemburg*.[12] All on the orders or at least under the protection of the ruling bourgeois canaille, which has not abdicated but indeed elevated itself, desecrating Weimar, that sacred grove of German retrospection, with its presence and its enterprise. Friends of law and order will reply: "The majority of the people cannot and will not allow itself to be terrorized by a small minority; we are acting in self-defense; we cannot control this violent horde without weapons." Our answer: Then become their slaves, for this is better than becoming a violent horde in turn! And where is your self-defense when innocent people are arrested and locked up in dirty cellars, when the defenseless, when peace envoys are shot and slain? Where is your self-defense when. . . . The pen struggles to continue. What are the most sanguine social autocrats of Wilhelmstrasse against the striking doctors of Greifswald?[13] Doctors on strike! Because someone dared to raise a red flag above their heads! Did they, too, act in "self-defense"? Were they attacked by those patients whose pain their Christian hearts had no compunction to increase, whose healing they delayed, whose deaths they expedited? The evening edition of the *Berliner Tageblatt* for January 31 reports:

> The doctors of the university clinic in Greifswald have announced the following protest: "Over the objection of the directors and all the doctors of the university hospital, a red flag was forcibly [*gewaltsam*] raised over the clinics by order of the Greifswald Council of Workers and Soldiers. The doctors had explained to the council that they would respond to such a violation with a walkout. Since trespassers nevertheless raised the flag, all the doctors and office personnel of the clinic have ceased all activities, which they will not resume until such time as they receive satisfaction. No new patients can be admitted to the Greifswald clinic. *Nor can those patients who are currently in the clinic receive medical treatment.* The outpatient clinic is likewise closed."[14]

Under certain circumstances striking workers put lives in danger—in the water or electric works, for example—but without intent. These doctors—it's a shame we don't know their names—should quite literally have the excrement of their dysentery patients poured down their throats. And these lowlifes would hardly have had the courage for such villainy had they not known that the government would cover for them. To sympathize with every conspiracy against the vital welfare of a German—this, too, is among your counterrevolutionary black arts, you monsters of Noske! Only conspiracy against the welfare of certain German pocketbooks gets your hackles up. You think you're breaking the bones of this uprising? You're only strengthening the next one, furnishing it with arguments and passion! Your methods are not just opprobrious; they're also stupid. Perhaps the validity of these lines will have been proven already by the time they appear in print. For time is moving quickly. Today's minority is tomorrow's majority. And even if it should remain the minority—what does that prove? If a minority is led by intellect, is brave and pure, is firmly determined to realize the good, the just, the reasonable, to realize a new order and do it quickly—doesn't that minority override a sluggish majority that adheres to something already overcome? Isn't the "right of the majority" a highly questionable dogma, one fully contrary to revolution? "Reason has still rank'd only with the few,"[15] and only revolutions permit those few to restore reason to power. The bandwagon revolutionaries who make up this butchers' regime render reason powerless. Self-defense? Oh, the proletarian knows self-defense: millennia of self-defense against an offensive of oppression that shall not last forever; eons with the master's knee upon his breast. But not subdued by these eons, the slave knows that the moment has finally come when he can rebel and, with luck, rise up for good. . . . I do not justify his counterviolence if it uses guns and grenades; but I do pardon it and am disgusted by those trigger-happy "socialists" who call it a crime—for no one who uses terror himself may be indignant when others use it, whether against another class or another nation. The instigators and endorsers of the world war were terrorists. Their terror was bloodier than that of Spartacus . . . and what is more, it was filthy, because it was possible only through lies. So what right do they have now to object? Because their wallets and bank accounts are in danger! War brings them money but communism costs them, so they play the shocked meekling and inveigh against "terror"!—But we, we say to the Reds and to the Whites: no, we would have let the Spartacists do as they liked on the fifth of January. What would have happened? Their actions included violence but not vandalism. In times of semi-anarchy, every agitated crowd engages in rabble and plunder (the government soldiery wreaked more havoc later than the rebels had). Their leaders were full of idealism, humanity, and purity. They occupied a few editorial offices; does that mean they infringed upon the freedom of the press?[16] Only as the criminal who arrests the crook infringes upon the freedom of the individual. To use the freedom of the press to lie, suppress, obfuscate is to misuse it. To use it again and again against intellect and to stir up hatred for intellect—is intellect not more deserving of protection than freedom? Since freedom finds its very basis in intellect? "But intellect can only flourish in freedom; they are interdependent." Be that as it may: if the occupation of the liberal newspapers had lasted, the gentle conquerors would have chucked out the handsome princes of advertisement (more dangerous than most actual princes) in favor of their own workforce (and, indeed, to the good of the general public); would have smoked out, fumigated, and de-swined the editorial offices; would have consigned all of the rubbish (and I stress: *only* the rubbish) above and below the line to the trash heap where it belongs; would have placed the chairs thus cleaned and sanitized at the disposal of the intellectual movement of this city and filled them with capable journalists and educators from their own ranks; and suddenly one day many hundreds of thousands of people in this country would have been addressed not by rabble-rousers and gossipers and swindlers and skunks of economic boom, but by intellect. Would such a development, such a revolution (for that finally would have been one) have called for lament? Even a radical left-wing government would have been anything but a catastrophic result: even as it reflected daily upon its decisions, it would have had to decide quickly in favor of reflection; it would have been unable to dispense with the best forces of the bourgeoisie; it would have achieved that great success of unifying the proletariat. And had it ruled sensibly amidst the ranting and raving of the rich, it would have enjoyed centuries of glory and fame; had it ruled senselessly (who could deny this possibility, especially given the lack of a leader of any caliber), it would have suffocated within a few weeks in the fat of its own impotence. So what need was there for massacres?

We Germans must make a start. Abhor Cain's instrument unconditionally. If other nations do not want to take off their armor, we must take off ours. Completely. Otherwise we will awaken mistrust as we always have, psychologically preventing others from disarming and sowing the seeds of a new war. We should have done it when we were "strong"; we should have invoked that great day of which *Nietzsche* dreams (in *Human, All-Too-Human*), that "great day on which a nation distinguished for wars and victories and for the highest development of military discipline and thinking, and accustomed to making the heaviest sacrifices on behalf of these things, will cry of its own free will, '*we shall shatter the sword*'—and demolish its entire military machine down to its last foundations. *To disarm while being the best armed*, out of an *elevation* of sensibility—that is the means to *real* peace."[17] We should have done it when we were "strong"; to do it now that we are "weak," going above and beyond what the enemy imposes upon us, is still better than not doing it at all. Listen to the counsel of *Norman Angell*, the great English pacifist: "Not a single warship, not a single piece of artillery! Then, the militarists of other countries will no longer be in a position to defend their policies to their own people. You must speak to the nations with a dramatic transformation from the old to a new Germany, so that there can be no other image of Germany in their eyes!" Thus Angell called recently upon his "friends in Germany" via a correspondent for the *Nationalzeitung* in Basel. Our scholars of pacifism are wise but not bold. Reduce the size of the army? We must abolish it! A militia instead of a standing army? Arm all the people? *Disarm* all the people! *All* the people, mind you. And if the French, the Czechoslovakians, the Poles, the Bolsheviks, the cannibals, or the devils come for us—the only effective weapon is to be unarmed. "Only through non-resistance to evil will humanity be led to substitute the law of love for the law of force [*Gewalt*]," writes *Tolstoy*, the prophet of the modern salons.[18] But do not intoxicate yourselves with Tolstoy or put on airs with Tolstoy—act according to Tolstoy! Without force of arms, we cannot prevent foreigners from invading our homeland, you say? Let us not prevent them! Let us finally be satisfied with faith in the force of law. The League of Nations or the world community will bring an end to all nationalist disgrace and align national borders with linguistic borders. And where that is not successful, where barbarians can still thwart the self-determination of the people, let us not play the liberator! The freedom brought to tens of thousands would not offset a single life taken in the process. And even if you continue to believe, however deeply, "better to be dead than a slave," you cannot turn that into the duty of another, cannot compel anyone to allow himself to be killed if he would rather be a slave than dead. There is no permissible war, but if there were, it could only be a war in which every single person involved desired to fight. He who is ready to give his life may do what he must; but to impose self-sacrifice upon his brother—a brother who may have far more valuable things to give to his people and to the world—is despotism. Compulsory military service is the cruelest form of slavery; states that have compulsory military service are wretched slave states. They deserve to be cursed and despised, whether they are capitalist or communist. The state, provided to the people by reason to be the instrument of their happiness, becomes an autotelic Moloch that eats the people instead. To cauterize this madness that has continued to spread throughout history, this cancer of the earth, would be revolutionary. A socialism that liberates people economically while continuing its tyrannical claim on their bodies exhausts itself in secondary concerns and misses the main point. Socialism with conscription is the world's most laughable reform doctrine. It ensures full stomachs without protecting the beating heart. It guarantees a certain quality of life but not life itself. Progressive in secondary concerns but conservative in elementary ones, as a revolutionary orientation it becomes too big for its britches.

The fundamental demand of political freedom is the abolition of conscription. Abolition of conscription in all countries, of course. (And if most of them hesitate, then Germany must lead by example, as it once did in social policy, defying the toads of inertia; the League of Nations and the de-anarchized world will be as loath to infringe upon the freedom of a great unarmed civilization as the anarchic world was to violate the freedom of small neutral countries . . . with the exception of the crimes against Belgium.) International law must also prohibit the recruitment of "volunteers," the establishment of mercenary armies, indeed all military institutions. The nations must prohibit them via multilateral agreement, and each nation must include the prohibition in its constitution. Germany must be the first. And if it thereby puts itself in a "worse" position than other nations from the standpoint of a traditional politics of force [*Gewaltpolitik*]—what has it lost? It is better positioned in terms of intellect, morality, immortality. War breaks out because one day the profusely accumulated cannons go off by themselves; a permanent condition of peace will not draw near until all implements of murder have been truly destroyed. Under appropriate supervision, all existing stores of weapons and other instruments of death and destruction must be literally annihilated: broken, smashed, melted down, exploded, sunk into the ocean. A modest remnant may of course remain—for policing and hunting purposes. And for these purposes the production of new weapons and munition may be allowed, but only in very small quantities; this must happen in factories that belong to the state and are closely inspected. The entire border-control racket must be exposed. "Children should guard our borders with flowers in their hands," as the Swiss writer Felix Möschlin says in his drama *The Revolution of the Heart*.[19]

This is possible. We need only to desire it. We need only the will to make a start. We need only to recognize the full fecklessness of Cain's methods and to resolve to draw any and all consequences from this recognition. Teach it and proclaim it among your friends and family; in cafés and on trains; from the pulpits and lecterns; in schools, cinemas, newspapers, and books: *Thou shalt not kill. Thou shalt not kill even for the sake of an idea. For no idea is more sublime than the living* [*der Lebendige*].

—*Trans. Lisa Marie Anderson*

GEORGES SOREL, FROM *REFLECTIONS ON VIOLENCE*

Translator's Preface

In chapter 34 of Thomas Mann's 1947 novel *Doctor Faustus*, the narrator, Serenus Zeitbloom, recounts the meeting of a reactionary intellectual salon, the Kridwiss Circle, which draws many of its lucubrations about a coming age of barbarism from Georges Sorel's *Réflexions sur la violence* (Reflections on violence). As Zeitbloom tells it, the book, "which had appeared seven years before the war, played a significant role in the discussions of this cultural avant-garde.... This was in fact the book's crude and intriguing prophecy: that henceforth popular myths, or better, myths trimmed for the masses, would be the vehicle of political action-fables, chimeras, phantasms that needed to have nothing whatever to do with truth, reason, or science in order to be productive nonetheless, to determine life and history, and thereby to prove themselves dynamic realities. It is easy to see that the book did not bear its menacing title in vain, for it dealt with violence as the triumphant counterpart of truth."[1] Zeitbloom's claim that Sorel's was "the book of the age" because of its "characterization of Europe as the soil of armed cataclysms" is as inaccurate about the contents of *Reflections* as it is in keeping with the sulfurous stereotype that continues to accompany the book—one that is bound to taint by association anyone, including Benjamin, drawing upon it for conceptual orientation in the understanding of violence.

It is significant, if not necessarily correct, that in his *Story of a Friendship*, Gershom Scholem indicates 1919 as the moment of Benjamin's first interest in the writings of the French thinker. Scholem tells that Benjamin had been spurred by exchanges with Ernst Bloch and Hugo Ball in Bern, where he was completing his dissertation on the concept of criticism in German Romanticism, to begin reading Sorel's *Reflections*. In October 1920, having already undertaken to write a series of articles on politics, Benjamin, at the recommendation of Adolf Otto, writes to Bernhard Kampffmeyer to send him a copy of *Reflections*, "which I have up until now not been able to procure" (*GB* 2:101). Kampffmeyer asks the historian of anarchism Max Nettlau, for whom he is serving as secretary, to fulfill the request. As Chryssoula Kambas recounts in her study of Benjamin's reading of Sorel, Benjamin at the time was living in Berlin-Grünau, one of the communal settlements organized by the Kropotkinian German Garden-City Society, of which Kampffmeyer—who lived in Bergisch-Gladbach, while Otto was with Benjamin in Grünau—was a founder.[2] Whether Nettlau eventually procured *Reflections* for Benjamin is not recorded, though we do know that, as he told Scholem himself in a letter, he was still waiting for a copy in January 1921.[3] The letter to Kampffmeyer, which refers to Benjamin's planned essay as dealing with the dismantling and not the critique of violence (*Abbau der Gewalt*), frames his interest in Sorel in terms of a wider anarchist literature, and especially in those authors dealing specifically with violence—both condemning the violence of the state and offering apologias for revolutionary violence. Whatever the exact facts regarding Benjamin's reading of Sorel (could he have consulted someone else's copy during his sojourn in Switzerland, and when precisely did he actually read *Reflections*?), it is evident that the intellectual and political context for his reception of the French theorist was almost the diametrical opposite of the one back-projected into 1919 by Thomas Mann, shaped as it was by the dilemmas of pacifism, experiments in anarchist forms of life, and the possibilities of revolutionary violence.

To treat Georges Sorel as belonging to the domain of anarchist literature is in itself not unproblematic. Sorel subscribed to Marx's critique of Bakunin as only superficially opposed to the state and ever tempted by the dictatorial coup. As he wrote in a 1906 letter to Édouard Berth, "the violence of Bakunin is violence put in the hands of politicians. Bakunin never had the idea of revolutionary syndicalism, whose result will be to form characters."[4] Sorel's commitment to Proudhon, on the other hand, was remarkably constant, ranging all the way from his "Essai sur la philosophie de Proudhon" (1892) to his claim in the 1920 "Aperçu sur les utopies, les soviets et le droit nouveau" (1920) that the Russian Revolution had birthed institutions closer to Proudhon's thinking than to "the schools which have so poorly exploited Marx's heritage."[5] Sorel's critical engagement with these "schools," together with their political avatars, had preoccupied him ever since his rather belated discovery of Marx in 1893, a year after his retirement at age forty-five from his position as chief engineer of waterworks in Perpignan. Having published in the prior decade numerous studies concerned especially with the critique of positivism in the domain of psychology, as well as monographs in philosophy and religious history (*Contribution à l'étude profane de la Bible* and *Le procés de Socrate*; 1889), with the text "Science et socialisme" (1893) Sorel would salute "Marx's new metaphysics" and collaborate assiduously with the first Marxist theoretical journals in France, *L'ère nouvelle* and *Le devenir social*, publishing in them important studies of Vico as well as of the Italian Marxist Antonio Labriola. Toward the end of 1897, spurred by his dialogue with his friend the Italian philosopher Benedetto Croce (who would pen the preface to the Italian translation of *Reflections*), as well as by the book *Pro e contro il socialismo* by Saverio Merlino, Sorel joined the ranks of Marxist "revisionism" and played a prominent role in the Europe-wide "crisis of Marxism."

While it has become identified with its author as his signature work, *Reflections* belongs to a rather circumscribed period of Sorel's theoretical activism, one identified with the revolutionary syndicalist movement that provided the only "organic" referent that Sorel's thinking ever enjoyed.[6] Central to syndicalism was the tactical and strategic emphasis on industrial direct action, along with a profound belief in proletarian self-education and self-government, accompanied by scepticism or downright hostility toward the parliamentary sphere and the representative capacities of parties, socialist ones included. In his first systematic study on trade-unions, "L'avenir socialiste des syndicats" (1898), Sorel, already involved in the revisionism debates, stressed that, notwithstanding the Marxist belief in the centrality of the industrial proletariat to the politics of revolution, no contemporary Marxist had really embraced Marx's own thesis, according to which the working class needs to develop its political and juridical capacities, its capacities for self-government, *before* a revolutionary triumph.[7] In 1900, an essay on strikes ("Les grèves," in the journal *La science sociale*) defended this manifestation of workers' power as the exercise of a real, if yet unrecognized, juridical right, in which any workplace violence is ultimately nothing but an infraction committed by an owner defending his goods.[8] But it was only after 1902, with the combative embrace of the strike by the Confédération Générale du Travail, that Sorel threw himself into the syndicalist cause. The acceleration of the syndicalist current in France was accompanied by its forceful irruption into the Italian socialist movement. The year 1904 saw a general strike impelled by syndicalists that was inspired, among others, by Sorel. In 1905, Enrico Leone founded the journal *Il divenire sociale* along expressly Sorelian lines, while in the same year the journal *Critica sociale* depicted him as the "idol" of Italian revolutionaries.[9] Articles later incorporated into *Reflections* were published starting in 1905 in *Il divenire sociale* (and subsequently in the journal *Le mouvement socialiste*), and in 1906 a first version of *Reflections* was published in Italian under the title *Lo sciopero generale e la violenza*.[10] By 1909, compromises of the French syndicalist movement with party politics led Sorel to turn away from it and, briefly, toward the French antiparliamentary nationalist right of the Action Française, while many of his Italian followers became involved in various nationalist-syndicalist amalgams. In the end, the self-styled "disinterested servant of the proletariat" would greet the Bolshevik revolution as the paradoxical vehicle for Proudhonian institutions of workers' self-rule and self-education.

Reflections is the most cited text in "Toward the Critique of Violence," and yet, as though Benjamin were anticipating his own later counsel to develop concepts that are "completely useless for the purposes of Fascism" (1:435; *SW* 3:102), Sorel's meditations on the violence of the general strike as myth—often taken to be the sole contribution of this fascinatingly digressive and compendious book—go entirely unmentioned. In drawing on Sorel's distinction between the political and the revolutionary general strike so as to explore the possibility of a sphere of pure means capable of deposing that (state) power at the heart of every mythic lawmaking—in other words, by counterposing the revolutionary general strike *to* myth—Benjamin is neutralizing the characteristically fascist use of Sorel, which takes the form of subtracting the general strike from his conception of myth. The connotations of Benjaminian myth, together with mythic violence, in which the references to ancient Greek religion and tragedy are paramount, are largely incommensurable with Sorel's own Bergsonian use of the term to designate a kind of *connaissance totale* (total knowledge) that would be intuitive, indivisible, and instantaneous, and which would be conveyed by ensembles or blocs of images. And yet without so much as mentioning that the general strike is a myth for Sorel, Benjamin subscribes to Sorel's understanding of what it is not, namely, a utopia—a future program managed by those who think their profession is to think for the proletariat, that is, the intellectuals. The intransigent polemic against the nexus of state power, intellectual protagonism, and party politics that governs *Reflections* and underlies the distinction between the political and revolutionary general strike also animates Benjamin's appropriation of Sorel—that much is evident in the parenthetical remark about the identity between the political general strike and the German Revolution. Benjamin endorses, as "deep, moral, and genuinely revolutionary" (53), Sorel's repudiation of utopia without thereby accepting his affirmation of myth. He also does not reproduce Sorel's crucial distinction between state force and revolutionary violence; though he translates the latter as *Kraft* and notes its articulation with the power (*Macht* or *Staatsgewalt*) of the state, he makes a distinction within *Gewalt*, between the mythical and the divine, which at best partially overlaps with Sorel's own entirely nontheological distinction.

Affinities with, and perhaps traces of, Sorel's own critique of the political consequences of natural law (*le droit naturel*) can also be registered in Benjamin's essay. In the first of the excerpts included herein from *Reflections*, these affinities and traces can be seen to originate in the influence on the French thinker of a "liberal conservative" anti-Jacobin tradition, ranging from Tocqueville to Taine. Benjamin's parenthetical remark on natural law as the ideological foundation of French revolutionary terrorism certainly echoes Sorel. But Benjamin's exclusive reference to *Reflections* perforce obscures the "primacy of the juridical over the political"[11] across the whole of Sorel's work. Sorel drew from Proudhon a conception of an autonomy of right (*droit*) vis-à-vis morality, a view crystallized in the notion of a *droit de la force* and an "immanentist vision of the juridical phenomenon."[12] He turned to Vico to differentiate between two kinds of social struggle—one concerned with the conquest of political and material power, the other targeting the ethical life and socio-juridical structure of an entire society.[13] He saw a concern with the development of a juridical capacity or consciousness by the proletariat as a dimension of Marx's thought neglected by Marxists, while conceiving of the appropriation of the means of production as a juridical formula. It is interesting to note that Sorel's abiding idea that class struggles were juridical struggles drew in part on Rudolf von Jhering's *Der Zweck im Recht* (Purpose in law; 1877–83), a text that Benjamin would cite first in Notes 19 and 20 of this volume on "objective mendacity" and then in relation to his study of fashion in *The Arcades Project*.[14] Jhering's *Der Kampf ums Recht* (The struggle for law; 1872) also corroborated Sorel's Marxian insight regarding struggle as something belonging to the essence of law.[15] While it has been claimed that Jhering, along with Sorel, provides some of the conceptual infrastructure for Benjamin's "negativistic image of law," attention to the presence of Jhering in Sorel's work, in the broader context of the French thinker's abiding concern with "the juridical aims of the struggle" should go some way toward problematizing the notion that one can find in *Reflections* an idea of law as "merely an instrumental institution for the maintenance of social order" and that this supposedly Sorelian idea, supplemented by a reading of Jhering, ultimately shaped Benjamin's "thoroughly negative conception of law."[16]

Benjamin's suggestion in "Toward the Critique of Violence" that the violence of the strike is feared by the state because of its threatening ability to found and modify juridical relationships would chime with Sorel's excavation of the juridical dimensions of revolutionary syndicalism, were it not for the fact that this production of "new law" (*droit nouveau*) is for Sorel something that takes place *within* the world of the producers and *before* any destructive violence. In that sense, while Benjamin is right to note that the revolutionary general strike imagined by Sorel is not a coercive instrument aimed at concessions and ameliorations but rather directly enacts a subversion of the very conditions of work against and outside the state, the idea that the political general strike is law-positing while the revolutionary general strike is anarchic jars with the juridical dimension of Sorel's thought. For the latter, the violence of the strike could ultimately do without the force of the state only to the extent that a juridical capacity underlies and precedes the irruption of the strike. Indeed, strikes provide evidence of how violence "serves the genesis and progress of juridical ideas."[17] In the foreword to his 1914 *Matériaux d'une théorie du proletariat*, Sorel notes that methodological imperatives compelled him to leave the juridical face of struggles in the shadows, as he was preoccupied with the question of proletarian violence, while in one of his very last texts he would justify his preference, in the light of the experience of the Soviets, for Proudhon over Marx, because of the former's attention to the juridical consciousness gestated by proletarian institutions and the latter's illusion that "the new world would be born in the middle of the juridical night."[18]

After the intense confrontation with Sorel in "Toward the Critique of Violence," references to the French thinker are few and far between in Benjamin's oeuvre. In 1927, Benjamin conducted an interview with the French politician and journalist Georges Valois for *Die literarische Welt* under the title (chosen by the editors) "Für die Diktatur [For dictatorship]: Interview mit Georges

Valois." While Benjamin did indeed conduct an interview, the article takes the form of a series of theses about French fascism. Benjamin calls Valois a "student of Sorel," while Sorel is described as "the great, truly significant theoretician of syndicalism" (4:489). As a member of the right-wing nationalist Action Française, Valois had occupied himself with the workers' movement and penned a text with Sorelian echoes on *The Monarchy and the Working Class*. In 1911, he had founded the nationalist-syndicalist (and anti-Semitic) *Cercle Proudhon* and played a role in Sorel's short-lived rapprochement with the radical right.[19] By the time of Benjamin's interview, Valois had founded the first explicitly fascist party outside of Italy, Le Faisceau. It is noteworthy that Benjamin explicitly distances Sorel's theory of the mass strike from Valois's own dubious views for a "bloodless revolution" anchored in fear and obedience—here one is reminded by contrast of the allusion in "Toward the Critique of Violence" to the way in which "a rigorous conception of the general strike is liable to diminish the deployment of actual violence in revolutions" (53). In "The Paris of the Second Empire in Baudelaire" (1938), Benjamin associated the *culte de la blague* in Sorel back with Baudelaire and forward with fascist propaganda—a passing mention that cannot really be treated as evidence of a shift in his estimation of the author of *Reflections*.[20] A diary entry by Werner Kraft from May 20, 1934, regarding a conversation with Benjamin about whether the latter still subscribed to the positions sketched out in "Toward the Critique of Violence," even hints at a further rapprochement with the French revolutionary syndicalist. As Kraft summarizes: "In substance, he argues today the following position: just law [*gerechtes Recht*] is what benefits the oppressed in class conflict. — Class conflict is the center of all philosophical questions, even the highest. — What he earlier called divine ("pending" [*waltende*]) violence was an empty spot, a limit concept, a regulative idea. Today, he knows that it *is* class conflict." Whatever the faithfulness of Kraft's jottings, his own account of his reply is indicative of how much the name of Sorel could be used as a polemical weapon against Benjamin's reflections on violence: "Me: class struggle is part of the sphere of myth exactly like the general strike in Sorel."[21]

— *Alberto Toscano*

GEORGES SOREL,
FROM *REFLECTIONS ON VIOLENCE*

[145–51] The Third Estate, which packed the assemblies during the revolutionary period—what we could term the official Third Estate—was not composed of the sum of farmers and heads of industry; power [*pouvoir*] was never in the hands of the men of production but in those of lawyer's clerks [*basochiens*].[1] Taine was struck by the fact that of the 577 deputies of the Third Estate in the Constituent Assembly, there were 373 "unknown lawyers and people occupying inferior positions in the profession, notaries, royal attorneys, register-commissaries, judges and assessors of the *présidial*,[2] bailiffs and lieutenants of the bailiwick, simple practitioners confined from their youth to the narrow circle of an inferior jurisdiction or to a routine of scribbling with no escape but philosophical excursions in imaginary space under the guidance of Rousseau and Raynal."[3] Today, we struggle to understand the importance of men of law [*gens de loi*] in the old France; there existed a multitude of jurisdictions; property-owners invested an extreme amount of self-regard [*amour-propre*] in the adjudication of questions that today seem to us of little note but that they considered of enormous significance owing to the overlapping of feudal law and property law. Everywhere, one could find functionaries of the judicial system, and they enjoyed the greatest prestige among the population.

This class brought to the revolution considerable administrative capacities. It is thanks to it that the country was able to withstand with relative ease the crisis that shook it for a decade and that Napoleon could so rapidly reconstitute quite orderly state services; but this class also brought with it a mass of prejudices that led its highest-placed representatives to commit the gravest mistakes. It is impossible, for instance, to understand the behavior of Robespierre if we compare him to contemporary politicians; we must always perceive in him the serious man of law, preoccupied by his duties, careful not to tarnish the professional honor of the orator at the bar. What's more, we must recall he was a well-read disciple of Rousseau. He had legal scruples that astonish contemporary historians; when he was forced to take decisions of supreme importance and to defend himself against the convention, he made show of a naïveté bordering on foolishness. The famous law of 22 Prairial,[4] for which he has often been reproached and which lent the revolutionary tribunal its brisk pace, is the masterpiece of his type of mindset; in it, we can find the entirety of the ancien régime expressed in lapidary formulas.

One of the fundamental ideas of the ancien régime was the employment of penal procedure to undermine all the powers that could hinder the monarchy [*royauté*]. It seems that in all primitive societies, criminal law [*droit pénal*] began as a protection accorded to the chief and to some privileged individuals to which he granted special favor; it was only very late that legal force [*force légale*] was used without distinction to safeguard the persons and goods of all the inhabitants of a country.[5] Since the Middle Ages were a return to the ancient customs, it was natural that they once again engendered rather archaic ideas about justice and that they treated the main mission of tribunals as assuring royal greatness. A historical accident favored the extraordinary development of this criminal regime. The Inquisition offered the model for tribunals that, having been set in motion by the feeblest of evidences, doggedly pursued individuals who troubled authority and made it impossible for them to harm that authority. The royal state borrowed from the Inquisition many of its procedures and almost unfailingly followed its principles.

Monarchy constantly demanded from its tribunals that they work to expand its territory; today, it seems strange that Louis XIV had annexations announced by commissions of magistrates, but he was faithful to tradition—many of his predecessors had Parliament confiscate feudal seigneuries for quite arbitrary reasons. Justice, which today appears to us as made in order to guarantee the prosperity of production and allow it to develop, in all liberty, in ever vaster proportions, seemed in the past to be designed to assure royal greatness: *its essential aim was not law* [*droit*], *but the state.*

It was very difficult to establish a rigorous discipline in the services constituted by the monarchy for the sake of war and administration; at every moment, it was necessary to undertake investigations in order to punish unfaithful or unruly employees. For these missions, kings employed men selected from their tribunals; they thus ended up confusing acts of disciplinary surveillance with the repression of crimes. Men of law transformed everything in keeping with their habits of mind; thus negligence, ill will, or carelessness turned into revolt against authority, assaults, or treason.

The revolution piously relayed this tradition, lending imaginary crimes an importance all the more magnified in that its political tribunals operated amid a population panic-stricken by the gravity of the danger. It seemed entirely natural to explain the defeats of generals in terms of criminal intentions and to guillotine those who had been unable to realize the hopes dreamed up by a public opinion repeatedly thrown back onto childish superstitions. Our penal code still contains a good number of paradoxical articles originating in this period: today it is difficult to understand how one can seriously accuse a citizen of weaving intrigues or conspiring with foreign powers or their agents in order to induce them to commit hostile acts or to wage war against France, or to procure them with the means to do so. Such a crime presupposes that the state can be put in danger as a whole by the deeds of one person, something that to us seems scarcely believable.[6]

Trials against enemies of the king were always carried out in an exceptional manner. Procedures were simplified as far as possible: one made do with mediocre evidence, which would not have sufficed for ordinary crimes; one sought to make terrible and profoundly intimidating examples. All of this can be found again in Robespierrean legislation. The law of 22 Prairial is content with rather vague definitions of political crime, so as not to let any enemy of the revolution slip through its grasp. As for standards of evidence [*preuves*], they are worthy of the purest tradition of the ancien régime and the Inquisition. "The proof [*preuve*] necessary to convict the *enemies of the people* comprises every kind of document, whether material or moral, oral or written, which can naturally secure the approval of every just and reasonable mind. The rule of judgments is the conscience of the jurors, enlightened by love of the fatherland; their aim is the *triumph of the Republic and the ruin of its enemies*." In this famous terrorist law, we find the strongest expression of the doctrine of the state.[7]

The philosophy of the eighteenth century contributed to making these methods even more redoubtable. It claimed, in effect, to articulate a return to natural law [*droit naturel*]; humanity had hitherto been corrupted by a small number of people who had an interest in deceiving it; but the means to return to the principle of primitive goodness, truth, and justice had at last been discovered. Every opposition to such a beautiful reform, so easy to apply and graced with such certain success, was the most criminal act imaginable; the innovators were resolved to remain unbending in order to destroy the nefarious influence that these bad citizens could exert in their efforts to impede the regeneration of humanity. Leniency was a culpable weakness, because it tended toward nothing short of the sacrifice of the happiness of multitudes for the whims of incorrigible people [*gens*] who demonstrated an incomprehensible obstinacy, refusing to recognize the self-evident and living on nothing but lies.

From the Inquisition to the political justice of the monarchy and from that to revolutionary tribunals, there was a constant progression in the direction of the arbitrary character of rules, the extension of force, and the amplification of authority. For a long time, the church harbored doubts regarding the exceptional procedures practiced by its inquisitors.[8] The monarchy did not have as many scruples, especially once it attained full maturity; but the revolution displayed for all to see the scandal of its superstitious cult of the state.

→→←←

[189–200] A. First, I will speak of class struggle, which is the starting point of any socialist reflection and which is in such need of clarification after sophists have sought to present a false idea of it.

1. Marx speaks of society as though it were split into two profoundly antagonistic groups; this dichotomic thesis has often been fought against in the name of observation, and it is true that a certain mental effort is required to find it verified in the phenomena of ordinary life.

The running of a capitalist workshop furnishes an initial approximation, and piecework plays an essential role in the formation of the idea of class. In effect, it illuminates a very clear opposition of interests emerging over the price of objects:[9] workers feel dominated by owners in an analogous manner as peasants feel dominated by urban traders and money-lenders. History shows that there is no economic opposition more clearly felt than this one; the countryside and the towns have constituted two enemy countries ever since there's been any civilization.¹⁰ Piecework also shows that in the world of wage-workers there is a group of men somewhat analogous to retailers [*marchands de détail*] who enjoy the trust of the owner and who do not belong to the world of the proletariat.

The strike brings a new clarity: it separates, better than the quotidian circumstances of life, the interests and ways of thinking of the two groups of wage-workers. It then becomes clear that the administrative group has a natural tendency to constitute a small aristocracy; it is these people who would gain an advantage from state socialism, because they would move up a notch in the social hierarchy.

But all oppositions gain an extraordinary sharpness when we consider conflicts magnified to the point of the general strike. Then all parts of the economic-juridical structure, inasmuch as it is considered from the point of view of class struggle, are brought to their perfection; society is indeed divided into two camps, and only two, on a battlefield. No philosophical explanation of the facts observed in practice could furnish such bright illumination as the simple picture [*tableau*] that the evocation of the general strike puts before our eyes.

2. It is impossible to conceive of the disappearance of capitalist command if we do not assume the existence of a burning feeling of revolt that ceaselessly dominates the soul of the worker; but experience shows that, very often, one-day revolts are far from possessing the tone that is truly specific to socialism. More than once, the most violent anger has stemmed from passions that could find satisfaction in the bourgeois world; we see many revolutionaries abandoning their former intransigence when they find a favourable path.¹¹ It is not just satisfactions of a material order that produce these frequent and scandalous conversions; self-love is, even more than money, the great driver of the passage from revolt to the bourgeoisie. This would be of little moment if we were only dealing with exceptional figures; but it has often been argued that the psychology of the working masses is so easily adaptable to the capitalist order that social peace would be quickly attained were the owners to make some concessions.

Gustave Le Bon claims it is a great mistake to believe in the revolutionary instincts of the crowds [*foules*]: that their tendencies are conservative, that the entire power [*puissance*] of socialism comes from the passably unhinged mental state of the bourgeoisie; he's convinced that the masses will always go toward a Caesar.¹² There is much truth in these judgments, grounded as they are in a very extensive knowledge of civilizations; but we must add a corrective to Le Bon's theses: they only apply to societies in which the notion of class struggle is missing.

Observation shows that this notion abides with indestructible force in all the milieus touched by the idea of the general strike: no more possibility of social peace, no more resigned routine, no more enthusiasm for beneficent or glorious masters; the day that the smallest incidents of daily life become symptoms of the state of struggle between the classes, where every conflict is an incident in the social war, where every strike engenders the perspective of a total catastrophe. The idea of the general strike has such motive force that it drags into its revolutionary wake everything it touches. Thanks to it, socialism remains forever young; attempts to realize social peace appear infantile; and the desertions of gentrified [*qui s'embourgeoisient*] comrades, far from discouraging the masses, excite them further to revolt. In a word, scission is never in danger of disappearing.

3. The successes obtained by politicians in their efforts to make what they call proletarian influence felt in bourgeois institutions constitute a very sizeable obstacle to the preservation of the notion of class struggle. The world has always lived through transactions between parties, and order has always been provisional; there is no change, as considerable as it may be, that could be regarded as impossible in a time such as our own, which has witnessed so many novelties arising unpredictably. It is through successive compromises that modern progress has realized itself—why not pursue the ends of socialism through procedures that have succeeded so well? One can imagine countless means capable of satisfying the most pressing desires of the unfortunate classes. For a long time, these ameliorative projects were inspired by a conservative, feudal or Catholic, spirit; as their inventors put it, it was a matter of wresting the masses away from the influence of radicals. The latter, menaced less by their ancient enemies than by socialist politicians, today imagine projects displaying progressive, democratic, free-thinking colors. At last, we are being threatened with socialist compromises!

It is not always noted that many political organizations, systems of administration, and financial regimes can be reconciled with the domination of a bourgeoisie. We need not always accord great value to violent attacks that target the bourgeoisie; they can be motivated by the desire to reform and perfect capitalism.[13] It seems that today many people would gladly sacrifice inheritance, like the Saint-Simonians, while being far from desiring the disappearance of the capitalist regime.[14]

The general strike eliminates all the ideological consequences of any possible social policy. Its partisans regard reforms, even the most popular, as being bourgeois in character;[15] for them nothing can attenuate the fundamental opposition of the class struggle. The more the politics of social reform become preponderant, the more socialism will feel the need to contrast the picture of progress that it strives to realize with the picture of the total catastrophe that the general strike furnishes in a truly perfect manner.

B. Let us now examine several essential aspects of the Marxist revolution by relating them to the general strike.

1. Marx says that the proletariat will present itself, on the day of the revolution, disciplined, united, and organized by the very mechanism of production. This extremely condensed formula is not so clear if we don't relate it back to its context: according to Marx, the working class feels the burden of a regime in which "the mass of misery, oppression, slavery, degradation, and exploitation grows," and against which it organizes an ever-growing resistance, until the day when the entire social structure collapses.[16] The exactness of this famous description, which seems far more suited to the time of the *Manifesto* (1847) than to that of *Capital* (1867), has been contested many times; but this objection should not block us, and it must be shunted aside through the theory of myths. The various terms that Marx employs to depict the preparation of the decisive combat must not be taken for direct and temporally determinate material observations; it is the ensemble alone that must strike us, and this ensemble is perfectly clear. Marx wants us to understand that the entire preparation of the proletariat depends solely on the organization of an obstinate, growing, and passionate resistance against the existing order of things.

This thesis is of the utmost importance for a healthy understanding of Marxism; but it has often been contested, if not in theory, then at least in practice. It has been argued that the proletariat must prepare itself for its future role through avenues other than those of revolutionary syndicalism. It is thus that the doctors of cooperation argue that their prescription must be given pride of place in the work of emancipation; democrats say it is essential to eliminate all the prejudices stemming from age-old Catholic influence, and so on. Many revolutionaries believe that, as useful as syndicalism may be, it is insufficient for the organization of a society that also needs a philosophy, a new legal system [*un droit nouveau*], and so forth. Since the division of labor is a fundamental law of the world, socialism must not shy away from turning to the many specialists in matters of philosophy and law [*droit*]. Jaurès never tires of repeating this twaddle.[17] This *enlargement* of socialism is contrary to Marxist theory as well as to the conception of the general strike; but it is obvious that the general strike commands thinking in an infinitely clearer way than any formula whatsoever.

2. I have called attention to the danger that revolutions taking place in an era of economic decline [*déchéance*] represent for the future of a civilization. Not all Marxists seem to have really understood Marx's thinking on this point: he believed that the great catastrophe would be preceded by an immense economic crisis, but we should not confuse the crises that Marx studied with a decline [*déchéance*]; crises appeared to him as the result of an excessively risky adventure of production, generating productive forces out of proportion with the regulatory means automatically available to the capitalism of the time. Such an adventure presupposes the vision of a future open to the most powerful firms and implies that the notion of economic progress was completely dominant at the time. For the middle classes, who can still find passable conditions of existence within the capitalist regime, to be able to join the proletariat, it is necessary that future production be capable of appearing to them as brightly as the conquest of America once appeared to English peasants who left old Europe to throw themselves into a life of adventure.

The general strike leads to the same considerations. Workers are used to seeing their revolt against the necessities imposed by capitalism succeed during periods of prosperity, so we can say that the fact alone of identifying revolution and general strike wards off any thought that an essential transformation of the world can result from economic decadence. Workers are also well aware that peasants and artisans will not march alongside them unless the future appears so beautiful that industry will be capable of bettering the fate not only of the producers but also of everyone else.[18]

It is very important always to foreground the high level of prosperity that must be enjoyed by industry in order to allow for the realization of socialism, for experience shows us that it is by trying to fight against the progress of capitalism and save the means of existence of classes on the path to decadence that the prophets of social peace try especially to garner popular favor. It is necessary to present, in a persuasive manner, the bonds that tie revolution to the constant and rapid progress of industry.[19]

3. It is difficult to overstress the fact that Marxism condemns any hypothesis about the future constructed by utopians. Professor Brentano,[20] from Munich, recounts that in 1869, Marx wrote to his friend Beesly (who had published an article on the future of the working class) that he had regarded him until then as the only revolutionary Englishman and that he now considered him a reactionary—because, he said, "Whoever composes a program for the future is a reactionary."[21] He judged that the proletariat needed not to follow the lessons of learned inventors of social solutions but simply to follow capitalism's lead. No need of programs for the future; programs are already realized in the workshop. The idea of technological continuity dominates all of Marxist thought.

The practice of strikes leads us to a conception identical to that of Marx. The workers who stop working do not present their bosses with projects for the superior organization of work, nor do they offer their contribution to better manage their bosses' affairs; in brief, utopia has no place in economic conflicts. Jaurès and his friends feel acutely that this represents a strong objection to their conception of how socialism should be realized. They would like the practice of strikes already to incorporate fragments of the industrial programs fabricated by learned sociologists and accepted by the workers; they would like to see the development of what they call *industrial parliamentarianism*, which would involve, like every political parliamentarianism, masses being led and rhetoricians imparting direction to them. It is the apprenticeship of their mendacious socialism that would need to begin straightaway.

With the general strike, all these pretty things disappear; the revolution appears as a pure and simple revolt, and no place is reserved for the sociologists, for the worldly friends of social reform, for the Intellectuals who have embraced the *profession of thinking for the proletariat.*[22]

→►◄←

[246–50] B. The great differences that exist between the two general strikes (or the two socialisms) become even more marked when we relate social struggles and war: the latter is in fact also liable to give rise to two opposed systems, so that one can say the most contradictory things about war, all the while referring to incontestable facts.

One may consider its noble side, namely, by considering it after the fashion of poets celebrating especially illustrious armies. Proceeding in this manner, we encounter:

1. the idea that the military profession can be compared to no other—that it raises the man who devotes himself to it to a category above the common conditions of life—that history rests in its entirety on the adventures of these men of war, so that the economy only exists to sustain them;

2. that feeling of glory which Renan so rightly regarded as one of the most unique and powerful creations of human genius and which has been found to be an unparalleled value in history;[23]

3. the burning desire to test oneself in great battles, to undergo the ordeal by dint of which the military trade lays claim to its superiority, and to conquer glory at the risk of one's life.

I need not insist on calling my readers' attention to these characteristics in order to make them grasp the role that this conception of war played in ancient Greece. The whole of classical history is dominated by the heroic conception of war. The institutions of Greek republics originally had as their basis the organization of citizens' armies; Greek art attained its apogee in the citadels; philosophers could conceive of no education other than the one that could sustain a heroic tradition among the youth, and if they endeavored to regulate music, it was because they did not want it to give free rein to feelings alien to this discipline; social utopias were fashioned with the aim of maintaining a core of Homeric warriors within the cities, and so forth. In our own time, the wars of liberty have been no less fecund in ideas than those of the Greeks.

There is another aspect of war that is instead devoid of any trait of nobility and that pacifists always stress.[24] War no longer has its ends in itself: its objective is to allow politicians to satisfy their ambitions; the foreigner must be conquered in order to procure great and immediate material advantages; it is also necessary that victory give the party who led the country during the time of success such preeminence that it is able to distribute many favors to its supporters; finally, it is hoped that the prestige of triumph will so intoxicate the citizens that they will cease properly perceiving the sacrifices demanded of them and abandon themselves to enthusiastic conceptions of the future. Under the influence of such a state of mind, the people [*peuple*] easily lets its government develop its organism abusively, so that every external conquest can be considered as having as its corollary an internal conquest, carried out by the party that holds power [*pouvoir*].

The syndicalist general strike offers the greatest analogies with the first aspect of war: the proletariat organizes itself for battle by clearly separating itself from the other parts of the nation, by regarding itself as the great motor of history, by subordinating every social consideration to its fight. It has the very distinct feeling of the glory that must attach itself to its historical role and of the heroism of its militant attitude; it aspires to the decisive test in which it will give the full measure of its value. Since it does not pursue any kind of conquest, it has no use for plans about how it may use its victories; it counts on expelling the capitalists from the domain of production and straightaway returning to its place in the workshop created by capitalism.

This general strike very clearly signals its indifference to the material profits of conquest by affirming that it aims to eliminate the state; the state has in effect been the organizer of the war of conquest, the dispenser of its fruits, and the raison d'être of the dominant groups who profit from all the undertakings whose costs are borne by the whole of society.[25]

Politicians take up the opposite point of view. They reflect on social conflicts in the exact same way as diplomats reflect on international affairs; the entire properly martial machinery of war interests them only feebly, and they see combatants only as instruments. The proletariat is their army, which they love with the love that a colonial administrator may have for the armed bands that allow him to subject countless Negroes to his whims. They seek to pull the proletariat along because they are in a hurry to quickly win the great battles that will deliver them the state; they stoke the ardor of their men, in the same way that the ardor of mercenary troops has always been stoked, by exhorting them to the impending pillage and by appeals to hatred, as well as by the minor favors that are already permitted by the distribution of some political posts. But for them the proletariat is *cannon fodder* and nothing else, as Marx himself said in 1873.[26]

The reinforcement of the state is at the basis of all their conceptions; in their current organizations politicians already prepare the cadres of a strong, centralized, disciplined power, which will be untroubled by the criticisms of an opposition, which will impose silence and decree its lies.[27]

→→←←

[256–57] The study of the political strike leads us to a better understanding of a distinction that must always be kept in mind when one reflects upon contemporary social questions. The terms "force" and "violence" are sometimes employed when speaking of acts of authority, sometimes when speaking of acts of revolt. It is clear that the two cases give rise to very different consequences. In my view it would be very beneficial to adopt a terminology devoid of ambiguity by reserving the term "violence" for the latter sense; we will therefore say that the object of force is to impose the organization of a certain social order in which a minority governs, while violence tends toward the destruction of that order. The bourgeoisie has employed force ever since the beginning of modern times, while the proletariat now reacts against the bourgeoisie and the state with violence.

→>-<←

[265–67] The political general strike distills this entire conception into an easily understood picture; it shows us how the state would lose none of its force, how a transmission from the privileged to the privileged would take place, how the people [*peuple*] of producers would achieve a change in masters.[28] These masters would probably be less skilled than the current ones; they would make more beautiful speeches than the capitalists, but everything leads us to believe that they would be far harsher and more brazen than their predecessors.

The *new school* argues in a diametrically opposed manner. It cannot accept the idea that the proletariat's historical mission is to imitate the bourgeoisie; it cannot understand how a revolution as prodigious as the one that would suppress capitalism could be attempted for the sake of such a minor and dubious result, for a change in masters, for the satisfaction of ideologues, politicians, and speculators—all worshippers and exploiters of the state. It does not wish to limit itself to Marx's formula; if the latter only theorized bourgeois force, that is not a reason in its eyes to stick rigorously to the imitation of bourgeois force.

During the course of his revolutionary career, Marx was not always felicitously inspired, and too often he followed inspirations belonging to the past. In his writings, he even ended up introducing a host of shop-worn ideas deriving from the utopians. The *new school* does not feel itself at all obliged to admire the illusions, faults, and errors of the one who did so much to develop revolutionary ideas; it strives to establish a separation between what blemishes Marx's work and what must immortalize his name. It thereby counters those official socialists who wish to admire in Marx above all what is not Marxist. We will accordingly attach no importance to the numerous texts that can be cited against us to show that Marx often understood history along the same lines as the politicians.

We now know the reason for his attitude: Marx was not aware of the distinction, which today appears so clear to us, between bourgeois force and proletarian violence, because he did not live in milieus that had acquired a satisfactory conception of the general strike.[29] Today we know enough to understand the syndicalist strike as well as the political strike; we know how the proletarian movement differentiates itself from the bourgeois movements of the past. We find in the attitude of revolutionaries faced with the state the means of distinguishing notions that were still quite confused in the mind of Marx.

— *Trans. Alberto Toscano*

ERICH UNGER,
FROM *POLITICS AND METAPHYSICS*

Translator's Preface

In a letter to Gerhard (later, Gershom) Scholem dated simply "January, 1921," Walter Benjamin informed his friend that in just the previous week he had attended two evening lectures by the philosopher Erich Unger (1887–1950) in which Unger presented readings from his soon-to-be-published book, *Politik und Metaphysik* (Politics and metaphysics; hereafter *PM*).[1] This book, Benjamin went on to say, promises to be "the most significant piece of writing on politics in our time" (*GB* 2:127; *C* 172). In what follows, I will offer a brief account of what Benjamin found so compelling in *PM*, but this requires some background about the wider context of left-wing political thought dubbed "Aktivismus" (Activism) in prewar Wilhelmine Germany. Aktivismus was given its name and theoretical adumbration by Kurt Hiller, a friend and associate of Unger. Since Hiller is represented in this volume with his own text, my comments about Aktivismus will be limited and focused on Unger's critical turn away from his earlier engagement with Hiller.

According to the curriculum vitae attached to his 1922 dissertation in philosophy, Erich Unger attended the Friedrichs-Gymnasium in Berlin from 1897 to 1906, after which he matriculated at the University of Berlin, where he studied law and philosophy until 1913. Together with some of his friends from his years at the Friedrichs-Gymnasium, especially Erwin Loewenson, Unger joined the anti-anti-Semitic Berlin University student group, the Freie Wissenschaftliche Vereinigung (Free Scholarly Union, abbreviated FWV). This group, dedicated to advocating for socially progressive causes and to freewheeling discussions about the latest developments in the human and natural sciences, was founded in 1881 by Jewish students in response to the publication of a controversial essay on the Jewish question by the Berlin professor Heinrich von Treitschke several years earlier, inciting the so-called Berliner Antisemitismusstreit.[2] At the center of this student group when Unger and Loewenson joined it in 1906 was Kurt Hiller.[3] Hans Davidson, the poet who later published under the name Jacob von Hoddis, was another important member of this student group at the time. Jacob von Hoddis, together with Kurt Hiller and the poet Georg Heym, became the literary triumvirate at the heart of the early expressionist circle in Berlin that called itself the New Club, which was formed in 1909 by Hiller and Loewenson as an offshoot of the FWV. The New Club served as a forum for new poets who shared a disdain for the bourgeois "philistinism" of the older generation, and who sought to forge a unity between critical (and even "nihilistic") rationality and emotional vitality. Unger, Hiller, and Loewenson were the core theoreticians of the New Club, and Aktivismus was the group's core program from the outset, although the term was only coined in 1915 by Hiller. As the Hiller scholar Lewis Wurgaft has persuasively shown, the most significant term in this program was *Geist*: "The Activists were convinced that a radical change was needed in the conventionally understood function of *Geist* (creative spirit) in social life. In response to the apparent remoteness of much German intellectual endeavor, they stressed the social impact of cultural activity. They attempted to unite the artistic and theoretical preoccupations of the *geistig* community with the needs of society as a whole."[4] At the center of *PM* is also a concern with how to integrate *Geist* and society in such a way that a radical transformation in the political orientation of Germany might be achieved. *PM* can be understood as a postwar revision of the basic principles of Aktivismus in light of the cataclysmic failure of *Geist* to redeem Germany from the feudal rigidity of Prussian social conservatism and the imperialist ambitions to which its rapid industrialization was tied.

After the war, Unger turned away from Aktivismus's (and expressionism's) concentration on the *geistig* power of the individual artist-poet and focused instead on a level of *Geist* beneath the threshold of individual consciousness, a level that was linked to the biological processes through which the human body is fabricated within the womb and maintained in existence throughout its lifespan. Relying on medical studies of altered states of consciousness such as those achieved by Yogi masters, Unger argued that this subthreshold level of *Geist* can affect the metabolism and general physiology of the individual, raising the possibility that the bioenergetic forces at work could be harnessed for the benefit of the social group. Unger also relied on the work of ethnologists who studied the relationship between the shaman and the tribal group to argue for the possibility of reactivating this tribal-mythic dimension of *Geist* in modern society. In turning away from the more attenuated forms of cultural expression that were the focus of Aktivismus's projects, Unger was not so much breaking with his and Hiller's earlier commitments as reinscribing them within a different theoretical frame, the so-called psychophysical problem, as I will shortly explain. Before turning to this, however, I must add one more name to the list of Unger's early intellectual collaborators: Oskar Goldberg (1885–1952).

Unger's *PM* was the first publication out of a total of four in a series titled Die Theorie: Versuche zu philosophischer Politik (Theory: Essays toward a philosophical politics), all of which were manifestos of a radical Jewish group whose spiritual guide and mentor was Oskar Goldberg. Most notable among these four volumes was Goldberg's magnum opus *Die Wirklichkeit der Hebräer* (The reality of the Hebrews; 1925).[5] After his father's early death, Goldberg was raised in an Orthodox Berlin home by his mother and paternal grandfather, who introduced Goldberg at the age of six to a circle of kabbalistic adepts in Berlin, possibly of East European origin. They judged Goldberg to have an exceptional potential for the Kabbalah and therefore agreed to train him despite his young age. Goldberg published a work on the numerical structures of the Pentateuch (*gematria*) in 1908 that received positive reviews from a number of Germany's leading rabbis.[6] Goldberg also shared with Unger and Loewenson his ideas about the metaphysical underpinnings of the Pentateuch's numerical edifice in discussions he held with them during their *Gymnasium* years. Unger came to believe that Goldberg's ideas held the key to the reactivation of *Geist* in the modern world. Goldberg claimed to have demonstrated that the Pentateuch contained a detailed blueprint for how a group of individuals can become united by means of their interlinked and vastly intensified biological power, achieved through their ability to experience the full influx of the transcendental life force at the pulsating heart of the supernal realm, what Goldberg called the I-Force (*I-Kraft*, where "I" represents the first letter, *yod*, of the four-letter name of God). Unger found Goldberg's kabbalistically inspired vitalist metaphysics of the Pentateuch to be perfectly attuned to his quest for a radically transformative *Geist*.

Benjamin mentions Goldberg and the group that saw him as their spiritual guide in the same letter to Scholem in which he discusses Unger's *PM*: "The Hebraic side of these people goes back to a Mr. Goldberg—to be sure I know very little about him, but his impure aura repelled me emphatically every time I was forced to see him, to the extent that I was unable to shake hands with him" (*GB* 2:128; *C* 173). In his recollections about his friendship with Benjamin, Scholem explains that in the early 1920s Benjamin was in frequent contact with the "Goldberg circle," some of whom he had known from his prewar days in Berlin. Unger was apparently a new acquaintance of Benjamin's, although Benjamin had known other members of the New Club. Scholem relates that Benjamin made a special effort at "maintaining his connection with Unger" despite his personal antipathy toward Goldberg, who was usually present at their meetings.[7]

Soon after his attendance at Unger's evening lectures in January 1921, Benjamin invited him to contribute to a journal that he was planning to launch, *Angelus Novus*. In a statement announcing the goals of this journal, Benjamin adverts to a theme that is central to *PM*, the dissolution of society into competing parties without any organizing unity. Benjamin hoped that the formal disunity of the journal's contributions would hold a mirror to the wider social and political disunity in Germany at that time: "Nothing appears more important to the editor than that the journal ... express the truth of the situation, which is that ... *the different collaborators will prove unable to create any unity* [*Einheit*], *let alone a community* [*Gemeinschaft*]. The journal should proclaim through the mutual alienness of their contributions *how impossible it is in our age to give voice to any community*" (2:246; *SW* 1:296). The opening of the second section of *PM*, not translated here, provides Unger's succinct formulation of a similar judgment about "our age" and the need for a transformative theoretical stance in relation to "the situation": "It is necessary to completely alter the atmosphere of our political world. There are no *possibilities* that today exist in this world. ... For anyone to become conscious of the monstrous, choking sterility of this sociological realm, he needs first to have sensed the existence of a sphere of other constellations" (*PM* 30). Benjamin, sharing Unger's assessment of the age, conceived of his journal *Angelus Novus* as carrying a message from what Unger called "a sphere of other constellations," if only by its rejection of fake aesthetic unity.

In the letter describing his impressions of Unger's lectures, Benjamin informs Scholem that he has "an extremely lively interest in his [Unger's] ideas."

Of particular interest, Benjamin goes on to explain, are Unger's ideas concerning "the psychophysical problem," which "surprisingly have some points in common with my own" (GB 2:128; C 173).[8] The psychophysical problem, that is, the relationship between consciousness and its organic basis, is indeed central to Unger's *PM*, as well as to his philosophical interests more generally. In 1922, the year after *PM* was published, Unger presented his doctoral dissertation in philosophy at the University of Erlangen. It was titled "Das psychophysiologische Problem und sein Arbeitsgebiet: Eine methodologische Einleitung" (The psychophysiological problem and its disciplinary treatment: A methodological introduction).[9]

Unger's answer to the psychophysical problem is to posit a "fabrication-causality" that binds the body into a perduring organic unity as an individual member of a species. Consciousness is the interface between the centripetal force that at every instant fabricates the body into a unified whole and the organism's external environment. Consciousness in the human organism is capable of self-reflexivity, but it is typically unable to experience the operation of the fabrication-causality within the body. Human consciousness only sees its own body as a separate entity from the world of its fellow humans, when in fact it is tied to its fellow humans at the deep level of the species-defining fabrication-causality. If a political leader were able to gain consciousness of the fabrication-causality within his own body, he would be able to operate the lever to effectuate a massive shift in the way that his society is constructed. Under such a leader, an "ethically satisfactory order of human togetherness" (*PM* 4) can come *instantly* into being. The fabrication-causality acts in an "all at once" (*einmalig*) manner that can generate a psychophysiological transformation in the social body in a kind of atomic chain reaction (the metaphor is Goldberg's; see *Die Wirklichkeit der Hebräer*, 24). Such, at least, is the guiding hypothesis of *PM*.

Unger certainly does not want to refocus politics away from economics to more "spiritual" concerns but rather to take politics *deeper* into human materiality, into the unitary source—the "archetypal-causal" nexus—underlying both the biological and economic existence of every human collectivity. Since this is where all the body's energies are concentrated (see esp. 227), it can serve as a means to unify the collectivity into a conflict-free social totality. A political program that fails to draw upon the concentrated life energy of the individuals within the society can, at best, resolve conflicting material interests by means of some temporary compromise, but every unity achieved in this way is purely mechanical, imposed by external pressure to accept a situation that no party to the compromise really desires (see 225). An organic unity, on the other hand, arises from a deeper source where each element of the organism finds its place in a whole whose structure is prefigured as an "*all-at-once* reality of all the separate forces" (*Realität des Auf-ein-Mal aller beteiligten Kräfte*) (225). Adapting Goldberg's ideas about the ancient Hebrews, Unger argues in *PM* that the fabrication-causality was, in ancient times, shared across a group of individuals belonging to a *Volk* (folk). When the group activated this fabrication-causality together in certain rituals, the biological energy bound together by this causality was intensified. The intensified bioenergy of the *Volk* at the center of the cult has the potential to be collected in certain specially prepared vessels. Goldberg would argue in *The Reality of the Hebrews* that the power attributed to the Ark of the Covenant in the Hebrew Bible is an example of this bioenergy-collecting device. In a paragraph from *PM* omitted here, Unger alludes to this heightened biological energy as it once was controlled by the "priests of the ancient peoples, who were also invested as healers and rulers" (*PM* 27). Unger thus holds out hope for a new "prophetic" figure whose heightened power of *Geist* can provide the metaphysical-biological focus for a new social order.

— Bruce Rosenstock

ERICH UNGER,
FROM *POLITICS AND METAPHYSICS*

[3] There is a single idea, a single alteration in the way we perceive the real world, which will guide both this programmatic enterprise and the more extensive discussions that will follow from it. This idea touches on the question of the divergence or conjunction of two ways in which life expresses itself; it touches on the assessment of a relation that we regard as nothing less than a vital point—one might also call it a *lethal knot* [*nodus letalis*]—in all of human existence.

The establishment of a noncatastrophic human order and the survival of any such order—any kind of noncatastrophic politics—is impossible as long as it is not metaphysical. Politics and metaphysics are the two areas whose conjunction stands in question before us. How is such a conjunction possible? The one—politics—is a concern that in every moment places upon us an unavoidable demand for practical results; the other—metaphysics—is a concern that has always seemed theoretically incapable of a single result, even in the most remote future. How could the two concerns be conjoined except in some fictional universe? How can one "unitize" a tangible and an intangible, [or in other words] harmonize something that is finite and concrete like every political reality with something that is unforeseeable? And from such a "unity" how in the world can a line lead to the dissolution of a rigid, concrete-social problematic other than as a floating unreality?

Nonetheless, we hold that this most fantastic conjunction is, at the same time, the most realistic and sober way, indeed the only way, to conceive of a noncatastrophic human order, provided that we succeed in opening our eyes to the character of finality [*Endgültigkeit*] in temporary and seemingly changeable periods of time, on the one hand, and manage to sharpen our understanding of the concepts of metaphysics and politics to such an extent that we can make effective use of both, on the other. The completion of the first task will offer us the means for methodically unfolding and assessing the objective possibilities that exist in the state and society. The completion of the second will provide us with a pathway toward praxis.

It is appropriate to identify right away the kind of intellectual orientation that is required of anyone who might wish to undertake this programmatic reflection with us. Only this orientation is of any avail against the thousands of objections that threaten to overwhelm us in advance and will only be discussed in later, more extensive treatments of the problem. The attitude in question is the one that appears to entail a maximum of hopelessness: *assessing all the elements and factors at work in present and past political experience, it finds that no ethically satisfactory order of human togetherness has ever emerged from them; but it nonetheless refuses either to give up on the claim that it makes for the value of this goal or—which amounts to the same thing—to defer its achievement to the distant future.* [4] This intellectual attitude allows us to recognize in its most starkly conceivable form the tense opposition between the two horns of the dilemma that we face today. Accordingly, the line of thought developed here addresses itself, above all, to those who find in the political facts of this generation no forces [*Kräfte*] that would be ethically more productive than those found in the political facts of prior generations and for whom "history" is only a "history of debacle" [*Geschichte des Fehlschlagens*]. Any history cut off from ethical normativity is a course [*Ablauf*] whose stigma is failure (whereas myth is a course whose stigma is success).

Accordingly, the following is the most fundamental presupposition of what is developed here: every apparent "approximation" [*Annäherung*] to any kind of "ideal condition" [*Idealzustand*] is to be seen as a marching-in-place, and every maneuver that is geared toward such an "approximation" is to be rejected in the sharpest possible terms. Talk of "approximation" is simply the way that *every* generation rationalizes its failure to realize within *its* lifetime and without remainder an idea or ethically demanded content. A contributing factor to this attitude is a particular moral sensibility, one for whom the realization of a final [*endgültig*] ethical condition would be a "supreme achievement" of humankind—that is, a goal that would constitute a perfection [*Vollkommenheit*] if it were reached. The assumption is, however, that the achievement of a perfection must "hover" in our minds as something that can only take place in the most distant future; for we are apparently unable to conceive of what to do with the world after the realization of "ideal conditions." In short, for this kind of moral sensibility the world ends, rather than begins, at a stage of fulfillment. Indeed, we lack any "mental image of the *experience*" [Erfahrungs*bild im Geiste*] of the situation *after* ideal conditions have been realized, yet such an image would appear necessary for the concretization of any intention to realize them, and so, *for this very reason*, ideal conditions are deemed "unattainable." In all seriousness, battle, conflict, disharmony, and their elimination are indeed *contents*—contents of experience—whereas a finality [*Endgültigkeit*] seemingly leaves no space for anything, except for *repetition*. For a moral sensibility, then, for which the realization of the ideal condition would *imply the end of all days*, conceiving of the ideal condition as something that may be realized immediately must be a ridiculous absurdity that is unworthy of discussion. But our attitude is the very opposite of this: it is possible to specify contents for the time *after* a perfect situation has been realized. The ideal condition is not an end point; it is not at all a matter that we endlessly "approximate" but rather a necessary presupposition whose realization is not an "achievement" and whose lack of realization constitutes the maximum of ethical and any other kind of inferiority that can be found anywhere in the world. We presuppose this view. It is shared by a movement that also considers the creation of ethically normative conditions as a mere presupposition, yet this movement is unable to specify the *contents* [5] for which the realization of these conditions is the presupposition. The movement in question is that of *communism* and *anarchism* of every possible stripe. At least communism recognizes the *temporal* problem of social change inasmuch as it is convinced—as we are—that humans do not have to regard themselves as *objects* of human history, as if human affairs were like things in the natural world, so that the way humans ought to be is made subordinate to how they actually are. Communism sees the required ethical condition as a whole, rather than just a part of it, as something that is demanded *instantaneously*; that is, the movement does not include *in advance* a possible break in reaching the ideal condition in its program. The communist program is not at all set to put up with partial measures, or "small contributions," or "getting closer, step by step." The approximation to a condition that has been "set before" one's mind [*Geist*] is the result of a *later* intuition of the path leading from the intention to its concretization; only the *retrospective* view of a line leading up to a point that has already been reached is able to determine segments of approximation.[1] By contrast, the *intention* cannot really take into account points of approximation if it is to *aim* in actual fact at the target point rather than the first intermediary point. If the intention or will were already to include, in its program, the breaks between different stages of concretization, it would affirm the resistance of the opposing matter to an inadmissible extent. Negating matter *in any case*, however, is the sole task of the intention or will, whereas determining the special *mode* of this negation is the task of reason. The method of "approximation" is a transposition [*Übertragung*] of the historical way of thinking onto teleological relations. In purely *ethical* terms, one is never able to identify an approximation to a condition that would correspond to an *idea* within the course of rational history (which is already proven by the fact that a "rational" principle of history only exists for philosophical speculation, but not for empirical science). In purely *causal* terms, one can only identify approximations to some more or less arbitrarily chosen historical situations. On both logical and empirical grounds, we thus eliminate the principle of *approximating* behavior [*Annäherungs-Verhalten*] from the attitude that we seek to outline here.

→>-<+-

[7] *Politics—today that means essentially the same as: the economy.* We do not want to play off "the spiritual" [*Geist*] against "the material" when we say this—in the sense that we would blame "materialism" in the usual manner, point to the spiritual [*ideell*] "values" of life, find salvation in the "rejection" of the material, and take "refuge" in the "spiritual realm" [*Geistigen*]. We do not intend to set up the following alternative: body *or* spirit [*Körper* oder *Geist*].[2] Indeed, we dare to assert that we in no way want to deny the importance that has come to be attached to the material realm or—in more or less "transposed" [*übertragen*] terms—the bodily interests of human beings. But we do wish to insist that these interests cannot be represented and protected by the material realm alone. We want to put forward a reversal [*Umkehrung*] that goes against the basic tendency of contemporary politics and must appear outrageous to it. Politics today is guided by the allegedly self-evident proposition that no one except the interested party itself looks after its interests. We want to oppose to this view the possibility that the interested party is wholly incompetent [*unzuständig*] so far as representing its interests when

it finds itself in the middle of a chaos of interests. Someone might object and say that the incompetence of the interested party will be corrected by a *counterinterest*, which will be represented by the "government" no matter what the system of representation may be, and interest and counterinterest must then find a balance for there to be objective justice. Even in the most just case, however, what is called "government" today is merely a theater of war for a *reduced* set of partisan interests and a reductive representation of the *quanta of power* that are raging in full force within the state. How in the world could anything of ethical consequence come to pass through such a *reduction*, that is, how can the essential nature of every *battle*—according to which the stronger will prevail and the weaker will submit—be avoided simply by turning the direct struggle of economic classes into a struggle among their representatives? Some will say that the essential nature of battle is not really *supposed* to be avoided by representative government; [8] rather, the battle is played out as a "peaceful battle" whose end point is a *compromise* to which all the parties must agree. But this "peaceful battle" or compromise, which is the main element of our present politics, is just the latent form of open battle. Compromise is always and must always be a mere postponement of rape [*Vergewaltigung*]: it is a temporary agreement among enemies as long as neither one of them can muster the strength to defeat the other. Every compromise is a product situated within the mentality of violence [*Mentalität der Gewalt*], no matter how much it may disdain all open violence, because the effort toward compromise is motivated not *internally* but from outside, indeed by the opposing effort, for no compromise, however freely accepted, is conceivable without a compulsory character. "It would be better otherwise" is the basic feeling belonging to every compromise.[3] Although compromise, understood as the resultant of competing political or economic tendencies, is the expression of a temporary distribution of forces [*Kraft-Verteilung*], it is never the expression of an *ethically* normative situation. The latter is never identical with compromise, unless one makes power [*Macht*] or the balance of power the standard of right or law [*Recht*]. But then this "law" will bear full responsibility for all the catastrophes that are caused by a shift in power, and we, who posited earlier that the complete absence of any destructive upheaval is the symptom of a moral order, cannot support the identification of right and might—and so we cannot allow conflict in any form, not even the "peaceful" one called *compromise*, to serve as a substitute for justice [*Gerechtigkeit*].

In opposition to the concept of compromise as a "balance of forces," we must indicate at the very least another way in which a complex of forces can behave: forces can achieve a "balance" either *mechanically*, such that they are added to one another or subtracted from another, or they can form a "system." A *system* of forces is the very opposite of a compromise of forces. A compromise of forces in the sense of a balance or a resultant force is found *everywhere* in nature, even in the most arbitrary or chaotic constellation, whereas a *system* of forces is found only in an "organism." In a mechanical balance of forces, each force acts by itself, and only at the point where it *meets* the other forces is it influenced by them, either to be decreased or increased in its magnitude; the balancing-out thus works *mechanically*. In a system of forces, by contrast, each force acts as if the others had been included in it from the *beginning*. Each force acts as if an *all-at-once* reality of all the forces involved had existed and been effective *before* any individual force came into being, as if there had been a prior reality of *togetherness* from which a force-differentiating and force-ordering tendency had proceeded—as if each force from its *beginning, right away*, at the *point of its emergence*, had experienced the action and influence of all the other forces. In this way, they all emerge immediately ordered—the balancing-out works *organically*.

[9] This moment of interaction among forces before their emergence, of the existence of the *entire* reality *before* the existence of its parts, is not found within the realm of individual forces, precisely because they have become independent of one another, which they could not have done if they had not emerged *one after the other*, as elements of a "development," in the course of which they eventually collide with one another mechanically. These forces could not have become independent of each other if they had emerged as tendencies that determine each other *in advance, simultaneously*, and have to adapt to each other like the elements of an organism. At the outset, however, the scene of such an original coexistence of the individual forces would have been an intellectual [*geistig*] one: their organic structure would at first have existed in the form of a *conception* [*Conception*].

The unity of the whole cannot be derived from the complete collection of parts because the latter have become *independent* of each other.

If we want to illustrate this abstract train of thought with our concrete case, we can say this: The tendencies of the economic world are found in a state of conflict. Thus, they are independent forces that can at best maintain a *mechanical* balance.

However, the original unity of these forces or an analogon of their organ-like coexistence can no longer be determined, because these tendencies, inasmuch as they make conflict possible, that is, inasmuch as they have become independent of each other, have acquired *a different form* and taken *a different direction* than they would have if they had remained in a state of organic connectedness.

No combination or permutation of the tendencies of parties can result in an ethically normative order of the whole domain of the economy because the economy is, *for the parties*, more or less a formula for economic ups and downs [*Konjunkturformel*]. What the economy *in truth* is cannot be deduced from individual phenomena in a pathological economic world but, as with any organic whole, can only be grasped and put into effect on the basis of a notion of purpose [*Zweckvorstellung*] that lies *beyond* the economy.

This means: *The problem of the economy*—the main problem of all human conflicts—*cannot be resolved from within its own domain*.

But it cannot be resolved purely on the level of "spirit" [*Geist*] either.

⟶⟵

[18] *This problem is nothing but an expression of the psychophysiological one*, and we once more have an opportunity to take advantage of a seeming accumulation of obstacles; for as the open questions of *two* different areas meet in one zone, new factors are introduced into our calculation.

[19] In the most condensed fashion, we want to indicate what these factors are. We may suspect—and we will find our suspicion is confirmed—that the extraordinary recalcitrance shown by the question of how the psychophysiological linkage takes place is due in large part to the fact that we continue to look for the point of connection between a psychical magnitude and materiality *within the individual* [*Einzelindividuum*]. Quite possibly, the point of connection cannot be found there, or it would have to be there when seen from the physiological side of the connection but not necessarily when seen from its psychical side. For the mind [*Geist*] and its organism are inhomogeneous and cannot be made commensurable with one another insofar as the body is placed in a biological plurality-nexus [*Vielheits-Nexus*], for which there is no analogon or evidence in any of the elements of "naturally given" consciousness. As a consequence, consciousness—which can only grasp what can be deduced from within it—experiences [*empfindet*] the body as something that came into being *outside of it*, something that is literally

"hetero-geneous" to it. With respect to the body, the reach of consciousness is in a sense *too short*. There is apparently no part of my consciousness that communicates to me the construction [*Konstruktion*] of my body. Whereas the mind has forms of intuition [*Anschauungsformen*] for the *use* of my body, there does not seem to be anything like that for intuiting the body's *disposition* [*Anlage*]. There are forms for intuiting bodies *from the outside*, but there are none for intuiting them *from the inside*. The sensorium of the individual [*Einzel-Sinnlichkeit*], as a matter of *logic* (and not as a matter of history), does not extend as far as the genetics [*Genetik*] of its own body, and it *cannot* extend that far because what matters for the complete grasp of our own materiality—which would in effect be the solution to the psychophysiological problem—is *not* the cyclical-biological genesis of the body but its unique causal genesis. In contrast to the ever-repeating biological cause that predetermines a course of development [*Ablauf*], the unique causal genesis refers to the cause of this predetermination—that is, the cause of the construction of the body that would operate not merely, as one might naïvely suspect, the way a single cause does, at the very *"beginning,"* but *transversally* as a concentrating cause. An intuition of the unique causal genesis of the body, however, cannot possibly be found within the sensorium of the individual, since the latter is, in turn, not a psychic magnitude that would be commensurable with the scope of an event such as the causality that concentrates the entirety of the biological cycle.

Thus, our psychical and physiological data do not fit together; that is, the psychophysiological problem continues to resist treatment *because of the total lack of clarity about the aspect of plurality* involved in the issue.

Accordingly, the reality of a plurality-existence [*Vielheitsexistenz*] is the point upon which both the psychophysiological problem and, at its deepest foundation, the sociological problem depend. [20] And so it is imperative that we take a position in relation to the limit question confronting the natural sciences; for it is only in the consideration of this question that a new political beginning will become possible, one that will inaugurate the true power of reflection.

Historically speaking, "politics" has always proceeded as if only the individual existed, albeit the individual repeated *n* times. "Politics" has overlooked the fact that this repetition must have a meaning, one according to which *the plurality* [*Vielheit*] *as such* could have an equally originary validity of existence as a *"single entity"* [*Einzelheit*]. Plurality is not to be understood as a merely "intellectual bond" [*geistiges Band*] holding together the "only real" entities, namely, individuals; rather, it needs to be seen as a reality in its own right whose meaning needs to be determined. If we want to avoid taking the logically and ethically dangerous step of splitting apart questions of purpose and meaning from questions of existence—all that matters for philosophical systems that establish a transcendent reality is that the latter not be confused with empirical reality, for empirical reality is irrelevant for the question of meaning, while transcendent reality is decisive in that regard—then we should not posit relations between psychic units without a foundation in reality. In that case, however, there remain only two options: either we embrace the doctrine of strict materialism, according to which a factually existent plurality has meaning only in a quantitative regard, or we choose the following option.

Since *addition* is not something that one can do with psychical entities, the existence of a plurality must indeed imply the possibility of an elevation [*Steigerbarkeit*] if a plurality is to have meaning on the level of psychic reality at all. However, this elevation can neither be a lateral expansion, as though it were the result of a physiological agglomeration, nor depend on numerical multiplication [*Vervielfachung*]. Since consciousness is in principle an "*innerness*" of unlimited exclusiveness, an elevation of consciousness can only lie in the expandability of this innerness—that is, *in the inclusion of originally alien psychical factors within a single consciousness.*[4]

All the questions of philosophy, and not just of philosophy, as we are going to show, lead in the end to the psychophysiological problem. This problem cuts across any and every system, from the most materialistic to the most idealistic, causing a rift in thinking that neither materialism nor idealism nor psychophysical parallelism is able to mend. This rift imposes itself on these explanatory hypotheses in the form of a lack of connection between, on the one hand, a psychical event whose bodiliness is at the very least intangible, and, on the other, its parallel physical process. Or, to rephrase the issue in terms of another doctrine, there is no connection between the sensation of consciousness, on the one hand, and the sensation of extension, on the other (for by comprehending both in a subjective manner and calling them "sensations" or something similar, I have in no way bridged the divergence in *content* between these sensations)....

[22] We are presented with the following possibilities. If the psychophysiological problem is amenable to solution, then two things are possible in principle.

First, the consciousness of certain physiologically separate individuals is not a fixed magnitude but is open to modification by psychical factors of a plurality for which there exists, in a nonmetaphorical sense, a psychophysiological nexus.

Second, by raising the power of consciousness in this manner (techniques for which are the subject of an entire scientific discipline) it becomes possible to advance to the experience of one's own materiality, that is, one's body, in the direction of its construction. In other words, what becomes possible is a coming together and coincidence of consciousness and the genetic and constructive forces of the organism (which were far beyond the reach of consciousness before). This amounts to nothing more or less than the principle of *handling* these forces. Areas that were closed off before now become accessible.

These two possibilities circumscribe the paradigm of an expanded sensorium [*Sinnenhaftigkeit*] that would have to use the immediate effectiveness of mental processes [*geistige Leistungen*] for political purposes. We have to spell out once more and *in concreto* the political significance of this possibility.

All progress in philosophy depends upon increasing the analyzability of our own materiality or our consciousness of it. And just as the exactitude of mathematics and the rule-governed understanding of the entire *physical* world with it follows from a particular state of *our* sensorium, attaining a rule-governed intuition of the *sociological* world requires an elevated sensorium that allows for the experience of *our own* materiality. When it comes to the sociological world, all exactitude lies in such an elevated sensorium, or if you will, in its "pure form."

[23] The relationship between, on the one hand, our unmodified sensorium and objective nature (in the narrower sense) and, on the other hand, between our modified "intuition" and our "fellow-being world" [*Seinesgleichen-Welt*] (that is, the assessment of the repetition of the individual as a natural fact) is also evident from a systematic point of view. (Incidentally, one should not misunderstand the term "intuition," which also applies, for instance, to *time* as a *form* of "*intuition*.") Our experience of objective nature is structured as if there were only one single human being; the fact of human plurality is irrelevant, but it is decisive for the problematic of sociology. Sociology, however, treats the concept of nature as if it came to an end at the point where its problematic begins. Its normative evaluations are, therefore, uprooted and proceed *without* making a decision regarding

the existential foundation of plurality (thereby overlooking the necessity of a transcendent reality, which is acknowledged elsewhere), as if "*one's own nature*" were a problem already solved. (The idea, by the way, that the autonomy of normative evaluations or the freedom of the will would somehow be annulled by knowledge of the rule-bound structure of an area of experience has little force when the rules arise from out of the human personality [*Personalität*] itself.) As already noted, the experience of nature is structured as if there were only one single human being. Apart from the extremely noteworthy fact of the so-called universal validity of natural laws, in which one can already discern an *intensive* manifestation of the possibility of *external* consciousness, the experience of nature is essentially the experience of myself inasmuch as I am a biological individual. However, the perception of a plurality is also a perception of myself, but not of myself as a biologically individuated entity but as a biologically unique and archetypically causal being. The difference between these two types of perception is the difference (to put it in mythological terms) between procreation [*Zeugung*] and ("creation" [*Schöpfung*] or) construction. The body, insofar as it is an arbitrary instrument of experience, belongs to the biological individual, whereas the body with regard to its *construction* belongs to a unity in which biological multiplication [*Vervielfachung*] has been undone.

If the theme of plurality, the central theme of all sociological research, thus becomes relevant for the clarification of nature's most authentic problem and, accordingly, is drawn into the natural sciences, then one may very well assume that sociology will be decisively transformed by *this* assessment of plurality as a fact of nature.

The state will become nature; the antithesis between the two will cease, not in some banal Rousseauvian return to a *long-lost* unity with nature but through the further development of *both* poles of the antithesis, not only of the state but also of—psychophysiological—nature beyond their present limits. It is, however, nothing other than the elevated [*gesteigert*] perception of myself that permits such development in the direction of the constructive element and a modified, rule-governed intuition.

→>-<←

[29] If consciousness, insofar as it rises to the level of "knowing [*Wissen*]" in the widest sense of the word, must essentially be a form of *knowing in advance* [*Vorher-Wissen*], then the metaphysical perspective must, if it is to accomplish

anything at all, realize the most concrete goal of the mind [*Geist*]: to *overtake the course of things in the material realm*.

This overtaking cannot count as an "ideal," since it is practically indispensable; there is no other thought that would identify in theory the Archimedean point that allows one to tame the blind compulsions at work in the movements found in social totalities [*Gesamtheiten*]. If anyone, it is the "statesman" who is *obligated*—to know in advance.

However, the clarification of these metaphysical relations is also binding for the plurality, for the simple reason that the latter remains *impenetrable without consideration of the element of its real totality*. There is a need for the plurality to *behave* as a totality [*Verhalten der Gesamtheit*] so that something can be accomplished at a level that currently regards the plurality as the least significant thing in the whole world.

This behavior was the subject of the metaphysical laws among the ancient peoples. And with this behavior something emerged that in recent times has been discussed only infrequently, in a vague and unscientific manner, and has remained completely unknown as a form of praxis: *the people* [*Volk*] as a plurality with a clearly identifiable *program*—a purpose [*Bestimmung*] that goes far beyond the mere economy (which presently provides the main principle of orientation) inasmuch as this purpose addresses the living embodiment [*Leiblichkeit*] of human beings even more radically than does the economy.

Here an extreme "idealism" makes use of an extreme "materialism" as an argument—for in the body the most unconditional instinct of matter meets the path of the most remote intellectual pursuit [*Geistigen*].

Within a people, a metaphysical purpose makes its presence felt not as an "idealistic" postulate forever reverberating in deaf ears but as the very condition of corporeal existence. In the presence of this teleological but nonetheless directly corporeal orientation of movement, both body and mind [*Geist*] operate together as a motivating force. For the resulting totality, the danger of a rift is thus avoided—a rift that threatens to burst open whenever the body-tendencies of individuals or groups of individuals begin to work against each other, which is something that is bound to happen if they are independent from each other rather than joined together in this psychophysical unity. Where such unity exists, the connection between individual organic *life* and the totality becomes visible, and accordingly, the economy is only of secondary importance. The economy necessarily moves into first place, however, if the metaphysical nexus joining the corporeal and the intellectual [*Geistiges*] is ripped apart. In the best of circumstances, "economy" means: a compromise of opposed forces. But the appeal to a *merely intellectual* [*bloß-geistig*] or *historical* or remote generative source of unity, one that might resolve this conflict, is bound to ring hollow and fail of its purpose if the real unity, the totality of the most intense, theoretical-concrete interests, has been lost.

[30] The people—this once meant, before the intellectual [*Geistiges*] and the corporeal had begun to diverge, the tribal totality, for this totality enclosed within itself the psychical [*Seelisches*].

Today, there are no more such peoples.

And what will come into being will be a tribal- and problem-community, a community of the most urgent theoretical-corporeal questions.

— *Trans. Bruce Rosenstock and Markus Hardtmann*

EMIL LEDERER, "SOCIOLOGY OF VIOLENCE: A CONTRIBUTION TO THE THEORY OF SOCIAL-FORMATIVE FORCES"

Translator's Preface

Emil Lederer's "Sociology of Violence" appeared in the spring of 1921 in *Die weißen Blätter* (The white pages), not long before Benjamin's essay in August of that year in the *Archiv für Sozialwissenschaft und Sozialpolitik* (Archive for social science and social policy), which Lederer also edited. Though not a source Benjamin could have consulted, it is presented here as the central statement on violence defended at the time by the figure responsible for publishing Benjamin's essay. In the early weeks of 1921, Lederer, then a professor of sociology at Heidelberg, had taken on a role as editor of *Die weißen Blätter* in a new (short-lived) series of the journal, which had previously been one of the foremost journals of literary expressionism in the German-speaking world, with a marked pacifist leaning during the war under the editorship of René Schickele. Around this time, Lederer had also been appointed managing editor of the *Archiv*, which was Germany's leading social-science periodical of the age, following the deaths of both Edgar Jaffé and Max Weber.

Born in 1882 to a German-Jewish family in the imperial Habsburg province of Bohemia, Lederer had studied in Vienna alongside Rudolf Hilferding, Joseph Schumpeter, and Ludwig von Mises, among others. In 1919 he assumed a position in Walter Rathenau's German Socialization Commission in Vienna (together with Hilferding and Schumpeter), and in the 1920s, after completing a *Habilitationsschrift* (qualifying dissertation) on German white-collar workers in 1916, became codirector of Heidelberg's Institut für Staats- und Sozialwissenschaften (Institute for Government and Social

Sciences) with Alfred Weber. The institute supported the work of figures such as Karl Mannheim and Norbert Elias, among others.[1] In 1925 Lederer joined the Social-Democratic Party, and generally all his work—which ranged from studies of the First World War through state-market relations and class conflict to parliamentary socialism—can be seen as articulating a politics in keeping with the ends and worldview of the party.[2] Lederer taught in Japan in the mid-1920s and later in the decade moved to the University of Berlin. Expelled from his post by the Nazis in 1933 because of Jewish heritage and SPD affiliation, Lederer fled via London to New York, where he helped establish the "University in Exile" at the New School for Social Research, becoming the institution's first dean and remaining in this position until his death in 1939, shortly before the arrival of some of Benjamin's former friends and associates, including Hannah Arendt and Leo Strauss. His literary archive resides in the SUNY Albany library as part of its German and Jewish Intellectual Émigré Collection, which includes a brief description of his life on its web page.[3]

How Benjamin's dealings with Lederer began remains something of a mystery. One possibility is that Ernst Bloch, with whom Benjamin had been friendly since 1919 and met repeatedly in that year during his studies in Bern, encouraged him to approach Lederer, or perhaps spoke to Lederer on Benjamin's behalf. As a figure with a marked expressionist as well as antimilitarist commitment in his early writings, and still with some contact to Lederer and other former mentors in the circle around Max Weber at Heidelberg, Bloch sent Lederer an essay, "Über den sittlichen und geistigen Führer" (On the moral and spiritual leader), which ultimately appeared in the same issue of *Die weißen Blätter* in which Lederer's own essay appeared—and Benjamin's did not.[4] From this small datum, it is at least a plausible conjecture that Bloch played a part in facilitating the relationship. In any case, we know from a letter of Benjamin to Gershom Scholem from late January 1921 that Lederer himself asked Benjamin to write something for him in late 1920 (see GB 2:127; C 172). In the same extended letter to Scholem, Benjamin indicates that he has been working on finalizing "Toward the Critique of Violence." He also notes that he sent the essay to Lederer, expecting it to appear in *Die weißen Blätter* (GB 2:130-31; C 173). In a letter to Scholem from February 14, however, Benjamin reports that Lederer has declined the essay on grounds of "length" and "difficulty" but that he will publish it instead in the *Archiv* (GB 2:138). In July 1921, shortly before the essay appeared in the August issue, Benjamin traveled to Heidelberg with plans to embark on a qualifying dissertation. He met with Lederer in July and then again in early August. Yet these meetings do not seem to have persisted into the fall. By December, Benjamin avers that he no longer considers Heidelberg a suitable venue for his plans, after certain unspecified "experiences." Lederer, for his part, ceased inviting him to his seminar (see *GB* 2:171, 173; *C* 183; *GB* 299; *C* 204).

Why exactly Lederer declined Benjamin's essay for *Die weißen Blätter*, and perhaps relatedly, why their relations deteriorated after the summer of 1921—this can only be a matter of guesswork from the extant documentation. It seems reasonable to suspect, however, that a substantive issue may have been the source of the rejection of the essay and, then again, the non-invitation to the fall seminars—a source beyond the essay's ostensible "length" and "difficulty."[5] As the editor of a journal with a more decidedly public mission than the *Archiv*, as well as a wider circulation than the latter, perhaps Lederer felt uncomfortable with Benjamin's position. Quite likely is that he may have felt perturbed by its distance from his own more developmentalist understanding of the fate of violence in European history after 1918, which Lederer defends in his contribution to the journal.

It is clear that, in contrast to Benjamin, "violence" (*Gewalt*) for Lederer is to be addressed fundamentally in some framework of social-evolutionary adaptation. As Lederer affirms at the outset of his essay, violence is to be considered structurally a thing of the past in European affairs of the age, although also something, as he notes, that—to paraphrase the opening sentence of the essay translated here—still survives in its obsolescence (see 237). In the passage of societies from feudal relations of organization via nascent capitalist economy to modern social-class arbitration under the parliamentary state, violent struggle, Lederer claims, ceases to form any lastingly "effective," "purposive," or "functional" (*zweckmäßig*) means of securing power-advantages for collective groups. Although conventional liberal narratives fail to grasp the extent to which violence recurrently eludes pacification by market economy, territorial expansionism ceases to suggest a sustainable modus operandi for an age in which societies find integration through complex global relations of interdependent individuals, in divisions of labor, and through the emergence of legislatures and intellectual public spheres as platforms of interclass bargaining. The First World War in this light is the consequence of a profound failure of European imperial states to manage their own dynamics of transformation, but it is nevertheless not a failure that must be seen as fated to recur.

There is a striking contrast between "Toward the Critique of Violence" and "The Sociology of Violence": where Lederer sees violent societal acts and events as increasingly contingent outcomes within a generally more necessary and consolidated process of conflict *institutionalization*, Benjamin sees essentially the opposite state of affairs. Where, for Lederer, Russia's and Germany's armed class insurrections remain unlikely to persist other than in some form of parliamentary incorporation, violence for Benjamin is the recurring fundament of modern structures of law, always underpinning the making and unmaking of law and liable to erupt at any moment, including in the form of the general strike. Modern social market economy, for Benjamin, is not a story of gradual interclass compromise and accommodation, as it is for Lederer; rather, it is something essentially more uncertain and labile. Nonetheless, in agreeing to publish Benjamin's essay, Lederer must surely also have sensed in it the very deep and disturbing challenges it posed. If perhaps he had been alienated by Benjamin's references to Sorel and apparent proximity to the thought of Schmitt, it is important to remember that it was Lederer, too, who, in 1927, accepted Schmitt's "Begriff des Politischen" (Concept of the political) for the *Archiv*.[6]

— *Austin Harrington*

EMIL LEDERER, "SOCIOLOGY OF VIOLENCE: A CONTRIBUTION TO THE THEORY OF SOCIAL-FORMATIVE FORCES"

In the paradoxes of today lie the truths of tomorrow. Such is the sense in which we can say that violence [*Gewalt*] outlives itself. In feudal and early capitalist societies, violence was a form to effect new distributions of social strengths [*Gewichte*]. Now, though, it is a thing of yesterday—for reasons not hard to see.

Primitive human beings tremble at the strong. In the Homeric epics is to be heard a limitless awe of physical force [*Kraft*]. Strong are those able to defeat enemies and thus to win followers; and if strength does not by itself create leadership, only the strong can contend for it, for the strong alone are the bearers of charisma—those alone in whom a divine force can dwell.

This basic outlook persists among many peoples today, whether primitive or advanced—in the one case naïvely, as nature-like bondedness, in the other as the elegiac longing for lost epochs. This link between the strong and that which is good and beautiful, indeed sublime, is the intellectual foundation of the belief in violence as the physical force that makes it possible to accomplish goals, and this belief has not even been shaken by Christianity, much less broken; only the ideology has changed. Behind every action of society and every dealing of peoples with one another lies, ultimately, in whatever symbolic refinement, an appeal to violence—as "ultima ratio," as it is tellingly called, such that reason is permitted to speak only "within the framework of power relations" (*Machtverhältnisse*), which, for their part, can be highly nonrational. All organization of social forces is, in the end, nothing but the replacement of dull, inanimate, impulsive violence by violence that is conscious, clear, ordered, and functionally structured [*zweckmäßig aufgebaut*]. Are not historians right to say that in the ways of the world, nothing has changed and nothing will?

Yet this resigned attitude remains a superficial one, for we must ask: under precisely what circumstances is violence a tool with which human beings can achieve something?

First, human beings must *believe* in violence; for even this most massive of social forms is not autochthonous. Nor are the power relations. The radius of power and violence is limited not only by their strength but also by the preparedness of human beings to acknowledge [*anerkennen*] them. The most clinically efficient and strongest state organization collapses in the very instant when human beings withdraw from it inwardly and cease to acknowledge it. Marx expressed this in his dictum that when a king views his citizens as subjects because he is their king, he does so in reality only because the citizens look up to him as his subjects.[1] The strongest power shatters like thin glass in the wake of a psychical crisis of those who are dominated. Clear-sighted despots have always known this. Despotism survives only for as long as the downtrodden believe in it, which is why rulers often sense the fragility of their position sooner than their underlings. Half of their success is simply not to draw attention to the fact and to maintain distance.

A rebellion, however, not against a given ruling power but against power as such, against power and violence as a social structure—here no such psychical shift is likely to occur for as long as the conditions for successful use of physical forces continue to be met. Although these forces have become extraordinarily refined over the course of millennia and remain, in large part, only symbolic in character, they have persisted in consciousness as a regulative principle.

Violence will be an effective means [*taugliches Mittel*] in social life—and the order of personal, interhuman, and social relations will play themselves out within the framework of power relations—only for as long as the general circumstances of life can be successfully extended, expanded, and secured by the application of force and the use of violence [*Gewaltanwendung*]. This is the case for all precapitalist epochs, where the production of goods has yet to unfold on the basis of rational business enterprise and waged labor. Certainly, capitalist systems, too, begin from violence, and within their structures, too, labor is not the source of ownership. Here, however, the relations of power no longer emanate from the sword and the whip but from social mechanisms, wherein what is decisive is not a force of arms (as is still the case even in the most refined feudal systems) but rather the intellectually calculated and directed process of production and market-"dominance" [Markt-"Beherrschung"]. Our language is still too saturated in the symbolic forms of feudalism for us adequately to articulate this basic difference. Economic domination in a capitalist age differs fundamentally from feudal domination in its functional adaptation to "economic laws," distinct from the exercise of directly physical means.

In a feudal world, encompassing not only agrarian but also artisanal production (in the form of slave labor or labor of the family), violence is an expedient [zweckmäßiges] resource for diffusing the bases of production. The powerful live from the labor of those subjected to them, requiring a surplus as the lord's basis of existence. The seigneur collects ground rent in the first instance, along with the produce of artisans. Generally, he lets "his people" produce for themselves. Not only in agriculture but also in manufacture, bondsmen work not for the market but for the master, who only occasionally brings products to a market or regularly only for particular reasons. Conquest of foreign lands thus means expulsion of a hostile ruling class, appropriation of land and labor, exploitation of revenues, and establishment of the means of settlement. Such outcomes of successful wars can be traced deep into the early capitalist period—as, for instance, after the Battle of White Mountain, with the destruction of the entire Czech aristocracy by the imperial Habsburg armies and the surrender of land and property to the Viennese high nobility.[2] For imperial colonels and field marshals, this involved conquest not only for the emperor and an abstract "state" but also direct personal extension of the means of existence. In such a world, violence was bound to appear as a last deciding instance [Kraft], and recurrent applications of violence [Gewaltanwendungen] would have been seen to follow from the most natural instincts of the human soul, from a drive for wealth, luxury, and supremacy—the sword being the sole European lingua franca, to whose arguments all inwardly acquiesced. Alongside this there stands Christianity as an at most innocuous legend, a fading ideology, frequently bending to the mentality of the age in contradictory ideals, such as in the notion of a "Christian chivalric class." Admittedly, the decline that occurs in an unquestioning faith in violence—increasingly after the eighteenth century, although widely interrupted again in the nineteenth century's wars—is one that cannot be attributed solely to changed material circumstances of life. Rather, a far-reaching psychical process [*seelischen Prozess*] is in play, one that addresses the most ancient habits of mind and can be understood concretely only in a spiritual manner [*geistig*]. Habits, thousands of years in the making, embodied in myriad institutions, in all forms of human life, in language, laws, and morals, even in forms of habitation and dress—all these undergo the deepest kind of inner transformation, such that only a revolution of the mind [*Revolution des Gemütes*] can posit itself and prevail against the outer world. Such a pause [*Einkehr*], like [Paul's] day in Damascus, is always and at all times possible. Still, it gains reality and effect only when it can set essential powers in motion, when it finds an alteration in social structure that makes its sacrifice, its personal conversion, its revolutionary deed—or however this conversion and pause [*Umkehr und Einkehr*] may express themselves—fruitful.

During the period in question, a silent and at first imperceptible transformation of social mechanisms creates an entirely new situation. Leaving aside all questions of how and why this happened, when human beings began to work not in order to consume directly but to acquire and accumulate wealth—when, that is, wealth became a goal and end in itself for the middle classes and aristocracies ceased self-evidently to hold wealth, inasmuch as wealth now itself generated seigneurial status—the seeds of a new reality of social forms were sown, now clearly setting limits to violence and doing so independently of all ideational developments. Admittedly, still today there is at work the millennia-old notion that wealth and booty stem from violence and that above all, in situations of rivalry among peoples, weapons decide in the last instance over the distribution of goods. This clearly indicates that even now the capitalist economy struggles to turn its own ideology into a mental habit.

Nevertheless, in the eighteenth century, in their attacks on mercantilism, the physiocrats saw instinctually that the mechanisms of economic relations had shifted. In its swashbuckling attitude, mercantilism had retained something of the mentality of the conquering knights. As the knights sought land, the mercantilists sought gold, preaching both peaceful and violent means to this end. But as [Lessing's character] Riccaut de la Marlinière asks at one point, so typically accentuating axioms in paradoxical turns of phrase: "So let me give you all the gold in the world; take it, have it; what now? There you are with all your riches and your goods. With whom now will you do business? Straight-away you will seek to put gold back into foreign hands, perhaps even to give it away, so that foreigners can buy your goods."[3] Riccaut's aperçu expresses our age's fundamental difference with feudal times, able to see riches as potentially a problem, capable of causing catastrophe, where victors on the battlefield become the bankrupters of others unless those riches are more functionally distributed. At first, this must have seemed paradoxical and yet obvious for an age that had ceased to think of wealth in its original form as accumulated treasure and, instead, henceforth in the derived, symbolic, and abstract form of money or "capital," which, although always convertible in physical form, never in fact *is* converted.

Wealth in this abstract form has always existed but until recently has not been the dominant, generally prevalent form. So long as the prevailing social type is the seigneurial lord as king, nobleman, military general, or indeed merchant of the crown, where capitalists appear at most as carpenters or yeomen, violence continues to be an instrument of advantage. A lord seizes the property and slaves of others. Wealth still consists mostly in consumable goods, not commodities. Capital as such is not abundant and is cherished only for its value in money. All distribution of wealth is thus nothing but a question of relations of power. But any distribution is possible. If wealth is in the hands of feudal lords, violence can always decide over its distribution. The luxuriously appointed manor house alongside the tumbledown huts of cottagers [*Kossäte*]; the courtly state of the absolute monarch amid a people of beggars: this is a stable socioeconomic condition only for as long as the downtrodden accept it—and they do accept it until capitalist processes and mechanisms make this structure impossible.

The capitalist system of production that makes wealth abstract and compels people to seek such wealth on pain of their own demise has therefore freed human beings in a very different sense from that of the system's prophets. It has not freed them by bursting any chains but, on the contrary, by establishing a coercive mechanism that breaks down the freedom of the original drives and instincts insofar as they are no longer functional [*zweckmäßig*] for it. Now let us imagine the settings discussed earlier transposed into a capitalist world: all wealth concentrated as capital in a few hands or in one hand, and many millions of free citizens without property, laboring yet acquiring no significant income and consuming but a tiny fraction of their own product. Here, instantly, the capitalist world and all its wealth would collapse for lack of circulation, because capitalists can only ever allow their products and profits to circulate freely in the economic sphere and cannot consume them.

And what is true of the national economy applies equally to the global plane: today's raging world crisis is but the sign of a world threatened by downfall for its reawakening of an obsolete structure of violence.

Clearly, violence's functionlessness [*Zwecklosigkeit*] in the economic domain has been insufficient to eliminate it from this sphere. Age-old instincts are slow to fade, and their objects are not always economic but often also political in nature, as closely interconnected as the two aspects may be today. And so we see that increasingly an *economic* argument is made for violence, which has to do not only with violence being a fact of life for humanity over millennia but also with its direct exercise appearing to have some benefits. A belligerent nation that expands its territory and thereby its wealth and power is one that seems to act purposively [*zweckvoll*]—yet in most cases only seems to do so. For a state must make so many sacrifices of its own organic, internal forces and possibilities of unfolding simply in order to be able to retain its power. No better example could be seen of this contradiction between expectations made of violence by the older habits of thought and violence's actual effect than in our recent world war. For the use of modern industry as a means of war entails that all human and material forces and potentialities of a country can and *must* be applied, with the result that by the war's end the victor stands just as exhausted as the defeated—and the latter no longer offers anything worth exploiting. Here is not the place to address this situation any further other than to underline that the contradictions inhere in the political as well as the economic and social mechanisms of our time; they have no other outcome than universal crisis. (In this crisis are contained the "critical arguments" of reality in a higher sense than any meaningless empirical content of our days.)

Only one question is still to be posed, because it particularly imposes itself in this connection and in the current moment: whether the same goes for violence within the circumference of social life, the confrontation between the classes. This is to ask, therefore, whether class conflict, civil war, must end only in destruction but without any result. Capitalist societies evolved out of the feudal order and still bear its features, although only in appearance. Feudal power relations depended on violence. In the era of the Peasants' Wars, the peasantry's unflinching will, even when fired by religious fervor, could in the end be broken because the feudal overlords operated with superior organization and could avail themselves of the age's entire *intellectual* apparatus. Today's difference lies in all classes not only being carriers of will but also possessing their own intellectual representation as sectors of "public opinion." If to this we add the present's increased class diversity (encompassing capitalists, workers, and peasants at a minimum), the likelihood is that change occurs more through evolutionary transformation than violent struggle. It is true that in particular situations, violence can occur as the last consequence of a long-drawn-out but not fully consciously and societally completed development, as with the wearing down of the once self-evident authority of the ruling elites of central Europe by 1918, where the social structure fell apart at this point and socialist or nationalist platforms took their place. Yet here violence was something largely accidental and was not even present in all cases where new forms of rule took the place of the old without a struggle. Moreover, just as important was a transformation of consciousness among previously dominated classes, generating a realization that they, too, could take power. This, and only this, completed the societal revolution because with the rise of new, stronger formations of will among classes previously inert, the basis of the old structures of rule fell away. Insofar as no state and no state form is possible without its citizens' either explicit or tacit consent, only a difference of degree exists between autocracy and democracy. Every autocracy evolves into democracy in the sense of moving to a *conscious* acceptance of prevailing forms of rule, so long as all social classes experience a process of both enlightenment and organization, such that each is able to defend itself against the currently dominant class and to make that class's long-term domination impossible.

Yet organized and informed classes, as carriers of will, have emerged only on the basis of capitalism. (Again, this is for reasons that can only be hinted at here, namely, that capitalism is *industrial* capitalism based on factories and waged, trained, and skilled labor, such that classes are not amorphous groups but well-organized, stratified, and ordered bodies capable of collective action, accompanied by a broad intelligentsia drawn from all classes, as well as by democracy as the prevailing political form, under which even members of the dominated classes can enter into a governing elite and bargain on their behalf and even attract advocates of their cause from other, superior classes.) Capitalism finally overcomes the bondage visible so frequently in social history and thereby also violence as an effective means of social struggles. It seems consistent with the circumstances of the time that in the medieval city republics, the different family factions [*die "Geschlechter"*] feuded violently with one another for power—and later also with the guilds—whereas it remains hard to imagine textile workers from Saxony battling today as an army with, say, peasant communities from central and southern Germany, in some way effectively or productively.

Yet what of Russia? Is not a new social form imposing itself here through violence, in the bitterest of class struggles, even if with a perhaps doubtful prospect of success? Our response is as follows. In 1917, Russia was still a feudal state, trapped, at least from our Western European gaze, in a long-bygone era and at most borrowing various technical means from the West. The Russian Revolution here offers one of the most interesting examples of ideas migrating and fundamentally changing in the process. Historically, when European societies moved politically from right to left, Russia moved from left to right, which is why the Russian proletariat first had to bring into existence its opponent, the bourgeoisie, as a conscious social class and to discriminate itself from this class, beyond all feudal relations. And herein lies the entire difference with the West, together with which is the fact that until now, the greatest drivers of the revolution have lain in seizure of land by the peasantry, demonstrating again how difficult it is to speak of both Russian and European developments in one breath.

In light of the above, it would seem appropriate to put the thesis of class conflict to the test and to determine more precisely its meaning for our time. By no means clear is that "all history is the history of class struggle."[4] Most often, the conflicts are those of one section of a class in conflict with another of that same class. Both the rise of the Romans and the Spanish colonial conquests involved struggles of feudal groupings with other such groupings. In both cases, social structures could change but did not *have* to change. Genuine class struggle, on the other hand, is represented by the wars of the early capitalist period, up to the wars and repercussions of the French Revolution, as struggles of merchant economic power with feudal power. Unless, however, we are to overextend the term, we must also distinguish this from disputes *within* capitalism concerning favorable market situations. Actions and events such as the driving out of competitors, or lockouts and strikes by workers, may in some degree involve violence, but these, in contrast to the cases just mentioned, are a contingent rather than necessary manifestation of what is meant by "struggle," which itself can and most often does play itself out through mechanisms of the market without changing them.

All the more evident is this with regard to the deciding instances of socioeconomic forms and relations of power today. In an age stamped by definite classes and by large representational apparatuses of class interest and corresponding class organization, such that no class is in a position to seize power permanently (for the reasons given), the only deciding factors of rationalization and control over social structure and form of development now remain the intensity of social currents of will and the energy of their representation, as well as the clarity of their goals and—other things being equal—the size of their support. In no way does this reduce the interplay of forces to a predictive formula, for will and agency always play their part in any given case. Nor does this preclude fundamental changes taking place in social structures. In the course of demographic, moral, and intellectual ascendance of once dominated classes, such changes increasingly become inevitable, although they must also be realized (and the fact of their inevitability is something a society only learns from the crises it falls into from their *not* being realized), which in turn requires conscious action and intention. Only a society that has been thrown off balance by war—in whose consciousness the effectiveness of finer social means [*feinerer gesellschaftlichen Mittel*] has been largely pushed into the background—will succumb to the illusion that the outbreak of a war between the classes can (according to the viewpoints of each class) either halt or accelerate this development.[5] For in our world today, will and action on the stage of society are no longer effective and at home in any predominantly physical form of compulsion—which is not to say that such will and action must be in some way more "moderate." No age of eternal harmony has arrived; but gone today is any time in which violence alone could create new situations with definitive outcomes. To be sure, far from human beings having in any sense advanced or "improved," we see that, even amid all the changes of their environment, they still cling to the old methods of violence. Nevertheless, this environment itself has changed, and even an Alexander the Great today would have to accept that the time is past in which one could cut the Gordian knot without the sword in some way springing back on the one who wields it.

— *Trans. Austin Harrington*

Glossary

"Toward the Critique of Violence"

Arbeiterschaft	organized labor	
aufheben	annul, abolish	One of Benjamin's translations of Sorel's *supprimer*. The term was famously adopted by Hegel, for it includes three senses: "cancel," "preserve," and "raise up." Benjamin uses this term in several contexts in his early writings, but in contrast with its use in some of his later writings, it does not generally include the sense of "preservation."
Ausgang	ending	In dramatic terms, the term designates a "denouement."

German	English	Notes
Auslösung	release	The term can also be translated as "trigger" and is associated with *Auslöser*, that is, "catalyst" in chemical reactions.
Ausschaltung, ausschalten	suspension, suspend; also abolish	Another term Benjamin uses to translate Sorel's *supprimer*; also used in the contemporaneous lexicon of phenomenology in conjunction with "epochē" and "putting into brackets."
Bannkreis	spell	The term suggests the idea of encirclement.
Bestand	standing resource	
das Bestehende	status quo	
dämonisch	demonic	
Darstellung	presentation	
Daseinslage	existential situation	
Einigung	agreement	
Entartung	degeneration	
Entfaltung	deployment	
Entsetzung	de-posing	The term has a specific legal sense equivalent to "relief," as in "to relieve someone of one's possession, power, or right."
Entsühnung	de-expiation	For a detailed discussion of the term, see 31–32.
Erlösung	redemption	As distinct from *Lösung* ("solution") and *Auslösung* ("release").

GLOSSARY

Ernstfall	a situation in which everything is at stake	The term, which can be literally translated as "serious-case," is used in such phrases as *das Eintreten eines für möglich gehaltenen (gefährlichen) Ereignisses*; hence, when something actually happens, in contrast to a drill; it also contrasts with the state of emergency (*Notstand*) and state of exception (*Ausnahmezustand*).
Erziehung	education	In modern contexts "education" is generally undertaken in institutional (hence, legal) contexts; Benjamin's use of the term is broader and should therefore be understood as "upbringing."
Gerechtigkeit	justice	Also translated in certain cases as "justness" (e.g., of means).
Gesetz, Gesetze	an individual act of legislation or (if plural) body of legislation	Like the English term "law" (derived from Old Norse), *Gesetz* is a modification of the word for "positing" or "setting" (*Setzen*).
Gespenst, gespentisch	spectral, ghostly	
Gestalt, gestaltlos	shape, shapeless, amorphous	As distinct from "form" and "formless."
Gewalt (including *gegebene Gewalten; eine Gewalt*); see also *Rechtsgewalt, Staatsgewalt; verwaltete Gewalt, schaltende Gewalt, waltende Gewalt*	violence; also in certain contexts "power," "authority"	Benjamin's translation for Sorel's *pouvoir; eine Gewalt* is generally translated as "a form of violence" with "form" sometimes in brackets; also "force" in conjunction with *Anwendung* (application).

Gewaltanwendung	use of violence, application of force	
Grenze (*Grenzsetzung*)	border	As with *Markstein*, translated as "border" rather than as "limit," in comparison with the Kantian distinction between *Grenze* ("boundary") and *Schranke* ("limit").
Handlung (*Tat*)	action	As distinct from *Akt* ("act").
Kraft	force	Benjamin's translation for Sorel's French term *force*.
Kriterium	criterion	
Kritik	critique	
Macht	power	
Machtvollkommenheit	full (legislative and executive) power	This is also translated (in Fragment 17) as "plenipotentiary authority"; the equivalent of the Latin term *plenitudo potestas*.
Maßstab	standard	
Menge	masses, in context of the people; also, multitude	The translation more commonly used for this word is "crowd," as distinct from its more organized form, "masses," which appears for instance in the title of Freud's *Massenpsychologie* published in the same year as Benjamin's essay. Benjamin may have had in mind Gustave Le Bon's *Psychologie des foules* (1895), which Sorel criticizes in his *Reflections on Violence* for not giving proper due to the propensity for groups to behave in accordance with a conception of themselves as a class—that is,

		with that "degree of reflection" that Benjamin identifies in those against whom the state finds no protection in its laws (48). With respect to the translation of the second instance of the word (60), it is worth noting that in Benjamin's contemporaneous translation of Baudelaire's poem "Les petites vieilles," he uses *Menge* to translate *tous* (everyone); see 4:36–37.
mittelbar (including *nicht mittelbar*, *unmittelbar*)	mediate, nonmediate, immediate	
Moral; moralisch	morality, moral	Benjamin tends to use this term as the abbreviation for morality in the Kantian sense.
Polizei	police "as an institution of the modern state"	
Polizeirecht	the "law" of the police, which Benjamin places in quotation marks	
prägnant	impressive	
rechtserhaltend	law-preserving	
rechtsetzend	law-positing	
Rechtsordnung	legal order	
Rechtsgewalt	legal violence, legal form of violence	A technical juridical term for power that has its basis in law; it may be contrasted with *Staatsgewalt*, or state power / authority that derives from sovereign power.
Sache, sachlich	thing, objective	

Satzung	statute	
schalten (including *walten* and *verwalten*)	attending, pending, and expending	*Schalten* can mean "to switch on" or "change gear"; *walten* can mean "to reign or prevail," but also "to exercise [power]"; *verwalten* can mean "to administer or manage"; *schalten und walten* is an idiomatic phrase that means "to be in a position to dispose of something as one pleases," in which case *schalten* and *walten* are essentially synonymous; for a detailed discussion, see the final note to the essay (293).
Schicksal, schicksalhaft	fate, fateful	The word derives from the verb *schicken* ("send") and can thus be translated as "destiny," but Benjamin's use does not tend to suggest any "destination" other than guilt-debt.
Schuld (see also *Verschuldung*)	guilt, debt; in certain contexts both are implied, hence "guilt-debt"	
Sinn	sense, meaning	In certain contexts (especially with respect to words), it must be translated as "meaning," but in others, especially those where "reality" is under discussion, "sense" is to be preferred, insofar as the English word, like the German, encompasses the totality of sensuous perception and is associated with the "sense of direction."

sittlich (cf. *Moral*)	moral	In contrast with *moralisch*, which is associated with the Kantian idea of "morality" (*Moral*), the adjective *sittlich* is a broader term for "morals" qua *mores* ("Sitte") as well as a term Benjamin tends to reserve for approbation and praise beyond (or against) moralizing attitudes and legalistic assessments.
Sonderverfügung	special decree	
Staatsgewalt	state power	Benjamin's translation of Sorel's *l'État*; to be contrasted with *Rechtsgewalt*, it refers to the power a sovereign exercises over a territory and its population, and also to the branches of a political administration (e.g., legislative, judiciary, executive *Staatsgewalten*).
Staatsrecht	constitutional law	
Sühne; sühnen	expiation; as verb, to expiate or atone	As Benjamin explains, *Sühne* and *sühnen* were originally juridical terms; for an extensive discussion, see 30.
Technik	technique	
Übereinkunft	accord	
Unterlassung	omission	The legal connotation of the term in German law goes beyond the contextual meaning of "withholding labor as part of a strike action"; omission is a legal act consisting of a legal subject's failure to act, from which liability might arise if the subject has a legally imposed duty to act.

Unterredung	discussion	
urbildlich	archetypal	
Verfügungsrecht	law pertaining to orders	A technical term in police administration; as distinct from *Verordnungsrecht*.
Verhalten	conduct	
Verhältnis (including *Verhältnisse*)	relation, but sometimes "circumstances" when in the plural, and also "proportion"	
Verordnung, Verordnungsrecht	ordinance, law pertaining to regulations	A technical term in police administration; as distinct from *Verfügungsrecht*.
Verschuldung	inculpation	The term used in situations where someone is blamed, thus incurring a debt and entering into the sphere of guilt.
Verstand	understanding (as a mental faculty)	As distinct from the faculty of reason (*Vernunft*).
Verständigung	coming-to-an-understanding	
verwerflich	to be rejected	An equivalent would be "reprehensible," but this word generally connotes only a breach of manners.
Volk	people	

GLOSSARY 255

Vollstreckung	dispatch	In a legal context, this word usually denotes the "execution" or "enforcement" of a judgment or order. Benjamin, by contrast, develops a notion of "dispatch without judgment" (*urteillose Vollstreckung*), as can be seen elsewhere, where he associates it specifically with humor; see for instance 2:287 and *SW* 2:54; cf. 2:628.
Zorn	rage	
zweideutig	ambiguous	As used in the essay, the term suggests two interpretations and directions.

Associated Fragments and Notes

Andacht	devotion	
Aufschub	reprieve	
ausdruckslos	expressionless	A key term in Benjamin's early writings; for a brief discussion, see 310.
aussöhnen	conciliation	
ausweglos, Ausweglosigkeit	hopeless, hopelessness	On the hopelessness of finding a literal translation of *ausweglos* ("without a way out"), see 307.
Bann	spell	
Bekenntnis	credo	
Belebung, beleben, Belebtheit	vivification, vivify, vivaciousness	

GLOSSARY

Darstellung, Darsteller, Darstellende	presentation; also performance, performer, act of performing	
Ehrlichkeit	sincerity	
Einsinnigkeit	unidirectionality	
Erkennbarkeit	knowability	
Erkenntnis	cognition	
erkenntnistheoretisch	cognitive-theoretical	
Geist	spirit, mind	For further discussions of the term in several contexts, see 215 and 332.
Geistesgeschichte	history of ideas	
Gesinnung	ethos	
Gestalt, Gestaltung	shape, shaping	
Gesteigert, ungesteigert (Steigern); cf. *Steigerung*	elevated, unelevated	See 301–2 for an extensive discussion.
Herrschaft	dominion	
Jüngstes Gericht	Last Judgment	
Körper	somatic body	
Leib, Leiblichkeit	living body, living-bodiliness	
Menschenhaftigkeit	humanness	
Neigung	inclination	The term suggests "affection" for that to which one is "inclined."
Permanenz	permanence	
Prägnanz	concision	
Sachverhalt	state of affairs	

Schauplatz	setting	
Schweigen	silence	
Sehnsucht	longing	
Steigerung	elevation	The term also suggests "enhancement" or "intensification" and is an important element in the lexicon of German Romanticism and Goethe, as well as Benjamin's dissertation; for further discussion, see 301.
Tateinheit	coincidence	
Überzeugung	conviction	
Untergang	demise	
Vergeltung	retribution	
Verlogenheit	mendacity	
Verschiebung	postponement	
Vollendung	completion	
Wahrnehmung	perception	
wahrnehmungstheoretisch	perception-theoretical	
Weltgericht	judgment of the nations	Cf. Matthew 25:31–32 (literally, "world-judgment").
Wesenserkenntnis	eidetic insight	
Wissen	knowledge, in the sense of knowing	Distinguished from *Erkenntnis* ("cognition") and associated with wisdom more than with the possession of disciplinary knowledge.
Zustand	state	

Notes

Introduction by Peter Fenves

1. A lucid description of Benjamin's complicated residency in this period can be found in Michael Jennings and Howard Eiland, *Walter Benjamin: A Critical Life* (Cambridge, MA: Harvard University Press, 2014), 117–76.

2. For a brief yet incisive account of the "aborted revolution," see Gordon Craig, *Germany: 1866–1945* (Oxford: Oxford University Press, 1978), 396–431. A detailed presentation of the events in Munich can be found in Allan Mitchell, *Revolution in Bavaria, 1918–1919: The Eisner Regime and the Soviet Republic* (Princeton, NJ: Princeton University Press, 1965); an analysis of the events in the Ruhr region stands at the center of Pierre Broué's massive study, *The German Revolution, 1917–1923*, trans. John Archer, ed. Ian Birchell and Brian Pearce (Chicago: Haymarket Books, 2006), 269–83. For a more recent attempt to grasp the dynamics of violence in this period, with particular attention to the magnifying function of media, see Mark Jones, *Founding Weimar: Violence and the German Revolution of 1918–19* (Cambridge: Cambridge University Press, 2016).

3. For more about these strikes, see 288–89, note 42.

4. In a letter Benjamin wrote to Scholem on New Year's Eve 1920/21, he recounts his response to a book that his brother had recently given him, Rosa Luxemburg's *Briefe aus dem Gefängnis* (Letters from prison): "I was struck by their incredible beauty and significance" (*GB* 2:120; C 171; cf. 7:447). Benjamin began the final composition of "Toward the Critique of Violence" only after he was able to obtain a copy of Sorel's *Reflections on Violence*. Nothing of Luxemburg's far more consequential writings on the mass strike makes its way into the argument of the

essay he wrote soon after reading her *Letters from Prison*. From this fact two conclusions can be drawn beyond the possibility that gender plays a role in his selection of appropriate political theorists: Benjamin did not want to align his argument with a standard version of Marxism (albeit in this case, one that opposed the policies of the SPD), and he wanted the contemporary trends in political theory with which he associates his argument to be surrounded by a degree of obscurity—which Luxemburg's work obviously did not enjoy a mere two years after her body was dumped in a Berlin canal.

5. See Alfons Paquet, "Wehrlosigkeit" [Defenselessness], in *Die neuen Ringe: Reden und Aufsätze zur deutschen Gegenwart* (Frankfurt am Main: Frankfurter Societäts-Druckerei, 1924), esp. 78, 119. Benjamin and Paquet contributed to the appendix Florens Christian Rang compiled for his *Deutsche Bauhütte: Ein Wort an uns Deutsche über mögliche Gerechtigkeit gegen Belgien und Frankreich und zur Philosophie der Politik* (orig. 1924), ed. Uwe Steiner (Göttingen: Wallstein, 2015). One version of the rumor that Schmitt entered into a correspondence with Benjamin can be found in Beatrice Hanssen, *Critiques of Violence: Between Poststructuralism and Critical Theory* (New York: Routledge, 2000), 16. Giorgio Agamben presents something akin to a "thought experiment" in the fourth chapter of *States of Exception* under the indisputable premise that Schmitt read the *Archiv* and could therefore have come across Benjamin's essay; see Agamben, *States of Exception*, trans. Kevin Attell (Chicago: University of Chicago Press, 2005), 52–64.

6. Leo Löwenthal, *Gewalt und Recht in der Staats- und Rechtsphilosophie Rousseaus und der deutschen Idealistischen Philosophie* (1926), first published in *Philosophische Frühschriften* (Frankfurt am Main: Suhrkamp, 1990), 1:174.

7. K. T. [= Karl Thieme], "Allgemeines," *Berichte deutschen Hochschule für Politik* 7, no. 3 (June 1929): 55.

8. See Michael Freund, *Georges Sorel: Der revolutionäre Konservatismus* (Frankfurt am Main: Klostermann, 1932), 346.

9. Karl Thieme, "Una Sancta Catholica: Rückblick und Ausblick 1933," *Religiöse Besinnung: Vierteljahrsschrift im Dienste christlicher Vertiefung und ökumenischer Verständigung* 5 (1933): 39; cf. 31–32, where Thieme refers to Benjamin's *Ursprung des deutschen Trauerspiels* (Origin of the German *Trauerspiel*) in conjunction with its description of a profound melancholia that overtakes Lutherans.

10. Barna Horváth, *Rechtssoziologie: Probleme der Gesellschaftslehre und der Geschichtslehre des Rechts*, in *Archiv für Rechts- und Wirtschaftsphilosophie*, suppl. no. 28 (Berlin: Verlag für Staatswissenschaften und Geschichte, 1934), 241.

11. Walter Benjamin, "Zur Kritik der Gewalt," in *Schriften*, ed. Theodor W. Adorno and Gretel Adorno (Frankfurt am Main: Suhrkamp, 1955), 1:3–30, esp. 26 (for the error).

12. Walter Benjamin, *Zur Kritik der Gewalt und andere Aufsätze* (Frankfurt am Main: Suhrkamp, 1965); the error identified in note 11 was not corrected for this edition of the essay (see p. 59).

13. Herbert Marcuse, "Nachwort," in Benjamin, *Zur Kritik der Gewalt*, 99.

14. See Jacques Derrida, "Force de loi: Le 'fondement mystique de l'autorité' / Force of Law: The 'Mystical Foundation of Authority,'" *Cardoza Law Review* 11 (July/August 1990): 919–1045; Werner Hamacher, "Afformativ, Streik," in *Was heißt ‚Darstellen'?*, ed. Christiaan Hart-Nibbrig (Frankfurt: Suhrkamp, 1994), 340–74; "Afformative, Strike," trans. Dana Hollander, in *Walter Benjamin's Philosophy: Destruction and Experience*, ed. Andrew Benjamin and Peter Osborne (London: Routledge 1993), 155–82; Giorgio Agamben, *Homo sacer: Il potere sovrano e la nuda vita* (Turin: Einaudi, 1995); Agamben, *Homo Sacer: Sovereign Power and Bare Life*, trans. Daniel Heller-Roazen (Stanford, CA: Stanford University Press, 1998); Judith Butler, *Parting Ways: Jewishness and the Critique of Zionism* (New York: Columbia University Press, 2012).

15. Friedrich Engels, *Die Rolle der Gewalt in der Geschichte* (1896; Berlin: Dietz, 1964); *The Role of Force in History: A Study of Bismarck's Policy of Blood and Iron*, trans. Jack Cohen (New York: International Publishers, 1968).

16. See Friedrich Engels, *Herrn Eugen Dührings Umwälzung der Wissenschaft*, 3rd ed. (Stuttgart: Dietz, 1894), 171; *Anti-Dühring: Herr Eugen Dühring's Revolution in Science* (Moscow: Progress Publishers, 1947), 112. The image of a midwife (masculine in Marx, transposed into the feminine form by Engels) can be found in *Das Kapital: Kritik der politischen Ökonomie*, vol. 1, ed. Friedrich Engels, 4th ed. (Hamburg: Meisnner, 1890), 716; *Capital: A Critique of Political Economy*, vol. 1, trans. Ben Fowkes (Harmondsworth, UK: Penguin, 1990), 916: "Force [*Die Gewalt*] is the midwife of every old society which is pregnant with a new one. It is an economic power [*Potenz*]." Benjamin would have been familiar with his famous image at the very least through his reading of Sorel, who quotes it in German in his overview of Marx's theory of force and correctly notes that the term *Potenz* is drawn from mathematics; see *Réflexions sur la violence*, 5th ed. (Paris: Marcel Rivière, 1921), 260; chap. 5, §4. For a reflection on this image without reference to the problem posed by the term *Potenz*, see Hannah Arendt, *Between Past and Future: Eight Exercises in Political Thought* (New York: Viking, 1968), 21–22. It is a curious circumstance that Arendt did not address "Toward the Critique of Violence" in this or other reflections on violence.

17. The conclusion to Fredric Jameson's *Political Unconscious* revolves around a famous dictum derived from one of Benjamin's last writings, "Über den Begriff der Geschichte" (On the concept of history), on the one hand, and Ernst Bloch's late treatise, *Das Prinzip der Hoffnung* (The principle of hope), on the other. The idea of the political unconscious, congruent with the "optical unconscious" (7:376; *SW* 3:117), could be developed anew in relation to the earlier versions of these two

texts, specifically Bloch's *Geist der Utopie* (Spirit of utopia; 1918) and "Toward the Critique of Violence." It should be emphasized, however, that the latter pointedly does not adopt anything from the former, least of all its concept of utopia, even as it associates itself, instead, with an anarcho-syndicalist line of argumentation that has little or nothing to do with "anarchist categories of the individual subject" (*The Political Unconscious: Narrative as a Socially Symbolic Act* [Ithaca, NY: Cornell University Press, 1982], 286). The structure of the "political unconscious" Benjamin uncovers in 1921 consists, above all, in the denial that violence can be a force except insofar as it is a tool; a corollary of this denial is described in Fragment 17 of this volume, where, for jurists, it is inconceivable that a "right to apply force" could be denied to the state, yet allowed to the "living community" (86). For "the true politician" (4: 122), by contrast, the structure of the political unconscious presumably begins to crack.

18. The next several paragraphs are indebted to Regis Factor, *Guide to the Archiv für Sozialwissenschaft und Sozialpolitik Group, 1904–1933: A History and Comprehensive Bibliography* (New York: Greenwood Press, 1988). Despite its brevity, Factor's history is highly informative; it should be noted, though, that even as Factor discusses several prominent thinkers who made a few contributions to the journal, he does not mention Benjamin beyond a standard bibliographical note.

19. Edgar Jaffé, Max Weber, and Werner Sombart, "Geleitwort," *Archiv für Sozialwissenschaft und Sozialpolitik* 19 (1904): vi.

20. Max Weber, "Die protestantische Ethik und der 'Geist' des Kapitalismus," *Archiv für Sozialwissenschaft und Sozialpolitik* 20 (1905): 1–54; Weber, *The Protestant Ethic and the Spirit of Capitalism*, trans. Peter Baehr and Gordon Wells (Harmondsworth, UK: Penguin, 2002). The scare quotes around "spirit" were eventually dropped.

21. Ernst Troeltsch, "Soziallehren der christlichen Kirche," *Archiv für Sozialwissenschaft und Sozialpolitik* 26 (1908): 1–55, 292–342, 649–92; *The Social Teaching of the Christian Churches*, trans. Olive Wyon (Louisville, KY: John Knox, 1992). Like Weber's *Protestant Ethics*, this appears in the bibliography Benjamin drew up for Fragment 18 in this volume, "Capitalism as Religion" (92).

22. The phrase "ideas of 1914" is closely associated with a like-titled book by Rudolf Kjellén, *Die Ideen von 1914* (Leipzig: Hirzel, 1915). Sombart's version of these "ideas" appears in Werner Sombart, *Händler und Helden: Patriotische Besinnungen* (Munich: Duncker & Humblot, 1915). Nowhere outside of a letter to Ludwig Strauß in September 1912 does Benjamin so much as mention Sombart—and only as an editor, not an author (see *GB* 1:64).

23. For further information on Lederer, see Austin Harrington's Preface to the translation of his essay in this volume, 233–36.

24. Ludwig von Mises, "Die Wirtschaftrechnung in sozialistischen Gemeinwesen," *Archiv für Sozialwissenschaft und Sozialpolitik* 47 (1920–21): 86–121. Arguments for socialism, von Mises concludes, can be formulated only in terms of "ethics."

25. Hans Kelsen, "Vom Wesen und Wert der Demokratie," *Archiv für Sozialwissenschaft und Sozialpolitik* 47 (1920–21): 50–85.

26. Emil Lederer, "Die Gewerkschaftsbewegung 1918/19," *Archiv für Sozialwissenschaft und Sozialpolitik* 47 (1920–21): 219–69.

27. See Gustav Mayer, *Friedrich Engels in seiner Frühzeit* (The Hague: Martinus Nijhoff, 1920). As Mayer notes, almost the entire manuscript of *The German Ideology* is in Engels's hand; but since Marx wrote the earlier critiques of Bruno Bauer, it is likely that he dictated the relevant pages to Engels, whose handwriting was more legible. A reliable translation of "On the Jewish Question" can be found in Karl Marx, *Early Political Writings*, ed. and trans. Joseph O'Malley (Cambridge: Cambridge University Press, 1994), 28–56; for an intermittently unreliable translation of *The Holy Family*, see Marx and Engels, *The Holy Family: or Critique of Critical Criticism against Bruno Bauer and Company* (Moscow: Foreign Language Publishing House, 1956).

28. Marx and Engels, "Das Leipziger Konzil," *Archiv für Sozialwissenschaft und Sozialpolitik* 47 (1920–21): 773–807, here 782; see Marx and Engels, *The German Ideology*, in *The Collected Works: 1845–47* (New York: International Publishers, 1976), 5:94.

29. The elements of Lederer's literary archive are available at the SUNY–Albany library; but it has no item earlier than 1922.

30. See Ernst Bloch, *Kampf, nicht Krieg*, ed. Martin Korol (Frankfurt am Main: Suhrkamp, 1985), 46; Ernst Bloch, "Über einige politische Programme und Utopien in der Schweiz," *Archiv für Sozialwissenschaft und Sozialpolitik* 46 (1918–19); 159–62; reprinted in *Kampf, nicht Krieg*, 532–59. As Michael Löwy notes, Bloch heavily revised the version that appeared in *Politische Messungen, Pestzeit, Vormärz*, 2nd ed. (Frankfurt: Suhrkamp, 1976); Löwy, *Redemption and Utopia: Jewish Libertarian Thought in Central Europe, a Study in Elective Affinity*, trans. Hope Heany (New York: Verso, 2017), 237. See also Alberto Toscano's Preface to the translation of Sorel's *Reflections on Violence* in this volume, 194–200.

31. Ernst-Erik Schwabach, "Von dem Charakter der kommenden Literatur," *Die weißen Blätter* 1 (1913): 1. For an account of the relation of the journal to German expressionism, see Paul Michael Lützeler, *Die Schriftsteller und Europa: Von der Romantik bis zur Gegenwart* (Munich: Piper, 1992); cf. Sven Arnold, *Das Spektrum des literarischen Expressionismus in den Zeitschriften "Der Sturm" und "Die Weissen Blätter"* (Frankfurt am Main: Peter Lang, 1998). In 1934, an entirely different journal appeared under the same name and became an anonymous vehicle of conservative-monarchical resistance to the Nazi regime.

32. For a description of this strange incident in the annals of literary prizes, see Rainer Stach, *Kafka: The Years of Insight*, trans. Shelley Frisch (Princeton, NJ: Princeton University Press, 2013), 37–43.

33. In this respect, Schickele edited a series of pacifist-oriented issues, culminating in *Menschliche Gedichte im Krieg* [Human poems during war] (Zurich: Rascher, 1918).

34. Emil Lederer, "Klassenkampf in der deutschen Revolution," *Die weißen Blätter* 7 (1920): 1–9, 70–79, here 79.

35. An earlier announcement of the "new series" describes the theme in a different way: "a few cultural problems of socialism" (Publisher's note, *Die weißen Blätter* 7 [December 1920]: 1). Lederer may have sought out Benjamin because he considered him capable of treating the theme of culture if not socialism.

36. Emil Lederer, "Zur Einführung," *Die weißen Blätter*, n.s., 1 (1921): 5–7, here 5.

37. See Ernst Bloch, "Über den sittlichen und geistigen Führer," *Die weißen Blätter*, n.s., 1 (1921): 8–15. There are several indications that the essay is a fragment of a longer work, beginning with the fact that Bloch republished the essay under a more expansive title, "Über den sittlichen und geistigen Führer oder die doppelte Weise des Menschengesichts," in *Durch die Wüste* (Berlin: Cassirer, 1923; repr., Frankfurt am Main: Suhrkamp, 1964), 95–104. When Benjamin encounters Bloch's essay in *Durch die Wüste*, he explicitly declines to say anything in response (see GB 2:438).

38. See esp. Lederer, "Klassenkampf in der deutschen Revolution," *Die weißen Blätter* 7 (1920): 8–9.

39. Karl Marx and Friedrich Engels, "Das Leipziger Konzil," 799–800; cf. *The German Ideology*, 109.

40. As discussed earlier in the Introduction (see 19–20 and its accompanying note), the status of *Gewalt* was of central importance both in the interpretation of Marx and in the expansion, retraction, and application of his work. The space of a note is not sufficient to describe this even in the roughest outline; see, however, Étienne Balibar, "*Gewalt*," *Historical Materialism* 17 (2009): 99–125. Balibar's concluding remarks on Benjamin are problematic (123), but this does not detract from the value of the article as a whole.

41. On this theme, see Jacques Derrida, *Specters of Marx: The State of the Debt, the Work of Mourning and the New International*, trans. Peggy Kamuf (New York: Routledge, 1994).

42. The subsequent interaction between Benjamin and Lederer repeats the rhythm of their epistolary relationship: initial receptiveness on Lederer's part, followed by enigmatic inertness. They first meet in the summer of 1921, when Benjamin takes a tour of Heidelberg: "The Lederers, especially the wife [Emma Lederer, a historian of modern Hungary], whom I highly esteem, are delightful to me. Bookstores,

new and used, were opened in celebration of my arrival. I entered a used bookstore as its first customer, where I was immediately welcomed by name" (*GB* 2:176–77). The incidents that first greet Benjamin in Heidelberg are so extraordinary that, alluding perhaps to Hölderlin's poem "Heidelberg," he describes them as "magic-things" (*GB* 2:176). Disenchantment soon follows. During a seminar led by Marianne Weber, his carefully prepared presentation on lyric poetry "ricocheted" (*GB* 2:299) back on him. It is difficult to conceive of what this means, but the phenomenon also characterizes his relation with Lederer, who stopped inviting him to his seminar after its initial meeting. Benjamin does not attribute any ill will to Lederer: "[I]t is certainly only because he cannot do anything for me, for lack of time" (*GB* 2:299). Since, however, Benjamin conceives of "the social" as a "manifestation of ghostly and demonic powers" (84), it is scarcely surprising that he was less than fully welcome among professors of sociology.

43. Benjamin, writing for himself and his wife, Dora, sent a note of condolence to Bloch that he included in his private memorial book for his wife: "You know that in every sense we were bound to your wife with love, not only as your spouse but also a human being who, in all of her vital expressions, embraced us in an incredibly comforting way" (cited in Ernst Bloch, *Tendenz, Latenz, Utopie* [Frankfurt am Main: Suhrkamp, 1978], 29–30). Another passage in the private memorial book is worth noting in conjunction with the theme of violence. In November 1921, Bloch records the following story: "The messiah does not bring a completely new world but rather shifts something in the already existing one, a little something, and everything is good" (Bloch, *Tendenz, Latenz, Utopie*, 15). In a letter Scholem sent Benjamin in July 1934, he claimed that the variants of this story that appeared in the publications of Bloch and Benjamin originated with none other than himself (see Gershom Scholem and Walter Benjamin, *The Correspondence of Walter Benjamin and Gershom Scholem: 1932–1940*, ed. Gershom Scholem [New York: Schocken, 1989], 123). In his memorial book, Bloch attributes the story to the "doctrine of the kabbalists," which may be a cipher for Benjamin or Scholem; in any case, Bloch adds this as well: "I don't believe it" (*Tendenz, Latenz, Utopie*, 15). Here is the version of the story that elicits Scholem's claim of authorship: "[A] great rabbi said [of the messiah] that he does not want to change the world with violence [*Gewalt*] but only to adjust [*zurechtstellen*] it a little" (2:432; *SW* 2:811). That Benjamin writes of *Gewalt* here may itself be a memorial to the circumstances around his 1921 essay. More importantly, however, he does not say whether he believes the "great rabbi" or not.

44. For Scholem's account of the incidents, see Gershom Scholem, *Walter Benjamin: The Story of a Friendship*, trans. Harry Zohn (New York: Schocken, 1988), 25–27.

45. For more on the incident, see Lisa Anderson's Preface, 181.

46. Martin Buber, "Die Losung," *Der Jude* 1, no. 1 (April 1916): 2.

47. Paul Mendes-Flohr argues that the change in Buber's view of the war occurred in conversations with his close friend Gustav Landauer from July 11 to July 14, 1916—which is precisely the time frame within which Buber received Benjamin's letter; see Mendes-Flohr, *Martin Buber: A Life of Faith and Dissent* (New Haven, CT: Yale University Press, 2019), 108. It makes psychological sense to suggest that a conversation with an old friend would have more effect than a letter from a near stranger; but perhaps it is the very strangeness of the letter that ignited a genuine shock. (Mendes-Flohr includes a sensitive discussion of Benjamin's letter that is slightly mistaken about the chronology of events; see p. 119.) Benjamin, for his part, (mistakenly) thought that the title of Buber's 1917 collection *Die Lehre, die Rede, das Lied: Drei Beispiele* (Frankfurt am Main: Insel, 1917), derived from his "unanswered letter" (*GB* 1:271), since the three kinds of speech Buber identifies in his title ("doctrine," "discourse," "song") are similar to the three modes of language outlined in his 1916 letter. The correspondence between Benjamin and Buber in the late 1920s, by contrast, was suffused with signs of friendship, even if each remained distant from the other. It is remarkable that Buber sent Benjamin a copy of the translation of the Pentateuch that he had prepared with Franz Rosenzweig (see *GB* 3:553); but this gesture, too, may refer back to the 1916 letter and the publication plans for "The True Politician."

48. In *One-Way Street*, Benjamin takes his readers through a "tour of the German inflation" (4:94–101; *SW* 1:450–55). For a comprehensive account, see Gerald Feldman, *The Great Disorder: Politics, Economics, and Society in the German Inflation, 1914–23* (Oxford: Oxford University Press, 1997).

49. Several years later, a project of this kind did find a publisher and began to appear under the title *Die Kreatur* (The creature). Unsolicited, Benjamin sent Buber an essay drawn from his experience in a Lenin-less Moscow (4:316–48; *SW* 2:22–46), and he made clear that he was available to make further contributions (*GB* 3:278; *C* 317).

50. Salomon later added "Delatour" to his surname in order to distinguish himself from another sociologist named Salomon; this is not needed here.

51. See Georges Sorel, *Über die Gewalt*, ed. Gottfried Salomon, trans. Ludwig Oppenheimer (Innsbruck: Wagner, 1928); see also Chryssoula Kambas, "Walter Benjamin liest Georges Sorel: 'Réflexions sur la violence,'" in *Aber ein Sturm weht vom Paradiese her*, ed. Michael Opitz and Erdmut Wizisla (Stuttgart: Reklam, 1992), 250–69, esp. 258–59.

52. This letter was discovered in the 1980s by Chryssoula Kambas in the archive of a major historian of anarchism, Max Nettlau; see also Alberto Toscano's Preface to the passages from Sorel in this volume, 195. On the basis of the cumulative index

Benjamin produced that accounts for the books and articles he read, the following anarchist-oriented works appear in relatively close proximity: Mikhail Bakunin's *Dieu et l'état* (God and state), Gustav Landauer's *Aufruf zum Sozialismus* (Call to socialism), Rudolf Stammler's *Die Theorie des Anarchismus* (The theory of anarchism), and Sorel's *Les illusions du progrès* (The illusions of progress), along with his *Reflections on Violence* (7:447).

53. See Walter Benjamin, *Briefe*, ed. Gershom Scholem and Theodor Adorno (Frankfurt am Main: Suhrkamp, 1966): 1:247. In his edition of the letters, Scholem insists that "The True Politician" is identical with the critique of Paul Scheerbart's science-fiction novel *Lesabéndio*; see *Briefe* 1:228, as well as Scholem, *Walter Benjamin: The Story of a Friendship*, 38. Benjamin says nothing of the kind, and the reconstruction of the letter suggests that this is unlikely; see the editorial remark at *GB* 2:111.

54. Benjamin's reflections on Scheerbart's novel can be found at 2:618–20; for a translation of the novel, see Paul Scheerbart, *Lesabéndio*, trans. Christina Svendsen (Cambridge, MA: Wakefield, 2012). Around 1922, Benjamin also drew up notes for a discussion of Scheerbart's "Berlin novel," *Münchhausen und Clarissa* (Berlin: Osterheld, 1906); see 6:147–48 and 298 below. Many years later, probably in the late 1930s, Benjamin wrote another reflection (in French) on Scheerbart; see 2:630–32; *SW* 4:386–88.

55. Benjamin suggests as much to Scholem in a letter from July 1927, when he speaks of losing a convolute of "irreplaceable manuscripts, en l'espèce [in this case] many-years preparatory studies toward 'Politics,' [namely,] the ur-text of *One-Way Street*, which of course contains only very little that does not exist in duplicate and diverse allotria" (*GB* 3:281). A thorough treatment of the provenance of *One-Way Street* can be found in *KGA*, vol. 8, ed. Detlev Schöttker; yet nowhere in this volume does it indicate that this remark to Salomon represents a plan for the book that would eventually appear in 1928—as the only part of Benjamin's "Politics" besides "Toward the Critique of Violence" that was published in his lifetime.

56. Saul Friedländer, "Der Antichrist und Ernst Bloch," *Das Ziel: Jahrbücher für das geistige Politik* 4 (1920): 103–16, here 104. (Friedländer is alluding to Hölderlin's poem "Hälfte des Lebens," in which water is called "holy-sober.") Hiller adds an editorial afterword to Friedländer's review that concludes with the designation of Bloch's book as a "vomative" (*Das Ziel* 4 [1920]: 117).

57. See *GB* 2:94 and Note 22 of this volume (109), where Benjamin identifies several of Radbruch's works for the further development of the argument proposed in the essay. It is not known how Benjamin came into contact with Radbruch, who had recently played an important legal role in support of labor during the Kapp-Lütwitz Putsch and became an SPD representative in the Reichstag as a result. For a succinct

account of Radbruch's activities during this period, see Martin Klein, *Demokratisches Denken bei Gustav Radbruch* (Berlin: Berliner Wissenschafts-Verlag, 2007), 31–32; Klein provides an extensive survey of Radbruch's relation to neo-Kantianism, 55–154. For further discussion of Radbruch, see the Afterword, esp. 125–26.

58. The coeditor of *Logos* was Richard Kroner, whose *Habilitation* thesis on the methodology of the biological sciences, directed by Heinrich Rickert, is briefly discussed below (269). After lamenting that *Logos* did not have sufficient funds for the special issue that was to have carried his review of Bloch, Benjamin nevertheless credits the review with some "important clarifications" (*GB* 2:131; *C* 174) of his own thought; for earlier remarks about the review, see *GB* 2:67–68; *C* 156; *GB* 2:72; *GB* 2:75; *C* 159. The wealth of remarks about this review contrasts with the paucity of comments about the content of "The True Politician," although it is only the latter that Benjamin continually tried to publish.

59. Benjamin probably chose the term *Abbau* (dismantling), above all, so that he could distinguish his "negation" of violence from "the anarchist demand that violence be abolished [*Abschaffung der Gewalt*] [which] makes sense only in relation to expended violence [*verwaltete Gewalt*]" (68). The implication of this remark is that the abolition of administrative violence, especially its policing functions, only concerns one form of state-related violence, and this form is secondary. Benjamin may have drawn the term *Abbauen* from the terminology of transcendental phenomenology, which did not present itself as a variety of neo-Kantianism but nevertheless identified itself with the program of recovering the original constitution of experience, whose access has been barred by an accumulation of metaphysical-scientific sedimentations. A contemporaneous use of the term *Abbauen* as a preliminary philosophical movement can be found in Heidegger; see, for instance, his Freiburg seminar *Grundprobleme der Phänomenologie* (1919/20) (Frankfurt am Main: Klostermann, 1993), 147. As discussed in the Afterword (318n7), Benjamin may have been averse to the use of the term because of its association with Silvio Gesell's *Der Abbau des Staates nach Einführung der Volksherrschaft* (Berlin: Verlag des Freiland-Freigeld-Bundes, 1919).

60. A copy of the official English-language version of the Treaty of Versailles is available at https://www.loc.gov/law/help/us-treaties/bevans/m-ust000002-0043.pdf. (Part II of the treaty describes the borders of Germany.)

61. See Matthias Erzberger, *Der Völkerbund: Der Weg zum Weltfrieden* (Berlin: Hobbing, 1918), 54–60; *The League of Nations: The Way to World Peace*, trans. Bernard Miall (New York: Henry Holt, 1919), 107–19. Erzberger was murdered in August 1921 by right-wing assassins. There is no evidence that Benjamin is responding to Erzberger's pamphlet; but on at least one point *The League of Nations* and "Toward the Critique of Violence" converge: Erzberger affirms that any peace modeled on the

Pax Romana "proceeds by way of a form of violence and repression that is *ambiguous and has two faces*" (38); cf. 45.

62. It should be noted that Kant proceeds to say here that "compromise" is out of the question; this, too, corresponds to a basic motif of Benjamin's essay, which he attributes, however, to Unger; see 49.

63. In conducting the research that forms the basis of an essay he wrote in conjunction with *Toward Eternal Peace*, namely, "Das Ende aller Dinge" (The end of all things), Kant may have come across a second- or third-hand account of Lurianic doctrines; see *Aka* 8:327–39. For a canonical treatment of this theme, see Gershom Scholem, *Major Trends in Jewish Mysticism* (New York: Schocken, 1988), 244–86.

64. Benjamin studied the Critique of Teleological Judgment with Moritz Geiger in Munich; see *GB* 1:295.

65. Richard Kroner, *Zweck und Gesetz in der Biologie: Eine logische Untersuchung* (Tübingen: Laupp, 1913), esp. 152–56; cf. 7:448. Kroner's study seeks to find the ultimate sources of the scientifically dubious yet philosophically valid "resistance" to physicochemical reductionism. He finds this source in the "categorial constitution of biological thinking" (163–64). An inquiry into the enigma of an organism that understands its task solely in physicochemical terms will always result only in physicochemical solutions—and thus ignore the exigency of "biological thinking" altogether. The primary category of such thinking is that of accomplishment, more exactly "accomplishment for life [*Leistung für das Leben*]," which is accordingly characterized as "metachemical" (152) and distinguished from Darwinian-inflected notions of "struggle for existence." As for any putative "final purpose" (70) in biological thinking, there is only that of the system of science (hence, thinking) itself. Benjamin may have abandoned his nascent plans for "Teleology without Final Purpose" because the phrase encapsulates a recognizably neo-Kantian program.

66. See Benjamin's description of his encounter with Unger, which occurred as he was completing "Toward the Critique of Violence" (*GB* 2:128; 172); see Bruce Rosenstock's Preface in this volume, 217–18. For a list of Benjamin's seminars in Bern, see *KGA*, vol. 3, ed. Uwe Steiner, 298–302, 304–8, and esp. 364–73.

67. Kant's famous preface to *Toward Eternal Peace* presents his treatise as a "game," the seriousness of which lies in the graveyard toward which the sign "Toward Eternal Peace" actually points; see *Aka* 8:343.

68. See especially the essay Benjamin wrote in the fall of 1919, "Schicksal und Charakter" (Fate and character), which appeared in the spring of 1921 in the first issue of *Die Argonauten*; reprinted in 2:171–79; *SW* 1:201–6.

69. For a more detailed (although still schematic) discussion, see the Preface to the translation of Cohen in this volume, 161–63.

70. The absence of any relation between the two parts of *The Metaphysics of Morals* is also astonishing from the perspective of the *Critique of the Power of Judgment*, which is itself prompted by a certain "embarrassment" that derives from the "gulf" (*Aka* 5:175) between the domain of nature, understood in terms of mechanical causality, and the rule of freedom, which consists in its noumenal counterpart. At a certain moment in *The Metaphysics of Morals*, Kant almost admits that a transition between its two parts is necessary; but he does so solely within the scope of the *Doctrine of Virtue*: "[J]ust as a passage from the metaphysics of nature to physics ... is required, so something similar is rightly [*mit Recht*] requested from the metaphysics of morals" (*Aka* 6:468). Kant may have compensated for the nonfulfillment of this request by turning toward universal history in a contemporaneous reflection, which he placed at the center of his *Streit der Fakultäten* (Conflict of the faculties; 1798). Ostensibly concerned with the conflict between the faculties of law and philosophy, this "renewal" of the question whether human beings are constantly improving revolves around a "sign of history" (*Geschichtszeichen*) that Kant discovers in the "near enthusiasm" with which German spectators greeted the French Revolution—a quasi-moral yet still emotive condition that can be attributed to an otherwise hidden connection between moral advancement and the alteration of positive legislation in the direction of a republican constitution; see *Aka* 7:85–89. In the major program of research Benjamin undertakes in conjunction with his "political essays," namely, his critique of Goethe's novel *Die Wahlverwandtschaften* (Elective affinities), Benjamin draws attention to the abyssal-sublime character of *The Metaphysics of Morals* in light of its mechanized doctrine of matrimonial law, which is wholly lacking in any virtue, to say nothing of love (see 1:127–29; *SW* 1:299–300). A discussion along these lines that relates "Toward the Critique of Violence" to his essay on Goethe's novel would require a study of its own.

71. See Kant, *Critique of the Power of Judgment*, *Aka* 5:260; §28; on *Gewalt* in the third *Critique* and Benjamin's use of the term, see Kevin McLaughlin, *Poetic Force: Poetry after Kant* (Stanford, CA: Stanford University Press, 2014), 1–28.

72. Benjamin concludes his *Origin of the German Trauerspiel* in a similar manner. By means of the last quotation in the book, he explains the enigmatic phrase "ponderación misteriosa" that serves as the title of its final section: it lies in "the intervention of God [*das Eingreifen Gottes*] into the work of art" (1:408; *O* 258).

73. For a concise account of *Sühne* that Benjamin may have consulted, see Friedrich Kluge, *Etymologisches Wörterbuch der deutschen Sprache*, 4th ed. (Strasburg: Trübner, 1889), 348–49.

74. The locus classicus for the differentiation between mechanical and "organic" (reciprocal) laws is a much-cited remark from the *Critique of the Power of Judgment* in which Kant denies that there will ever be a Newton "who could make comprehensible

even the generation of a blade of grass according to natural laws that no intention has ordered" (*Aka* 5:400); for Kroner's revision, see *Zweck und Gesetz*, 10–11.

75. The typescript of Rickert's fall 1913 lecture, formally listed under *Logik*, resides in the University Library Archive at Heidelberg University under the title "Heid. Hs. 2740." I thank the University Library and Clemens Rohfleisch in particular for giving me access to this typescript. The first pages of the typescript, where Rickert clearly discusses "mere natural life," are missing; the very first words on the extant manuscript are "natural life." The typescript was worked over several times in Rickert's hand, and it served as the preliminary draft of the only volume of the "philosophical system" he published; see Rickert, *System der Philosophie: Erster Teil, Allgemeine Grundlegung der Philosophie* (Tübingen: Mohr, 1921), vii. A more plaintive version of the same argument appears in Rickert, *Philosophie des Lebens: Darstellung und Kritik der philosophischen Modeströmungen unserer Zeit* (Tübingen: Mohr, 1920). Benjamin's amusing remarks on Rickert's lectures on "completed life" can be found in *GB* 1:117.

76. The term Benjamin uses in the essay, *Auslösung*, has been translated as "release"; the modern chemical term "catalyst" derives from the equivalent Greek roots. (*Auslöser* is an outmoded synonym for *Katalysator*.) The significance of chemistry in the construction of Benjamin's argument can be seen from the use of the term "aggregate state [*Aggregatzustand*]" (59) in his (negative) elucidation of the meaning of existence. Benjamin is clearly attracted to chemical terminology. At the end of his dissertation Benjamin presents *Darstellung* in chemical terms as "preparation" (1:109; *SW* 1:178), and at the beginning of his critique of Goethe's chemical novel, *Elective Affinities*, he compares the commentator with the chemist and the critic with the alchemist (1:126; *SW* 1:298). Both of these chemical analogies converge in the thought of inculpation as a catalyst of legal violence, the limits of which appear in the "a-chemical" light of critique. Similarly, in several of his later writings, he is attracted to the work of natural catalysts, that is, enzymes (*Fermente*). See especially his discussion of the "metaphysical enzymes" (1:307; *O* 127) that help form the German baroque *Trauerspiel*. More suggestive still is the following remark about his now-famous reflection on the "decline of the aura": "Perhaps it is necessary to experiment with the concept of an aura purified of cultic enzymes [*von kultischen Fermenten gereinigten Aura*]. Perhaps the decline of the aura is only a transitional stage in which its cultic enzymes are excreted in order to approach one that is not yet recognizable" (7:753).

77. See Fyodor Dostoyevsky, *Schuld und Sühne*, trans. Hans Moser (Leipzig: Reclam, 1890). Benjamin read the novel under this title (see 7:468). In the *Origin of the German Trauerspiel*, Benjamin departs from stereotypical interpretations of tragedy in terms of *Schuld* and *Sühne*, understood as the element of the "moral world order" (1:279; *O* 92).

78. See Kurt Eisner, *Schuld und Sühne*, intro. Heinrich Ströbel (Berlin: Verlag Neues Vaterland, 1919). Eisner closes his speech by saying the following about Jean Jaurès, who was assassinated on the eve of the First World War: "He was, like all true politicians [*alle wahre Politiker*], a prophet. The sea of blood he foresaw has come to pass; but fortunately, it lies behind us. But now help us, as we all help ourselves through the redemption [*Erlösung*] and construction of the new world" (31). Were the words of this speech an impetus for Benjamin's essay "The True Politician"? Unfortunately, we do not know. Much more unfortunately, Eisner was wrong: the "sea of blood" did not lie behind him.

79. Grimm, *Deutsches Wörterbuch* (Leipzig: Hirzel, 1854–1961; Leipzig, 1971), http://woerterbuchnetz.de/cgi-bin/WBNetz/wbgui_py?sigle=DWB&mode=Vernetzung&lemid=GS56279#XGS56279. The discussion of *Entsühnung* here only concerns its use in "Toward the Critique of Violence." It should be noted, though, that from around 1919 to 1923, Benjamin experimented with the term in several different contexts: first, his short, unpublished critique of George Bernard Shaw's play about prostitution, *Mrs. Warren's Profession* (2:613–15); second, "Fate and Character" (2:175; *SW* 1:204); third, Fragment 18 of this volume, "Capitalism as Religion" (90); and fourth, his essay on *Elective Affinities* (1:138; *SW* 1:308, 1:140; *SW* 1:309, esp. 1:176; *SW* 1:336). Finally, in *Origin of the German Trauerspiel*, he evokes the idea of *Entsühnung* in quoting a passage from his own "Fate and Character" (1:288–89; *O* 104). Nowhere in any of these discussions does he develop the distinction between *Sühne* and *Entsühnung* with such exactness and intensity as in "Toward the Critique of Violence." In "Capitalism as Religion" he maintains a distinction between *Sühne* and *Entsühnung*, but the direction of the argument leads toward a certain diminishment of this distinction in light of an image of God who, finding himself caught in capitalism's net, ultimately de-expiates himself from its cultic (inculpating-expiating) processes. As for Benjamin's use of the terms in *Elective Affinities*, the clarity of the figure who succumbs to expiation in "Toward the Critique of Violence," namely, Niobe in all her fecundity, becomes cloudy in her replacement, that is Ottilie, who, although "untouched," also loses a child who is ambiguously her own. The afterlives of Niobe and Ottilie—one a "petrifact" (78), the other a still-beautiful form—resonate with each other in suggestive ways. Several of the themes thus associated with the category of de-expiation, from the prostitute-mother (Mrs. Warren) to affinitive motherhood in mourning (Ottilie), point toward a missing inquiry into sexual difference; see, however, Benjamin's contemporaneous fragment "Über Liebe und Verwandtes: (Ein europäisches Problem) [On love and what is related to it: (A European problem)]" (6:72–73; *SW* 1:229–30).

80. Jacob Grimm and Wilhelm Grimm, *Deutsches Wörterbuch* (Leipzig: Hirzel, 1862), 3:637–38. As Jacob Grimm notes, *ent-* can be either (*entweder!*) positive or

negative; and in the relation to the former, it can mark the beginning of a process, as in "die Pflanze entblühen" (*Deutsches Wörterbuch* [1862], 3:488), hence the function of the Latin *ex-*. The examples of *entsühnen* are drawn from the last two acts of Goethe's *Iphigenie auf Tauris*, which revolves around the house of Orestes's absolution from matricide-born miasma; see Johann Wolfgang von Goethe, *Werke: Hamburger Ausgabe in 14 Bänden* (Munich: C. H. Beck, 1977), 5:51–66, specifically lines 1617, 1702, 1969, 2138. The last of these is especially revealing: Orestes, wanting to inhabit an "entsühntes" house, asks that "Gewalt und List" (violence and cunning), which have hitherto been the sources of human fame, become matters of shame instead.

81. See Martin Heidegger, *Sein und Zeit* (Frankfurt am Main: Klostermann, 1927), 105; English translations include the pagination of the original edition. For varied accounts of the complicated relation between Benjamin and Heidegger, see Andrew Benjamin and Dimitris Vardoulakis, eds., *Sparks Will Fly: Heidegger and Benjamin* (Albany: SUNY Press, 2015).

82. Martin Heidegger, *Die Kategorien- und Bedeutungslehre des Duns Scotus* (Tübingen: Mohr, 1916). At the beginning of the letter in which Benjamin sketches his "Politics" project he dismisses Heidegger's *Habilitation* thesis as "only a piece of good translation" (*GB* 2:108; *C* 168); but at the beginning of the long letter in which he documents his progress on "Toward the Critique of Violence," he rescinds his earlier judgment and concedes that it "perhaps reproduces the most essential stratum of scholastic thought for my problem—although, of course, in an entirely opaque manner" (*GB* 2:127; *C* 172). For Benjamin's notes, which form an element of what would become the "task of the translator," see 6:22–23; *SW* 1:228.

83. In classical Latin, *de-*, like *ex-*, includes a semantic sense of (extensive or intensive) completion (because *de-* originally denoted "down" and could thus be understood as an abbreviation of "from top to bottom"); this does not survive into the use of *de-* for English constructions.

84. Hermann Cohen, *Religion der Vernunft aus den Quellen des Judentums* (Leipzig: Fock, 1919), 509. (Cohen, like Benjamin, transcribes the name as "Korah," which is preserved in citations of their work. A contemporary transcription of the name would be "Qórah." Outside of quotations I use a combination of the two, "Korah.") The claim advanced by Anselm Haverkamp that Benjamin drew the example of Korah from *Religion of Reason* depends on the dubious supposition that he had no other access to biblical scholarship than Cohen's posthumously published treatise, which, as noted in the Preface to the translation associated with this volume (165), he delicately mocks; see Anselm Haverkamp, "Ein unabwerfbarer Schatten: Gewalt und Trauer in Benjamins 'Kritik der Gewalt,'" in *Gewalt und Gerechtigkeit: Derrida-Benjamin*, ed. A. Haverkamp (Frankfurt am Main: Suhrkamp, 1994), 175. A broader and more judicious treatment of possible sources for Benjamin's discussion of Korah

can be found in Petar Bojanić, *Violence and Messianism: Jewish Philosophy and the Great Conflicts of the Twentieth Century*, trans. Edward Djordjevic (New York: Routledge, 2018), 99–114.

85. The extent of the devastation is recognized, as Benjamin Sommer notes, in certain passages of rabbinical writings, especially accounts of "the Talmudic-era sage Rabba son of Bar Hana [who] found the place in the desert where Korah and his band went underground, and heard them confessing, 'Moses is true and his Torah is true, and we are liars' (Bavli Bava Batra 74a; Sanhedrin 110a)" (Benjamin Sommer, email to the author). Under the premise that "[t]here is nothing new under the sun" (Eccl. 1:9), the novelty of the earth opening its mouth can be understood as a drift in the underground passage that leads to *Gehinnom* (viz., Sheol, the locus of the afterlife), such that it becomes aligned with an already existing surface feature, specifically a chasm that "a certain Arab merchant" showed the Talmudic sage (Numbers Rabbah, 18). Benjamin, for his part, could have learned of these midrashim from a variety of sources, beginning with Scholem. Similarly, he may have encountered versions of related midrashim that Louis Ginzberg wove together in such a way that the story of the devastation that befell Koraḥ and company sounds as though its author were Kafka, with whose works Benjamin had yet to engage: "Even the linen that was [at] the launderer's or a pin belonging to them rolled toward the mouth of the earth and vanished therein. Nowhere upon earth remained a trace of them or of their possessions, and even their names disappeared from the documents upon which they were written" (Louis Ginzberg, *The Legends of the Jews*, trans. Paul Radin [Philadelphia: Jewish Publication Society of America, 1911], 3:298).

86. It is worth noting that Benjamin was intermittently and ambivalently studying Hebrew in this period; see *GB* 2:98, 104. Even if Benjamin could not read the biblical texts unaided, he would still have been able to discern the words with the help of a dictionary. (He was seeking to improve his scholastic Latin as well.) In reflecting on the issue of atonement, he may have consulted Michael Sachs's widely used *maḥzor* for Yom Kippur (in German, *Versöhnungstag* or *Sühnetag*). At certain moments in the afternoon prayer, Sachs introduces the strange verb *entsünen*; see *Festgebete der Israeliten: Yom Kippur*, trans. Michael Sachs (Berlin: Gerschel, 1864), 426, 514. Benjamin may have known of this translation through Scholem, who intended to write a "linguistic-metaphysical" examination of Sachs's translation practices; see *TB* 2:442 ("Sachs helps the language—his advantage and disadvantage at the same time"). What is silently striking about Sachs's translation is the absence of the "h" in *entsünt*, which, like Benjamin's use of *entsühnen*, removes it from the assumption that it is largely synonymous with *sühnt*. As for what *entsünt* then means, this is less clear.

87. In an appendix to "Force of Law" that has generated some controversy, Derrida connects the theme of bloodless violence with the gas chambers used by the Nazi regime (see "Force of Law," 1040–45). In responding to Derrida, Burkhart Lindner aptly cites Benjamin's ominous reflections on gas warfare; see Lindner, "Derrida. Benjamin. Holocaust: Zur politischen Problematik der 'Kritik der Gewalt,'" *Zeitschrift für kritische Theorie* 5 (1997): 65–100, here 94–95. The most deadly form of gas warfare in the First World War, so-called mustard gas, is not bloodless; on the contrary, as a contact poison (unlike earlier poisons, which required inhalation), it leaves visible signs on the surface of the body in the form of scarring blisters. For Benjamin's discussion of mustard gas, see "Theories of German Fascism" (3:240; *SW* 2:312–21) and esp. "Die Waffen von morgen" (Tomorrow's weapons), where he describes its chemical formula (4:474–75). Benjamin's concern about modern weaponry was shared by Dora Kellner-Benjamin, who wrote a novel titled *Gas gegen Gas* (Gas against gas) that was serialized in several newspapers in the early 1930s.

88. Buber, "Die Losung," *Der Jude* 1, no. 1 (April 1916), 2; see also Buber, *Drei Reden über das Judentum* (Frankfurt am Main: Rütten & Loening, 1920), 22: "[B]lood is the deepest level of power in the soul." Similar formulations appear throughout Buber's early writings.

89. The literature around the principle expressed in Leviticus 17:11 is understandably enormous. The following are helpful guides for the perplexed. For a thorough investigation of the biblical text as well as contemporary commentaries throughout the twentieth century, see William Gilders, *Blood Ritual in the Hebrew Bible* (Baltimore: Johns Hopkins University Press, 2004). For a consistently insightful examination of how blood sacrifice was reinterpreted in rabbinical Judaism, see Mira Balberg, *Blood for Thought: The Reinvention of Sacrifice in Early Rabbinic Judaism* (Oakland: University of California Press, 2017). Finally, for a broad and profound analysis of the theme of blood in Judaism and Christianity, see David Biale, *Blood and Belief: The Circulation of a Symbol between Jews and Christians* (Berkeley: University of California Press, 2007). (In an email, Professor Biale indicated to me that he was unaware of the provenance of Benjamin's remarks on Koraḥ; for his own inquiry into the afterlife of the incidents recounted in Numbers 16, see David Biale, "Korah in the Midrash: The Hairless Heretic as Hero," *Jewish History* 30 [2016]: 15–28.)

90. A more comprehensive account of what's missing from this volume can be obtained through a comparison of its contents with the Suhrkamp volume *Zur Kritik der Gewalt*, for which Marcuse provided an afterword. It includes "On the Program of the Coming Philosophy," which would certainly belong to a larger volume dedicated to the same set of problems as this one; but it would also need to include a variety of associated notes and fragments along with hitherto untranslated texts to which Benjamin refers, especially Cohen's *Logik der reinen Erkenntnis* (Logic of

pure knowledge). Something similar is the case with another essay included in Marcuse's edition, "Fate and Character," which at the very least should be supplemented by Benjamin's review of Dostoyevsky's *The Idiot* (2:237–41; SW 1:78–81) and Benjamin's critique of George Bernard Shaw's play *Mrs. Warren's Profession*, where he distinguishes between protecting one's personal "purity" (chastity) and something like "purification" (*Entsühnung*) (2:613–15). Two other items are found in Marcuse's volume, the so-called "Theologisch-Politisches Fragment" (Theological-political fragment) and a version of "Über den Begriff der Geschichte" (On the concept of history). Neither of these, though, would be appropriate for this volume, since both of them—the latter certainly, the former probably—stem from different circumstances, which would require different sets of associated writings; on the dating of the "Theological-Political Fragment," see 301.

One further document related to "Toward the Critique of Violence" does not appear as an independent item in this volume: some notes Werner Kraft drafted in the spring of 1934 that derive from his conversations with Benjamin. One set of notes, dated May 20, 1934, begins with Benjamin, prompted by Kraft's query, repudiating the "standpoint" of "Toward the Critique of Violence." Kraft indicates that he is unable to reproduce the entire course of their conversation and records instead a series of largely isolated remarks that are meant to outline Benjamin's new "position," beginning with the following: "Just law [*gerechtes Recht*] is what benefits the oppressed in class conflict. — Class conflict is the center of all philosophical questions, even the highest. — What he [Benjamin] earlier called divine ("pending" [*waltende*]) violence was an empty spot [*leerer Fleck*], a limit concept [*Grenzbegriff*], a regulative idea. Today, he knows that it *is* class conflict.... The 'just [sic] war' at the end of the violence essay: class conflict" (*Für Walter Benjamin*, ed. I. and K. Scheuermann [Frankfurt am Main: Suhrkamp, 1992], 47. Clearly the Kantian provenance of the essay remained alive for Benjamin. Unlike the remarks Scholem inscribes in his diary, which are here translated as Note 1, however, the notes from Kraft's diary do not derive from anything he wrote. There are reasons, moreover, to doubt the accuracy of the transcription, including that fact that several of its formulations are unpunctuated or otherwise unintelligible (which is itself understandable, for they are, after all, only jottings in a diary). What is "it" (*es*), specifically, that Benjamin is said to know "today"? If the subject matter of this knowledge were "pending violence" (60), it would have been designated by *sie*. As for the claim that the term "true war" (60) should now be reinterpreted as a reference to class conflict, this is less a change in standpoint than a shift in emphasis, for the "proletarian" in "proletarian general strike" can scarcely be understood in any other way. Nevertheless, for Benjamin, there is something new, and it begins, as Kraft's notes suggest, with the idea of "*just* law," which points toward a "philosophy of law" (108) that exhausts itself in its usefulness to oppressed classes.

Walter Benjamin, "Toward the Critique of Violence"

1. "Natural law" is generally understood as a term drawn from ancient Greek and Latin sources for a theory in which morality is understood as an objective feature of the cosmos; law of this kind can be discovered through the natural light of reason. In the history of European public law, "natural law" was the general doctrine from which *ius publicum universale* emerged in late seventeenth-century juridical reasoning and came to be known as "natural constitutional law" (*natürliches Staatsrecht*) by the mid-eighteenth century. During the nineteenth century, especially in Germany, the "natural law" origins of constitutional law underwent several terminological transformations: "natural law" as a discipline became synonymous with "legal philosophy" (*Rechtsphilosophie*), and "natural" or "general constitutional law" (*natürliches* or *allgemeines Staatsrecht*) split into the "common constitutional law of the German states" (*gemeines deutsches Staatsrecht*) and a "general theory of state" (*allgemeine Staatslehre*) concerned with foundational questions rather than with existing legislation. With the rise of legal positivism, practical interest in *allgemeine Staatslehre* receded in favor of the application of empirical methods to the dispensation of positive law, which had proliferated with the expansion of the state's administrative functions; at the same time, the natural-law tradition persisted in the writings of liberal jurists who resisted any tendency that would present law, state, and constitution as self-evident objects of study. In reaction to the revolutionary potential of certain theories of natural law, Carl von Savigny proposed in the early nineteenth century that it be replaced by a historical view of the provenance of positive law. By the second half of the nineteenth century, a group of jurists and philosophers came to oppose Savigny's view and sought to discern a "purpose" or "end" (*Zweck*) in law for which any reasonable person has the duty to struggle—a view associated, above all, with Rudolf von Jhering, whose work Benjamin calls "important!" (93). In referring to a "major trend in legal philosophy," Benjamin may be alluding to the more recent revival of natural law during the "recently elapsed German Revolution" (52). It was self-evident to some observers and participants that the new German constitution should conform with ideals of justice or morality that would be universally accessible to all educated citizens. For an authoritative account of these terminological and disciplinary developments, see Michael Stolleis, *Geschichte des öffentlichen Rechts in Deutschland* (Munich: Beck, 1988–2012), 2:122–23, 423–26; 3:94–95, 170–71.

2. Benjamin may be referring to several articles of the Declaration of the Rights of Man and Citizen, 1789, especially the second, which defines natural law as the basis of such rights, and the twelfth, which prescribes a "public military force" required to secure rights given by nature. This would be the "ideological foundation" for the Committee on Public Safety, created in the spring of 1793 and inextricably associated with the Reign of Terror. A translation of the declaration can be found at https://avalon.law.yale.edu/18th_century/rightsof.asp.

3. Benjamin is probably referring to chapter 16 of Spinoza's *Tractatus Theologico-Politicus*: "The Basis of the State; the Natural and Civil Right of the Individual, and the Right of Sovereign Powers," which opens in the following way: "By the right and established order of Nature I mean simply the rules governing the nature of every individual thing, according to which we conceive it as naturally determined to exist and to act in a definite way. For example, fish are determined by nature to swim, and the big ones to eat the smaller ones. Thus it is by sovereign natural right that fish inhabit water, and the big ones eat the smaller ones. For it is certain that Nature, taken in the absolute sense, has the sovereign right to do all that she can do; that is, Nature's right is co-extensive with her power. For Nature's power is the very power of God, who has sovereign right over all things. . . . Whatever an individual thing does by the laws of its own nature, it does with sovereign right, inasmuch as it acts as determined by Nature, and can do no other. Therefore among men, as long as they are considered as living under the rule of Nature alone, he who is not yet acquainted with reason or has not yet acquired a virtuous disposition lives under the sole control of appetite with as much sovereign right as he who conducts his life under the rule of reason. . . . Thus the natural right of every man is determined not by sound reason, but by his desire and power. . . . Thus whatever every man, when he is considered as solely under the dominion of Nature, believes to be to his advantage, whether under the guidance of sound reason or under passion's sway, he may by sovereign natural right seek and get for himself by any means, by force, deceit, entreaty or in any other way he best can, and he may consequently regard as his enemy anyone who tries to hinder him from getting what he wants" (Baruch Spinoza, *Complete Works*, trans. Samuel Shirley, ed. Michael L. Morgan [Indianapolis: Hackett, 2002], 526–28).

4. Popularizers of Darwin's biology such as Ernst Haeckel and Houston Stewart Chamberlain facilitated the widespread acceptance of the belief that physical power produced its own source of legitimacy for the state. Such a biologistic view of state power as deriving from the assertion of the strongest had been "revived" by social Darwinism most "recently" from, among other possible sources, the major work of Swiss jurist Karl Ludwig von Haller, *Restauration der Staats-Wissenschaft oder Theorie des natürlich-geselligen Zustandes, der Chimäre des künstlich-bürgerlichen entgegengesetzt* (Restoration of statecraft or a theory of the natural-social condition, as opposed to the chimera of the artificial-civil one; 1816–34). Despite his intermittent concern with certain aspects of the biological sciences (see 20 and 72), Benjamin showed little interest in Darwinism except insofar as it suffered a crisis; see his review of a lecture by the dubious paleontologist Edgar Daqué under the title "Krisis des Darwinismus?" (Crisis of Darwinism) (4:534–36). The issue of evolution (understood as autonomous development in nature) and violence is implicitly treated in Fragment 3 of this volume.

5. Theorists of positive law hold that "legitimate" is what has been posited regardless of its merits vis-à-vis such "natural givens" as ideals of justice, efficiency, prudence, or moral standards. A major source of the doctrine of legal positivism can be found in the work of Austrian jurist Hans Kelsen, especially *Hauptprobleme der Staatsrechtslehre, entwickelt aus der Lehre vom Rechtssatze* [Main problems in constitutional legal theory, developed from the theory of the legal norm] (Tübingen: Mohr, 1911), which lays the foundations for a program of rendering law as a chain of a priori norms that have their meanings conferred upon them by other, successively "higher" norms without ever referring to any other domain (or "ends"), including and up to the highest norm, the constitution. Kelsen argued that the legal validity of the first, historical norm must simply be presupposed; he expands his program to the area of government and public law in an essay on the "essence and value of democracy" ("Vom Wesen und Wert der Demokratie"), which was published in the same number of the *Archiv für Sozialwissenschaft und Sozialpolitik* and which reflects his experience in drafting the democratic-liberal constitution for the State of Austria. Several of Kelsen's major works, including *Main Problems*, appear in the bibliography Benjamin kept for the expansion of his own critique of violence, included in this volume as Note 22; see also the Afterword, 127–37.

6. In this sentence, what might otherwise appear as "justice" (*Gerechtigkeit*) is a function of law (*Recht*), inasmuch as positive law arrives at so-called justice through "justification" (*Berechtigung*), which can be translated more literally as "rendering legal" or "rendering justifiable through law." *Gerechtigkeit* is thus translated here as "justness" (as a quality of what emerges from a legal process) rather than "justice."

7. In the *Critique of Pure Reason*, Kant identifies several antinomies that emerge when reason comes into conflict with itself, and each of his subsequent *Critiques* includes its own antinomies; see esp. A 405–8; B 432–35. The last of the antinomies Kant identifies appears in a section of his *Rechtslehre* (Doctrine of law) with the following subtitle: "Toward the Critique of Legal-Practical Reason in the Concept of the External Mine and Thine" (*Zur Kritik der rechtlich-praktischen Vernunft im Begriffe des äußeren Mein und Dein*) (Aka 6:254; §7 in the original order of the paragraphs, which is unfortunately altered in several contemporary versions of the text).

8. The distinction between historically recognized and nonrecognized *Gewalt* finds in legal positivism one prominent source in Georg Jellinek, who in his *Allgemeine Staatslehre* (General theory of state; several editions from 1900–1914) derived the validity of law from what he called the "normative power of the factual" (*normative Kraft des Faktischen*); the very fact that state power (*Staatsgewalt*) asserts itself in the formation of a constitution implies the "recognition" of this claim by the citizen-recipients of these norms, which is sufficient to legitimize the legal order in question. For Jellinek, this sort of normative-factual "recognition" clarifies how the

"open violence" (*offene Gewalt*) often involved in the dissolution and formation of new states can nevertheless transform into legitimate "state power" through a legal constitution (*Staatsrecht*), even if the new constitution is exploitative or despotic. See Georg Jellinek, *Allgemeine Staatslehre* (Berlin: Häring, 1914), 337–44.

9. Benjamin does not further pursue the theme of "value," but here it is presented in a manner broadly consistent with the distinction between fact and value that is of paramount importance for the "Southwest" neo-Kantian school initiated by Wilhelm Windelband and developed by his student, Heinrich Rickert, who in turn taught Benjamin for several semesters at the university in Freiburg-im-Breisgau. For a relatively lucid presentation of the principles of "value philosophy," see Rickert, "Über logische und ethische Geltung" [On logical and ethical validity], *Logos* 19 (1914): 182–221. Benjamin was also familiar with the work of Leonard Nelson, the founder of a circle devoted to the renewal of the ideas of Jakob Fries who for a time was also associated with Gustav Wyneken and the school reform movement; Nelson's *Rechtswissenschaft ohne Recht* (Jurisprudence without right), to which Benjamin refers in Note 22, criticizes legal positivism for conflating the "end of law" with its value and failing to recognize the value of the "nonvalue" that accrues to all that is not "correct" law and therefore, according to the legal positivist, cannot be law.

10. The term *Rechtsgewalt* dates back to 1514 and denotes power (*Gewalt*) that has a legal basis or power on the basis of law; in this sense it would be synonymous with *Rechtsmacht* (legal power). In the history of the concept of the state, *Rechtsgewalt* may be contrasted to *Obrigkeitsgewalt*, that is, "power that derives from an authority such as a head of state or of a community." (An *Obrigkeitsstaat* denotes an "authoritarian state.") A contemporaneous account of the distinction can be found in Heiner Krabbe, *Obrigkeitsgewalt und Rechtsgewalt in der Geschichte*, in *Die Moderne Staats-Idee* (Dordrecht: Springer, 1919), 12–38; see also *Deutsches Rechtswörterbuch*, http://www.rzuser.uni-heidelberg.de/~cd2/drw/e/re/chtg/ewal/rechtgewalt.htm.

11. With the term *Rechtszwecken* (legal ends), Benjamin may be alluding to Jhering's *Das Zweck im Recht* (Purpose in law; 1877, partially translated as *Law as a Means to an End* by Isaac Husik [Boston: Boston Book Company, 1913]); see Note 19 and the accompanying editorial remarks.

12. By restricting his analysis to "contemporary Europe" while at the same time referring to earlier legal conditions, Benjamin signals an awareness of a then-recent development in jurisprudence, comparative (history of) law. Comparative law regarded states as historical facts whose emergence, specificity, and decline were classifiable as historically differentiated concepts; see Christian Starck, "Rechtsvergleichung im öffentlichen Recht," *Juristenzeitung* 52, no. 21 (November 7, 1997): 1021–76; Stolleis, *Geschichte des öffentlichen Rechts in Deutschland*, 2:436–38. One prominent comparative jurist was Josef Kohler, whose work appears in Note 22 in

connection with the name of an Americanist, Walter Lehmann, whose seminars on ancient Mesoamerican cultures Benjamin eagerly attended during his first semesters in Munich (*GB* 1:290–91, 300); for an extensive account of their relationship, see the Afterword, esp. 145.

13. The term "purposively" (*zweckmäßigerweise*) is drawn from a Kantian lexicon, in which purposiveness is given a precise formulation as an element of both practical and theoretical philosophy (as well as in aesthetics); the canonical treatment of the concept of purposiveness can be found in §§7 and 8 of the introduction to the *Critique of the Power of Judgment*, Aka 5:188–94.

14. Benjamin's remarks on "education" (*Erziehung*) are troubling insofar as his discussion of "educative violence" (58) seems to promote corporal punishment under the presumption that it not draw blood. It should be emphasized, however, that every single one of Benjamin's publications prior to 1921, with the exception of his dissertation, is associated with the theory of education in a broad sense. This is especially true of the essay that summarizes his reflections on the current educational situation, "Das Leben der Studenten" (The life of students), which appeared twice in print, the second time in Kurt Hiller's journal *Das Ziel* (2:75–87; *SW* 1:37–47). To the small extent that Benjamin's name was known in the public sphere, it was associated with this essay. As for the direction of the educational theory Benjamin therein promotes, it can be negatively described as one in which student life is freed from the "falsification of creative spirit into vocational spirit" (2:81; *SW* 1:41). The best and most succinct guide, however, to what "education" means in the context of his "political essays" (*GB* 2:101) can be found in the final aphorism of *Einbahnstraße* (One-way street), which, as argued elsewhere in this volume (see 17 and 117), is the culmination of the project of which "Toward the Critique of Violence" was originally a part: "The mastery of nature [*Naturbeherrschung*]—so teach the imperialists—is the meaning of technology. But who would trust a cane-master who explained that the meaning of education lies in the mastery of children by adults? Is not education, above all, the indispensable ordering of the relations among generations and therefore, if one wants to use the term 'mastery,' the mastery of these relations, not of children?" (4:147; *SW* 1:487).

15. The term *Notwehr* (self-defense) first appears as *nôtwer* in Middle High German at the end of the twelfth century as a translation of *Vim vi repellere licet*, which in Roman law was described by the jurist Cassius in terms of natural right in the context of armed struggle: "It is permissible to repel force by force, and this right is conferred by nature" (*The Digest of Justinian*, trans. and ed. Alan Watson [Philadelphia: University of Pennsylvania Press, 1985], 4:97; §43, 16, 1, 27). The formulation still current in German law today (as it was in 1921) was introduced into the Prussian Penal Code in 1851 (§41), which then became §53 of the *Reichsstrafgesetzbuch* of 1871, where it

states that "a punishable action is not present when the action was demanded by self-defense. Self-defense is defense that is required in order to protect oneself or another against a present, unlawful attack. Excessive self-defense is not punishable if the perpetrator exceeded the boundaries of self-defense out of confusion, fear, or intimidation" (Hans Rüdorff, *Deutsches Strafgesetzbuch*, 2nd ed. [Berlin: Guttentag, 1871], 186). For a broader discussion, see *Deutsches Rechtswörterbuch*, https://drw-www.adw.uni-heidelberg.de/drw-cgi/zeige?term=notwehr&index=lemmata); for an account of Benjamin's later expansion of his ideas concerning the troubling place of self-defense in the history of law and colonial regimes, see the Afterword, esp. 152.

16. The legal notion that the state enjoys a monopoly on violence was famously formulated by Max Weber in his 1919 lecture "Politik als Beruf" (Politics as vocation), in which he identifies "physical violence" (*physische Gewaltsamkeit*) as the sole criterion by which a modern state can be defined in sociological terms: "[The modern] state is that human community that, within a certain area—and exclusively within this 'area'—lays a (successful) claim on the *monopoly of legitimate physical violence*" (Max Weber, *Politik als Beruf* [Munich: Duncker & Humblot, 1919], 4; "The Profession and Vocation of Politics," in *Max Weber: Political Writings*, trans. Ronald Speirs [Cambridge: Cambridge University Press, 1994], 310). As the sole source of the "right" to use violence, the state can expect its constituents to relinquish their claim to any such use in their own right and has exclusive power to employ means (administrative power, police) necessary to maintain the continuity of the *Rechtsstaat* (constitutional state). The need to uphold the state's monopoly on legitimate violence was sometimes used as a counterargument by opponents of the right of self-defense.

17. The figure of the "great criminal" appears in criminological textbooks of the period; see esp. Erich Wulffen, *Psychologie des Verbrechers* (Berlin: Landgenscheidt, 1908), 2:106–8; Max Kauffmann, *Die Psychologie des Verbrechens: Eine Kritik* (Berlin: Springer, 1912), esp. 161. Both Wulffen and Kauffmann emphasize that the "greatness" of criminals lies in their understanding of their criminality as a "vocation" (*Beruf*) that requires training, dedication, and consummate skill. Among the historical figures with whom the term "great criminal" was often associated—besides both historical and fictional figures such as those that populate the literature of the *Sturm und Drang*, including works by Goethe and Schiller—is that of the seventeenth-century Swiss politician-conspirator-traitor-apostate Jörg Jenatsch, not least because of Conrad Ferdinand Meyer's novel *Jürg Jenatsch* (1876), which Benjamin probably read while completing the essay (see 7:452).

18. The right to strike first appears in §152 of the Industrial Code of the North German Confederation of 1869 (Gewerbeordnung des Norddeutschen Bundes), which later becomes the code for the entire Reich (Reichsgewerbeordnung); see *Bundesgesetzblatt des Norddeutschen Bundes, No. 26: Gewerbeordnung für den Norddeutschen Bund* (Berlin: Gesetz-Sammlungs-Debits- und Zeitungs-Komtoir, 1869), 281.

19. As a legal term, *Unterlassung* denotes the failure to take some action that is required of the legal subject. In German law, *Unterlassung* (or *Unterlassen*) is an alternative to doing (*Tun*) and tolerating (*Dulden*) that consists in the subject's nonactivity but technically remains an action (*Handlung*) under law, which decides whether or not it is punishable under the circumstances. "Omission" is the English equivalent in legal terminology.

20. *Staatsgewalt* refers to the authority over a state and its territory that derives from its sovereign power; in this sense, it is synonymous with *Staatsmacht* (state power). There is a historical as well as categorical distinction between *Staatsgewalt* and *Rechtsgewalt*.

21. The law of war (as a component of international law) that was generally recognized during the First World War was formalized in the Geneva Convention (1906) and the Hague Convention (1907).

22. As Kant emphasizes in his 1795 treatise *Toward Eternal Peace*, the word "peace," as used by "statesmen" and "political moralists," means perpetual preparation for war; by contrast, the condition of peace that Kant's treatise—which is written in the form of an international treaty—seeks to establish has nothing to do with war preparation, and all of its provisions are meant to reduce both its psychological incentives and its material (financial) means of support. As Kant notes in the preamble, the term "eternal peace" in its popular formulation means something else, namely, "resting in peace" under a gravestone—and this, he suggests, is because the word "peace" has hitherto only meant "preparation for war." Kant's proposal for an international community of republican states (where republicanism consists in the separation of the legislative from executive power, such that the legislative power alone can declare war) was the implicit model for the preamble to the Treaty of Versailles that established the League of Nations; see also 18.

23. Benjamin is referring to pacifist proposals that emerged from the carnage of the First World War, doubtless including Kurt Hiller's "Anti-Cain" (see 185). Benjamin has a dim view of some of the major forms of post-WWI pacifism; see in particular his critique of Fritz von Unruh's *Flügel der Nike—Buch einer Reise* (Wings of Nike—book on a journey) that appeared under the telling title "Friedensware" (Peace commodity), 3:23–28.

24. Universal conscription was codified in the law regarding the duty to perform military service (*Gesetz, betreffend die Verpflichtung zum Kriegsdienste*) of the North German Confederation of November 9, 1867; Article 57 of the Constitution of the German Reich of 1871; and the Reich military law of May 2, 1874 (see *Deutsches Reichsgesetzblatt, No. 15: Reichsmilitärgesetz* [Berlin: Kaiserliche Post-Zeitungsamt, 1874], 45–64). It was relinquished in 1919 as a consequence of the Treaty of Versailles.

25. The phrase "Erlaubt ist, was gefällt" is taken from act 2, scene 1, of Goethe's *Torquato Tasso*, in which Tasso reminisces about a "golden age" in which humans

and animals roamed freely and happily together on earth: "Where every bird in the open air / And every beast that roamed through hill and valley, / Said to human kind: What pleases is permitted." (Johann Wolfgang von Goethe, *Torquato Tasso*, reprinted in *Werke: Hamburger Ausgabe in 14 Bänden* (Munich: C. H. Beck, 1977), 5:100; Goethe, *Torquato Tasso*, in *The Essential Goethe*, trans. Michael Hamburger, ed. Matthew Bell [Princeton, NJ: Princeton University Press, 2016], 188). For Benjamin's attempt to gain insight into "anarchist literature" (*GB* 2:101) in preparation for this essay, see 16 and 195.

26. In several of the associated writings included in this volume, Benjamin develops the line of thought sketched here, whereby ethics is "applied" to history. From within the general purview of both Kantian and neo-Kantian programs, a concept acquires its "meaning" (*Sinn*) through its "application." Without the applicability of moral concepts, as suggested here, reality itself would lose its sense, for reality would thus be constituted solely by causal laws, which, unlike "historical occurrences," are reversible, hence directionless and thus, at bottom, senseless; see 16 and 195.

27. The quotation is drawn from Kant's 1785 treatise *Grundlegung zur Metaphysik der Sitten* (Groundwork for the metaphysics of morals), *Aka* 4:429. In speaking of a "minimal program," Kant is adopting the lexicon used by Friedrich Schlegel in his commentary on *Toward Eternal Peace*; see Schlegel's 1797 "Versuch über den Begriff des Republikanismus, veranlaßt durch die Kantische Schrift zum ewigen Frieden," which is reprinted in the seventh volume of the *Kritische Friedrich-Schlegel Ausgabe*, ed. Ernst Behler, Jean Jacques Anstett, and Hans Eichner (Munich: Schöningh, 1958–); "Essay on the Concept of Republicanism Occasioned by the Kantian Tract 'Perpetual Peace,'" in *The Early Political Writings of the German Romantics*, ed. Frederick Beiser (Cambridge: Cambridge University Press, 1996), 93–111.

28. Several of Benjamin's major early writings, from "Fate and Character" through his essay on Goethe's *Elective Affinities*, to the first part of his *Origin of the German Trauerspiel*, are directly concerned with the construction of a certain concept of "destiny" or "fate" (*Schicksal*). The argument proposed in the earliest of these, "Fate and Character," runs approximately as follows: fate has no relation to good fortune or to innocence, only to misfortune and guilt; its order is therefore not that of religion but of law, which "elevates" misfortune and guilt to "measures of the person" (2:174; *SW* 1:203). Every "inculpation by law" (*rechtliche Verschuldung*) is a misfortune, that is, an element on the order of fate. The only reason why the order of law has managed to outlast the demise of the "demonic stage of human existence" (2:174; *SW* 1:203) is due to law's having been confused with the realm of justice. Accordingly, "law condemns one not to punishment" that might atone for some wrongdoing "but to guilt. Fate is the guilt nexus of the living [*der Schuldzusammenhang des Lebendigen*]" (2:174–75; *SW* 1:204; cf. 1:138; *SW* 1:307). Guilt is thus the sole "fate" to which law is oriented, insofar as it is entirely irrelevant what (or who) it punishes or

expiates: "the judge can see fate wherever he wishes; with every punishment he has to blindly dictate [*mitdiktieren*] fate." Law targets not the individual but "the mere life" (*das bloße Leben*) (2:175; SW 1:204) in them. In his *Origin of the German Trauerspiel*, Benjamin quotes from the paragraphs from which the passages cited above are drawn (1:288–89; O 104); but it remains a question—as indicated by the passage he chooses to cite—whether the concept of fate developed in "Toward the Critique of Violence" is entirely consonant with the one he proposed in the earlier essay.

29. Deterrence (*Abschreckungstheorie*) is a theory in penology that regards punishment as preventing crime by virtue of the threat that it will certainly be carried out. One version of this theory was formulated by Paul Johann Anselm von Feuerbach; see his *Lehrbuch des gemeinen, in Deutschland geltenden peinlichen Rechts* [Textbook on common penal law in Germany] (Gießen: Georg Friedrich Heyer, 1801), where he also originated a key postulate of the constitutional state: *nullum crimen, nulla poena sine lege*, or, "there is no crime and no punishment without law."

30. One such critic was Rosa Luxemburg, who in the first issue of the newspaper *Die Rote Fahne* (The red flag), dated November 18, 1918 (hence only a few days after the beginning the German Revolution), called for the immediate abolition of the death penalty, which she described as a "duty of honor" and a necessary step in the dismantling of the entire penal code along with the class system in which it is rooted; see Rosa Luxemburg, "Against Capital Punishment," *International Socialist Review* 3, no. 1 (January–February 1969): 5–6.

31. Beginning in the sixteenth century, practical administration was known as *gute policey*, though prior to 1800 *Policey* and *Policeyrecht* were considered merely reactive instruments of the state and did not have a "law" of their own. Nevertheless, *gute policey* symbolized the modernity of the state inasmuch as it signaled the means by which felicity (*Glückseligkeit*) and good order under the prince were attained and maintained. With the emergence of the constitutional movement and the *Rechtsstaat* (constitutional state, rule of law) as a desideratum after 1800, *Polizeirecht* came to denote governance by policy that was subordinated to, and therefore also distinct from, constitutional law. *Polizeirecht* and *Rechsstaat* are thus bound up with one another; "police law" was conceived as an aspect of administrative law (*Verwaltungsrecht*) in order to legally restrict police powers to matters of security and the protection of citizens' rights, while administrative law was rewritten to include the juridical capacity to place limits on the absolutist *Policey* of which it was once a mere instrument; see Robert von Mohl's *Die Polizei-Wissenschaft nach den Grundsätzen des Rechtsstaats* (1832–33), which, while establishing the term *Rechtsstaat*, also articulated the first theory of the police as an independent force situated between state legislation and its everyday delivery to its subjects. By 1900, it was generally accepted that the constitutional state required a well-defined and separate police law in order to set out its relationship to the everyday delivery of administration. Yet the principles of police law

governed concrete relations (such as police operations) without containing any legal norms themselves; *Verwaltung* was both "executive" in the sense that it implemented law as determined by the state and "creative" in that it remained bound to law that presented itself as a limit on the state. This dual sense of *Verwaltung* corresponds roughly with Benjamin's notion that the police "annul" the distinction between "law-positing" and "law-preserving" *Gewalt*. For an extensive account of the history of police and administrative law, see Stolleis, *Geschichte des öffentlichen Rechts in Deutschland*, 1:334–404, chaps. 8–10; 2:229–65, 381–422, chaps. 5, 9; 3:203–45, chap. 6.

32. *Polizeiverordnungen* are police regulations and refer to a general administrative act consisting in the delegation of legislation and operate like legal norms. The foundation for *Polizeiverordnung* in Prussia is the Law of Police Administration (Gesetz über die Polizei-Verwaltung) of March 11, 1850, which later became the Regulation for Police Administration in the Newly Acquired Territories (Verordnung über die Polizeiverwaltung in den neu erworbenen Landestheilen) in 1867. *Polizeiverfügungen* are police orders that relate to concrete cases oriented toward restrictions on private right, and they are based solely on the General State Laws for the Prussian States of 1794; see §10 II 17. Whereas *Verordnungsrecht* refers to the prevention of present danger to members of the public, *Verfügungsrecht* refers to the maintenance of public order and security.

33. Among Benjamin's sources for this conception of the decision is the second volume of Kierkegaard's *Either/Or*, written by the pseudonymous "Judge Wilhelm," who, representing law, formulates a version of Kantian morality that insists on the spatiotemporal uniqueness of the decision that corresponds to the uniqueness of the one chosen as a spouse for no (finite, definable) reason. Benjamin adopted Kierkegaard's idea of the "decisive either/or" in his essay on "Die religiöse Stellung der neuen Jugend" (The religious attitude of the new youth) (2:73; Benjamin, *Early Writings, 1910–1917*, trans. Howard Eiland [Cambridge, MA: Harvard University Press, 2011], 168).

34. As the German translation of *plenitudo potestas*, *Machtvollkommenheit* refers to the concept of princely power; it was introduced in the twelfth and thirteenth centuries as a device with which church and state could justify changing the hitherto statically conceived legal order according to their will. The prince could act within the established order and, on the basis of his *plenitudo potestas*, just as legitimately act against it. See Holger Erwin, "Machtspruch," in *Handwörterbuch zur deutschen Rechtsgeschichte* (Berlin: Erich Schmidt, 2020), 3:1119–21, www.HRGdigital.de/HRG.machtspruch.

35. In the General State Laws for the Prussian States of 1794, for instance, the contract is defined as a reciprocal consent to acquire or express a law between two or more persons; every contract thus explicitly confirms the power of the law (*Rechtsgewalt*) to regulate or make good on the duties and obligations of the contractual parties.

36. By "syndicalist," Benjamin is clearly referring to Sorel, whom he quotes extensively in what follows. He does not do the same with respect to the Bolsheviks or, in the German context, Spartacists such as Rosa Luxemburg, especially in her (pre-Spartacist) "Social Democracy and Parliamentiarism" (1905), a translation of which can be found at https://www.marxists.org/archive/luxemburg/1904/06/05.htm. In the context in which his essay was received, however, Luxemburg's name would probably be associated with Bolshevism. A widely known version of Lenin's critique can be found in his 1917 treatise, *The State and Revolution*, where Marx is said to favor the abolition of parliaments; see Vladimir Lenin, *The State and Revolution* (Beijing: Foreign Language Press, 1976), 51–61.

37. For a use of the term "pure means" circa 1900, see Bruno Wille, *Philosophie der Befreiung durch das reine Mittel: Ein Beitrag zur Pädagogie des Menschengeschlechts* [Philosophy of liberation by pure means: A contribution to the pedagogy of the human race] (Berlin: Fischer, 1894). Wille condemns the use of violence (*Gewalt*) in a variety of cases, from corporal punishment in schools and military force to religious authority and economic exploitation as "impure." "Pure means," by contrast, is nonviolent, without compulsion or threat and therefore free.

38. Benjamin is clearly distinguishing lying from bearing false witness (in a court-like setting), since the latter is self-evidently a legal matter. The remarks in this paragraph are elements of the larger project he developed around the concept of "objective mendacity," which ranges from moral and political considerations to logical and metaphysical inquiries that take their point of departure from the Liar's Paradox; see 93 in this volume, as well as the discussion in the Afterword, 159.

39. The maxim *ius civile vigilantibus scriptum est* ("Civil law is written for the vigilant") can be traced back to a fragment from Quintus Cervidius Scaevola's *Liber singularis quaestionum publice tractatarum* (Questions publicly discussed), which is preserved in Justinian's Digest (§42.8.24), in the section pertaining to the "Restoration of What Is Done in Fraud of Creditors"; see Digest of Justinian 4:79. *Augen für Geld* ("eyes for money") is one among a group of legal proverbs, including "Augen auf, Kauf ist Kauf" (Keep your eyes open, a sale is a sale) and "Wer die Augen nicht auftut, tut den Beutel auf" (He who does not open his eyes opens his purse). They refer to the law that protects the seller against liability for goods that are later discovered to be damaged. According to this principle, the onus is on the buyer to inspect the goods prior to purchase; after purchase, the buyer bears the risk for any defects. While the phrase itself was likely first coined in the nineteenth century, the principle already appears among the rulings made by the Upper Court of Lübeck, which had existed since the mid-thirteenth century; see Andreas Ludwig Jakob Michelsen, *Der ehemalige Oberhof zu Lübeck und seine Rechtssprüche* (Altona: J. F. Hammerich, 1839), 286–87, no. 217. Indications of the proverb's provenance can be found in Eduard Heilfron, *Das bürgerliche Recht des deutschen Reichs*, pt. 1, §2, *Deutsche Rechtsgeschichte* (Berlin:

Speyer and Peters, 1905), 326; *Bürgerliches Gesetzbuch*, ed. Heinrich Rosenthal, 7th ed. (Graudenz: Röthe, 1906), 891; Pierre Siméon, *Recht und Rechtsgang im Deutschen Reiche* (Berlin: Heimann, 1908), 1:350; Eduard Graf and Matthias Dietherr, *Deutsche Rechtssprichwörter* (Nördlingen: C. H. Beck, 1869), 259–60.

40. The bracketed expressions derive from Benjamin. Of note is the fact that Benjamin chooses to translate Sorel's *l'État* with *Staatsgewalt*, which, as remarked above, refers in German legal theory to state power (as distinct from open violence, *offene Gewalt*) inasmuch as it is recognized as possessing a legal constitution; as the sovereign power (or authority) exercised over a state's territory, *Staatsgewalt* is also distinct from *Rechtsgewalt*, the power that issues from law. The French *l'État* denotes the state as a defined and delimited population living within a territory and subject to a government, and the modern sense of the term is arguably the achievement of Louis XIV's century; *Staatsgewalt* specifically is the equivalent of *autorité de l'État*. Also noteworthy is that Benjamin uses *Gewalt* here as his translation for Sorel's *pouvoir*, which he has therewith interpreted as the legal term denoting a power as an organ of decision, or (*Staats*)*gewalt*. With his word choices, Benjamin makes a small but significant adjustment to German legal language and thereby formulates a constitutional theory in nuce: for him, *Gewalt* rather than *Macht* signifies *pouvoir* (even though *Macht* can evidently also mean "power"), and *Gewalt* is not to be taken for granted as *autorité*; for Benjamin, the co-implication of power and violence, of power *qua* violence, is ineluctable and represents a problem (as opposed to a state of affairs) for the constitution of the state both as a territory and as an authority. Such a view lays bare what might otherwise be hidden or taken for granted, which is the transaction of sheer power, *Macht*, that grants the constitutional state its authority; accordingly, in the following quote, where Sorel only writes of *la transmission* between the privileged, Benjamin inserts the term "power" (*Macht*). In the third quote, Benjamin translates Sorel's *supprimer*, meaning "eliminate" or "abolish" and usually rendered as *löschen* or *beseitigen*, with *ausschalten* ("suspend" or "switch off"). By suggesting its synonymity with the proletarian general strike's "annihilation" (*Vernichtung*) of state power in the previous sentence, Benjamin's *ausschalten* retains the sense of the temporary and secondary character of state power and the "ideological consequences" in which it consists. In the fourth quote, finally, Benjamin also translates *supprimer* as *aufheben*, which can mean "abolish," one of the lexical meanings of the French term. In doing so, Benjamin makes clear that he does not associate the "suspension" or "abolition" of state power with the use of *aufheben* by Hegel and his successors (including Marx) as a dialectical process of canceling and preserving at a higher level.

41. See 338, where Sorel refers to an apocryphal remark Marx supposedly made to the historian Edward Spenser Beesly: "[T]he man who draws up a program for the future is a reactionary."

42. In early 1919, there were doctors who refused to treat wounded participants in the German Revolution. This can be seen as part of a broader movement

of counterstrikes by members of the bourgeoisie against the Spartacist movement. Strikes of this kind occurred on January 9 in Halle, where three thousand wounded were left unattended; March 31 in Stuttgart; and April 9 in Braunschweig. See Eberhard Wolff, "Mehr als nur materielle Interessen: Die organisierte Ärzteschaft im Ersten Weltkrieg und in der Weimarer Republik 1914–1933," in *Geschichte der deutschen Ärzteschaft: Organisierte Berufs- und Gesundheitspolitik im 19. und 20. Jahrhundert*, ed. Robert Jütte (Cologne: Deutsche Ärzteverlag, 1997), 97, 110–11; Walter Hänsle, *Streik und Daseinsvorsorge: Verfassungsrechtliche Grenzen des Streikrechts in der Daseinsvorsorge* (Tübingen: Mohr Siebeck, 2016), 145–46.

43. Benjamin is likely referring to a satirical drawing by George Grosz from 1917, which was published in *Die Pleite* [The bankrupt], April 1919, 2. In the drawing, a commission of military doctors sits at a table while one of them examines a soldier's cadaver consisting of scraps of flesh hanging off a skeleton; the commission declares that the soldier is "KV," that is, *kriegsverwendungsfähig* (suitable for use in war). The

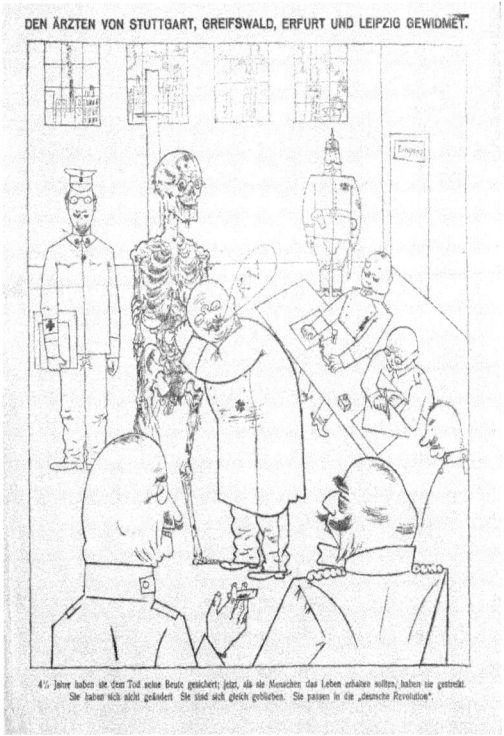

To the Doctors of Stuttgart, Greifswald, Erfurt, and Leipzig: For 4½ years they have secured death its prey, and now, just as they should be saving people's lives, they are on strike. — George Grosz, *Die Pleite* [The bankrupt], April 1919, 2.

print was inscribed with the dedication "To the Doctors of Stuttgart, Greifswald, Erfurt and Leipzig" and given the caption "For 4½ years they have secured death its prey, and now, just as they should be saving people's lives, they are on strike. They have not changed. They have remained the same. They fit right into the 'German Revolution.'" It was reprinted in June 1920 in the portfolio *Gott mit Uns* (God with us), published by Malik-Verlag, where it was given a new title: "*Le triomphe des sciences exactes, Die Gesundbeter* (The triumph of the exact sciences, the faith healers), German doctors fighting the blockade" (pl. 5).

44. The claim that reason does not decide on justness or justice of ends may sound "dogmatic," to use the term Benjamin had recently introduced (40); but it corresponds to the conclusion of Kant's *Doctrine of Virtue*, which concerns the idea of divine justice; see *Aka* 8:488–92. Divine justice, for Kant, is not in itself inconceivable; but the concept cannot be applied to any concrete case; the same is true, for Benjamin, with the regard to the justice (justness) of any conceivable end, which would require a cognition unavailable to human beings for the assessment of its moral status. The determination of the justness of ends must therefore be "left" to a being capable of such cognition. Far from being dogmatic, Benjamin's invocation of God at this point in his argument is "critical" in the sense Kant assigns to the term.

45. The myth of Niobe is recounted in Homer's *Iliad*, bk. 24, lines 602–17; Benjamin read Johann Heinrich Voss's famous translation, which was published in 1793 and reprinted in *Homers Werke in zwei Bänden, Erster Band: Ilias* (Leipzig: Max Hesse, 1900); cf. 7:440. Benjamin may also have been familiar with Ovid's version in the *Metamorphoses* (bk. 6, lines 145–310), as well as her appearance in Sophocles' *Antigone* and thus in Hölderlin's translation of the tragedy, which had recently been republished by Norbert von Hellingrath (act 3, scene 2, lines 852–66). Among the many other sources that would have been available are Kierkegaard's brief remark on Niobe in the section on "The Unhappiest Man" in *Either/Or*, and Nietzsche's mentions in *Human, All Too Human* ("The Wanderer and His Shadow") and "Homer's Contest." In a letter dated July 23, 1920, Benjamin thanks Scholem for a "Niobe" he has not yet had a chance to read but describes as "a mythological work that, coming from you [Scholem], fills me with the greatest expectation, and the subject matter is significant [*bedeutend*]" (*GB* 2:94; *C* 166).

46. Benjamin is referring to an element of the Prometheus myth adopted in Aeschylus' (or pseudo-Aeschylus') *Prometheus Bound*. In his *Origin of the German Trauerspiel*, Benjamin adopts a formula drawn from Nietzsche's *Die Geburt der Tragödie* (The birth of tragedy), "the deep Aeschylean trait of justice" (1:288; *O* 104). Strangely enough, though, Benjamin attributes this apt formula to Max Wundt; see Nietzsche, *Sämtliche Werke: Kritische Studienausgabe*, ed. Giorgio Colli and Mazzino Montinari (Berlin: Walter de Gruyter, 1988), 1:71; §9.

47. *Urphänomen* is a term borrowed from Goethe's morphological studies. Benjamin first uses the term around 1917 in a fragment on "perception" (*Wahrnehmung*) with reference to Goethe and the biological sciences; see "Zum verlorenen Abschluß der Notiz über die Symbolik in der Erkenntnis [On the lost conclusion to the note on symbolism in cognition]" (6:38).

48. Benjamin is referring to the following passage from Anatole France's *Le lys rouge* (Paris: Calmann Lévy, 1894), 118; *The Red Lily*, trans. Winifred Stephens (New York: Lane, 1908), 94–95): "In the days of Saint Louis no one would have dreamt of sending a man of learning and intelligence into battle. Neither was the labourer dragged from his plough and forced to join the army. Now it is considered the duty of a poor peasant to serve as a soldier.... We in France are soldiers and we are citizens. Our citizenship is another occasion for pride! For the poor it consists in supporting and maintaining the rich in their power and their idleness. At this task they must labour in the face of the majestic equality of the laws, which forbid rich and poor alike to sleep under the bridges, to beg in the streets, and to steal their bread. This equality is one of the benefits of the Revolution. Why, that revolution was effected by madmen and idiots for the benefit of those who had acquired the wealth of the crown."

49. Benjamin may be referring to a passage in which Sorel discusses criminal law in "primitive societies" (202). As described in note 46 above, which describes Benjamin's attribution of a passage from one of Nietzsche's works to Max Wundt, here he attributes to Sorel a major theme of Nietzsche's *Antichrist* (Anti-Christ or Anti-Christian), which includes the succinct formula "A right is a privilege" (*Ein Recht ist ein Vorrecht*) (Nietzsche, *Sämtliche Werke*, 6:243; §57).

50. For a discussion of this and the following remarks, where Benjamin distinguishes between "expiation" (*Sühne*) and "de-expiation" (*Entsühnung*), see 31–32.

51. This quote reappears verbatim in Benjamin's long essay from 1934 on Kafka (2:412; SW 2:797).

52. See Num. 16:1–50. There is a vast field of commentary on Koraḥ and his "horde" in Jewish, Christian, and Muslim traditions; it is not clear what drew Benjamin's attention to Koraḥ's rebellion, which is mentioned nowhere else in his extant work; see 33–34 for further discussion and references.

53. Compare Lev. 17:11, "For the life of the flesh is in the blood: and I have given it to you upon the altar to make an atonement for your souls: for it is the blood that maketh an atonement for the soul" (King James Bible). Luther translates the Hebrew word given here as "flesh" (in other versions as "creature"), בשר (*basar*) as Leib (living body) and "atonement," in Hebrew כפור (*kippur*) as *Versöhnung*, which is also often translated as "reconciliation." On the original context of this passage as well as the term "mere life" (*bloßes Leben*), see 35.

54. In the version published by Adorno in his inaugural collection of Benjamin's writings from 1955, Adorno mis-transcribed *Auslösung* (meaning "release" in the sense of "trigger" or "catalyze") as *Auflösung*, which was then translated into English (and reproduced in all subsequent reprints of that translation) as "dissolution" based on this mis-transcription; see Benjamin, *Schriften*, ed. Theodor W. Adorno and Gretel Adorno with Friedrich Podszus (Frankfurt am Main: Suhrkamp, 1955), 1:26; cf. *SW* 1:250.

55. Ex. 20:13; Deut. 5:17. The Hebrew term רצח (*ratsah*) is properly translated as "murder." In Luther's versions (which Benjamin is citing here, doubtless because of its familiarity to his readers), *ratsah* is translated as *töten* (kill); in the King James Bible, it is likewise translated as "kill."

56. For a helpful discussion of the figurative sense of *davor* (viz. *dafür*) *sein* (literally, to stand "in front of," hence block), see paragraph I.3 in the entry for *Davor* in the dictionary begun by Jacob and Wilhelm Grimm, *Deutsches Wörterbuch*, available at http://woerterbuchnetz.de/cgi-bin/WBNetz/wbgui_py?sigle=DWB&mode=Vernetzung&lemid=GD01041#XGD01041. Benjamin may have in mind a midrash (or series of midrashim) concerning the potent character of the divine presence; but the editors have been unable to identify any one in particular.

57. A statement to this effect (Judaism does not recognize in the commandment "Thou shalt not kill" any hindrance to killing in self-defense) is already evident in light of the remark concerning the more appropriate English and German translation of *ratsah* in note 55 above; insofar as the commandment proscribes "murder," it permits self-defense. See also the discussion in Fragment 17 (89), where Benjamin invokes the idea of *kiddush haShem* (sanctification of the Name) in relation to an argument that closely approximates the one pursued here.

58. It is in light of this remark that Benjamin undertakes his investigation into the "psychophysical problem," which can briefly be described as the problem of determining how the human being is unified beyond its aggregate somatic shape (*physis*) and its putative unity of consciousness (*psychē*).

59. "Vielleicht, ja wahrscheinlich ist es jung, als die letzte Verirrung der geschwächten abendländischen Tradition, den Heiligen, den sie verlor, im kosmologisch Undurchdringlichen zu suchen." The original is ungrammatical inasmuch as it omits a "zu" from the first clause. The translation makes sense of the sentence by inserting a "too" to complete the "too *x* to do *y*" construction. Notably, Benjamin writes not of "das Heilige" (the sacred) but of "den Heiligen," which is normally translated as "the saint." Benjamin seems to be suggesting that the institution of sainthood, which identifies sacred ones among those who have died, somehow corresponds to the same tendency in the Western tradition that has more recently promoted the dogma of the sanctity of all life, understood as "mere life."

60. A juridical term, *entsetzen* means "to relieve someone of their possession, power, or right." An *Entsetzung* of *Recht* can occur, for instance, in the sense of the

withdrawal of a right by the power of a judge. Benjamin transforms the meaning of *entsetzen* such that both law and any authority founded on law are "relieved" of their power to relieve and, indeed, to "posit" (*setzen*) at all.

61. In German: "Verwerflich aber ist alle mythische Gewalt, die rechtsetzende, welche die schaltende genannt werden darf. Verwerflich auch die rechtserhaltende, die verwaltete Gewalt, die ihr dient. Die göttliche Gewalt, welche Insignium und Siegel, niemals Mittel heiliger Vollstreckung ist, mag die waltende heißen." In these final lines, Benjamin decomposes a well-known idiom, "schalten und walten," which means "to be given free rein" or "to be in a position to dispose of something as one pleases." The verb *schalten*, for its part, can mean "to switch (on or off)" and thus "to change gear," while *walten* generally means "to reign," "to prevail over," "to hold sway," or "to be available as an operative force." As used in the aforementioned idiom, *schalten* and *walten* are placed in a relation of synonymity that reinforces the operational senses of both terms. Benjamin, by contrast, makes them categorically different from each other—so much so that the final sentences of the essay transform a colloquial both-and ("schalten *und* walten") into a quasi-technical either-or: either law-positing violence or another form of violence, which is here identified with a *walten* that, dissociated from the shifting function denoted by *schalten*, has nothing to do with the (legal-mythic) illusion of "free rein," which is pictured as an ability to shift from one path to another and then shift back again. To draw on a phenomenological vocabulary with which Benjamin was well acquainted: the dynamics of *schalten*—whereby lines of power and communication can be turned on and off at will—are *ausgeschaltet* (suspended, excluded, placed in brackets, and thus "reduced"). Benjamin's conclusion is more suggestive still. The paragraph opens with the appeal to an "ending" (*Ausgang*) that will make possible the breaking of the apparent dialectic of law-positing and law-preserving violence through the incisive and decisive examination of their "temporal data." The ending of the essay provides such a point of departure, since Benjamin calls law-preserving violence *verwaltete*, which as a past participle of *verwalten* ("to administer, to manage") indicates that the "preservation" of law-related violence consists in its having been used up, hence "expended." Administrators of legal force do not "have" power at their disposal; rather, they merely represent a power that is already dissipating. The translation offered here attempts to capture Benjamin's diction by proceeding along parallel lines: *walten* deposes *verwalten* of its attenuating prefix, and something similar happens with "expended" and "pending." "Pending" violence is fundamentally different from "attending" violence: the former "hangs over," while the latter "stretches across." It seems appropriate to qualify divine violence as "pending," moreover, since Benjamin has just associated it with a "standing reserve" that cannot be canceled—and is therefore "pending" in a precise sense. Finally, the translation seeks to approximate a subtle but important feature of these strange last sentences in which Benjamin presents a vocabulary that he never uses

in the essay itself, as if the actual language of violence were pending as well: the suggestion of rhyme. Benjamin says of rhyme in a corresponding context that it "ascends out of the creaturely world" (2:362; SW 2:453). Nothing of this rhyme can be preserved in translation, of course; but each of the English terms used here to identify a mode of violence includes "-end-" in accordance with the "idea" to which "Toward the Critique of Violence" as a whole is dedicated: "the idea of its ending."

Notes and Fragments

1. Notes toward a Work on the Category of Justice

Scholem Arc 4° 1599 / File 265 MS 45–46. "Notizen zu einer Arbeit über die Kategorie der Gerechtigkeit" was probably written in the summer or early fall of 1916. Scholem copied the "Notes" from "the notebook lent to me by W.B." (as Scholem writes at the top of the page) into his diary entry of October 8–9, 1916. Three final paragraphs (which are reproduced in note 3 below) are separated from the preceding text by two horizontal lines in the manuscript; it is unclear whether or not Scholem also copied them from Benjamin's notebook. These paragraphs originate from conversations Scholem and Benjamin had concerning the theme of "historical time" in August 1916; see also 6:90 and 92; cf. Note 8 in this volume, 73.

1. This sentence has no direct object that would determine what is protected.
2. See Matt. 6:9–13; Luke 11:2–4.
3. The following paragraphs are added below two horizontal lines: "The problem of historical time is already posed through the peculiar form of historical time-reckoning. The years are countable but, in contrast to most countables, not numerable [cf. 2:601]. / Jean Paul on the Romantics: 'a school that is now halfway collapsed, whose pupils and writing exercises, for instance, the Friedrich-Schlegelian ones, outlived their brief moment of immortality' [see Jean Paul, *Kleine Nachschule zur ästhetischen Vorschule*, in *Sämmtliche Werke*, 3rd ed. (Berlin: Reimer, 1860–62), 13:326)]. From a lecture on Greek philosophy: / Thoughtlessness goes overboard: the elements are 'the personifications of the shapes of the gods.'"

2. Vivification and Violence

Scholem Coll. Untitled in the original, the fragment, here called "Vivification and Violence" (rather than "Der Centaur" as in *GS*), could have been written either in the second half of 1917 or in the first half of 1921 (see 7:566–67). The only extant manuscript includes the date "15 July 1921," written in Benjamin's hand. This was his twenty-ninth birthday, and Benjamin may have inscribed the date when he presented the text as a gift rather than as a mark of its completion. In another hand—presumed by the editors of *GS* to be Jula Cohn's—the manuscript includes the following inscription: "By Walter Benjamin, written in Jula Cohn's copy of Maurice de Guérin, *Der Centaur*, translated by Rainer Maria Rilke, Leipzig 1919" (7:566). Maurice de Guérin was a French poet primarily known for writings on nature; *Le centaure* was published a year after his death in 1839. Benjamin received an edition of Guérin's collected works from Ernst Schoen in the summer of 1917, and Benjamin wrote some "thoughts" (*GB* 1:415) later in the year. Around the same time he read the last of Friedrich Hölderlin's so-called Pindar commentaries, "Das Belebende" (The vivifying element) in the appendix to an edition of Hölderlin's Pindar translations prepared by Norbert von Hellingrath, whose edition along with its accompanying dissertation, *Pindarübertragungen von Hölderlin: Prolegomena zu einer Erstausgabe* (Jena: Diederich, 1911), rescued Hölderlin's poetry from obscurity and established a perspective under which the poet's "late" writings, previously viewed as early evidence of his benightedness, for the first time became widely admired. Benjamin briefly mentions Hölderlin's centaur poem, "Chiron," in "Two Poems of Friedrich Hölderlin" (*GS* 2:119; *SW* 1:30–31). A note Benjamin probably wrote around the same time as the fragment outlines its argument: "Sadness in the shape of centaurs: the vivifying element, violence [*das Belebende, die Gewalt*], creation from development and the contrary. The firmer, one-time, *word*-born Jewish creation" (6:196). Both Hölderlin and (more likely) Benjamin may also be responding obliquely to a remark Machiavelli makes in an infamous chapter of *The Prince*: "[A] ruler must know well how to imitate beasts as well as employing properly human means. This policy was taught to rulers allegorically by ancient writers: they tell how Achilles and many other ancient rulers were entrusted to Chiron the centaur, to be raised carefully by him. Having a mentor who was half-beast and half-man signifies that a ruler needs to use both natures, and that one without the other is not effective" (Niccolò Machiavelli, *The Prince*, trans. Quentin Skinner [Cambridge: Cambridge University Press, 1988], 61). In Fragment 21 of this volume, Benjamin returns to the theme of running water (103) without reference to the issue of creation.

1. See Aristotle, *Metaphysics*, 983b21–22. Thales of Miletus is often called the earliest Greek philosopher.

2. In the aforementioned letter to Ernst Schoen, Benjamin refers him to the edition of "Das Belebende" in *Hölderlins Pindar-Übertragungen*, ed. Norbert von Hellingrath (Berlin: Verlag der Blätter für die Kunst, 1910), 66–67. A more accurate edition was also available a few years later; see Friedrich Hölderlin, *Sämtliche Werke: Historisch-kritische Ausgabe*, ed. Norbert von Hellingrath and Friedrich Seebass (Munich: Müller, 1913), 5:272–73; cf. Hölderlin, *Essays and Letters*, ed. and trans. Jeremy Adler and Charlie Louth (Harmondsworth, UK: Penguin, 2009), 338–39. A detailed discussion of the relation between Hölderlin and Benjamin's centaur-related fragments is beyond the scope of a note, but two points are immediately relevant to

the themes of this volume: Hölderlin uses *Gewalt* to translate Pindar's ῥιπή ("force with which anything is thrown," according to Liddell and Scott's authoritative *Greek-English Lexicon*), as he names the initial violence or force with which the surface of the earth is divided against itself; and Benjamin draws on the account of "*word*-born" (6:196) creation that he sketched in a "little treatise" (*GB* 1:343; *C* 81) that he wrote in 1916 titled "Über die Sprache überhaupt und über die Sprache des Menschen" [On language as such and on human language] (2:140–57; *SW* 1:62–74).

3. From "Life and Violence"

WBA 1152 [= I MS 505ᵛ]. Untitled in the original, the fragment was written in Dora Kellner-Benjamin's hand (as dictated presumably by Benjamin) on the back side of an extensive of schematization of certain problems in logic and linguistic theory under the title "The Word" (6:19–21). As the editors of *GS* indicate, the fragment probably derives from a "short, very topical [*aktuelle*] note on 'Life and Violence' ... of which I may very well say that it is written from my heart" (*GB* 2:85; *C* 162). The text may have been written as early as 1916 or 1917 or as late as the first months of 1920; see Note 16, where Benjamin refers to his lost reflections on "Life and Violence" (87). As discussed in the Introduction (36), Fragments 2 and 3 may be related to each other.

1. For a description of Benjamin's interest in "anarchist literature" (*GB* 2:101), see 16 and 195; for the translation of *verwaltete* (often rendered by "administered" or "administrative") as "expended," see the note to the final sentence of "Toward the Critique of Violence" (293).

2. Benjamin develops the idea of inclination (*Neigung*) in several other contexts, including Fragment 6 (71) and the final section of his essay on Goethe's *Elective Affinities*; see 1:186–88; *SW* 1:344–45. Like "inclination," *Neigung* suggests a stance that partially gives way to a certain force such as gravity; it contrasts with uprightness, which diametrically opposes the relevant force and (heroically) seeks to overcome it through a counterforce.

4. On Morality

WBA 400/35 [= I MS 708]. "Zur Moral" is dated in *GS* as "around 1917/18" (6:667). It is also possible, however, that the fragment was written in the fall of 1915 or spring of 1916, when Benjamin attended the University of Munich, in whose vicinity he could have overheard the Bavarian prayer to which he refers. Furthermore, while in Munich, he took classes with Moritz Geiger, who made important early contributions to the phenomenological movement, while also reading Edmund Husserl's "difficult, principal groundwork" (*GB* 1:302), which could refer to either *Logische Untersuchungen* (Logical investigations,) or, more likely, *Ideen zur reinen*

Phänomenologie und phänomenologischen Philosophie (Ideas for a pure phenomenology and phenomenological philosophy). Benjamin's use of the term "intention" (viz., "intentionality") is indebted to his studies of phenomenology. This fragment comes from the same notepad ("Erster Notizblock") as Fragments/Notes 6, 7, 8, 9, 10, 11, 12, 13, and 18 in this volume.

5. All Unconditionality of the Will Leads to Evil

WBA 1185 [= I MS 783]. Untitled in the original, "Alle Unbedingtheit des Willens" is dated in *GS* as "early summer 1918" (6:667). As with Fragment 4, this fragment may be related to Benjamin's studies of phenomenology in 1915–16, as is suggested by its use of the term "intention." As with Fragments 6 and 7, however, the fragment may have been written in 1917 or 1918, when Benjamin was undertaking an extensive "altercation with Kant and Cohen" (*GB* 1:441; *C* 119).

1. Benjamin develops the theme of *Andacht* in several later writings, including "The Work of Art in the Age of Its Technical Reproducibility" (1:465; *SW* 3:119; cf. 1:1043–44).

6. On Kantian Ethics

WBA 400/26r [= I MS 699]. "Zur Kantischen Ethik" is dated in *GS* as "early summer 1918" (6:667).

1. This sentence could also be understood to begin as follows: "The doctrine of 'rational beings' as subjects of ethics has at least one thing in common with ethics [*ihr*] ..."

2. Throughout his writings Kant refers to intelligent beings on planets other than Earth, beginning with his spectacular description of the "inhabitants of the stars" (that is, the known planets, concluding with Saturn, which houses the most quick-witted species of rational beings) in his 1755 treatise *Allgemeine Naturgeschichte und Theorie des Himmels* (Universal natural history and theory of the heavens), *Aka* 1:351–66.

3. See also 68.

7. The Spontaneity of the I

WBA 400/17r [= I MS 690]. Untitled in the original, "Die Spontaneität des Ich" is dated in *GS* as "early summer 1918" (6:668).

1. An essential element of Kant's theory of knowledge consists in drawing a distinction between the spontaneity of the faculty of the understanding and the receptivity that characterizes (human) sensibility; see *Critique of Pure Reason*, A 50; B 74, esp. B 158. Kant also distinguishes (theoretical) spontaneity from (practical, ethical) freedom; see *Critique of Pure Reason*, A 445; B 473.

8. Ethics, Applied to History

WBA 400/20r–21v [= I MS 693–94]. Untitled in the original, "Ethik, auf die Geschichte angewendet" is dated in GS as "early summer to late fall 1918" (6:684). It is possible, however, that Benjamin's use of the term *Weltgericht* (judgment of the nations) alludes to a volume of writings about the war that Karl Kraus published in 1919 under this title.

1. See Matt. 25:31–33: "All the nations will be gathered in front of him [the Son of Man]. He will separate them from each other, just as a shepherd separates the sheep from the goats" (Common English Bible).

2. This remark alludes to Kant's Third Antinomy of Pure Reason in the *Critique of Pure Reason*, A 445–51; B 473–79.

9. Modes of History

WBA 400/14 [= I MS 687]. "Arten der Geschichte" is dated in GS as "early summer to late fall 1918" (6:684). The format given here corrects the one given in GS.

1. Benjamin is probably referring to the first volume of Herder's *Ideen zur Philosophie der Geschichte der Menschheit* (Ideas for the philosophy of human history; orig. 1784), reprinted in the fourth volume of his *Ausgewählte Werke*, ed. Bernhard Suphan (Berlin: Weidmannsche Buchhandlung, 1887); partially translated in *Herder on Social and Political Culture*, ed. F. M. Barnard (Cambridge: Cambridge University Press, 2010). Benjamin may also be alluding to, or drawing from, Kant's negative reviews of Herder's *Ideas* (Aka 8:45–58). In a set of notes on Paul Scheerbart's "Berlin novel" *Münchhausen und Clarissa* (Berlin: Osterheld, 1906), Benjamin proposes a kindred theme: "Since the earth forms a living body [*Leib*] together with humanity, it is naturally vivified [*belebt*]" (6:148).

2. *Anthropos* is the Greek word for "human being."

10. Methodical Modes of History

WBA 400/19 [= I MS 692]. "Methodische Arten der Geschichte" is dated in GS as "early summer to late fall 1918" (6:685). In a letter to Scholem from February 1921, Benjamin indicates that, while in Switzerland (hence around 1918), he wrote out "some thoughts on philology" (GB 2:137; C 176) that may include this fragment.

1. Benjamin is probably deriving the term "pragmatic" along with "pragmata" (the things that emerge through certain purposive activities) from their Kantian usage. In the preface to his *Anthropologie in pragmatischer Hinsicht* (Anthropology in a pragmatic perspective), Kant understands the term in relation to what a "free being makes of itself" (Aka 7:119), such that "pragmata" are at once the source and product of this process of self-making.

2. Goethe helped introduce the term "morphology" in *Zur Morphologie* (On morphology; 1817), which includes his "Metamorphose der Pflanze" (1790); see *The*

Metamorphosis of Plants, trans. Gordon Miller (Cambridge, MA: MIT Press, 2009). Benjamin read "The Metamorphosis of Plants" as well as "much else from Morphology I" (7:442) in conjunction with his research for his dissertation.

11. Death

WBA 400/23r [= I MS 696]. "Tod" is dated in *GS* as "around 1920, perhaps earlier" (6:676). The typography here corrects the version produced in *GS*.

12. As Many Pagan Religions, So Many Natural Concepts of Guilt

WBA 400/41r [= I MS 714]. Untitled in the original, "Soviel heidnische Religionen, soviel natürliche Schuldbegriffe" is dated in *GS* as "summer 1918" (6:669). As with Note 13, this fragment may have served as a preparatory note for the essay Benjamin wrote between the spring of 1918 and the summer of 1919 under the title "Schicksal und Charakter" (Fate and character), where he reflects on the concept of *Schuld*, here translated as "guilt" (see 2:171–79; *SW* 1:201–6).

1. An intricately devised version of this widely recognizable thesis, whereby Judaism rejects the notions of original (inherited) sin, can be found in Hermann Cohen's extensive discussion of fate, tragedy, and religion in *Ethics of Pure Will*, chaps. 10 and 11; Cohen emphasizes the importance of the concept of שגגה (*shegagah*), that is, unwitting or inadvertent sin; see the preface to the portion of *Ethics of Pure Will* included in this volume, 163.

2. A note Benjamin probably wrote around the same time as the fragment responds to this question as follows: "Jewish thought: the integrity of guilt [*Schuld*]; contrasts with Christian 'sin.' [That] life is *guilt* is ancient and Jewish; 'original-inherited sin' [*Erbsünde*] is Christian" (6:196).

13. On the Problem of Physiognomy and Prediction

WBA 400/33r [= I MS 706]. "Zum Problem der Physiognomik und Vorhersagung" is dated in *GS* as "between March 1918 and June 1919" (6:683); like Fragment 12, this note is probably a preparatory study for "Fate and Character" (see 2:176; *SW* 1:204; see also a discussion of "parasitic time" in Benjamin's *Origin of the German Trauerspiel* (1:313–14; *O* 135). The version of the note in *GS* reproduces only the upper part of the manuscript page; three sets of keywords and phrases that appear in the lower part of the page are reproduced in separate volumes (with the second and third sets conjoined to other notes on the "grin"). The first set, which is written in the same black ink as the preceding notes, is related to the primary themes of "Fate and Character" as well as associated notes on comedy; the second set, which is also written in the same black ink, concerns a pair of terms ("expressionlessness" and "the expressive") that play an important role in a number of other writings, including Benjamin's essay on Goethe's *Elective Affinities* and the notes on objective mendacity, translated as Note 19 in this volume; see

310 for further references. The third set, which is written in a blue ink, likewise concerns the dyad "expressionless"/"expressive." The bibliographic entry at the bottom of the page, written in black ink, is omitted from *GS* altogether and is reproduced here with the permission of the Walter Benjamin Archive. Prepared by Julia Ng.

1. Emily Nevill Jackson, *The History of Silhouettes* (London: The Connoisseur, 1911). This is one of the very few books in English Benjamin seems to have consulted, perhaps because the history it recounts requires little or no knowledge of English.

14. The Meaning of Time in the Moral World

WBA 1211 [= I MS 798]. "Die Bedeutung der Zeit in der moralischen Welt" is dated in *GS* as 1920 or 1921 (6:687–88). The fragment may have been written in response to Scholem's reflections on justice, which were themselves developed in response to Note 1 in this volume; see Scholem's essay "Über das Buch Jona und den Begriff der Gerechtigkeit" (*TB* 2:522–32; see also *TB* 2:335–36); "On Jonah and the Concept of Justice," trans. Eric Schwab, *Critical Inquiry* 25 (1999): 353–61. In an essay titled "Ein Jakobiner von Heute" (A contemporary Jacobin), which discusses Werner Hegemann's sociopolitical history of tenement housing in Berlin, Benjamin briefly reprises the argument of this fragment by associating the forced air through which tenement housing must be ventilated with the "cool wind of the past": "Even on the Day of Judgment, the fact that it all lies so long ago must count as an extenuating circumstance. For the course of time [*Zeitverlauf*] is itself a moral accomplishment [*Vollzug*]—not in its advancement of today into tomorrow but in the sudden reversal [*Umschlag*] of today into yesterday" (3:264).

1. Homer describes Atē in the *Iliad* (bk. 19, lines 91–92) as the oldest daughter of Zeus, who is able to "bewilder" (ἀᾶται) human beings as well as gods; in Hesiod's *Theogony*, l. 230, she is the daughter of Eris ("strife").

2. As Benjamin suggests in the following paragraph, this image is obscure; it may allude to the storms in the book of Jonah, to which Scholem devotes his reflections on justice, as noted above.

15. 1) World and Time

WBA 1202r [= I MS 811]. Untitled in the original, "1) Welt und Zeit" is dated in *GS* as "sometime between fall 1919 and December 1920" (6:689).

1. The idea of the "coming world" is a significant element in Jewish thought under the Hebrew term העולם הבא (*haolam haba*); a contemporaneous compendium of sources in Jewish antiquity for the term can be found in Joseph Klausner's inaugural

dissertation, *Die messianische Vorstellungen des jüdischen Volkes* (Cracow: Fischer, 1903), 17–23.

2. The editors of *GS* suggest that Benjamin may be referring to a lost essay titled "Phantasie über eine Stelle aus dem Geist der Utopie" (Fantasy on a passage from the *Spirit of Utopia*), which he mentions in a letter to Scholem (*GB* 2:118; *C* 170). The rationale for this suggestion is a remark with which Benjamin begins his so-called "Theologisch-politisches Fragment" (Theological-political fragment): "The greatest service of Bloch's *Spirit of Utopia* is to have denied the political significance of theocracy with total intensity" (2:203; *SW* 3:305). In the same vein, it could be suggested that the "Theological-Political Fragment"—the title seems to stem from Theodor Adorno—constitute the "notes" in question. One major problem with both of these suggestions is that Bloch's book scarcely mentions theocracy, much less engages in an especially intensive critique of it. Why, then, does the "Theological-Political Fragment" present Bloch's book in this manner? Because Benjamin remembered it in this way when he wrote the "fragment" circa 1937, as Adorno contends (see 2:946). The past-tense formulation in the previously quoted passage suggests as much: Bloch's book is no longer a matter of public discussion, but it had significance for an earlier generation. As for the "notes" to which he refers here, they appear to have been lost; but one of their elements is perhaps captured by a remark that can be found in Note 8, "Morality: doctrine of theocracy" (73). This implies the provocative thesis that the critique of morality in the Kantian sense (*Moral*) is at the same time, contra Kant, a critique of theocracy.

3. Several sources lead Benjamin to this evidently obscure "definition" of politics, the key elements of which are the concept of *Steigerung* (elevation) and the use of *Menschhaftigkeit* (humanness) rather than *Mensch* (human being), *Menschheit* (humanity), or *Humanität*. The concept of *Steigerung* is of some importance in Benjamin's doctoral dissertation, *Der Begriff der Kunstkritik in der deutschen Romantik* (The concept of art-critique in German Romanticism), since Friedrich Schlegel and Friedrich von Hardenberg (Novalis), like Goethe, have occasion to use the term, which combines an image of upward movement with a suggestion of higher intensity. Adding a footnote to the use of *Steigerung* in a section of the dissertation concerned with the theory of the natural sciences, Benjamin interrupts his otherwise immanent analysis of early Romantic thought and raises an objection: "[W]here knowledge is concerned, it can be a question only of an elevation [*Steigerung*], a potentiation of reflection.... Only a breaking off, never a diminishment, of reflection-elevations is thinkable. Therefore, all relations among centers of reflection—not to mention their relations to the absolute—can rest on elevations of reflection. This objection seems warranted at least by inner experience, which is, of course, difficult to clarify with any definitiveness" (1:57; *SW* 1:191–92). An element of this objection becomes part

of his own concept of critique, which he summarily presents in a letter to Florens Christian Rang from December 1923: "I define: critique is mortification of works. Not elevation of consciousness in them (romantic!) but rather knowing [*Wissen*] settling in them" (*GB* 2:393; *C* 224; cf. *Origin of the German Trauerspiel*, 1:357; *O* 193). In "1) World and Time," written several years earlier, Benjamin defines politics in a similar manner: negatively spoken, politics is not a matter of raising consciousness; its positive determination follows from the idea of humanness. The advantage of the term "humanness" over similar terms is that it does not carry any suggestion of a criterion that would yield an intraspecies principle of distinction; it is something like a minimal condition that requires no "spiritual" or "mental" addenda, such as "rationality" or "a capacity for self-consciousness." Benjamin may have been drawn to present politics as "unelevated" as an implicit criticism of Unger's *Politics and Metaphysics*, which identifies "elevation" as a decisive element of the coming politics, insofar as it designates "the inclusion of originally alien psychical factors within a single consciousness" (228). Alternatively, Benjamin may have been drawn to Unger's work because, after having defined politics in terms of its "unelevated" character, *Politics and Metaphysics* represents a notable challenge.

4. Benjamin may be alluding to Martin Buber's concept of "realization" (*Verwirklichung*), which is a central feature of the novel he wrote under the inspiration of Nietzsche's *Also sprach Zarathustra*, namely, *Daniel: Gespräche von der Verwirklichung* (Leipzig: Insel, 1913); *Daniel: Dialogues on Realization*, trans. Maurice Friedman (Syracuse, NY: Syracuse University Press, 2018).

16. Morality, Ethics

WBA 1162r [= I MS 528]. Untitled in the original, this schema derives from a set of ring-binder pages that Benjamin used over the course of several years, beginning in 1916 and ending as late as 1922. Most of the other notes, which begin on the reverse side of the page on which this schema is drawn, concern the theory of color and the concept of "appearance" or "illusion" (*Schein*); see 6:114–21. The editors of *GS* suggest that this was composed in 1918 (see 6:699), and the themes under discussion suggest that it was written between 1918 and 1920.

The schema occupies the lower half of the manuscript page. On the upper half is a brief text that was copied by Scholem together with several others into a notebook that is held today in the Scholem Archive. This set of writings was published under the heading "Aphorismen" (Aphorisms) in 2:601 by the editors of *GS*, who note that Scholem kept his transcription among his copies of Benjamin's essays from 1916 and 1917; see 2:1411. The editors of *GS* thus suggest that the short text that appears on WBA 1162r was written in 1916. What follows is a translation of the text as it appears above the schema on "Morality, Ethics," which we include because of the themes it shares with several other Notes and Fragments, most notably 2 ("Vivification and Violence") and 21 (the discussion of dreams toward the end of the "Schemata for the Psychophysical Problem"). The text differs from Scholem's transcription (and thus the version at 2:601) with regard to several words, most notably "existence" (*Dasein*), which Scholem had replaced with "river" (*Fluß*): "The language of dreams lies not in words but rather among words. In the dream, words are chance products of the meaning [*Sinn*] that is found in a wordless continuity of existence [*Dasein*]. In dream language, meaning is hidden in the way a figure is hidden in a picture puzzle [*Vexierbild*]. It is even possible that the origin of picture puzzles is to be found in such a direction, namely, as shorthand for a dream [*Traumstenogramm*]."

The entire page is crossed through with a large "X" in the manuscript. The format and typography given here correct the ones given in *GS*.

17. The Right to Apply Force / Use Violence

WBA 1205 [= I MS 812]. "Das Recht zur Gewaltanwendung" is dated in *GS* as "not before April 1920" (6:691); it was also doubtless completed before the end of 1920, when Benjamin began "Toward the Critique of Violence." The title is triple underlined. The fragment appears to be the draft of a formal response to Herbert Vorwerk, "Das Recht zur Gewaltanwendung," *Blätter für religiösen Sozialismus* [Magazine for religious socialism] 1 (1920): 14–16. In line with the general orientation of his scholarship and pedagogical activities, Carl Mennicke established the journal in 1920 for the propagation of religious socialism. He entered into a conversation with the theologian Paul Tillich concerning the "use of force" in the context of the Kapp-Lüttwitz Putsch of March 1920, which Benjamin, for his part, does not mention, despite the fact that he was in Berlin when it occurred. For the inauguration of the journal, Mennicke convened a discussion of the question raised by his conversation with Tillich and asked Herbert Vorwerk to prepare a formal response. Vorwerk was a German jurist who had completed a dissertation at the University of Marburg in 1918 under the title "Die seekriegsrechtliche Bedeutung von Flottenstützpunkten" (The juridical significance of fleet bases for the law of war). Throughout this fragment, *Gewaltanwendung* is translated by both "use of violence" and "application of force" as a reminder of the manner in which, from a juridical perspective, violence becomes force.

1. Vorwerk, "Das Recht zur Gewaltanwendung," 14; all of the quotations in Benjamin's fragment derive from the three pages of his article, which are not hereafter individually identified.

2. The handwriting is unclear; "good" is the most likely option.

3. The editors of *GS* refer at this point to Benjamin's "Theological-Political Fragment," presumably because it also includes remarks on messianic rhythm (see 6:692; 2:204; *SW* 3:306). It should be noted, however, that the two remarks on rhythm

positively contradict each other—which indicates that, as noted earlier (see 301), the date Adorno assigned the fragment (ca. 1937) is more likely than the date upon which Scholem insisted, the early 1920s (cf. 2:946–47).

4. Benjamin is alluding to Rudolf von Jhering's influential manifesto *Der Kampf um's Recht* (The struggle for law), originally published in 1872 and republished dozens of times afterwards.

5. The term *quaternio terminorum*, or "fallacy of four terms," derives from the structure of the syllogism, which is supposed to have only three terms (concepts) that are subordinated to one another. A *quaternio terminorum* occurs when a fourth term is added either in the minor premise or the conclusion, such that the conclusion does not follow, since two premises do not suffice to connect four terms. The fallacy often comes about when one of the terms alternates between two meanings.

6. A draft or portion of this lost essay is perhaps preserved in Fragment 2 in this volume, 68.

7. On the phrase "monopoly on violence," which was borrowed from a recent lecture by Max Weber on "Politics as Vocation," see 168; the term *Machtvollkommenheit* refers to a form of "perfect power" that remains undivided in its application (in contrast to the "division of powers" introduced by Montesquieu, among others, against the pretensions of the absolutist state); see also 286.

8. Mignon is a character in Goethe's novel *Wilhelm Meisters Lehrjahre* (Wilhelm Meister's years of apprenticeship); the phrase appears in book 8, chapter 2. Mignon, incidentally, dies soon after singing the phrase in question.

9. Benjamin is doubtless referring to the series of pogroms to which Galician Jews were subjected, especially those that occurred in 1898 and 1905. These and other atrocities elicited a renewed discussion of what is entailed by the "sanctification of the Name" (*kiddush HaShem*), that is, martyrdom.

18. Capitalism as Religion

WBA 400/27-29 [= I MS 700–702]. "Kapitalismus als Religion," which could also be translated as "Capitalism as a Religion," was probably written between 1920 and 1922. Benjamin may have drawn up these notes for seminars in which he participated at the University of Heidelberg, especially those conducted by Emil Lederer and Marianne Weber; this would date the fragment to the second half of 1921. Benjamin repurposed several elements of these notes, including the fragment below, in a section of *One-Way Street* titled "Steuerberatung" (Tax advice) (4:139; *SW* 1:481).

On the recto side of MS 702 [= WBA 400/29r], Benjamin wrote a fragment under the title "Money and Weather (with respect to the *Lesabéndio* critique)": "Rain is the symbol of this-worldly misfortune. / The curtain before the drama of world demise [*Weltuntergang*] / The frightening expectation of the sun / Seeing through weather and money / In neither is there unidirectional movement / The utopian condition of the world without weather / Weather itself a frontier [*Grenze*] for the relation of the human being to the apocalyptic condition of the world (bad weather [*Unwetter*]), blessedness (without weather, cloudless), money designates another, still unfamiliar term [*Terminus*]. / Rain, thunderstorms: parade/foil of world demise [*Weltuntergangsparade*]. They are to this [demise] as a sniffle is to death. / Money belongs together with rain, not with the likes of the sun. / The weatherless space of the pure planetary event before which: weather is the veil. / In Kubin's *Die Andere Seite* [The other side] money [is] exactly like weather" (4:941). For an English translation of the novel to which Benjamin refers, see Alfred Kubin, *The Other Side*, trans. Mike Mitchell (Sawtry, UK: Dedalus, 2014); a brief discussion of *Lesabéndio* can be found at 116.

1. Benjamin is clearly referring to Max Weber's *The Protestant Ethic and the Spirit of Capitalism*; see 7 and 234.

2. Throughout this fragment Benjamin uses terms derived from *ziehen* (to draw), including *Zug* (trait) in the following sentence.

3. In *GS* this phrase is mis-transcribed as *sans rêve et sans merci* ("without dream and without mercy") (6:100). Eduardo Mendieta has suggested that the phrase *sans trêve et sans merci* ("without truce and without mercy") was intended to allude to the "Medieval Decalogue of Chivalry," as recorded by Léon Gautier, *The Everyday Life of the Medieval Knight* (orig. 1884); see *The Frankfurt School on Religion*, ed. Eduardo Mendieta (New York: Routledge, 2005), 262. According to the sixth chivalric commandment, "[Y]ou will wage war on Infidels without truce and without mercy" (Léon Gautier, *La chevalerie* [Paris: Palmé, 1884], 33).

4. For an extensive discussion of *Entsühnung*, here translated as "de-expiation," in relation to *Sühne* (expiation), see 32–33.

5. The last phrase is ambiguous: "the ethos defining Nietzsche" could also be translated as "the ethos Nietzsche defines," which would presumably be an ethos one defines for oneself rather than a universal ethical norm or particular mores adopted in accordance with "herd instincts," to quote from the first part of *Jenseits von Gut und Böse* (Beyond good and evil), reprinted in Nietzsche, *Sämtliche Werke: Kritische Studienausgabe*, ed. Giorgio Colli and Mazzino Montinari (Berlin: Walter de Gruyter, 1988), 5:124; §202.

6. See the discussion of this term in a note to Fragment 15 (301n3). Nietzsche is fond of the term *Steigerung*, especially in the later sections of *The Birth of Tragedy*.

7. A shortened version of the widely quoted dictum "Natura non facit saltum" (Nature does not make any leaps), often associated with Leibniz; see, for one of many examples, the opening of the series of letters Leibniz addressed to Burcher de Volder at the turn of the seventeenth century: "This is the axiom that I use—*no transition is*

made through a leap" (Gottfried Wilhelm Leibniz, *Philosophical Papers and Letters*, ed. Leroy Loemker, 2nd ed. [Boston: Reidel, 1976], 515). Benjamin discusses the "dialectical opposite" (3:153) of this principle in his 1928 review of Karl Bloßfeldt's photographic album, *Urformen der Kunst* (Primordial forms of art); see "Neues von Blumen" (Something new about flowers) (3:151–53), which may derive in part from the inquiries into the biological sciences congruent with Benjamin's writing of political essays in the early 1920s; see 20.

8. On page 262 of *Reflections on Violence* (in the edition Benjamin read), the following can be found: "Economists today are little disposed to believe that the natural laws that impose themselves are due to Nature: they see that the capitalist regime came about slowly, but they think that it came into being through a process that should enchant the soul of enlightened man."

9. On page 44 of *Politics and Metaphysics* (Berlin: Verlag David, 1921), Unger writes: "There is a logical either-or: either frictionless commerce or a wandering of peoples; that is, either the transport of goods contributing to physiological existence or the search for such goods. . . . The assault on capitalism must remain forever futile in the place where it reigns supreme. Capitalism is the most powerful and most profound of all systems, and it can integrate every objection raised against its existence in the region where it remains in force. In order to organize anything against capitalism in general, the following is indispensable: to step away from its effective area. For within its own area, it can absorb every countereffect. The spatial abandonment of the region where it holds dominion is, therefore, an unavoidable command for all congregations that aspire for themselves some other basic plan of material existence, and for those who have no such aspirations, this detachment would ultimately still amount to the liberation from a power that can just as little be rejected as it can be satiated."

10. See Bruno Archibald Fuchs, *Der Geist der bürgerlich-kapitalistischen Gesellschaft: Eine Untersuchung über seine Grundlage und Voraussetzungen* (Munich: Oldenbourg, 1914), in which he expands on Max Weber's thesis in *The Protestant Ethic* that modern capitalism's high regard for the abstraction and rationalization of work results from a generalization of Calvinism's asceticism and doctrine of predestination.

11. See Weber, *Gesammelte Aufsätze zur Religionssoziologie* (Tübingen: Mohr, 1920), which contains the revised second editions of both *The Protestant Ethic and the Spirit of Capitalism* (1904–5) and *Confucianism and Taoism* (1915), translated as *The Religion of China: Confucianism and Taoism*, trans. and ed. Hans H. Gerth (Glencoe, IL: Free Press, 1951). The dates Benjamin gives correspond with the publication date of volume 1; in referring to "two volumes," he may have been thinking of the inclusion of both treatises in the 1920 volume. (The second volume of the *Gesammelte Aufsätze zur Religionssoziologie*, which contains *Hinduismus und Buddhismus*, appeared in 1921.)

12. Weber asked Ernst Troeltsch to respond to his *Protestant Ethic*, which resulted in articles that appeared in the *Archiv* and a subsequent treatise. The version to which Benjamin refers here is Troeltsch, *Die Soziallehren der christlichen Kirchen und Gruppen*, in *Gesammelte Werke* (Tübingen: Mohr, 1912); cf. *The Social Teaching of the Christian Church*, trans. Olive Wyan (Louisville, KY: John Knox, 1992).

13. Benjamin is presumably referring to Weber's editorial work in revising Gustav von Sternberg's *Handbuch von politischen Ökonomie* (Handbook of political economy), which led him toward his further inquiries into the sociology of religion. For a description of the academic conflict that ensued around this revision, see Vittorio Cotesta, *Max Weber on China: Modernism and Capitalism in a Global Context*, trans. Kay McCarthy (Newcastle, UK: Cambridge Scholars, 2018), 90–91.

14. Gustav Landauer, *Aufruf zum Sozialismus: Revolutionsausgabe*, 2nd ed. (Berlin: Cassirer, 1919), 144: "Fritz Mauthner (*Dictionary of Philosophy*) has shown that the word 'God' was originally identical with 'idol' and that both mean 'poured (metal).' God is a product made by men that comes to life, draws the life of men to itself and finally becomes more powerful than all mankind. The only 'poured metal,' the only idol, the only God that men have ever created physically is money. Money is artificial and alive, money breeds money, and money and money and money has all power on earth. / Who however fails to see, still fails to see today that money, this God, is nothing else but spirit that has exited from man and become a living thing, an un-thing, that it is the meaning of life changed to madness? Money does not create wealth, money is wealth; wealth *per se*; there is no one rich except money. Money gets its powers and its life from somewhere; it can get them only from us; and as rich and generatively productive as we have made money, we have impoverished and sapped ourselves, all of us. It has almost become literally true that human women by the hundreds of thousands can no longer become mothers because hideous money bears offspring and hard metal like a vampire sucks the animal warmth out of men and women and the blood out of their veins. We are all beggars and poor wretches and fools, because money is God, and because money has become cannibalistic. / Socialism is a reversal of this. Socialism is a new beginning. Socialism is a return to nature, a re-endowment with spirit, a regaining of relationships" (*For Socialism*, trans. David J. Parent [St. Louis: Telos Press, 1978], 135). *Aufruf zum Sozialismus* also appears as item 736 in 7:447; in addition, Landauer's *Skepsis und Mystik: Versuche im Anschluss an Mauthners Sprachkritik* is listed as item 708 in 7:446. Landauer, a close friend of Martin Buber's, was assassinated in May 1919.

15. Unfortunately, there is no English equivalent of *ausweglos* (without a way out) that captures the sense of the word as well as "hopeless," even though Benjamin is specifically not speaking of hope in this paragraph; he may, however, be referring to the famous scene in the final act of Goethe's *Faust*, part II, where Faust's

otherwise perfectly secured mansion is incapable of preventing *Sorge* (care, worry) from entering—and eventually blinding him.

16. *Wergeld* is the price set upon someone's life; the term is often used in the context of the juridical process of expiation (*Sühne*).

17. See Adam Müller, *Zwölf Reden über die Beredsamkeit und deren Verfall in Deutschland* (Leipzig: Göschen, 1816), 56–57: "In times before this beneficial, but also pernicious invention, the art of writing was only employed for those absent and for posterity. Living speech, however, was dominant for the contemporaries, for everyone whom one could reach with his breast and his voice. It was the same with money matters; where one could reach each other, there everyone repaid each other with the strength of his hands and with services. One paid those present and contemporary with one's own person; only for those far off, for those absent, for the future, did one make use of gold and silver. Gold and silver are to the living deed exactly as writing is to the living word. Thus all of man's practical relations dissolved into money relations [*Geldverhältnisse*]" (Müller, *Twelve Lectures on Rhetoric*, ed. and trans. Dennis Bormann and Elisabeth Leinfellner [Ann Arbor: University Microfilms for University of Nebraska Press, 1978], 139). In a letter to Scholem from February 1921, Benjamin describes his interest in Müller's *Lectures* and further notes that it gives him some "stimulus" for the "expansion of 'The True Politician'" (*GB* 2:141). Even as Benjamin criticizes Müller in this letter for his "enormous flaccidity," he finds "wonderful insights," especially in the sixth chapter, to which this item refers as well.

19. Notes on "Objective Mendacity" I

WBA 1173 [= I MS 768]. "Notizen über 'objektives Verlogenheit' I" is dated in *GS* as "1922/23" (6:671). The notes are elements of a larger project around the theme of lying that intersects with the central paragraphs of "Toward the Critique of Violence," 50–51. Note 20 also belongs to the broader project, as do Benjamin's reflections "On the 'Cretan'" (6:57–59), which are concerned with the logical and metaphysical dimensions of the so-called Liar's Paradox, whose importance had recently been revived through its association with Russell's Paradox (to which Benjamin proposes his own solution; see 6:10–11).

1. Benjamin may be alluding to the opening sentence of Carl Schmitt's *Politische Theologie* (Political theology): "Sovereign is the one who decides on the state of exception [*Ausnahmezustand*]" (*Politische Theologie. Vier Kapitel zur Lehre von der Souveränität* [Munich: Düncker & Humblot, 1922], 17); Schmitt, *Political Theology: Four Chapters on the Concept of Sovereignty*, trans. George D. Schwab (Chicago: University of Chicago Press, 2004), 5; for an extensive discussion of Benjamin's relation to Schmitt, see the Afterword, 127–37.

2. See bibliographical note to Fragment 14, esp. 300.

3. See Rudolf Borchardt, *Die Päpstin Iutta, ein dramatisches Gedicht*, erster Teil, *Die Verkündigung* [Pope Joan, a verse drama, pt. 1: The announcement] (Berlin: Rowolt, 1920). In a May 1918 letter to Ernst Schoen, Benjamin describes his conception of Borchardt's work, which he connects to his concept of objective mendacity. After claiming that Borchardt's "moral essence" consists in a "*will* to lying" (*GB* 1:457; C 126), he qualifies this judgment: "He is not himself the lie, but the lie grabs hold of him each time he determines his relation to the public" (*GB* 1:460; C 128).

4. A translation of this story, originally in Norwegian, can be found in Knut Hamsun, *Tales of Love and Loss*, trans. Robert Ferguson (London: Souvenir Press, 1997).

5. See Maxim Gorki, *Reminiscences of Leo Nikolaevich Tolstoy*, trans. S. S. Koteliansky and Leonard Woolf (New York: Huebsch, 1920); Johan Bojer's 1903 novel *The Power of a Lie*, originally published in Norwegian under the title *Troens makt* (The power of faith), appeared in German translation as *Macht der Lüge* (Munich: Beck, 1922); see Bojer, *The Power of a Lie*, trans. Jessie Muir (New York: Moffat, Yard, 1920).

6. Detlev von Liliencron's autobiographical *Leben und Lüge* (Life and lie) can be found in the sixth volume of his *Gesammelte Werke* (Berlin: Schuster & Loeffler, 1918). The title of Liliencron's work recalls Goethe's autobiographical reflections, *Dichtung und Wahrheit* (Truth and poetry). Benjamin is presumably referring to Nietzsche's posthumously published essay "Über Wahrheit und Lüge im außermoralischen Sinn" (*Sämtliche Werke: Kritische Studienausgabe*, 1:873–90; "On Truth and Lie in an Extra-Moral Sense," in *The Portable Nietzsche*, ed. and trans. Walter Kaufmann [New York: Penguin, 1976], 42–46).

7. See Anatole France, *Le génie Latin* (Paris: Lemerre, 1913); cf. *The Latin Genius*, trans. Wilfrid Jackson (New York: Lane, 1924).

8. As Benjamin indicates, Rudolph von Jhering's *Der Zweck im Recht* is an important work for the lines of thought that congregate around "Toward the Critique of Violence"; see Jhering, *Der Zweck im Recht*, 4th ed. (Leipzig: Breitkopf and Härtel, 1904–5); *Law as a Means to an End*, trans. Isaac Husik (Boston: Boston Book Company, 1913). For Jhering's extensive discussion of the juridical significance of lying, see *Der Zweck im Recht*, 2:459–91 (not included in the English version).

9. Christoph Friedrich (Fritz) Heinle was a poet and close friend of Benjamin's during their involvement with *Der Anfang*, the periodical of the Jugendbewegung (German Youth Movement) helmed by school reformer Gustav Wyneken. This quotation may have been an offhand comment, as were several similar passages in his notes of the period, where he included quotations from Heinle, who committed suicide at the beginning of the First World War. In his *Berliner Chronik* (A Berlin chronicle), Benjamin describes in relatively extensive terms his relation to Heinle; see 6:477–83; *SW* 2:604–9. An edition of Heinle's extant writings can be found in

Christoph Friedrich Heinle, *Lyrik und Prosa*, ed. Johannes Steizinger (Berlin: Kadmos, 1916).

10. *Ehrlichkeit*, here translated as "sincerity," is a term that Benjamin discusses extensively in a text from 1912, "Dialog über die Religiösität der Gegenwart" (Dialogue on the religiosity of the present); see 2:16–35; *Early Writings*, 62–84. It is also a term that appeared alongside *Echtheit* (authenticity) and *Wahrhaftigkeit* (truthfulness) in slogans of the German Youth Movement. Wyneken had a particular predilection for the term, writing, for instance in *Schule und Jugendkultur* (School and youth culture) at the height of the movement in 1913, that "we need youth like we need nature in order to find our way in it back to sincerity and naturalness again and again. A youth that is allowed to be truly young is society's great remedy against conventionalism, philistinism, and fearfulness" (Gustav Wyneken, *Schule und Jugendkultur* [Jena: Diederichs, 1913], 39).

11. Benjamin is referring to the lengthy controversy between François Fénelon and Jacques Bossuet concerning the nature of perfect prayer.

12. In relation to this term, the following section from the fragment titled "Arten des Wissens" (Modes of knowing) is illuminating: "IV. The kind of knowing that determines [*Das bestimmende Wissen*]. This, action-determinative knowing, does exist. It is, however, determinative not as 'motive' but rather by virtue of its linguistic structure. The linguistic moment in morality is connected to knowing. It is certain that this knowing, which determines action, leads to silence. It is therefore not teachable. The knowing that determines action may have a close affinity with the concept of Dao. By contrast, it is strictly opposed to knowing in the form of the Socratic doctrine of virtue. For this knowing motivates action; it is not agent-determinative" (6: 48–49).

13. "Expressionless" is a cardinal term in Benjamin's lexicon of this period; it attains an especially dense formulation in his essay on Goethe's *Elective Affinities*, where it is identified with "critical force" or "critical violence" (*kritische Gewalt*) that is itself connected with a "moral word" (*moralisches Wort*) (1:181; *SW* 1:340), "Expressionless" is conceived as part of a pair together with "expressive"; see also Note 13 in this volume, 80.

20. Notes toward a Work on Lying II

WBA 1216 [= I MS 794]. "Notizen zu einer Arbeit über die Lüge II" is dated in *GS* as "1922/23" (6:672).

1. The legal terms *Tateinheit* and *Tateneinheit* designate "unity of the crime," whereby several crimes can be committed in a single act.

2. In accordance with the Jewish tradition, the commandment translated as "Thou shall not bear false witness against thy neighbor" (King James Bible, Ex.

20:16) is not viewed as a prohibition on lying as such but rather as a specific legal proscription; listed among seven other similar proscriptions on false testimony, it is the 576th of 613 commandments in Maimonides' *Sefer Hamitzvot* (Book of Commandments). There is, incidentally, another set of commandments concerning honesty in commercial dealings. For Benjamin's interest in Maimonides in this period, see *GB* 2:138. See also Benjamin's exegesis of the biblical commandment against killing, that is, murder, in "Toward the Critique of Violence" (58) and the accompanying note.

3. It seems as though "sincerity" is the object of the demand in this sentence.

21. Schemata for the Psychophysical Problem

WBA 1218/1–5 [= I MS 1965–69]. "Schemata zum psychophysischen Problem" is dated in *GS* as "around 1922/23" (6:678). As Uwe Steiner has shown, Benjamin's interest in the "psychophysical problem" dates at least back to the seminars he attended at the University of Bern conducted by Paul Häberlin (*KGA* 3:310–11). Benjamin continued to correspond with Häberlin until at least 1925; see especially Benjamin's December 1922 letter to Häberlin, in which he refers to a review of Häberlin's *Der Leib und die Seele* (Basel: Spittlers Nachfolge, 1923), which, as he likewise indicates, was the subject matter of one of the seminars he attended (*KGA* 3:368–69). A remarkable feature of the five manuscript items gathered under the rubric "Schemata for the Psychophysical Problem" is the sparsity of the literature to which they refer; only the works of Ludwig Klages are listed. Both Häberlin and Unger produced monographs on the subject in 1922 (although the short dissertation Unger submitted to the University of Erlangen was never published). These lacunae may indicate that the manuscripts comprising this fragment were written in the spring or summer of 1922, when the last of Ludwig Klages's treatises, *Vom kosmogonischen Eros* (On cosmogonic eros), first appeared.

1. Benjamin is referring to the circle of friends and acquaintances around the poet Stefan George, one of whom, Friedrich Gundolf, wrote a book on Goethe that Benjamin subjects to an eviscerating critique in his contemporaneous essay on Goethe's *Elective Affinities* (1:158–63; *SW* 1:322–26).

2. A Latin term that can acquire a variety of meanings, including "innate quality," "constitution," and "temperament," especially the temperament associated with "insight" or "genius" (with which it is obviously cognate).

3. The distinction between substance and function is closely associated with the Marburg School of neo-Kantianism and finds canonical expression in Ernst Cassirer's *Substanzbegriff und Funktionsbegriff* (Berlin: Cassirer, 1910); *Substance and Function, and Einstein's Theory of Relativity*, trans. William Curtis Swabey and Marie Collins Swabey (New York: Dover, 1953).

4. In the original, Benjamin writes "Ausdeutung" (interpretation) but presumably meant to write "Ausdehnung" (extension), a slip that the editors of *GS* point out in 6:80.

5. Benjamin lists several of Ludwig Klages's works below. Benjamin attended a lecture by Klages on graphology in 1914 (see 2:879) and later read his graphological handbook, *Handschrift und Charakter* [Handwriting and character] (Leipzig: Barthes, 1917); cf. 7:447, and see his essay on graphology, 4:596–98; *SW* 2:398–99. In December 1920, he wrote Klages an unsolicited letter that describes his interest in "Vom Traumbewußtsein" [On dream consciousness], *Zeitschrift für Pathopsychologie* 3 (1919): 1–38. Benjamin asks Klages whether he could send him a copy of its continuation (*GB* 2:114). Among the many places in his writings where he returns to Klages is a brief but incisive discussion of the relation between Klages and George (see note 1 above) in his essay on Johann Jakob Bachofen (*GS* 2:229–30; *SW* 3:18–19).

6. Benjamin provides a relatively full bibliographical citation for each work. With regard to the first of these, *Vom Wesen des Bewußtseins* (On the essence of consciousness), Benjamin was under the impression that Klages would publish a third part to his "On Dream Consciousness," but this did not occur. As for the others, the full bibliographical citations are as follows: "Geist und Seele: Psychologische Grundbegriffe" [Spirit and soul: Fundamental concepts of psychology], *Deutsche Psychologie* 1 (1917): 281–314, 361–97, 245–70, 171–96; *Vom Wesen des Bewußtseins* [On the essence of consciousness] (Leipzig: Barth, 1921); *Mensch und Erde* [Human being and earth] (Munich: Müller, 1920); *Vom kosmogonischen Eros* (Munich: Müller, 1922). The latter text is listed among the books Benjamin read (7:451).

7. A quotation from Goethe's "Selige Sehnsucht" (Blessed longing) in his late collection, modeled on the Persian poet Hafiz, *West-östlicher Divan* (see 313).

8. Benjamin may be referring to the following passage from Dante's *Paradiso*, where the poet places "la dolce donna" among the stars and at the same time identifies the source of his own *ingenium*: "O, glorious stars, o lights suffused by great force [*virtù*], all my genius [*ingegno*], whatever it may be, I recognize comes from you" (canto 22, lines 112–14).

9. This appears to be Benjamin's own translation of the passage from Plato's *Symposium* 202d–203a; in any case, it departs significantly from Friedrich Schleiermacher's widely used translation.

10. Benjamin is clearly alluding to one of the phrases through which Nietzsche understands his own work and likewise executes his critique of moral philosophy, namely, "pathos of distance"; see *Zur Genealogie der Moral* (Toward the genealogy of morality), reprinted in *Sämtliche Werke: Kritische Studienausgabe*, 5:205; §257.

11. Benjamin is probably referring to certain salacious passages in the posthumously published parts of August Strindberg's autobiography, which had recently

appeared in German; see *Der Sohn einer Magd*, trans. Emil Schering (Munich: Müller, 1918); *The Son of a Servant*, trans. Claud Feld (New York: Putman, 1913).

12. See Karl Kraus, "Die Verlassenen" [The abandoned ones], in *Worte in Verse* [Words in verse], vol. 5 (1922; repr., *Worte in Versen*, ed. Heinrich Fischer [Munich: Kösel, 1959], 263). A similar pairing of Kraus's poem with Goethe's can be found in *One-Way Street* (4:121; *SW* 1:469). In typographic terms, Benjamin may have written "Gegensatz" (opposite) before correcting to "Gegenstück" (counterpart); *Gegenstück* is a term Benjamin generally used to describe a relation of weak or improbable similarity between texts, particularly his own.

22. Literatur zu einer ausgeführteren Kritik der Gewalt und zur Rechtsphilosophie / Literature for a More Fully Developed Critique of Violence and Philosophy of Law

WBA 508/16 [= I MS 1858]. "Literatur zu einer ausgeführteren Kritik der Gewalt und zur Rechtsphilosophie" is mentioned via a mis-transcribed title by the *GS* editors in 7:724. While Benjamin uses the same black ink throughout, the opacity differs, suggesting that he added to it over a period of time. Judging from the publication dates of the items listed, Benjamin worked on this bibliography on and off up until 1925 at the earliest and possibly until 1927 or 1928, depending on which edition of Felix Somló, Hans Kelsen, or Carl Schmitt he used. Curiously, Benjamin refers to the 1921 first edition of Schmitt's *Diktatur* (Dictatorship); in his letter to Schmitt from December 9, 1930 (*GB* 3:559), he refers to this book as counting among the works Schmitt composed after *Political Theology*—which he cites in *Origin of the German Trauerspiel*—suggesting that Benjamin had the second, 1928 edition of *Dictatorship* on hand when he wrote the letter. Several further names and/or titles appear in other of Benjamin's writings, (unpublished) working bibliographies, and correspondence, most notably Dante, Lessing, Machiavelli, Natorp, Latte, von Eicken, Nelson, Reinach, Binder, Stammler, and Wilamowitz-Moellendorff; some, like Rosenstock and Radbruch, were also acquaintances. Any infelicities concerning titles, spelling, or publication dates are corrected in note 1 below. Prepared and translated by Julia Ng.

1. In what follows, I have provided the complete bibliographic information for each of the texts Benjamin includes in WBA 508/16 [= I MS 1858]; where relevant, I have corrected the date and spelling and included the dates for multiple editions in cases where Benjamin does not definitively indicate which one he is referring to. In a couple of instances, I have provided the names of texts Benjamin may have had in mind by extrapolating from his shorthand and the dates he gives; I have marked such conjectures with a "[?]" following the titles in question.

> Jakob Fries, *Philosophische Rechtslehre und Kritik aller positiven Gesetzgebung: Mit Beleuchtung der gewöhnlichen Fehler in der Bearbeitung des Naturrechts*, with a

new index and ed. Jakob-Friedrich-Fries-Gesellschaft (Leipzig: Meiner, 1914). (Original = Jena: Johann Michael Mauke, 1803.)

Hugo Grotius, *Des Hugo Grotius drei Bücher über das Recht des Krieges und Friedens, in welchem das Natur- und Völkerrecht und das Wichtigste aus dem öffentlichen Recht erklärt werden*, trans. J. H. von Kirchmann, 2 vols. (1st ed., Berlin: Heimann, 1869; 2nd ed., 1877) = Philosophische Bibliothek (Hamburg [Leipzig: Meiner, 1868–]). (Original = *De jure belli ac pacis libri tres* [Paris: Buon, 1625].)

Cesare Beccaria, *Über Verbrechen und Strafen*, trans. K. Esselborn (Leipzig: W. Engelmann [= Felix Meiner], 1905). (Original = 1764.)

Dante Alighieri, *Über die Monarchie*, trans. Oskar Hubatsch (Berlin: Heimann, 1872) = Philosophische Bibliothek (Leipzig: Verlag Felix Meiner). (Original = 1312–13.)

Eugen Rosenstock-Huessy, "Der ewige Prozess des Rechts gegen den Staat," *Zeitschrift für Rechtsphilosophie in Lehre und Praxis* 2 (1919): 219–41.

Theodor Lessing, *Studien zur Wertaxiomatik: Untersuchungen über reine Ethik und reines Recht* (1st ed., Leipzig: Verlag Felix Meiner, 1908; exp. ed., 1914).

Niccolò Machiavelli, *Vom Staate: Erörterungen über die erste Dekade des Titus Livius*, trans. W. Grüzmacher (Berlin: Heimann, 1870) = Philosophische Bibliothek (Leipzig: Verlag Felix Meiner).

Plato, *Platons Gesetze*, trans. Otto Apelt, 2 vols. (Leipzig: Verlag Felix Meiner, 1916).

Zeitschrift für Rechtsphilosophie in Lehre und Praxis, ed. Felix Holldack, Rudolf Joerges, and Rudolf Stammler (vols. 1–3); Felix Holldack, Erich Jung, and Hans Friedrich Reichel (vols. 4–6) (Leipzig: Verlag Felix Meiner, 1914–35?).

Felix Somló, *Juristische Grundlehre* (1st ed., Leipzig: Verlag Felix Meiner, 1917; 2nd ed., 1927).

Rudolf Stammler, *Theorie der Rechtswissenschaft* (Halle: Buchhandlung des Waisenhauses, 1911).

Adolf Menzel, *Naturrecht und Soziologie* (Vienna: Carl Fromme, 1912).

L'année sociologique, ed. Émile Durkheim (1898–).

Mordché Rapaport, *Das religiöse Recht und dessen Charakterisierung als Rechtstheologie*, foreword by Josef Kohler (Berlin: Walther Rothschild, 1913).

Heinrich von Eicken, *Geschichte und System der mittelalterlichen Weltanschauung* (1st ed., Stuttgart: Cotta, 1887; 2nd ed., 1913).

Hans Kelsen, *Die Staatslehre des Dante Alighieri* (Vienna: Deuticke, 1905). [?]

———, *Hauptprobleme der Staatsrechtslehre entwickelt aus der Lehre vom Rechtssatze* (1st ed., Tübingen: Mohr, 1911; 2nd ed., 1923). [?]

———, *Allgemeine Staatslehre* (Berlin: Julius Springer, 1925).

———, *Der soziologische und der juristische Staatsbegriff* (1st ed., Tübingen: Mohr, 1922; 2nd ed., 1928).

Gamschei Abraham Wielikowski, *Die Neukantianer in der Rechtsphilosophie* (Munich: Beck, 1914).

Georg Büttner, *Im Banne des logischen Zwanges: Ethische Grundfragen in erkenntniskritischer Beleuchtung nebst einem pädagogischen und religionsphilosophischen Ausblick* (Leipzig: E. Wunderlich, 1914).

Albert Görland, *Ethik als Kritik der Weltgeschichte* (Leipzig: Teubner, 1914).

———, *Die Idee des Schicksals in der Geschichte der Tragödie: Ein Kapitel einer Ästhetik* (Tübingen: Mohr, 1913).

Paul Natorp, "Recht und Sittlichkeit: Ein Beitrag zur kategorialen Begründung der praktischen Philosophie," *Kant-Studien* 18 (1913): 1–79.

Friedrich Carl von Savigny, *Vom Beruf unsrer Zeit für Gesetzgebung und Rechtswissenschaft* (1st ed., Heidelberg: Mohr und Zimmer, 1814; 2nd ed., 1828; 3rd ed., 1840).

Adolf Reinach, "Über die apriorischen Grundlagen des bürgerlichen Rechts," *Jahrbuch für Philosophie und phänomenologischen Forschung* 1 (1913): 685–847.

Gustav Radbruch, *Grundzüge der Rechtsphilosophie* (Leipzig: Quelle & Meyer, 1914).

Rudolf Stammler, *Recht und Macht* (Berlin: C. Heymanns, 1918).

Fritz Münch, review of *Das Problem des natürlichen Rechts*, by Erich Jung, *Zeitschrift für Rechtsphilosophie in Lehre und Praxis* 1 (1914): 111–33.

Erich Jung, *Das Problem des natürlichen Rechts* (Leipzig: Duncker & Humblot, 1912).

Kurt Latte, *Heiliges Recht: Untersuchungen zur Geschichte der sakralen Rechtsformen in Griechenland* (Tübingen: Mohr, 1920).

Georg Fraenkel, *Die kritische Rechtsphilosophie bei Fries und bei Stammler* (Göttingen: Vandenhoeck & Ruprecht, 1912).

Julius Binder, *Rechtsbegriff und Rechtsidee: Bemerkungen zur Rechtsphilosophie* (Leipzig: A. Deichert, 1915).

Rudolf Stammler, *Rechtsphilosophische Abhandlungen und Vorträge*, 2 vols. (Charlottenburg: Pan-Verlag, Heise, 1925).

Gustav Radbruch and Paul Tillich, *Religionsphilosophie der Kultur: Zwei Entwürfe* (1st ed., Berlin: Reuther & Reichard, 1919; 2nd ed., 1921).

Josef Kohler, *Das Recht der Azteken* (Stuttgart: Enke, 1892).

Felix Kaufmann, *Logik und Rechtswissenschaft: Grundriss eines Systems der reinen Rechtslehre* (Tübingen: Mohr, 1922).

Ulrich von Wilamowitz-Moellendorf, *Griechische Verskunst* (Berlin: Weidmann, 1921).

Max Ernst Mayer, *Rechtsphilosophie* (Berlin: Julius Springer, 1922) = Enzyklopädie der Rechts- und Staatswissenschaft, Abteilung Rechtswissenschaft, vol. 1, ed. E. Kohlrausch, W. Kaskel, and A. Spiethoff (Berlin: Julius Springer, 1922).

Louis Gabriel Ambroise, vicomte de Bonald, *Die Urgesetzgebung* (Mainz: Simon Müller, 1825).

———, *Législation primitive considérée dans les derniers temps par les seules lumières de la raison: Suivie de divers traités et discours politiques*, 2nd ed. (Paris: A. Le Clere, 1817).

Hermann Lucas, "Aus der Geschichte der Todesstrafe," *Der Greif: Cotta'sche Monatsschrift* 1, no. 2 (August 1914): 388–401.

Carl Schmitt-Dorotić, *Die Diktatur: Von den Anfänen des modernen Souveränitätsgedankens bis zum proletarischen Klassenkampf* (1st ed., Munich: Duncker & Humblot, 1921; 2nd ed., 1928).

———, *Politische Romantik* (Munich: Duncker & Humblot, 1919).

———, *Politische Theologie* (Munich: Duncker & Humblot, 1922).

———, "Soziologie des Souveränitätsbegriffes und politische Theologie," in *Hauptprobleme der Soziologie: Erinnerungsausgabe für Max Weber*, vol. 2, ed. Melchior Palyi (Munich: Duncker & Humblot, 1923), 3–35.

Leonard Nelson, *Die Rechtswissenschaft ohne Recht: Kritische Betrachtungen über die Grundlagen des Staats- und Völkerrechts, insbesondere über die Lehre von der Souveränität* (Leipzig: Veit, 1917).

2. Hugo Grotius, *Hugo Grotius on the Law of War and Peace*, trans. Stephen C. Neff (Cambridge: Cambridge University Press, 2012).

3. Cesare Beccaria, *"On Crimes and Punishments" and Other Writings*, ed. Richard Bellamy, trans. Richard Davies (Cambridge: Cambridge University Press, 1995).

4. Dante Alighieri, *Monarchy*, trans. Prue Shaw (Cambridge: Cambridge University Press, 1996).

5. Niccolò Machiavelli, *The Discourses*, ed. Bernard Crick, trans. Leslie J. Walker (London: Penguin, 1984); also in *Machiavelli: The Chief Works and Others*, ed. and trans. Allan Gilbert, 3 vols. (Durham, NC: Duke University Press, 1989), 1:175–532.

6. Plato, *The Laws*, ed. Malcolm Schofield, trans. Tom Griffith (Cambridge: Cambridge University Press, 2016).

7. Friedrich Karl von Savigny, *Of the Vocation of Our Age for Legislation and Jurisprudence*, trans. Abraham Hayward (London: Littlewood, 1831).

8. Adolf Reinach, *The Apriori Foundations of the Civil Law: Along with the Lecture "Concerning Phenomenology,"* trans. John F. Crosby (Frankfurt: Ontos, 2012).

9. Gustav Radbruch, "Legal Philosophy," in *The Legal Philosophies of Lask, Radbruch, and Dabin*, trans. Kurt Wilk (Cambridge, MA: Harvard University Press, 1950).

10. Paul Tillich, "On the Idea of a Theology of Culture," trans. William Baillie Green, in Tillich, *What Is Religion?*, ed. James Luther Adams (New York: Harper & Row, 1969), 155–81.

11. Carl Schmitt, *Dictatorship: from the Origin of the Modern Concept of Sovereignty to Proletarian Class Struggle*, trans. Michael Hoelzl and Graham Ward (Cambridge, UK: Polity, 2014).

12. Carl Schmitt, *Political Romanticism*, trans. Guy Oakes (Cambridge, MA: MIT Press, 1986).

13. Carl Schmitt, *Political Theology: Four Chapters on the Concept of Sovereignty*, trans. George Schwab (Cambridge, MA: MIT Press, 1985).

Afterword by Julia Ng

1. Benjamin, "Für die Diktatur: Interview mit Georges Valois" (4:487–92). The theme of "Dictatorship" was assigned by the journal's editors. As the prefatory note accompanying the issue states, the pair of interviews was to be the first in a series devoted to "The Great Antitheses of Our Time" (4:1035).

2. Benjamin must of course have been aware that Sorel himself had briefly turned towards the antiparliamentary right; for a succinct discussion, see the preface to Sorel in this volume (197).

3. See, for instance, his letter to Scholem from October 17, 1925, in which he still says that it "must get done" (*GB* 3:90).

4. In his letter to Bernhard Kampffmeyer from October 1920, Benjamin had asked for recommendations in "anarchist literature" to be sent to him along with a copy of Sorel's *Reflections on Violence* (*GB* 2:101). Several titles listed in Benjamin's "Verzeichnis der gelesenen Schriften" (Roster of books read) might have been among these recommendations, including Rudolf Stammler's *Die Theorie des Anarchismus* (The theory of anarchism; 1894) (see 7:447). It is unsurprising that Stammler's book did not make an impression on "Toward the Critique of Violence," since it does the exact opposite of what Benjamin was looking for: instead of defending revolutionary violence as pitted against state violence, Stammler accuses anarchist theory (as represented in the works of Proudhon and Stirner) of being confused and unsubstantiated in regard to the possibility of a naturally harmonious, unregulated, and extrajuridical social life. However, it seems possible that Stammler's book, which launches a defense of the necessity of juridical norms for human community, provided an impetus for Benjamin's self-guided study of the canonical works of legal philosophy. For one, Stammler himself was a predominant figure in the philosophy of law. Another reason why Stammler's book might have inspired much of Benjamin's further reading is the argument Stammler

mounts against anarchist theory (and Stirner's in particular) that it does not sufficiently distinguish between "state" and "legal order" and thus also fails to recognize the objective characteristics of law as a (mere) concept of the validity of a norm. See Rudolf Stammler, *Die Theorie des Anarchismus* (Berlin: Häring, 1894), 21–25.

5. The Felix Meiner Verlag was founded in 1911; its series Philosophische Bibliothek had been acquired from its founder, the jurist and philosopher Julius Hermann von Kirchmann, along with the list of the Verlag der Dürr'schen Buchhandlung, as its initial stock. See https://meiner.de/der-verlag/chronik.

6. Julius Hermann von Kirchmann, who founded the series Philosophische Bibliothek in 1868, was a member of the Reichstag from its founding in 1871 until 1876. For a history of the series, see Rainer A. Bast, *Die Philosophische Bibliothek: Geschichte und Bibliographie einer philosophischen Textreihe seit 1868* (Leipzig: Verlag Felix Meiner, 1991).

7. Benjamin announces this iteration of the title of his project twice at the end of 1920: the first time in the letter he writes to Bernhard Kampffmeyer in October asking for recommendations of anarchist literature to help him in his completion of his essay (*GB* 2:101), and then in a letter to Scholem around December 1 (*GB* 2:109). Benjamin may ultimately have been repelled by the term *Abbau* as it was used in the "free economist" Silvio Gesell's pamphlet *Der Abbau des Staates nach Einführung der Volksherrschaft* (1919). Gesell called for a process by which the state would be eliminated upon the introduction of sweeping land and monetary reforms to replace interest and rent with a "natural economic order" consisting of free competition based solely on natural ability. In his usage, *Abbau* is a metaphor drawn most likely from the term's meaning in agriculture, where it denotes the abandonment of fields or plants, and in that sense, their nonactive "decultivation." Gesell's ideas of free economy and "free money" were praised by Gustav Landauer in *Aufruf zum Sozialismus* (1911), which may have been one of the pieces of "anarchist literature" Kampffmeyer recommended to Benjamin and which Benjamin included on his "Roster of Books Read" (7:447). Gesell was a brief but active participant in the 1919 Bavarian Soviet Republic but was also a welcome figure at meetings of the anti-Semitic German Socialist Party from as early as 1920. He also acquired a later admirer in John Maynard Keynes. See Silvio Gesell, *Der Abbau des Staates nach Einführung der Volksherrschaft—Denkschrift an die zu Weimar versammelten Nationalräte* (Berlin: Verlag des Freiland-Freigeld-Bundes, 1919); Udo Kissenkötter: *Gregor Strasser und die NSDAP* (Berlin: Walter de Gruyter, 1978), 96.

8. German law in 1921 was by and large the German law whose codification began in the 1870s with the political unification of the German states under the

Hohenzollerns. Many of the sources of these laws have been documented in the notes to the essay.

9. In the case of the German legal code, the codification of law went hand in hand with the progress of legal positivism, the dominant school of legal theory in the late nineteenth century. All the codes and statutes were drafted by university professors or judges and civil servants trained in scientific positivism, which assumed that law and justice are entirely contained in the norms without gaps.

10. Adolf Menzel, *Naturrecht und Soziologie* (Vienna: Carl Fromme, 1912).

11. Menzel, 5, 24.

12. Hans Kelsen, review of *Naturrecht und Soziologie*, by Adolf Menzel, *Archiv für die Geschichte des Sozialismus und der Arbeiterbewegung* 5 (1915): 225.

13. Max Ernst Mayer, *Rechtsphilosophie* (Berlin: Julius Springer, 1922), 10.

14. Mayer, 22.

15. Mayer, 22; Alfred Friters, *Revolutionsgewalt und Notstandsrecht: Rechtsstaatliches und Naturrechtliches* (Berlin: J. Guttentag, 1919), 26.

16. Friters, 30, 37.

17. For further details in regard to this point, see Michael Stolleis, *Geschichte des öffentlichen Rechts in Deutschland*, vol. 3: *1914–1945* (Munich: C. H. Beck, 2002), 170–71.

18. Justus Möser, *Patriotische Phantasien* (Berlin: Nicolai, 1775–86); Menzel, *Naturrecht*, 9.

19. Benjamin also includes Stammler's *Theory of Anarchism* (*Theorie des Anarchismus* [Berlin: Häring, 1894]) in his "Roster of Books Read"; see 7:447.

20. Mayer, *Rechtsphilosophie*, 20.

21. Rudolf Stammler, *Theorie der Rechtswissenschaft* (Halle: Buchhandlung des Waisenhauses, 1911).

22. Rudolf Stammler, *Recht und Macht* (Berlin: C. Heymanns, 1918), 3.

23. Stammler, 3.

24. Stammler, 3, 19–20.

25. Stammler, 22.

26. See, for instance, Mayer, *Rechtsphilosophie*, 7.

27. Gustav Radbruch, *Grundzüge der Rechtsphilosophie* (Leipzig: Quelle & Meyer, 1914). Radbruch was also the person Benjamin hoped would place his (now lost) review of Bloch's *Spirit of Utopia* with the *Kant-Studien*, which for reasons that are unclear never happened. See 267n57 for a discussion of the relation between Radbruch and Benjamin.

28. Gustav Radbruch, "Über Religionsphilosophie des Rechts," in Radbruch and Paul Tillich, *Religionsphilosophie der Kultur: Zwei Entwürfe* (Berlin: Reuther & Reichard, 1919, 1921), 17.

29. Mordché Rapaport, *Das religiöse Recht und dessen Charakterisierung als Rechtstheologie*, with a foreword by Josef Kohler (Berlin: Walther Rothschild, 1913); Hermann Lucas, "Aus der Geschichte der Todesstrafe," *Der Greif: Cotta'sche Monatsschrift* 1, no. 2 (August 1914): 388–401; Kurt Latte, *Heiliges Recht: Untersuchungen zur Geschichte der sakralen Rechtsformen in Griechenland* (Tübingen: Mohr, 1920).

30. Erich Jung, *Das Problem des natürlichen Rechts* (Leipzig: Duncker & Humblot, 1912).

31. Kelsen and Schmitt's debate, which took the form of a series of papers, a book, and a review, was the culmination of their years-long quarrel over whether the constitution was founded in the coextensivity of state (*Staat*) and rule of law (*Rechtsstaat*), or in a moment of political will. For an extensive discussion and partial translations of the documents in question, see Lars Vinx, ed., *The Guardian of the Constitution: Hans Kelsen and Carl Schmitt on the Limits of Constitutional Law* (Cambridge: Cambridge University Press, 2015).

32. Vereinigung der Deutschen Staatsrechtslehrer, ed., *Die Gleichheit vor dem Gesetz im Sinne des Art. 109 der Reichsverfassung. Der Einfluß des Steuerrechts auf die Begriffsbildung des öffentlichen Rechts: Verhandlungen der Tagung der Vereinigung der Deutschen Staatsrechtslehrer zu Münster i. W. am 29. und 30. März 1926* (Berlin: Walter de Gruyter, 1927).

33. Erich Kaufmann, "Bericht von Professor Dr. Erich Kaufmann in Bonn," in Vereinigung der Deutschen Staatsrechtslehrer, *Die Gleichheit vor dem Gesetz im Sinne des Art*, 2–23.

34. Hans Kelsen, "Aussprache," in *Die Gleichheit vor dem Gesetz im Sinne des Art. 109 der Reichsverfassung*, 53–55.

35. One indication of its status is the fact that, in the same year that it appeared in the *Archiv für Sozialwissenschaft und Sozialpolitik*, Kelsen's "Vom Wesen und Wert der Demokratie" was also published as an independent brochure by J. C. B. Mohr in Tübingen in 1920.

36. Hans Kelsen, "Vom Wesen und Wert der Demokratie," *Archiv für Sozialwissenschaft und Sozialpolitik* 47 (1920–21): 50–85.

37. Kelsen, 54.

38. Kelsen, 55–56.

39. Kelsen, 72–73.

40. Karl Kautsky, *Terrorismus und Kommunismus: Ein Beitrag zur Naturgeschichte der Revolution* (Berlin: Verlag Neues Vaterland, 1919); *Terrorism and Communism: A Contribution to the Natural History of Revolution*, trans. W. H. Kerridge (1920; London: National Labour Press, 1921).

41. Kelsen, "Vom Wesen und Wert der Demokratie," 56.

42. Kelsen, "Aussprache," 55.

43. Benjamin's initial unfamiliarity with Kelsen seems to have left a trace in the bibliography in the form of the "?" he inserts after the abbreviated, first title he lists by Kelsen's name, *Staatslehre*. Referring to Kelsen's *Staatslehre* would have been shorthand used by someone more familiar with his work, and Benjamin seems unsure at first which title he ought to read between the two that it might refer to. Given the inclusion of Dante's *De Monarchia* earlier in the list, it is intriguing to imagine that he eventually read both the dissertation on Dante and the more likely candidate, the *Hauptprobleme der Staatslehre*, particularly in view of the oblique reference to Dante's political theology (as mediated through the work of Erich Auerbach) later in his essay on surrealism.

44. Hans Kelsen, *Die Staatslehre des Dante Alighieri* (Vienna: Deuticke, 1905).

45. Carl Schmitt, *Politische Romantik* (Munich: Duncker & Humblot, 1919); Schmitt, *Political Romanticism*, trans. Guy Oakes (Cambridge, MA: MIT Press, 1986).

46. Hans Kelsen, *Hauptprobleme der Staatsrechtslehre entwickelt aus der Lehre vom Rechtssatze* (1st ed., Tübingen: Mohr, 1911; 2nd ed., 1923). For a succinct restatement of the continuity between Kelsen's thesis on Dante and his habilitation thesis, "Main Problems," I am indebted to Maurizio Cau's illuminating essay "To the Roots of the Universal Juridical Order: Hans Kelsen and the *Staatslehre* of Dante Alighieri," in *Hans Kelsen and the Natural Law Tradition*, ed. Peter Langford, Ian Bryan, and John McGarry (Leiden: Brill, 2019), 94–117.

47. Schmitt, *Politische Theologie*, 19; Schmitt, *Political Theology: Four Chapters on the Concept of Sovereignty*, trans. George Schwab, with a new foreword by Tracy B. Strong (Chicago: University of Chicago Press, 2005), 13.

48. Hans Kelsen, *Allgemeine Staatslehre* (Berlin: Julius Springer, 1925).

49. Schmitt, *Political Theology*, 9; Schmitt, *Die Diktatur: Von den Anfängen des modernen Souveränitätsgedankens bis zum proletarischen Klassenkampf* (1st ed., Munich: Duncker & Humblot, 1921; 2nd ed., 1928); Carl Schmitt, *Dictatorship: from the Origin of the Modern Concept of Sovereignty to Proletarian Class Struggle*, trans. Michael Hoelzl and Graham Ward (Cambridge, UK: Polity, 2014), xlii.

50. See 2:1097. See also Tracy B. Strong's foreword to Schmitt's *Political Theology* for a discussion of the evidence that Schmitt regarded the friend/enemy distinction as a "transcendental presupposition" for politics (xvi).

51. Hans Kelsen, *Der soziologische und der juristische Staatsbegriff* (1st ed., Tübingen: Mohr, 1922; 2nd ed., 1928); Karl Löwith, "Max Weber und seine Nachfolger," *Maß und Wert* 3 (1940): 166–76.

52. Letter to Richard Weissbach, March 23, 1923, *GB* 2:327.

53. Letter to Gottfried Salomon, December 21, 1923, *GB* 2:400.

54. Schmitt's understanding of "secularization" is indebted to his teacher Max

Weber's theory of the world's progressive "disenchantment" across historical periods and cultural situations. Among the vast literature on the topic, one item bears particular mention in the present context: Benjamin's fragment on "Capitalism as Religion," included as Fragment 18 in this volume (90), which interrogates in concise form the emergence of legal and economic concepts in tandem with periods of religious transformation, as well as, implicitly, the differences with other doctrinal or non-Western "times."

55. Schmitt's own summary of Kelsen's argument is that "the state is nothing else than the legal order itself, which is conceived as a unity. . . . The state, meaning the legal order, is a system of ascriptions to a last point of ascription and to a last basic norm." See Schmitt, *Political Theology*, 19.

56. Schmitt, 9.

57. Schmitt, 5, 13.

58. Schmitt, 35–38.

59. Schmitt, 35–38.

60. Schmitt, 14.

61. Schmitt, 14.

62. Schmitt, *Dictatorship*, xxxix.

63. Schmitt, xxxix–xl.

64. Schmitt, xliii. Schmitt here cites Rudolf Jhering's *Der Zweck im Recht*.

65. Schmitt, *Dictatorship*, 166, 119.

66. Schmitt, 119, 123.

67. In a lengthy footnote on dictatorship's relation to the philosophy of history that was amended for a later edition, Schmitt writes that "the essence of the concept of dictatorship is that it constitutes an exception to organic development in order to justify the task of eliminating any mechanical hindrance that obstructs the immanent flow of history. Through this concept, of an immanent historical development, an opposition arises to the mechanistic and centralizing state." See Schmitt, 279n22.

68. Schmitt, *Political Theology*, 35.

69. Some years later, Benjamin reprises this line of thought in a review of *Krieg und Krieger* (War and warriors; 1930), Ernst Jünger's edited collection of essays written by members of the German right-wing nationalist and fascist intelligentsia on their ideas concerning war. Opening with a reflection on a remark made by Léon Daudet, editor of the journal *Action française*, in which Valois too had been involved, Benjamin excoriates the volume's authors for their "symptomatic" (3:240; *SW* 2.1:314) refusal to grasp the role played by the amorality of means—technology—in modern imperialist war. Some, he notes, even complain that war had been reduced to "administration [*verwaltet*]" (3:243; *SW* 2.1:316). See Benjamin, "Theorien des deutschen Faschismus" [Theories of German fascism], 3:238–50; *SW* 2.1:312–21.

70. Georg [György] Lukács, "Reification and the Consciousness of the Proletariat," in *History and Class Consciousness: Studies in Marxist Dialectics*, trans. Rodney Livingstone (Cambridge, MA: MIT Press, 1971), 83–222.

71. Johannes Volkelt, *Ästhetik des Tragischen* (Munich: Beck, 1917), 469–70; cited in 1:279; *O* 92.

72. Here, too, the *Trauerspiel* book contains the kernel of an argument Benjamin later reprises in "Theories of German Fascism," as well as his essays on art and technology. Referring to Ernst Jünger's own essay in his edited volume *War and Warriors*, Benjamin writes in his 1930 review essay: "The German feeling for nature has found an unanticipated upsurge in view of [Jünger's idea of] the total mobilization of the landscape.... [A]ll the surroundings had become the terrain of German Idealism itself.... Technology wanted to retrace the heroic traits in the countenance of German Idealism with ribbons of fire and communications trenches. It erred. For what it regarded as heroic were Hippocratic traits, the traits of death. Deeply imbued with its own abjectness [*Verworfenheit*], technology shaped the apocalyptic face of nature, reduced it to silence, even though it was the power that could have given to nature its language. War in metaphysical abstraction, to which the new nationalism is committed, is nothing other than the attempt to solve the enigma of an idealistically understood nature, mystically and without mediation, through technology, rather than using and illuminating this secret via technology as mediated by a detour through the human scheme of things. 'Fate' and 'hero' occupy them like Gog and Magog." See 3:247; *SW* 2.1:319.

73. The letter, which Unger wrote to Kurt Breysig on February 7, 1915, is partially reproduced in Manfred Voigts, "Metaphysische Politik und psychophysisches Problem," *Neue Deutsche Hefte* 35, no. 2 (1988): 798–808.

74. Kurt Latte, *Heiliges Recht: Untersuchungen zur Geschichte der sakralen Rechtsformen in Griechenland* (Tübingen: Mohr, 1920), 2–3.

75. Latte, 2–3.

76. Latte, 2–3; cited in *GS* 1:295; *O* 111. As Benjamin notes elsewhere, *Sühne* is originally a juridical term; see 323. Latte uses the term *Staat* (state) to refer to the "state" in a generalized sense that he derives from the modern use of the word, as indicated by his use of the toponyms *Hellas* and *Griechenland* throughout, as well as his references to *Staatsrecht* (constitutional law) in a transhistorical sense. In his usage, *Staat* is not a translation of *polis* (which would be *Stadtstaat*), and his discussion does not therefore restrict itself to matters concerning the specific legal and political configuration that is the Athenian *polis*.

77. Latte, *Heiliges Recht*, 48. Latte writes that the recovery of debts remained a private matter until the late Hellenistic period, and because the state had no means of enforcement, the debtor who refused to pay would simply be shut out of

the community. See Latte, *Heiliges Recht*, 48–49. On *exoulēs dikē*, see the entry by Gerhard Thür, "*Exoulēs dikē*," in *Brill's New Pauly: Antiquity Volumes*, ed. Hubert Cancik and Helmuth Schneider, English ed. Christine F. Salazar, http://dx.doi.org/10.1163/1574-9347_bnp_e408090.

78. Latte, *Heiliges Recht*, 3.

79. The passage in question is indebted to Florens Christian Rang's letter of January 24, 1924, to Benjamin concerning theater and agon, part of which was preserved in Rang's diary and is reproduced in *GB* 2:425–27. In his letter—specifically, the part that Benjamin skips over in the *Trauerspiel* book—Rang speculates that the origin of the ancient Greek juridical process lies in "dialogue [that] is originally a clash of weapons, the *persecution* of right [*Rechts*-Verfolgung]; the injured chases after the injurer with sword in hand (in the context of which there is no difference between civil law and penal law) and right [*Recht*] becomes the people's political right [*Volksrecht*] only by virtue of self-redress (clan against clan)" (*GB* 2:427). He surmises that law comes to be delimited from vengeance when the theatrical-juridical agon intersects with the astrological order of things. Yet Rang is reticent about revealing his sources and doubts that "our archaeological sciences and history of religions have any knowledge or can provide ancient textual evidence to support" (*GB* 2:426) his hypothesis that a "free word" (*GB* 2:425) is capable of founding a higher order of law by breaking out of the judicial situation of the feud altogether, including its linguistic practices of oaths and guarantees. Latte, whose work in comparative law draws heavily on the history of religion, is of course one such resource, but in view of his placement immediately above a selective recapitulation of Rang's letter in this passage, Benjamin seems to have intended for him to provide a perspective on a question on which Rang declined to elaborate, namely, the structural relevance of ancient legal procedure for issues concerning post-ancient constitutional theory. Not only does Latte use the term *Staat* (state) to refer to "Hellas" throughout, but the "word" that breaks through the agon, which Benjamin attributes to the hero's "cry of indignation" (1:295; *O* 112), is for Latte also precisely the oath [*Eid*], which is one of the "sacral forms of proof and verdict" to which he refers in the lines Benjamin cites. For Benjamin, the tragic hero's cry registers both the "entry" of such interruptive forms into the juridical process and the seed of the reconfiguration of legal procedure into an "expiatory negotiation" (1:295; *O* 112), setting the stage for the transition out of the bodily-mythic confines of guilt and fate.

80. Latte, *Heiliges Recht*, 6, 11.

81. Latte, 44.

82. Latte, 44–46.

83. See §14 of *The Birth of Tragedy*.

84. Latte, *Heiliges Recht*, 113.

85. Benjamin refers to Rosenzweig as having pointed out this actual significance of the doctrine of the unities: a remaining immobile amid incessant change. See 1:296; O 113.

86. Thus, in the years leading up to 1927 but possibly as early as 1921, Benjamin was considering a critique of political economy specifically within the framework of a critique of fascism. In the fragment "Capitalism as Religion" that is included in this volume as Fragment 18, Benjamin refers to a passage in Sorel's *Reflections on Violence* where, he suggests, Sorel provides a description of capitalism's relation to law as being of "pagan character" (91). In the passage in question, Sorel writes that contemporary economists attribute the emergence of capitalist political economy to the enchantment of nature, which takes on the guise of natural laws; see 306n8.

87. Diego de Saavedra Fajardo, *Idea de un príncipe político christiano representada en cien empresas* (Munich: Nicolao Enrico, 1640); translated into German as *Abris eines christlich-politischen Printzens*, in *CI Sinn-Bildern vnd mercklichen Symbolischen Sprüchen Gestelt von A. Didaco Saavedra Faxardo, Spanischen Ritter [et]c. Zuvor auß dem spanischen ins Lateinisch, Nun in Teutsch versetzet* (Cologne: Sumptibus Ioannis Conradi Münch, 1674).

88. Saavedra Fajardo, *Abris eines christlich-politischen Printzens*, 897. For an account of Saavedra's use of astrology in the *Idea de un príncipe político-cristiano* and the broader political background of this work, see the illuminating discussion in Abel A. Alves, "Complicated Cosmos: Astrology and Anti-Machiavellianism in Saavedra's *Empresas Politicas*," *Sixteenth Century Journal* 25, no. 1 (Spring 1994): 67–84.

89. [Walter Benjamin, "Zur Kritik der Gewalt"], dated Berlin, June 29, 1922 (in pencil), W179/7, Nachlass Walter Lehmann, Ibero-Amerikanisches Institut [IAI] Berlin.

90. Josef Kohler, *Das Recht der Azteken* (Stuttgart: Enke, 1892).

91. Walter Benjamin to Walter Lehmann, Munich, February 4, 1916, Nachlass Walter Lehmann, IAI Berlin. Most of Lehmann's personal papers are still uncatalogued, and they include almost all of the materials used in the ensuing discussion. I am grateful to the Ibero-American Institute for granting me permission to cite from these documents.

92. Walter Lehmann Personalakten, L 080, Universitätsarchiv, Humboldt Universität Bibliothek.

93. Walter Lehmann, *Zentral-Amerika*, 2 vols. (Berlin: Dietrich Reimer, 1920); Bernhard Riese, "Walter Lehmann. Eine Bio-Bibliographie," *Indiana* 8 (1983): 312–13.

94. William Werner has succinctly reconstructed the lucrative entanglement of Lehmann's archaeological research with the transnational capitalist enterprises of the

regional German expatriates from Lehmann's unpublished travel diaries. See William Werner, "Culture Concepts and Capitalism: Walter Lehmann's 1907–1909 Central America Expedition," *Antiquity: A Review of World Archaeology* 84, no. 323 (March 2010), http://antiquity.ac.uk/projgall/werner323/.

95. Lehmann seems to have retained for his own use a significant library and collection of artifacts. After his early retirement he was granted space for this collection at the Ibero-American Institute in Berlin, which today still houses his archive.

96. Walter Lehmann Personalakten. See also Riese, "Walter Lehmann. Eine Bio-Bibliographie," 315.

97. Eduard Seler, "Die mexikanischen Bilderhandschriften Alexander von Humboldts in der Königlichen Bibliothek zu Berlin (1893)," in Seler, *Gesammelte Abhandlungen zur Sprach- und Alterthumskunde*, vol. 1: *Sprachliches—Bilderschriften—Kalender und Hierglyphenentzifferung* (Berlin: Asher, 1902), 163. Hereafter cited as *GA*.

98. Eduard Seler, "The Mexican Chronology," in Eduard Seler, E. Förstemann, Paul Schellhas, Carl Sapper, and E. P. Dieseldorff, *Mexican and Central American Antiquities, Calendar Systems, and History*, trans. Charles P. Bowditch (Washington, DC: Government Printing Office, 1904), 29, 35.

99. Eduard Seler, "The Significance of the Maya Calendar for Historic Chronology," in Seler et al., *Mexican and Central American Antiquities, Calendar Systems, and History*, 327–28; see also Seler, "The Venus Period in the Picture Writings of the Borgian Codex Group," in ibid., esp. 370.

100. Walter Lehmann, "Ein kostbares Räuchergefäß aus Guatemala," *Zeitschrift für Ethnologie* 48, no. 6 (1916): 335–39.

101. Lehmann, 339.

102. One reason why Lehmann did not publish this work initially may have been the same reason why he enjoyed such professional success relative to some of his peers: the protection and support he received from Eduard Seler, the most powerful figure in the field, seems to have come at the price of any public dissent with Seler's findings. For a detailed discussion of Lehmann's relationship to Seler as well as to his competitors, see the dissertation by Norbert Díaz de Arce, "Plagiatsvorwurf und Denunziation: Untersuchungen zur Geschichte der Altamerikanistik in Berlin (1900–1945)" (PhD diss., Freie Universität Berlin, 2004).

103. The Nachlass Walter Lehmann holds several copies of the fourteen documents comprising this project in both manuscript and typescript, scattered across several unmarked and uncatalogued cartons. The two most comprehensive sets are contained in the folders "Mond- und Sonnensystem im Mexico und Mittel-Amerika: München 1916" (which includes six typescripts in duplicate totaling seventy pages) and "Mss W.L. Abgeschriebene Mss. Maya-Gefäss Nachtrag 'Cipactli'" (which

includes an offprint of the article "Ein kostbares Räuchergefäß aus Guatemala," a third set of the aforementioned six typescripts, plus eight additional manuscripts totaling 105 pages). The original manuscripts are dated in his hand and range from March 25 to April 28, 1916; some of them specify Munich as their place of origin as well. Lehmann likely made these copies himself with the intention of expanding on them for eventual publication; on several of the manuscripts (and copied over onto the typescripts) Lehmann noted on "May 11, 1927" that they were "not yet mature," though "containing the correct basic ideas."

104. Seler, "The Venus Period in the Picture Writings of the Borgian Codex Group," 391.

105. "Mond- und Sonnensystem im Mexico und Mittel-Amerika," typescript dated "27.IV.1916," Nachlass Walter Lehmann, IAI Berlin.

106. "Mond- und Sonnensystem im Mexico und Mittel-Amerika," typescript without date, Nachlass Walter Lehmann, IAI Berlin.

107. Eduard Seler, "Das Tonalamatl der alten Mexikaner," in *GA* 1:600.

108. As noted in 294, these additional paragraphs originate from conversations Scholem and Benjamin had concerning the theme of historical time in August 1916; see 294n3.

109. For an extended discussion of Benjamin's relation to Lehmann and the mark that his study of Mesoamerican cultures made on his thinking on the concept of history, please see my essay on "Mesoamerica and 'Natural History': Walter Benjamin's Transition Problem" (in preparation).

110. "Mond- und Sonnensystem im Mexico und Mittel-Amerika," typescript dated "28. März 1916," Nachlass Walter Lehmann, IAI Berlin.

111. Walter Lehmann, "Toltecs," *Encyclopaedia Brittanica*, 11th ed. (Cambridge, UK: Encyclopaedia Brittanica, 1911).

112. "Mond- und Sonnensystem im Mexico und Mittel-Amerika," typescript dated "28. März 1916," Nachlass Walter Lehmann, IAI Berlin.

113. "Mond- und Sonnensystem im Mexico und Mittel-Amerika," typescript dated "27. – 28. April 1916," Nachlass Walter Lehmann, IAI Berlin.

114. Gershom Scholem, "Walter Benjamin und Felix Noeggerath," in *Walter Benjamin und sein Engel* (Frankfurt am Main: Suhrkamp, 1992), 79–80.

115. Vorlesungsverzeichnis der Friedrich Wilhelms Universität Berlin, Wintersemester 1921/22. See also *GB* 1:208.

116. For an indicative contemporaneous assessment of Kohler's work, see Leonhard Adam's intellectual-biographical essay included in the *Festschrift* for Kohler's seventieth birthday, "Josef Kohler und die vergleichende Rechtswissenschaft," *Zeitschrift für vergleichende Rechtswissenschaft* 37 (1920) (= "Festgabe für Josef Kohler zum siebzigsten Geburtstage," ed. Leonhard Adam): 1–32.

117. Josef Kohler, "Fragebogen zur Erforschung der Rechtsverhältnisse der sogenannten Naturvölker, namentlich in den deutschen Kolonialländern," *Zeitschrift für vergleichenden Rechtswissenschaft* 12 (1897): 427–40.

118. Kohler, *Lehrbuch der Rechtsphilosophie*, cited in Adam, "Josef Kohler und die vergleichende Rechtswissenschaft," 9.

119. Kant, *Aka* 8:374.

120. Kohler, *Das Recht der Azteken*, 78.

121. Kohler, 79–80.

122. Kohler, 7–9, 15.

123. Kohler, "Fragebogen zur Erforschung der Rechtsverhältnisse der sogenannten Naturvölker," 427.

124. Kant, *Anthropologie in pragmatischer Hinsicht*, *Aka* 7:119–20; "Anthropology from a Pragmatic Point of View," in Kant, *Anthropology, History, and Education*, trans. Robert B. Louden (Cambridge: Cambridge University Press, 2007), 231–32.

125. Alonso de Molina, *Vocabulario de la lengua mexicana*, ed. Julio Platzmann (Leipzig: Teubner, 1880); Gershom Scholem, *Walter Benjamin: Die Geschichte einer Freundschaft* (Frankfurt am Main: Suhrkamp, 1975), 47.

126. Molina, *Vocabulario de la lengua mexicana*, 6.

127. For a recent and illuminating discussion of Molina's colonization of the Nahua conception of the dream, see Heriberto Martínez Yépez, "¿Sueñan los marxistas con revoluciones aztecas? Poéticas del Náhuatl y el México de Karl Marx y Walter Benjamin" (PhD diss., University of California, Berkeley, 2018), esp. 16–26.

128. Molina, *Vocabulario de la lengua Mexicana*, 23, 74.

129. Adolf Reinach, "Über die apriorischen Grundlagen des bürgerlichen Rechts," *Jahrbuch für Philosophie und phänomenologischen Forschung* 1 (1913): 685–847; Adolf Reinach, *The Apriori Foundations of the Civil Law: Along with the Lecture "Concerning Phenomenology,"* trans. John F. Crosby (Frankfurt: Ontos, 2012), 4.

Hermann Cohen, from *Ethics of Pure Will*: Translator's Preface

1. Hermann Cohen, *Kants Theorie der Erfahrung* (Berlin: Dümmler, 1871). The first, second (1885), and third (1918) editions of this work are available in volume 1 (in 3 vols.) of Cohen, *Werke* (Hildesheim: Olms, 1987). For an examination of Cohen's life and work in the context of contemporaneous philosophical controversies, see Frederick Beiser, *Hermann Cohen: An Intellectual Biography* (Oxford: Oxford University Press, 2018). A general introduction to Cohen's philosophy is Andrea Poma, *The Critical Philosophy of Hermann Cohen*, trans. John Denton (1988; Albany: SUNY Press, 1997).

2. Hermann Cohen, *Deutschtum und Judentum: Mit grundlegenden Betrachtungen über Staat und Internationalismus* (1915; 2nd ed., 1916), in Cohen, *Werke*, vol. 16

(Hildesheim: Olms, 1997). (See also "Deutschtum und Judentum" [1916] in *Werke*, vol. 17 [2002].) A few sections of the pamphlet (which was written in part to convince American Jews to support neutrality during the First World War) can be found in Hermann Cohen, *Reason and Hope: Selections from the Jewish Writings of Hermann Cohen*, ed. and trans. Eva Jospe (Cincinnati: Hebrew Union College Press, 1993).

3. These three works are available in volumes 6–9 of the collected works edition, Hermann Cohen, *Werke* (Hildesheim: Olms, 1977–).

4. Hermann Cohen, *Die Religion der Vernunft aus den Quellen des Judentums* (Leipzig: Fock, 1919). This is a faulty edition, signaled by the mistaken title: Cohen did not present "the" religion of reason but rather "a" religion of reason, or simply "religion of reason." The correction was made in the second edition (Frankfurt am Main: Kauffmann, 1929), ed. Bruno Strauss, translated by Simon Kaplan as *Religion of Reason Out of the Sources of Judaism* (Atlanta: Scholars Press, 1995).

5. For a helpful introduction to this work, see chapter 6 of Poma, *The Critical Philosophy of Hermann Cohen*. Michael Zank provides a commentary to it in *The Idea of Atonement in the Philosophy of Hermann Cohen* (Providence, RI: Brown Judaic Studies, 2000; repr., Brown Judaic Studies Open Humanities Book Program, 2020, https://repository.library.brown.edu/studio/item/bdr:1111035, 260–315). See also Michael Zank, "The Ethics in Hermann Cohen's Philosophical System," in "Hermann Cohen's Ethics," ed. Robert Gibbs, special issue, *Journal of Jewish Thought and Philosophy* 13 (2004), nos. 1–2. An exploration of Cohen's ethics and philosophy of law can be found in Dana Hollander, *Ethics Out of Law: Hermann Cohen and the "Neighbor"* (Toronto: University of Toronto Press, forthcoming).

6. The German term *Recht* refers to a system of law, comprising the totality of legal institutions and norms; the term is the German equivalent of the Latin *ius* and the French *droit*, and has in philosophical contexts sometimes been translated into English as *right*.

7. Cohen, *Ethik des reinen Willens*, reprinted in *Werke*, 7:65–68, 70.

8. For a discussion of the relationship between this chapter and Benjamin's essay on Goethe's *Elective Affinities*, see Rochelle Tobias, "Irreconcilable: Ethics and Aesthetics for Hermann Cohen and Walter Benjamin," in "Walter Benjamin, Gershom Scholem and the Marburg School," ed. Julia Ng and Rochelle Tobias, special issue, *Modern Language Notes* 127, no. 3 (April 2012): 665–80.

9. See Cohen, *Religion of Reason*, chaps. 10 and 11; on *shegagah*, see esp. 199.

10. For a thorough guide to Benjamin's reception of Cohen, see Astrid Deuber-Mankowsky, *Der frühe Walter Benjamin und Hermann Cohen: Jüdische Werte, Kritische Philosophie, Vergängliche Erfahrung* (Berlin: Vorwerk 8, 2000). Beyond the citations discussed in the body of this preface, Benjamin mentions or cites Cohen in the following texts: "Fate and Character" (2:178; *SW* 1:206); and "Franz Kafka" (2:412;

SW 2:797), which includes the same citation as the one in "Toward the Critique of Violence." Cohen's work as a whole is discussed in the encyclopedia article "Juden in der deutschen Kultur" (Jews in German culture), 2:809. (As noted by Lisa Anderson in her preface [183]), Benjamin reviews a collection of Hiller's books in the early 1930s; but this only recapitulates the critique of his thought that finds expression in "Toward the Critique of Violence.")

11. Scholem, *Walter Benjamin: The Story of a Friendship*, 60. A contemporaneous record of this reading group, which reproduces Benjamin's evaluation of *Kant's Theory of Experience*, was preserved in Scholem's hand and retained in his personal archive; see the dossier containing the transcription and translation of these records, "Against the Metaphysical Exposition of Space" and "On Kant," as well as Julia Ng's introduction ("Walter Benjamin's and Gershom Scholem's Reading Group around Hermann Cohen's *Kants Theorie der Erfahrung* in 1918") and her accompanying analysis, "Kant's Theory of Experience at the End of the War: Scholem and Benjamin Read Cohen," *Modern Language Notes* 127 (April 2012): 433–84. Some remarks about this reading group can also be found in Scholem's diaries of the period, including *TB* 2:274–75.

12. In this regard, see esp. Werner Hamacher, "Intensive Languages," trans. Ira Allen and Steven Tester, *Modern Language Notes* 127 (April 2012): 485–541.

13. Benjamin also makes ambivalently critical remarks about *Aesthetics of Pure Feeling* in the *Origin of the German Trauerspiel* (1:352–53; O 187; 1:360; O 197).

14. In his essay on *Elective Affinities*, Benjamin also commends, with qualification, a long essay Cohen wrote on Mozart as a complement to his *Aesthetics* (1:129; *SW* 1:300); see Hermann Cohen, *Die dramatische Idee in Mozarts Operntexten* (Berlin: Cassirer, 1915); reprinted in *Werke*, vol. 17.

15. See *Das Leben Jesu nach jüdischen Quellen*, ed. Samuel Krauss (Berlin: Calvary, 1902). Krauss's work is now recognized as a critical edition of the *Toledot Yeshu*, which Scholem seems to have prized long before it became customary among scholars to do so (see *GB* 2:119; *C* 171); for a recent assessment of Krauss's work in this regard, see Catherine Hézser, "The International Context of Samuel Krauss's Scholarship," in *Modern Jewish Scholarship in Hungary*, ed. Tamás Turán and Carsten Wilke (Berlin: Walter de Gruyter, 2016), 190–91. As a final note, Benjamin mentions Cohen's *Religion* in conjunction with Franz Rosenzweig's *Stern der Erlösung* (Star of redemption) in a similarly ambivalent manner; see "Bücher, die lebendig geblieben sind" (Books that have remained alive), 3:171.

Hermann Cohen, from *Ethics of Pure Will*

Hermann Cohen, *Ethik des reinen Willens*, 2nd ed. (Berlin: Cassirer, 1907); *Werke* (Hildesheim: Olms, 1981), 7:357–72.

1. The term *Faktum* is translated throughout as "factum" in order to make clear that it is a technical term distinct from the English word "fact," the standard German equivalent of which would be *Tatsache*. —trans.

2. Famous for its ambiguity, the word *Geschlecht* means "sex," "race," "generation," or "dynasty," as well as "lineage," which is the translation used here; for a brief discussion of Atē, see the note to Benjamin's "Meaning of Time in the Moral World" (300n1). —trans.

3. The original sentence is ambiguous; it could also be translated, with subject and object reversed, as "This unity is accomplished precisely by fate." —trans.

4. Erinys in the singular is the oldest name of the Furies, who were the gods of vengeance. Aristotle famously defined tragedy in terms of catharsis or "purgation" (*Poetics* 1449b21–28). —trans.

5. Cohen discusses the book of Ezekiel in relation to the sin and individuation earlier in his argument; see *Ethik des reinen Willens*, 298–99, which cites Ezek. 18:4. —trans.

6. The Latin legal term *dolus* can be rendered in English as "fraud," in the sense of willful or intentional damage, as opposed to *culpa*, referring to a "fault" resulting from neglect or negligence. —trans.

7. See *Ethik des reinen Willens*, 318–23; Cohen regularly refers to Schopenhauer's thought, always as a point of contrast. —trans.

8. Cohen is referring to Franz Eduard Ritter von Liszt, a German jurist who is perhaps best known for "Der Zweckgedanke im Strafrecht" (The idea of purpose in criminal law; 1883). —trans.

9. The "character" in question here is that of being a moral (human) being. —trans.

Kurt Hiller, "Anti-Cain": Translator's Preface

1. Kurt Hiller, *Das Recht über sich selbst: Eine strafrechtsphilosophische Studie* (Heidelberg: Carl Winter's Universitätsbuchhandlung, 1908).

2. Daniel Münzner, "A Twisted Road to Pacifism: Kurt Hiller and the First World War," *Simon Dubnow Institute Yearbook* 13 (2014): 381.

3. Münzner, "A Twisted Road," 367–68, 384–86.

4. "Ein deutsches Herrenhaus," *Das Ziel* 2 (1918): 382; unless otherwise noted, translations are my own.

5. See Münzner, "A Twisted Road," 383–86.

6. "Der träumerische Schaffner," in *Die Weisheit der Langenweile: Eine Zeit- und Streitschrift* (Leipzig: Wolff, 1913): 1: 178–81.

7. See Walter Benjamin, "Das Leben der Studenten," *Das Ziel: Aufrufe zu tätigem Geist*, ed. Kurt Hiller (1916): 141–55; reprinted in 2:75–87; *SW* 1:37–47. "The Life of Students" had previously appeared in the journal *Der neue Merkur*, but Benjamin considered that version incomplete because it lacked the conclusion he had added to the lectures for print, including a quotation from Stefan George's 1897 poem cycle *Das Jahr der Seele* (Year of the soul).

8. See also Gershom Scholem, *Walter Benjamin: The Story of a Friendship*, trans. Harry Zohn (Philadelphia: Jewish Publication Society of America, 1981), 5–6, 15–16. For Werfel's essay, see "Brief an einen Staatsmann," *Das Ziel: Aufrufe zu tätigem Geist*, ed. Kurt Hiller (1916): 91–98.

9. Kurt Hiller, *Der Sprung ins Helle: Reden, Offne Briefe, Zwiegespräche, Essays, Thesen, Pamphlete gegen Krieg, Klerus und Kapitalismus* (Leipzig: Lindner, 1932), 13–19, 124–26.

Kurt Hiller, "Anti-Cain"

Kurt Hiller, "Anti-Kain: Ein Nachwort zu dem Vorhergehenden," *Das Ziel: Jahrbücher für geistige Politik* 3 (1919): 24–32.

1. As Hiller's subtitle indicates, his essay follows from the one that directly preceded it in the third volume of his journal *Das Ziel*, "Endkampf der Waffengegner," by the writer and left-wing activist Rudolf Leonhard, who premised his pacifist "battle against weapons" on the inherent goodness of man: "Der Mensch ist gut." See *Das Ziel: Drittes der Jahrbücher für geistige Politik*, ed. Kurt Hiller, 3, no. 1 (1919): 23. In the early 1930s, Benjamin came across Leonhard's small book *Das Wort* (Berlin: Graetz, 1932), and quoted one of its elucidations of the onomatopoetic source of language in his reflections on similarity and mimesis; see 2:207, 212; *SW* 2:696, 721). —trans.

2. As throughout this volume, *Gewalt* means both "violence" and "force." I have translated it as one of these two throughout the essay, depending on context. —trans.

3. Hiller's term, *Geist*, meant to him both "spirit" and "intellect/mind" simultaneously; it was the cornerstone of his doctrine of *Logokratie* (logocracy). Wherever my translation has him speaking of "intellect / intellectual / the mind," reference to "spirit" is also intended. —trans.

4. A close ally of Lenin's, Karl Bernhardovich Radek wrote for left-wing German newspapers and engaged in pacifist activism in Germany before participating in the German Revolution (1918–19) on behalf of the Bolsheviks. He was an influential speaker at the December 30, 1918, party congress that led to the founding of the German Communist Party (KPD), previously known as the Spartacus League. In 1923, Radek returned to Germany to prepare a revolution, the failure of which led to his ouster from the Comintern. He was later banished to the Urals and became a victim of Stalin's Great Purge. —trans.

5. Erich Ludendorff was quartermaster general of the German army during the First World War. The failure of his "spring offensive" (1918) was a major element in the German defeat; he would also play a leading role in the Kapp-Lüttwitz Putsch in March 1920. —trans.

6. Friedrich Ebert, who, as leader of the SPD, became the first president of the ("Weimar") German Republic. —trans.

7. René Schickele was a German-French writer and pacifist; beginning in 1915, he edited *Die weißen Blätter*, one of the most important expressionist journals and the journal where Benjamin originally expected to publish "Toward the Critique of Violence" (see also 23). —trans.

8. The Berlin Palace, which had housed the Hohenzollern family and Kaiser Wilhelm II, became the base of the revolutionary People's Navy Division. Eleven of its members died in this Christmas Eve skirmish with government troops. —trans.

9. Gustav Landauer was an anarcho-pacifist activist and one of the leaders of the revolutionary Munich Workers' Republic. He was murdered by the paramilitary *Freikorps* in May of 1919 after the Munich Republic was suppressed; see also 92 and 307. —trans.

10. Adolf Moritz Steinschneider studied law and business in Munich and Berlin before joining the Spartacist rebellion; he was imprisoned in Berlin in 1919 and 1920. I have not been able to find information about Heinrich Appel. —trans.

11. Karl Kautsky was a prominent Marxist theoretician and activist who served in the short-lived government established after the November Revolution; he was arrested on January 15, 1919, and released later that day. Hans Vorst was the pseudonym of Karl Johann von Voß, a German-Baltic journalist who wrote about Russia for the *Berliner Tageblatt*. The pacifist publisher and activist Hans Georg von Beerfelde was a leader in the revolutionary council government in Berlin. —trans.

12. This was written before that week in March whose barbarism overshadowed everything that came before. Martial law was declared *contra legem* on the basis of a lie ("mass murder of police officers in Lichtenberg"). Many people were shot without cause and without trial because they fought back when arrested, often based on a mere denunciation of carrying concealed weapons, including thirty-two sailors who were in no way involved in the events and had done nothing to violate martial law, simply because their faces displeased a brutish wretch of an "officer." Three weeks later, as of April 8, this beast is still living in freedom. The devil only knows what escalations of cannibalism will have become possible between this writing and the appearance of these lines. But God knows that the government that has tolerated or, in some cases, organized all of this—lower even than the lowest of the Wilhelmine rulers—will be judged by history, or indeed sooner by the present. [On March 9, 1919, numerous newspapers published the false report that Spartacists had murdered sixty people, including many police officers. Defense Minister Gustav Noske (SPD) declared martial law in Berlin, citing Spartacist barbarism and warning that anyone bearing arms against government troops would be shot on sight. —trans.]

13. The offices of the Spartacus League were on Wilhelmstrasse in Berlin. —trans.

14. "Ein Proteststreik Greifswalder Ärtze: Die rote Fahne" [A protest of Greifswald doctors: The red flag], *Berliner Tageblatt*, January 31, 1919, evening ed., 3. —trans.

15. A slightly altered quotation from Friedrich Schiller's 1805 play *Demetrius*, which speaks of *Verstand* (understanding, intellect) rather than *Vernunft* (reason), as Hiller has it; see Friedrich Schiller, *Works: Early Dramas and Romances*, trans. Henry G. Bohn (London: Henry G. Bohn, 1853), 346. —trans.

16. The uprising included an occupation, on January 5, 1919, of the newspaper district whose bourgeois papers had been extremely hostile toward the Spartacists. —trans.

17. Friedrich Nietzsche, *Human, All Too Human*, trans. R. J. Hollingdale (Cambridge: Cambridge University Press, 1996), 380. —trans.

18. From *The Pathway of Life*, vol. 1, trans. Archibald J. Wolfe (New York: International Book Publishing Company, 1919), 223. Hiller quotes the 1912 translation, *Der Lebensweg*, by Adolf Heß. —trans.

19. Felix Möschlin was a prolific Swiss writer and journalist, whose play *Die Revolution des Herzens: Ein Schweizerdrama* (Revolution of the heart: A Swiss drama) appeared in 1917. —trans.

Georges Sorel, from *Reflections on Violence*: Translator's Preface

1. Thomas Mann, *Doctor Faustus*, trans. John E. Woods (New York: Vintage, 1999), 385–86. See also André Gisselbrecht, "Thomas Mann et Georges Sorel ou la captation d'un penseur par un écrivain," *Cahiers Georges Sorel* 6 (1988): 78–90; Furio Jesi, *Spartakus: The Symbology of Revolt*, trans. Alberto Toscano (Calcutta: Seagull, 2013), 39.

2. Chryssoula Kambas, "Walter Benjamin lecteur des *Réflexions sur la violence*," *Cahiers Georges Sorel* 2 (1984): 80.

3. *Reflections on Violence* is also listed in the bibliography for Fragment 18 of this volume (91). *Les illusions du progrès* is numbered 726 on Benjamin's list of the books that he has read, and *Reflections* comes soon afterwards, number 734 (7:447). There does not seem to be any textual trace of *Les illusions* in Benjamin. Kambas notes that the treatment of Turgot in Sorel's text has important resonances with the place of the French physiocrat's *Oeuvres* in *The Arcades Project*; see Kambas, "Walter Benjamin lecteur," 87n41.

4. Quoted in Michel Prat, "Georges Sorel en Allemagne," in *Georges Sorel en son temps*, ed. Jacques Julliard and Shlomo Sand (Paris: Seuil, 1985), 416n17.

5. Quoted in Shlomo Sand, "Lutte de classes et conscience juridique dans la pensée de Georges Sorel," in Julliard and Sand, *Georges Sorel en son temps*, 243.

6. See J. R. Jennings, *Georges Sorel: The Character and Development of His Thought* (Basingstoke, UK: Macmillan, 1985), ch. 6.

7. Giovanna Cavallari, "Le idee giuridiche e la trasformazione della società democratico-borghese," in *Georges Sorel: Studi e richerche* (Florence: Leo S. Olschki, 1973), 68.

8. Cavallari, "Le idee giuridiche," 80.

9. Gian Biagio Furiozzi, "La fortuna Italiana di Sorel," in *Georges Sorel: Studi e richerche*, 93–112.

10. See Shlomo Sand, "Bibliographie des écrits de Sorel," in Julliard and Sand, *Georges Sorel en son temps*, 425–66.

11. Sand, "Lutte de classes et conscience juridique," 226.

12. Cavallari, "Le idee giuridiche," 49. This vision treats "juridical rules as temporary norms" (47).

13. Georges Sorel, "Étude sur Vico," *Le devenir social* 2 (October-December 1896): 787–817, 906–41, 1013–46.

14. Cavallari, "Le idee giuridiche," 83. Sorel discusses *Der Zweck im Recht* (in its French translation as *L'évolution du droit*) in his 1903 book on the "modern economy," drawing from him a distinction between *opportunity* as the creation of new productive forces and *right* (*droit*) as being concerned with their conservation; see Georges Sorel, *Introduction à l'économie moderne*, 2nd ed. (Paris: G. Jacques, 1929), 98. For Benjamin's reference to Jhering, see 93 and 5:128; *The Arcades Project*, trans. Howard Eiland and Kevin McLaughlin (Cambridge, MA: Harvard University Press, 2002), 75, 77.

15. Sorel also repeatedly cites Jhering's work on the development of Roman law in *The Illusions of Progress*.

16. The phrase "the juridical aims of the struggle" derives from Sand, "Lutte de classes et conscience juridique," 228; "thoroughly negative conception of law" from Axel Honneth, *Pathologies of Reason: On the Legacy of Critical Theory*, trans. James Ingram et al. (New York: Columbia University Press, 2009), 104. Honneth erroneously claims that Jhering's legal theory "is mentioned neither in [Benjamin's] letters nor in his works" (103).

17. Georges Sorel, "Le prétendu 'socialisme juridique'" (1907), in Carlos Miguel Herrera, ed., *Par le droit, au-delà du droit: Textes sur le socialisme juridique* (Paris: Kimé, 2003), 213. For Sorel, the social struggles crystallized in the pages of *Capital* amount to "an ensemble of violences which conceals from the eyes of a superficial observer [their] *juridical spirit* [*âme juridique*]"; see Sorel, "Les idées juridiques dans le marxisme" (1899), in Carlos Miguel Herrera, ed., *Georges Sorel et le droit* (Paris: Kimé, 2005), 27.

18. Sand, "Lutte de classes et conscience juridique," 241–42.

19. Zeev Sternhell, "Georges Sorel, le syndicalisme révolutionnaire et la droite radicale au début du siècle," Julliard and Sand, *Georges Sorel en son temps*, 75–100.

20. The same thought (almost verbatim) is found in a letter to Horkheimer (*GB* 6:96), but here Benjamin indicates his source, Julien Benda's *Discours à la Nation Européenne* (repr., Paris: Gallimard, 1992), 139.

21. Taken from an unpublished diary by Werner Kraft held by the Werner Kraft Archiv in Köln, this entry was published in *Für Walter Benjamin*, ed. I. and K. Scheuermann (Bonn: AsKI; Frankfurt am Main: Suhrkamp, 1992), 47–48; reproduced in Walter Benjamin, *Per la critica della violenza*, ed. and trans. Massimiliano Tomba (Roma: Edizioni Alegre, 2010), 117–18.

Georges Sorel, from *Reflections on Violence*

From Georges Sorel, *Réflexions sur la violence*, 5th ed. (Paris: Marcel Rivière, 1921).

1. The *basoche* was a company formed by the lawyers' clerks in the Parliament of Paris; a *basochien* was an officer of this company. —trans.

2. The *présidial* was a judicial tribunal in the ancien régime, abolished by decree of the National Assembly in 1790. —trans.

3. Hyppolite Adolphe Taine, *The French Revolution*, trans. John Durand (New York: Henry Holt, 1897), 1:117. —trans.

4. Enacted on June 10, 1794, this law, also known as the *loi de la Grande Terreur*, proposed by Georges Auguste Couthon but allegedly drafted by Robespierre himself, simplified the judicial process and accelerated the tempo of executions during the Terror. The law extended the jurisdiction of the Revolutionary Tribunal to cover the spreading of false news, the slander of patriotism, and so on; limited trials to three days; removed both witnesses and defense counsel; and dictated that trials could only end in acquittal or death. —trans.

5. For Benjamin's paraphrase of these remarks, see 56. —trans.

6. This was nevertheless the article that was applied to [Alfred] Dreyfus, without anyone having tried, moreover, to demonstrate that France was in danger.

7. The specifics of this law can themselves only be explained if we relate them back to the older rules of criminal law.

8. Some modern authors, interpreting to the letter certain instructions originating from the papacy, have argued that the Inquisition was relatively lenient in terms of the customs of the time.

9. I'm not sure that scientists [*savants*] have always properly understood the role of piecework. It is obvious that the famous formula, "The producer should be able to buy back his product," stems from a reflection on piecework.

10. "One might well say that the whole economic history of society is summed up in the movement of this antithesis" between town and country (Karl Marx, *Capital*, trans. Ben Fowkes [London: Penguin, 1976], 1:472).

11. Recall how the volcanic eruption in Martinique led to the demise of a governor who, in 1879, had been one of the protagonists of the socialist congress in Marseille. The Commune itself was not fatal to all its partisans; several enjoyed rather handsome careers. France's ambassador to Rome distinguished himself, in 1871, among those who demanded the death of hostages. [Louis Guillaume Mouttet (1857–1902) started on the extreme left and collaborated with the *Revue socialiste*, joined the colonial administration in 1887, and died in the eruption of Mount Pelée, a year after having taken up his governorship in Martinique. Camille Barrère (1851–1940), wrote for the militant paper *La sociale* during the Paris Commune and was ambassador to Rome between 1897 and 1924. —trans.]

12. Gustave Le Bon, *Psychologies du socialisme*, 3rd ed. (Paris: Alcan, 1902), 111, 457–59. The author, who some years back was treated as an idiot by the little braggarts of academic socialism, is one of the most original natural philosophers [*physiciens*] of our time.

13. I know, for example, of a very enlightened Catholic who manifests with singular acrimony his contempt for the French bourgeoisie; but his ideal is Americanism, namely, a very young and very active capitalism.

14. Paul de Rousiers was very struck by how in the United States rich fathers would force their children to make a living; he often met "Frenchmen profoundly shocked by what they called the egotism of American fathers. They find it revolting that a rich man forces his son to make a living, that he doesn't set him up [*établisse*]" (*La vie américaine, l'éducation et la société* [Paris: Firmin-Didot], 9). [Paul de Rousiers (1857–1934), French economist and economic geographer, disciple of Le Play who specialized in the United States, United Kingdom, and the comparative study of trade unions; in 1903 he became secretary general of the French shipowners' association. Beginning with *L'avenir socialiste des syndicats* (1898), Sorel would often draw on his work. See Antoine Savoye, "Paul de Rousiers, sociologue et praticien du syndicalisme," *Cahiers Georges Sorel* 6 (1988): 52–77. There are several references to de Rousiers in *Reflections*, both to *La vie américaine* and to *Le trade-unionisme en Angleterre*. Chapter 6, on the morality of violence, draws on de Rousiers's comments on the use of lynch law in the United States, while in chapter 7, on the morality of producers, his considerations on the United States are employed to argue that, if he had not been blinded by philology, Nietzsche would have recognized an analogy between his Homeric masters and Yankee pioneers. —trans.]

15. Benjamin's version: "[It] suspends [*supprime / schaltet aus*] all ideological

consequences of every possible social policy; its partisans regard even the most popular reforms as bourgeois" (52). —trans.

16. Marx, *Capital*, 1:929.

17. Jean Jaurès, leader of the French Socialist Party from 1902, was murdered for his antimilitarist stance in 1914. He is the frequent target of Sorel's polemic against socialist reformism in *Reflections*. In a note to the foreword, Sorel recalls how Jaurès ironically referred to him as the "metaphysician of syndicalism" in a May 11, 1907, speech at the Chamber of Deputies. —trans.

18. It is not hard to recognize that propagandists are compelled frequently to return to this aspect of social revolution: the latter will take place when the intermediate classes are still in existence but when they have become disgusted by the farce of social peace, and when the conditions are in place for such great economic progress that the future will be seen in a favorable light by everyone.

19. [Karl] Kautsky has often returned to this idea, which was particularly dear to [Friedrich] Engels.

20. Lujo Brentano (1844–1931), professor of economics, *Kathedersozialist* (*academic socialist*) and co-founder of the *Verein für Socialpolitik* (known in English as the German Economic Association); he carried out studies of English trade unions and in 1918 briefly served as a minister in Kurt Eisner's revolutionary government in Bavaria. —trans.

21. About this matter, [Eduard] Bernstein has said that Brentano may have exaggerated somewhat but that "the phrase quoted by him is not too distant from Marx's thought." What can utopias be made with? With the past and often with the very remote past. That is probably why Marx treated [Edward] Beesly as a *reactionary*, while everyone remained impressed by his revolutionary daring. Catholics are not alone in being hypnotized by the Middle Ages, and Yves Guyot is amused by Lafargue's "collectivist troubadourism" (Paul Lafargue and Yves Guyot, *La propriété: Origine et evolution* [Paris: Delagrave, 1895], 121–22). [The passage from Bernstein's article derives from "Des forces de la démocratie industrielle: Réponse à Mlle Luxemburg," *Le mouvement socialiste* (September 1, 1899): 270, which appeared in the same journal, founded by Hubert Lagardelle, in which Sorel published earlier versions of arguments later included in his *Reflections*, which he had first explored in articles for the Italian journal *Il divenire sociale*. As already noted by Isaiah Berlin in a 1971 essay on Georges Sorel, which was later collected in *Against the Current* (London: Pimlico, 1979), there is no evidence of such a letter by Marx to Beesly. Lafargue and Guyot's *La propriété* is divided into Lafargue's "communist thesis" and Guyot's "refutation," which precedes the thesis. Yves Guyot (1843–1928) was a French politician and free-trade economist, author of numerous antisocialist polemics, several of which were translated into English. Paul

Lafargue (1842–1911) was a revolutionary socialist, Marx's son-in-law, and author, among others, of *The Right to Be Lazy* and the farce *The Religion of Capital*. —trans.]

22. Benjamin's version: "With the general strike, all these fine things disappear; the revolution appears as a clear, simple revolt, and no place is reserved either for the sociologists or for the elegant amateurs of social reforms, nor for the intellectuals who have made it their profession to think for the proletariat" (53). —trans.

23. Ernest Renan, *Histoire du peuple d'Israël*, 5 vols. (Paris: Calmann Lévy, 1887–93), 4:199–200.

24. The distinction between these two aspects of war forms the basis of [Pierre-Joseph] Proudhon's book *War and Peace*.

25. Benjamin's version: "This general strike clearly announces its indifference toward material gain through conquest by declaring its intention to abolish [*supprimer/aufheben*] the state; the state was really . . . the basis of the existence of the ruling groups, who profit from all enterprises whose burdens are borne by the public" (52). —trans.

26. *L'alliance de la démocratie socialiste*, 15. [The expression "cannon fodder" is to be found in a parenthesis immediately following this passage from the secret statutes of Mikhail Bakunin's Alliance of Socialist Democracy: "All that a well-organized secret society can do is, first, to assist in the birth of the revolution by spreading among the masses ideas corresponding to their instincts, and to organize, not the army of the revolution—the army must always be the people." Marx and Engels's pamphlet *The Alliance of Socialist Democracy and the International Workingmen's Association* was published in London and Hamburg in 1873. An English translation can be found in Karl Marx and Frederick Engels, *Complete Works* (London: Lawrence & Wishart, 1988), 23:469. —trans.]

27. Benjamin's version: "The strengthening of state power [*le renforcement de l'État / Staatsgewalt*] is the basis of their conceptions; in their present organizations the politicians (namely, the moderate socialists) are already preparing the ground for a strong centralized and disciplined power [*pouvoir/Gewalt*] that will be impervious to criticism from the opposition, and capable of imposing silence and issuing its mendacious decrees" (52). —trans.

28. Benjamin's version: "The political general strike demonstrates how the state will lose none of its force [*force/Kraft*], how power is transferred [*la transmission / Macht*] from the privileged to the privileged, how the mass of producers will change their masters" (52). —trans.

29. The insufficiencies and errors contained in Marx's oeuvre, in everything that concerns the revolutionary organization of the proletariat, can be indicated as memorable illustrations of the law that prohibits us from *thinking* something other than what has real bases in life. Let us not confuse *thought* and *imagination*.

Erich Unger, from *Politics and Metaphysics*: Translator's Preface

1. For a general discussion of Unger's philosophical output, see Manfred Voigts, *Oskar Goldberg, der mythische Experimentalwissenschaftler: Ein verdrängtes Kapitel jüdischer Geschichte* (Berlin: Agora, 1992), 45–63. For a more detailed discussion of *Politik und Metaphysik*, see Bruce Rosenstock, *Transfinite Life: Oskar Goldberg and the Vitalist Imagination* (Bloomington: Indiana University Press, 2017), 76–118. For a full discussion of the relationship between Unger and Benjamin, see Manfred Voigts, "Walter Benjamin und Erich Unger: Eine jüdische Konstellation," in *Global Benjamin: Internationaler Benjamin Kongress 1992*, ed. Klaus Garber and Ludger Rhems, vol. 2 (Munich, 1999), 839–55. PM has been republished in Erich Unger, *Erich Unger: Politik und Metaphysik*, ed. Manfred Voigts (Würzburg: Königshausen & Neumann, 1989).

2. For a discussion of the historical circumstances of the group's founding and its importance, see Manfred Voigts, *Freie wissenschaftliche Vereinigung: Eine Berliner antiantisemitische Studentenorganisation stellt sich vor - 1908 und 1931* (Universitätsverlag Potsdam, 2008).

3. Peter Gust, "Studenten in der künstlerischen Avantgarde: Der 'Neue Club' und die Freie wissenschaftliche Vereinigung an der Berliner Universität," *Wissenschaftliche Zeitschrift der Humboldt-Universität zu Berlin, gesellschaftswissenschaftliche Reihe* 36 (1987): 607–15.

4. Lewis Wurgaft, "The Activists: Kurt Hiller and the Politics of Action on the German Left 1914–1933," *Transactions of the American Philosophical Society* 67, no. 8 (1977): 11.

5. Republished in Oskar Goldberg, *Die Wirklichkeit der Hebräer*, ed. Manfred Voigts (Wiesbaden: Harrassowitz, 2005).

6. Oskar Goldberg, *Die fünf Bücher Mosis: Ein Zahlengebäude* (Berlin: Verlag David, 1908); reprinted in Oskar Goldberg, *Zahlengebäude, Ontologie, Maimonides und Aufsätze 1933 bis 1947*, ed. Manfred Voigts (Würzburg: Königshausen & Neumann, 2013), 11–68.

7. Gershom Scholem, *Walter Benjamin: The Story of a Friendship*, trans. Harry Zohn (New York: New York Review Books, 2003), 120.

8. For a discussion of Benjamin's interest in the psychophysical problem in the years just before his encounter with Unger, see Uwe Steiner, "Von Bern nach Muri: Vier unveröffentlichte Briefe Walter Benjamins an Paul Häberlin im Kontext," *Deutsche Vierteljahrsschrift für Literaturwissenschaft und Geistesgeschichte* 75, no. 3 (2001): 463–90.

9. Erich Unger, "Der psychophysiologische Problem und sein Arbeitsgebiet: Eine methodologische Einleitung" (PhD diss., Erlangen University, 1922).

Erich Unger, from *Politics and Metaphysics*

From Erich Unger, *Politik und Metaphysik* (Berlin: Verlag David, 1921); reprinted in Unger, *Politik und Metaphysik*, ed. Manfred Voigts (Würzburg: Königshausen & Neumann, 1989).

1. On *Geist* and *geistig*, see the Translator's Preface, 215. —trans.
2. This phrase could also be translated as "body or mind." In Fragment 21 of this volume, Benjamin develops his own technical vocabulary around the "psychophysical problem," which can productively be compared with Unger's. Because Unger does not make a distinction between *Leib* (living body) and *Körper* (somatic body), the latter is translated simply as "body" throughout this text. Unger sometimes refers to *Leib-Seele-Verhältnis* (body-soul relation) and, like Benjamin, occasionally speaks of the *Seelische* (soul-like or psychic), including at the end of the excerpt in this volume, 232. —trans.
3. Benjamin adopts this passage into his argument; see 49. —trans.
4. On *Steigerung* (elevation), which is also a significant term for Benjamin in this period, especially through its negation, see 91 and 301. —trans.

Emil Lederer, "Sociology of Violence": Translator's Preface

1. See Reinhard Blomert, *Intellektuelle im Aufbruch: Karl Mannheim, Alfred Weber, Norbert Elias und die Heidelberger Sozialwissenschaften der Zwischenkriegszeit* (Munich: Hanser, 1999); Dirk Hoeges, *Kontroverse am Abgrund: Ernst Robert Curtius und Karl Mannheim: Intellektuelle und "freischwebende Intelligenz" in der Weimarer Republik* (Frankfurt am Main: Fischer, 1994); Austin Harrington, *German Cosmopolitan Social Thought and the Idea of the West: Voices from Weimar* (Cambridge: Cambridge University Press, 2016). On Lederer's extensive support for the career of Karl Mannheim, see also David Kettler and Volker Meja, *Karl Mannheim and the Crisis of Liberalism* (New Brunswick, NJ: Transaction, 1995).
2. See Emil Lederer, *Kapitalismus, Klassenstruktur und Probleme der Demokratie in Deutschland 1910–1940: Ausgewählte Aufsätze*, ed. Jürgen Kocka (Göttingen: Vandenhoeck & Ruprecht, 1979); *The State of the Masses: The Threat of the Classless Society* (New York: Norton, 1940); "On the Sociology of World War" (1915), *European Journal of Sociology / Archives européennes de sociologie* 47 (2006): 241–68.
3. See the M. E. Grenander Department of Special Collections and Archives at the State University of New York at Albany, https://archives.albany.edu/browse/ger.html.
4. See Ernst Bloch, "Über den sittlichen und geistigen Führer," *Die weißen Blätter*, n.s., 1 (1921): 8–15. In an interview much later in his life from 1974, Bloch spoke positively of Lederer as one of the few figures within the Weber circle who opposed the war from the outset; the others were Georg Lukács, Karl Jaspers, Gustav Radbruch, and himself. Bloch's personal relations with Lederer at the time may therefore have been quite cordial; see Michael Löwy and Vicki Williams Hill, "Interview with

Ernst Bloch," *New German Critique* 9 (1976): 35–45. Lederer's issue of the journal includes three other essays: Carl Brinkmann, "Zur Soziologie der Intelligenz" (On the sociology of intelligence), Gerhart Lükens, "Der Pazifismus und die sozialistische Idee" (Pacifism and the socialist idea), and Lotte Mendelsohn, "Möglichkeiten der Entwicklung Englands" (Possibilities for England's development).

5. For further discussion, see the Introduction, 10–11.

6. See Carl Schmitt, "Der Begriff des Politischen," *Archiv für Sozialwissenschaft und Sozialpolitik* 58 (1927): 1–33; *The Concept of the Political*, trans. George Schwab (Chicago: University of Chicago Press, 1996).

Emil Lederer, "Sociology of Violence"

Emil Lederer, "Soziologie der Gewalt: Ein Beitrag zur Theorie der gesellschaftsbildenden Kräfte," *Die weißen Blätter*, n.s., 1 (1921): 16–29.

1. See Karl Marx, *Capital: A Critique of Political Economy*, vol. 1, trans. Ben Fowkes (London: Penguin, 1990), 149n. —trans.

2. The Battle of White Mountain (Schlacht am Weißen Berg) was an important battle in the early stages of the Thirty Years' War, fought near Prague on November 8, 1620, resulting in the defeat of Protestant Bohemian forces by the combined armies of Ferdinand II, Holy Roman Emperor, and the German Catholic League, and consequently in the imposition of Roman Catholicism as the majority religion in Czech lands until the twentieth century. —trans.

3. Riccaut de la Marlinière is a character in Gotthold Ephraim Lessing's comedy *Minna von Barnhelm* (1767). He is not so much a physiocrat as a soldier-for-hire. The speech Lederer quotes is from act 4, scene 2. —trans.

4. Lederer alludes, of course, to Karl Marx and Friedrich Engels, *The Communist Manifesto* (London: Penguin, 2002), 3: "The history of all hitherto existing society is the history of class struggles." —trans.

5. This remark seems to be Lederer's ultimate response to Benjamin's essay, which also speaks of "finer feeling" (47). —trans.

Note on the Translators

Lisa Marie Anderson is professor and chair of German at Hunter College, City University of New York. She is the author of *German Expressionism and the Messianism of a Generation* (Rodopi, 2011) and the translator/editor of two books about Johann Georg Hamann (Northwestern University Press 2008, 2012). Recent articles and reviews have appeared with Iudicium Verlag, Peter Lang, and Fordham University Press, as well as in *The Goethe Yearbook*, *Studies in Twentieth and Twenty-First Century Literature*, *The German Studies Review*, *Germanistik in Ireland*, *The Yearbook of the Simon Dubnow Institute*, and *The Wilson Quarterly*. Her translation of Peter Sloterdijk's "Voices for Animals" was published by Lexington Books in 2012. She is currently coediting a new English translation of Ernst Toller's autobiographical book *A Youth in Germany*.

Markus Hardtmann is a teacher of German in the Modern Language Centre at King's College London, University of London. His research areas include critical and literary theory, media studies, and the intersection of literature and the sciences in German and comparative literature from the eighteenth century to the present. He has translated widely in these areas, including works by Ali Benmakhlouf, Andrew Buchwalter, Astrid Deuber-Mankowsky, Werner Hamacher, Douglas Moggach, and Terry Pinkard, as well as two exhibition catalogs on art and social media. Reviews have appeared with *Syndicate Lit* and *Modern Language Notes*. His current book project, *The Occasionality of*

Meaning: Robert Musil's Mathematical Modernism, examines Musil's writings in the context of contemporaneous debates surrounding the foundations of mathematics.

Austin Harrington is associate professor of sociology at the University of Leeds. His recent publications include *German Cosmopolitan Social Thought and the Idea of the West: Voices from Weimar* (Cambridge University Press, 2016) and, as editor, *Georg Simmel: Essays on Art and Aesthetics* (University of Chicago Press, 2020).

Dana Hollander is associate professor in the Department of Religious Studies at McMaster University, Hamilton, Ontario, where she is also an associate member of the Department of Philosophy and a member of the MA program in cultural studies and critical theory. Her research areas are twentieth-century French and German philosophy, modern Jewish thought, and German-Jewish studies. She is the author of *Exemplarity and Chosenness: Rosenzweig and Derrida on the Nation of Philosophy* (Stanford University Press, 2008) and the translator of Jacob Taubes, *The Political Theology of Paul* (Stanford University Press, 2004). Her monograph *Ethics Out of Law: Hermann Cohen on the "Neighbor"* is forthcoming from the University of Toronto Press.

Bruce Rosenstock is professor of religion at the University of Illinois at Urbana-Champaign. His most recent book is *Transfinite Life: Oskar Goldberg and the Vitalist Imagination* (Indiana University Press, 2017). His current book project is tentatively titled *Flesh of One's Flesh: The Racial Construction of Carnal Israel from the Bible to Black Judaism*. He maintains the digital library Folk Literature of the Sephardic Jews (http://sephardifolklit.illinois.edu).

Alberto Toscano is reader in critical theory and codirector of the Centre for Philosophy and Critical Thought at Goldsmiths, University of London. He is the author of *The Theatre of Production: Philosophy and Individuation between Kant and Deleuze* (Palgrave Macmillan, 2006), *Fanaticism: On the Uses of an Idea* (Verso, 2010; 2nd ed. 2017), and (with Jeff Kinkle) *Cartographies of the Absolute* (Zero Books, 2015). He has translated several works by Alain Badiou, as well as Antonio Negri, Furio Jesi, and Franco Fortini. He sits on the editorial board of the journal *Historical Materialism: Research in Critical Marxist Theory* and is series editor of The Italian List for Seagull Books.

Index

Aaron, 33
Adam, Leonhard, 327n116
Adorno, Gretel, 4
Adorno, Theodor, 4, 117, 184, 292n54, 301n2, 303n3
Aeschylus, 290n46
Agamben, Giorgio, 4, 260n5
Alves, Abel A., 325n88
Appel, Heinrich, 187
Angell, Norman, 191
Arendt, Hannah, 234, 261n16
Auerbach, Erich, 321n43

Bachofen, Johann Jakob, 312n5
Bakunin, Mikhail, 195, 267n52, 339n26
Balberg, Mira, 275n89
Balibar, Étienne, 264n40
Ball, Hugo, 195
Baudelaire, Charles, vii, 200, 251
Bauer, Bruno, 8, 11–12, 263n27
Beccaria, Cesare, 108, 110, 121
Beerfelde, Hans Georg von, 188, 333n11
Beesly, Edward, 209, 288n41, 338n21
Beiser, Frederick, 328n1
Benda, Julien, 336n20
Benjamin, Andrew, 273n81

Benjamin, Walter: *The Arcades Project*, 198; "The Author as Producer," 183; "The Concept of Art-Critique in German Romanticism," 195, 257, 301n3; "Fate and Character," 269n68, 272n79, 284n28, 299; "Für die Diktatur: Interview mit Georges Valois," 115, 199, 317n1; "Goethe's Elective Affinities," 165, 270n70, 271n76, 272n89, 284n28, 296n2, 299, 310n13, 311n1, 330n14; "The Life of Students," 13, 181, 184, 281n14, 331n7; "On Language as Such and on Human Language," 296n2; "On the Concept of History," 260n17, 276n90; "On the Program of the Coming Philosophy," 17, 21–22, 164, 275n90; *One-Way Street*, 17, 116–17, 120, 146, 156, 266n47, 267n55, 281n14, 304, 313n12; *Origin of the German Trauerspiel*, 16, 120, 132–46, 152, 155, 159, 164–65, 260n9, 270n72, 271nn76–77, 272n79, 284n28, 290n46, 299, 313, 323n72, 324n79, 330n13; "Peace Commodity," 283n23; *Tableaux Parisiens* (translation), vii, 15, 19, 165; "Theological-Political Fragment," 276n90, 301n2, 303n3; "Theories of Greman Fascism," 17,

345

275n87, 322n69, 323n72; "Tomorrow's Weapons," 275n87
Benjamin-Kellner, Dora, 265n43, 275n87, 296
Benn, Gottfried, 9
Bergson, Henri, 30, 197
Berlin, Isaiah, 338n21
Bernstein, Eduard, 338n21
Berth, Édouard, 195
Biale, David, 275n89
Bible (Hebrew), 33–35, 173, 273n84, 291n53, 292n55, 331n5. *See also* New Testament
Binder, Julius, 109, 111, 125, 313
Bismarck, Otto von, 5
Bloch, Ernst, 5, 9, 195, 263n30, 264n37, 265n43, 267n56, 268n58, 341n4; "On the Moral and Spiritual Leader," 10, 12, 234, 264n37; *The Principle of Hope*, 261n17; *Spirit of Utopia*, 17–18, 36, 261n17, 301n2, 319n27
Bloßfeldt, Karl, 306n7
Blumenthal, Herbert, 181
Bojanić, Petar, 274n84
Bojer, Johan, 93, 309n5
Bonald, Louis Gabriel Ambroise, 109, 111
Borchardt, Rudolf, 93, 309n3
Bossuet, Jacques, 94, 310n11
Brentano, Lujo, 209, 338nn20–21
Broué, Pierre, 259n2
Buber, Martin, 12–15, 23, 35, 266n47, 266n49, 275n88, 302n4, 307n14
Butler, Judith, 4, 264n41
Büttner, Georg, 108, 110

Cassirer, Ernst, 311n3
Cassirer, Paul, 10
Cau, Maurizio, 321n46
Chamberlain, Houston Stewart, 278n4
Cohen, Hermann, 17, 21–23, 138, 161–67, 297; *Aesthetics of Pure Feeling*, 162, 165, 330n13; *Germanism and Judaism*, 162; *Kant's Theory of Experience*, 161, 164, 330n10; *Ethics of Pure Will*, 3, 25–27, 33, 57, 162–63, 166, 299n1, 331n5; *Logic of Pure Knowledge*, 162, 164–65, 275n90; *Religion of Reason Out of the Sources of Judaism*, 162–63, 165, 273n84, 330n15
Cohn, Jula, 294–95
Cotesta, Vittorio, 307n13
Couthon, Georges Auguste, 336n4
Craig, Gordon, 259n2
Croce, Benedetto, 196

Dante Alighieri, 105–6, 108, 110, 121, 130, 312n8, 313, 321n43
Daqué, Edgar, 278n4
Darwin, Charles, 40, 278n4
Daudet, Léon, 322n69
Davidson, Hans, 215
Derrida, Jacques, 4, 264n41, 275n87
Deuber-Mankowsky, Astrid, 329n10
Díaz de Arce, Norbert, 326n102
Dostoyevsky, Fyodor, 31, 271n77
Dreyfus, Alfred, 336n6
Durkheim, Émile, 108, 110

Ebert, Friedrich, 1, 179, 181, 186, 333n6
Eicken, Heinrich von, 108, 110, 313
Eiland, Howard, 259n1
Einstein, Carl, 9
Eisner, Kurt, 1, 7, 31, 272n78, 338n20
Elias, Norbert, 234
Engels, Friedrich, 5, 8, 25, 61, 261n16, 263n27, 338n19, 339n26, 342n4
Engliš, Karl, 61
Erzberger, Matthias, 18, 268n61

Factor, Regis, 262n18
Feldman, Gerald, 266n48
Fénelon, François, 94, 310n11
Feuerbach, Paul Johann Anselm, 285n29
Fichte, Johann Gottlieb, 122
France, Anatole, 56, 93, 291n48, 309n7
Fränkel, Georg, 109, 111
Freud, Sigmund, 91, 250
Freund, Michael, 3
Friedländer, Salomon, 17–18, 267n56

INDEX 347

Fries, Jakob, 108, 110, 280n9
Friters, Alfred, 123
Fuchs, Bruno Archibald, 92, 306n10

Gautier, Léon, 305n3
Geiger, Moritz, 269n64, 296
George, Stefan, vii, 98, 311n1, 312n5, 331n7
Gesell, Silvio, 268n59, 318n7
Gilders, William, 275n89
Ginzberg, Louis, 274n85
Goethe, Johann Wolfgang von, 88, 107, 162, 165, 257, 282n17, 291n47, 301n3, 311n1, 313n12; *Elective Affinities*, 270n70, 271n76, 272n79; *Faust*, 307n15; *Iphigenia in Tauris*, 32, 273n80; *On Morphology*, 298n2; *Torquato Tasso*, 283n25; *Truth and Poetry*, 309n6; *Wilhelm Meister's Years of Apprenticeship*, 304n7
Goldberg, Oskar, 216–19
Gorki, Maxim, 93
Görland, Albert, 109, 111
Grimm, Jacob, 31–32, 272n80
Grosz, George, 289n43
Grotius, Hugo, 108, 110, 121
Guérin, Maurice de, 295
Gundolf, Friedrich, 311n1
Guyot, Yves, 338n21

Häberlin, Paul, 311
Haeckel, Ernst, 278n4
Haller, Karl Ludwig von, 278n4
Hamacher, Werner, 4, 330n12
Hamsun, Knut, 93, 309n4
Hanssen, Beatrice, 260n5
Haverkamp, Anselm, 273n84
Hegel, Georg Wilhelm Friedrich, 121, 184, 247, 288n40
Hegemann, Werner, 300
Heidegger, Martin, 32, 268n59, 273nn81–82
Heinle, Fritz, 94, 309n9
Hellingrath, Norbert von, 290n45, 295
Herder, Johann Gottfried, 75, 162, 298n1
Hesiod, 300n1

Heym, Georg, 215
Hézser, Catherine, 330n15
Hilferding, Rudolf, 233
Hiller, Kurt, 2, 5, 13, 36, 58–59, 179–84, 214–16, 267n56, 281n14, 283n23, 329n10
Hirschfeld, Magnus, 179–80
Hirschstein, Hans, 61
Hobbes, Thomas, 121
Hoddis, Jacob von. *See* Hans Davidson
Hofmannsthal, Hugo von, 117
Hölderlin, Friedrich, 36, 67, 265n42, 267n56, 290n45, 295, 295n2
Homer, 290n45, 300n1
Honneth, Axel, 335n16
Humboldt, Alexander von, 148
Husserl, Edmund, 184, 296

Jaffé, Edgar, 7–8, 233
Jameson, Fredric, 261n17
Jaspers, Karl, 341n4
Jaurès, Jean, 208–9, 272n78, 338n17
Jean Paul, 294n3
Jellinek, Georg, 279n8
Jenatsch, Jörg, 282n17
Jennings, Michael, 259n1
Jhering, Rudolph von, 93, 126, 198–99, 277n1, 280n11, 304n4, 309n8, 322n64, 335n14
Jones, Mark, 259n2
Jung, Erich, 109, 111, 126
Jünger, Ernst, 3, 322n69, 323n72

Kafka, Franz, 9, 274n85
Kambas, Chryssoula, 195, 266n52, 334n3
Kampffmeyer, Bernhard, 15–17, 118, 195, 317n4, 318n7
Kant, Immanuel, 17, 20–22, 29, 35, 71, 156, 161–62, 165, 251, 253, 269n62, 297n2, 298n1, 301n2; *Anthropology in a Pragmatic Perspective*, 298n1; *Critique of Pure Reason*, 27–28, 164, 279n7, 297n1, 298n2; *Critique of the Power of Judgment*, 19, 27, 270n74, 281n13; *Doctrine of Right*, 27; *Doctrine of Virtue*, 27, 290n44;

Groundwork for the Metaphysics of Morals, 284n27; *The Metaphysics of Morals*, 26–27, 270n70; *Toward Eternal Peace*, 2, 18–19, 29, 45, 153, 269n63, 269n67, 283n22, 284n27
Kantorowicz, Hermann, 126
Kassner, Rudolf, 184
Kauffmann, Max, 282n17
Kaufmann, Erich, 128–29
Kaufmann, Felix, 109, 111
Kautsky, Karl, 130, 135, 188, 333n11, 338n19
Kelsen, Hans, 8, 61, 108, 110, 118–20, 123, 127–36, 279n5, 313, 320n31, 321n43,46
Keynes, John Maynard, 318n7
Kierkegaard, Søren, 286n33, 290n45
Kirchmann, Julius Hermann von, 318nn5–6
Kjellén, Rudolf, 262n22
Klages, Ludwig, 103, 292n59, 311, 312n5
Klausner, Josef, 300n1
Klein, Martin, 268n57
Kohler, Josef, 109, 111, 146, 152–55, 280n12, 327n116
Koraḥ, 33–35, 273n84, 274n85, 275n89, 291n52
Krabbe, Heiner, 280n10
Kraft, Werner, 200, 276n90, 336n21
Kraus, Karl, 107, 131, 298, 313n12
Krauss, Samuel, 165, 330n15
Kroner, Richard, 20, 268n58, 269n65, 271n74
Kubin, Alfred, 305

Labriola, Antonio, 196
Lafargue, Paul, 338n21
Lagardelle, Hubert, 338n21
Landauer, Gustav, 1, 92, 187, 266n47, 267n52, 307n14, 318n7, 333n9
Lasalle, Ferdinand, 183
Lasker-Schüler, Else, 9
Latte, Kurt, 109, 111, 126, 140–42, 159, 313, 323nn76–77, 324n79
Le Bon, Gustave, 205–6, 250, 337n12
Lederer, Emil, 5–12, 17, 36, 233–36, 264n42, 304

Lehmann, Walter, 109, 120, 146–52, 156–58, 281n12, 326nn95,102–3
Leibniz, Gottfried Wilhelm, 305n7
Lenin, Vladimir, 130, 186, 287n36, 332n4
Leone, Enrico, 197
Leonhard, Rudolf, 180, 332n1
Lessing, Gotthold Ephraim, 342n3
Lessing, Theodor, 108, 110, 313
Liebknecht, Karl, 1, 188
Liliencron, Detlev von, 93, 309n6
Lindner, Burkhart, 275n87
Liszt, Franz von, 175, 179, 331n8
Loewenson, Erwin, 214–16
Louis XIV, 202
Löwenthal, Leo, 3
Löwith, Karl, 131
Löwy, Michael, 263n30
Lucas, Hermann, 109, 111, 126
Ludendorff, Erich, 186, 332n5
Lukács, Georg, 137, 341n4
Lützeler, Paul Michael, 263n31
Luxemburg, Rosa, 1, 188, 259n4, 285n30, 287n36

Machiavelli, Niccolò, 108, 110, 121, 295, 313
Maimonides, 311n2
Mann, Heinrich, 9, 181
Mann, Thomas, 132, 194–95, 334n1
Mannheim, Karl, 234
Marcuse, Herbert, 4, 275n90
Martínez Yépez, Heriberto, 328n127
Marx, Karl, 5, 10–11, 25, 52, 91, 121, 195–96, 198–99, 204, 207–9, 211–13, 238, 263n27, 264n40, 287n36, 288n40, 338n21, 339n26, 339n29; *Capital*, 12, 207, 261n16, 337n10; *The Communist Manifesto*, 342n4; *Contribution to the Critique of Political Economy*, 11; *The German Ideology*, 8, 263n27; *The Holy Family*, 8, 263n27; "The Leipzig Council," 8, 12, 61; "On the Jewish Question," 8, 263n27
Mauthner, Fritz, 307n14
Mayer, Max Ernst, 109, 111, 123

Mayer, Gustav, 8, 263n27
McLaughlin, Kevin, 270n71
Mendes-Flohr, Paul, 266n47
Mendieta, Eduardo, 305n3
Mennicke, Carl, 303
Menzel, Adolf, 108, 110, 122–24
Merlino, Saverio, 196
Michels, Robert, 61
Mises, Ludwig von, 8, 10, 61, 233, 263n24
Mitchell, Allen, 259n2
Moeller, Hero, 61
Molière, 80
Molina, Fray Alonso de, 157
Montesquieu, 304n7
Möschlin, Felix, 193, 334n19
Möser, Justus, 124
Moses, 33, 166, 274n85
Müller, Adam, 92, 308n17
Musil, Robert, 9, 181

Napoleon Bonaparte, 201
Natorp, Paul, 109, 111, 313
Nelson, Leonard, 109, 111, 123, 280n9, 313
Nettlau, Max, 195, 266n52
Nevill Jackson, Emily, 80
New Testament, 66, 298n1
Newton, Isaac, 270n74
Nietzsche, Friedrich, 21, 30, 91, 93, 106, 142, 191, 290n45–46, 291n49, 302n4, 305nn5–6, 309n6, 312n10, 337n14
Niobe, 33–34, 55, 57, 272n79, 290n45
Noeggerath, Felix, 148–49
Noske, Gustav, 181, 189, 333n12
Novalis (Friedrich Hardenberg), 301n3
Numbers Rabbah, 274n85

Oppenheimer, Franz, 61
Otto, Adolf, 195
Ovid, 290n45

Papen, Franz von, 128
Paquet, Alfons, 3, 260n5
Philip IV, 145

Plato, 108, 110, 121, 142, 179, 312n9
Poma, Andrea, 328n1, 329n5
Prometheus, 45, 114, 290n46
Proudhon, Pierre-Joseph, 195–99, 317n4, 339n24

Quetzalcoatl (Kucumatz), 149–51

Rabbah bar bar Hana, 274n85
Radbruch, Gustav, 17, 109, 111, 126, 267n57, 313, 319n27, 341n4
Radek, Karl Bernhardovich, 186, 332n4
Radt, Fritz, 146
Rang, Florens Christian, 141, 260n5, 302n3, 324n79
Rapaport, Mordché, 108, 110, 126
Rathenau, Walter, 233
Raynal, Guillaume Thomas, 201
Reinach, Adolf, 109, 111, 159–60, 313
Renan, Ernest, 210
Rickert, Heinrich, 20, 30, 268n58, 271n75, 280n9
Robespierre, Maximilien, 202, 336n4
Rosenstock, Eugen, 108, 110, 313
Rosenzweig, Franz, 266n47, 325n85, 330n15
Rousiers, Paul de, 337n14
Rousseau, Jean-Jacques, 121, 201–2

Saavedra Fajardo, Diego de, 145, 325n88
Sachs, Michael, 274n86
Salomon, Gottfried, 15, 17, 132
Salz, Arthur, 61
Sand, Shlomo, 335n16
Savigny, Carl von, 109, 111, 277n1
Scaevola, Quintus Cervidius, 287n39
Schaffner, Jakob, 181
Scheerbart, Paul, 16, 20, 267nn53–54, 298n1, 304
Schickele, René, 9–10, 186, 233, 264n33, 333n7
Schiller, Friedrich, 282n17, 334n15
Schlegel, Friedrich, 284n27, 301n3
Schmitt, Carl, 3, 109, 111, 118–20, 127–39, 143, 236, 260n5, 308n1, 313, 321n54, 322n55,67

Schoen, Ernst, 5, 16, 295, 309n3
Scholem, Gershom, 8–10, 13, 16–18, 20, 93, 115–16, 137, 152, 157, 164–66, 181, 194–95, 214, 217, 234, 265n43, 267n53, 267n55, 274nn85–86, 276n90, 290n45, 294, 298, 300–303, 318n7, 327n108, 330n11
Schopenhauer, Arthur, 174, 331n7
Schumpeter, Joseph, 7, 233
Schwabach, Ernst-Erik, 9
Seler, Eduard, 148–51, 153, 326n102
Shaw, George Bernard, 272n79, 276n90
Simmel, Georg, 179
Socrates, 106, 139, 141–43, 173
Sombart, Werner, 7, 262n22
Somló, Felix, 108, 110, 118, 125, 313
Sommer, Benjamin, 274n85
Sophocles, 290n45
Sorel, Georges, vii, 2–3, 11, 15–16, 24, 51–53, 56, 91, 115, 118, 144, 194–200, 236, 247–50, 253, 259n4, 261n16, 267n52, 287n36, 288n40, 291n49, 317n2, 317n4, 325n86
Spinoza, Baruch, 40, 278n3
Stach, Rainer, 264n32
Stammler, Rudolf, 108–11, 124–26, 267n52, 313, 317n4, 319n19
Steiner, Uwe, 311, 340n8
Steinschneider, Adolf, 187, 333n10
Sternheim, Carl, 9
Stirner, Max, 317n4
Stolleis, Michael, 277n1, 280n12, 286n31, 319n17
Strauss, Leo, 234
Strigl, Richard, 61
Strindberg, August, 106, 313n11
Strong, Tracy B., 321n50
Szende, Paul, 61

Taine, Hyppolite, 198, 201
Thales, 67
Thieme, Karl, 3, 260n9
Tillich, Paul, 109, 111, 303

Tobias, Rochelle, 329n8
Tocqueville, Alexis de, 198
Tolstoy, Leo, 191
Toltecs, 149–50
Treitschke, Heinrich von, 215
Troeltsch, Ernst, 7, 92, 307n12
Trotsky, Leon, 130

Unger, Erich, 2–3, 20, 49, 51, 92, 118, 139–40, 214–19, 269n62, 302n3, 306n9, 311, 323n73
Unruh, Fritz von, 283n23

Valois, Georges, 115–16, 119, 136–38, 144, 199–200, 322n69
Vardoulakis, Dimitris, 273n81
Vico, Giambattista, 196, 198
Vinx, Lars, 320n31
Voigts, Manfred, 340nn1–2
Vorst, Hans, 188
Vorwerk, Herbert, 303
Voß, Karl Johann von, 333n11

Weber, Alfred, 61, 234
Weber, Marianne, 265n42, 304
Weber, Max, 7–8, 61, 90, 92, 233–34, 282n16, 304n7, 305n1, 306n10, 11, 307n12, 321n54
Weissbach, Richard, 132
Werfel, Franz, 181
Werner, William, 325n94
Wielikowski, Gamschei Abraham, 108, 110
Wilamowitz-Möllendorf, Ulrich von, 109, 111, 313
Wilhelm II, 179, 333n8
Wille, Bruno, 287n37
Windelband, Wilhelm, 280n9
Wulffen, Erich, 282n17
Wundt, Max, 290n46
Wurgaft, Lewis, 215
Wyneken, Gustav, 280n9, 309n9, 310n10

Zank, Michael, 329n5

The authorized representative in the EU for product safety and compliance is:
Mare Nostrum Group
B.V Doelen 72
4831 GR Breda
The Netherlands

www.ingramcontent.com/pod-product-compliance
Lightning Source LLC
Chambersburg PA
CBHW020828160426
43192CB00007B/565